BARGOED AND GILFACH

A LOCAL HISTORY

by

GELLIGAER HISTORICAL SOCIETY

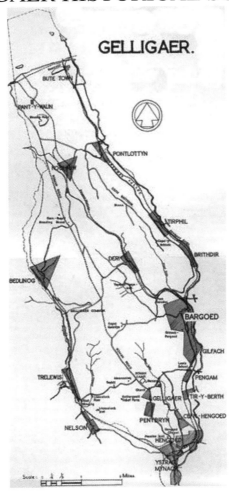

© Gelligaer Historical Society

First published in November 2011
All rights reserved

The right of Gelligaer Historical Society to be identified as author of this work
has been asserted in accordance with the
Copyright, Designs and Patents Act, 1993

ISBN 978-0-9570426-0-5

British Library Cataloguing in Publication Data: a catalogue record for this
book is available from the British Library.

Published by Gelligaer Publishing

Printed in Wales with the aid of

communities *first* **cymunedau** *yn gyntaf*

by
MWL Print Group
Units 10-13 Pontyfelin Industrial Estate,
New Inn, Pontypool, South Wales NP4 0DQ
Telephone : 01495 750033 Fax : 01495 751466
Email : sales@mwl.co.uk   www.mwl.co.uk

FOREWORD

"Pont Aberbargoed, lle hynod y byd
Pump ty tafarn sy ynddo i gyd
Dwy siop ragoral a gof a thri chrydd"

This is part of how Lewis James, brother of Ieuan ap Iago (Evan James) described Bargoed as it was in the old days. 'The loveliest place on earth with five pubs, two excellent shops, a smithy, and three shoemakers.' In addition there was a flourishing flannel factory with a fulling mill (pandy) and also a corn mill (melin).

The community described was transformed in the 1890s by the sinking of the coal pit, and remained a bustling, thriving town until after the end of mining in 1977. The Rhymney Railway Company had shortened the name from Pont Aberbargoed to Bargoed when it arrived in the late 1850s.

At last here is a definitive account of the history of Bargoed and Gilfach, which, whilst being typical of many Welsh valley towns, is very special to past and present inhabitants. In it are found many different factors in our story and these combine to explain why our community is unique.

David Williams MA. MB. BChir.

ACKNOWLEDGEMENTS

Gelligaer Historical Society gratefully acknowledges the help and support of countless local residents and exiles as well as Society members who have given of their time by searching their personal photograph collections or recalling memories of life and work in Bargoed and Gilfach over the decades.

Special thanks to Steve Kings and his staff in Bargoed Library, always on hand with guidance and encouragement even though our period of research coincided with their time in temporary accommodation. Thanks are also due to staff at Caerphilly County Borough's Winding House Museum, Glamorgan Archives, National Library of Wales and The National Archives for help and guidance.

Research and printing of this volume has been made possible by the financial assistance of Communities First Trust Fund scheme (which is administered by WCVA), Glamorgan County History Trust Fund, Greater Bargoed Partnership, Caerphilly County Borough Council and Gelligaer Community Council. The interest, support and encouragement of Bargoed Chamber of Trade and Bargoed Town Council is also acknowledged.

Finally, Gelligaer Historical Society is grateful to Gareth Williams, B.A. (Hons) Welsh for the Welsh version of the Preface.

DEDICATION

This book is dedicated to

past, present and future members of Gelligaer Historical Society

and to all who have played a part in shaping Bargoed and Gilfach.

PREFACE

Gelligaer Historical Society, founded in 1961, concerns itself with the history and heritage of the area covered by the former Gelligaer parish and Gelligaer Urban District Council. As the Golden Jubilee approached, members considered what would be most appropriate to mark this important landmark in its history and concluded that research and publication of a local history would leave a worthwhile and tangible souvenir at the end of Gelligaer Historical Society's first five decades. Eventually, having given thought to other research projects, it was decided to focus on Bargoed and Gilfach, the largest urban development in the area, and one currently undergoing great changes as it becomes part of Greater Bargoed.

Other than Gelligaer Urban District Council's *The Gelligaer Story*, Heolddu Comprehensive School's *Bargoed Bygones* and the photograph collections by Paul James, little has been published on the fascinating and unique history of this, the largest urban community and most important social and economic centre in the mid Rhymney Valley, on the river's Glamorgan bank.

Much of the book concerns the history of Bargoed and Gilfach in the last century and a half when transport and coal brought many changes that affected the character and appearance of the area, but pre-nineteenth century developments have not been ignored.

Mae Cymdeithas Hanes Gelligaer, a sefydlwyd yn 1961, yn ymwneud â hanes a threftadaeth yr ardal a gwmpasir gan Blwyf Gelligaer gynt a Chyngor Dosbarth Trefol Gelligaer. Fel y dynesai Jiwbilî Aur y gymdeithas, rhoddodd yr aelodau ystyriaeth i beth fyddai fwyaf priodol i nodi'r garreg filltir bwysig hon yn ei hanes a daethpwyd i'r casgliad y byddai ymchwil a chyhoeddiad ar hanes lleol yn fodd gwerth chweil o ddathlu'r achlysur ar ddiwedd pum degawd cyntaf Cymdeithas Hanes Gelligaer. Yn y pen draw, ar ôl ystyried prosiectau ymchwil eraill, penderfynwyd canolbwyntio ar Bargoed a Gilfach, y datblygiad trefol mwyaf yn yr ardal, ac un ar hyn o bryd sy'n mynd trwy newidiadau mawr fel y daw yn rhan o Fargoed Fwyaf.

Ar wahân i *The Gelligaer Story* gan Gyngor Dosbarth Trefol Gelligaer, *Bargoed Bygones* gan Ysgol Gyfun Heolddu a'r casgliadau o luniau gan Paul James, ychydig sydd wedi ei gyhoeddi am yr hanes diddorol ac unigryw sydd i'r ardal a hithau y gymyned drefol fwyaf a'r ardal bwysicaf yn economaidd a chymdeithasol sydd hanner ffordd i fyny'r cwm ar lan Morgannwg afon Rhymni.

Mae llawer o'r llyfr yn ymwneud â hanes Bargoed a Gilfach yn y ganrif a hanner ddiwethaf pan ddaeth trafnidiaeth a glo â llawer o newidiadau a effeithiodd ar gymeriad a golwg yr ardal, ond ni anwybyddwyd datblygiadau cyn y bedwaredd ganrif ar bymtheg ychwaith.

CONTRIBUTORS

Both *The Gelligaer Story*, a parish study that first appeared in the late 1950s to celebrate the Golden Jubilee of Gelligaer Urban District Council, and this local history of Bargoed and Gilfach reflect the work of sizeable research teams. The researchers in the 1950s, belonging to the renaissance of interest in local history in the post World War II era, relied heavily on printed material and the limited sources in archives such as Glamorgan Record Office, then in its infancy housed in a basement in Glamorgan County Hall. Those involved in preparing this history of Bargoed and Gilfach not only have access to a far wider range of sources in modern facilities such as the new Glamorgan Archives but also benefit from computer technology undreamed of by those earlier researchers.

The research team involved in this study of Bargoed and Gilfach, comprising members and friends of Gelligaer Historical Society coordinated by Annie Owen, M.A., has worked since November 2008 and used a variety of sources. Space does not permit inclusion of names of all those who have contributed to this publication but the following have been actively involved throughout and contributed to the text of this present work: Clive Andrewartha, B.Sc., M.A., Greg Buick, Judith Jones, M.A., Beryl Mapstone, B.A., Terry McCarthy, M.Sc., B.A., J.P., David Mills, Annie Owen, M.A., Iris Owens, B.A.(Hons) and Fay Swain, B.A.(Hons).

The cover, designed by Nesta Williams, shows an aerial view of Bargoed and Gilfach taken from the west by David Williams and a collage of photographs depicting the local area from early times to the present day.

TABLE OF CONTENTS

A view up Wood Street from Trafalgar Square.

Bargoed as seen from the Monmouthshire side of the valley.

CHAPTER 1
INTRODUCTION

The communities of Bargoed and Gilfach emerged in the early twentieth century as the Rhymney Valley's largest urban development between Rhymney, a nineteenth century iron-town at the head of the valley, and Caerphilly, a medieval castle and market town in the south. The map on the title page, taken from *The Gelligaer Story*, shows that Bargoed and Gilfach are on the west bank of the river Rhymney. Bedwellty, Monmouthshire's most north-westerly parish, lies to the east of that river and the east-bank communities of New Tredegar, Aberbargoed and Pengam are near neighbours of Bargoed and Gilfach.

Although primarily linked with coal for decades, the story of the Bargoed and Gilfach communities predates the sinking of Bargoed Colliery and owes much to the construction of Rhymney Railway Company's line through the area as well as to small pre-1900 coal-mining enterprises in the locality. These rail and coal developments were superimposed on a rural environment, home to generations of farmers and local craftsmen. Before that, and stretching back through medieval and Roman eras into prehistoric times, when the valley sides had been more wooded, there is evidence of human activity on the open moorland surrounding present day Bargoed and Gilfach.

Since the mid nineteenth century, the former rural area with a handful of farms and cottages between two small settlements (Pontaberbargoed and Pontaberpengam) at crossing points on the river Rhymney has changed dramatically. Bargoed started to develop southwards from Pontaberbargoed, a community that straddled both parish and county boundaries, after Rhymney Railway Company opened Bargoed Station in 1858 while Gilfach emerged as a coalmining community in the later nineteenth century. The sinking of Bargoed Colliery at the turn of the century was followed by such phenomenal local growth and rapid house-building that the two communities merged. However, local community spirit and pride remained strong and the smaller Gilfach, with its separate identity and village-like character, was never subsumed by a Bargoed developing not only as a coal-mining community but also as a service centre attracting people from an extensive hinterland to its impressive stores and places of entertainment.

In the twentieth century the economic, social and cultural life of Bargoed and Gilfach reflected the history of the local coal industry. In its early years Bargoed Colliery attracted people in their thousands. While the colliery was operating, the area was vibrant, but its closure paved the way for decline.

Local newspapers shed light on the way in which the communities of Bargoed and Gilfach developed. Early editions of *Merthyr Express*, a newspaper with a continuous history since November 1864, included very little on the Bargoed and Gilfach area, but some detailed reports on local people, events and developments appeared before the turn of the century. As the

9

communities grew following the sinking of Bargoed Colliery so the reports became more frequent and comprehensive. The newspaper, covering a wide area extending from the Cynon Valley to Ebbw Vale, and occasionally beyond, appeared in several editions. A Rhymney Valley edition with an extra four sides (one folded sheet) for Rhymney Valley news was issued in the mid twentieth century and since the 1990s events and organisations in Bargoed and Gilfach have been reported in an edition known as *Rhymney Valley Express*. More local and short-lived was *The Journal* (variously called *New Tredegar, Bargoed and Caerphilly* or *Bargoed Journal*). First published by editor and proprietor, Percy S. Phillips, on Thursday 16 June 1904, its pages shed some light on life and work in Bargoed and Gilfach.

While it is not possible to list all the other sources consulted, a few can be mentioned. Trade Directories such as those published by Kelly provide a useful source of information about Bargoed and Gilfach. They are printed books and usually include a brief description of the place followed by lists of the important residents and the businesses. In addition, the town directories published between 1911 and 1914 provide insight into the Bargoed and Gilfach communities at that crucial time in their development. School log books are another useful source as they shed light not only on the curriculum and the day-to-day school life of pupils and their teachers but also on the wider community. Some of those of the north Bargoed and Gilfach Schools as well as that of Bargoed Higher Elementary (later Secondary, Grammar and Grammar-Technical) are in Glamorgan Archives but the fate of those of the South Bargoed Schools is uncertain. It is worthy of note also that records in The National Archives in Kew include much information not only on local schools but also on local railways. However, in a study of this kind much information inevitably comes from residents and former residents, from their memories and their photograph albums.

The unpublished personal reminiscences of two former local residents, Rev. Gwilym Thomas and George Thompson, Ch.D., shed light on life and work in Bargoed and Gilfach in the past. When Rev. Gwilym Thomas (1870-1964) wrote his *Memories of a childhood in Bargoed* in the mid twentieth century he was one of the few people left alive who had met and spoken to his grandmother's brother, Evan James, the author of Wales' National Anthem. As an old man, he wrote so that his grandchildren and future descendants could understand his youth on the cusp when Pontaberbargoed still had a working mill and a lively Welsh culture with harpist and poets, yet the nearby railway station and the school he called the Board School pointed to a very different future for the people and the area. George Thompson, Ch.D. wrote *Tua'r Goleuni* from his South Australian home in 1991. It was a description of Bargoed about 1920, *a time when the town was young, striving towards the light, yet unaware of the perilous years that cast it into a state of impotence, powerless to give sustenance to its young: men and women drifting away, many never to return*. It is hoped that some of today's residents and exiles who read this present study may feel inspired to write their own memories of life and work in Bargoed and Gilfach to enhance the knowledge and understanding of future generations.

The story of Bargoed and Gilfach over the last century and a half is like a complex jigsaw puzzle: it comprises many parts and the more pieces that can be slotted in, the more complete the understanding and appreciation. Important though they were, it is not enough to understand how the railway companies, Powell Duffryn Steam Coal Company and local councils helped to shape the area and create the Bargoed and Gilfach of today. The contribution of local clergymen of all denominations, doctors, school teachers, solicitors, accountants and other professionals, those involved in commerce and business as well as the many who organised music, sport and other interest groups, have all helped enrich the quality of life in the local area. The jigsaw is not complete without the story of a myriad others: details of the daily life and work of those who earned a living on the railways and in the mining industry, in the shops, places of entertainment as well as the countless wives and mothers whose contribution has often been left untold, all add to the picture. Neither is it sufficient just to know about iconic structures such as Gilfach Fargoed Fawr (the area's oldest building), the majestic seven-arch railway viaduct standing proud in north Bargoed, fine town centre buildings like the Emporium at the Pierhead and the Police Court, Gilfach's New Bridge in the south and the places of learning and of worship. Just as important are the hundreds of local dwellings, ranging from the humble terraced house to the fairly palatial residence, all called home by many over the decades. They are all part of the local story.

The area is currently undergoing great changes as Bargoed and Gilfach merge with Aberbargoed and Britannia, their neighbours on the Monmouthshire side of the valley, to form Greater Bargoed. This is not a history of Greater Bargoed because historically those parts of Greater Bargoed on the east side of the river Rhymney were in the parish of Bedwellty and the county of Monmouthshire and so, although there are numerous occasions when the stories merge, their histories are different.

History makes a place special and helps its people take pride in its distinctive local characteristics. The history and heritage of Bargoed and Gilfach is as valuable in shaping the future of the local area as it is in remembering the past. The fabric of today's Bargoed and Gilfach, its public buildings, open spaces, streets and houses, as well as its economic activities, is the product of the past and present as well as being the canvas for the future. Successful planning and regeneration strategies to sustain and strengthen the local area for the future depend upon sound knowledge and understanding of the local past and of the traces of history on the ground.

Over the centuries, the local area has been influenced by and has in turn, touched the lives of many people, and its fascinating and unique history deserves to be widely known, understood and appreciated in its own right as well as in the context of the South Wales Coalfield in general. This local history starts by placing the area that became Bargoed and Gilfach in its geological and geographical context before tracing the main themes that characterised the area from prehistoric to historic times and on to the present day and tries to capture the flavour of the various developments over the centuries. It is hoped that it will help readers, whether local residents or from elsewhere in the country and further afield, reflect on the local distinctiveness of Bargoed and Gilfach, the largest urban development within the former Gelligaer parish and Urban District.

While this work takes the story of Bargoed and Gilfach to the present day and looks towards the future, it does not deal with the post World War II era in as much detail as the earlier part of the twentieth century. Not only is the available written source material for recent decades more limited but also researchers and readers alike are less likely to be able to stand back and assess the developments dispassionately. The concluding chapter suggests some ways in which readers may like to contribute their own memories of life and work in Bargoed and Gilfach in recent decades.

Prior to the last quarter of a century or so, local people used imperial weights and measures and pre-decimal coinage, and so these are used in the text in the following chapters. However, especially as today's younger people are not familiar with some of the imperial weights and measures, a simple conversion aid appears in an Appendix on page 336

Place names are spelled as in common use in the local area today. While Lewis James (see Foreword) used Pont Aberbargoed in the nineteenth century, sources suggest that by the early twentieth century that form was used to refer to the bridge itself while Pontaberbargoed (and Pontaberpengam) was in more common use when referring to the community. Pierhead appears in local newspapers of the early twentieth century to describe the corner occupied by the Emporium building where Lower and Upper High Street meet. In the decades prior to World War II it was common to use Gellygaer (including use in the name of the local council) but the usual form now is Gelligaer. Bargoed's square (triangular in shape) is variously known as Trafalgar Square, Hanbury Square or, simply, The Square. Historically the river that flows through Deri and joins the Rhymney River was Bargoed-Rhymney but is generally known as Darran by local people today.

It is commonly held that the early name for the growing community near Bargoed Railway Station was Charlestown. When writing about the New School (as opposed to that in Factory Road) Rev. Gwilym Thomas noted that it *was built above the Rhymney Railway in a part of the village that was known as Charlestown* while George Thompson refers to the hamlets of Pontaberbargoed and Charlestown. Writing in *Gelligaer*, the journal of Gelligaer Historical Society, in 1972 Bryn H. Rees recalled that in the 1920s old inhabitants had told him a man named *Charles* had built some of the first houses in what became

Bargoed so the people called the emerging town Charlestown (pronounced Chalston). However, research to date has not shed any light on the identity of *Charles* nor which houses he may have built.

Except for a few families the people of Gelligaer parish did not start using surnames until the eighteenth century: they used patronymic naming to identify people. Each individual had only a single name, for instance William, and, to distinguish him from others with the same name, the name of his father was added e.g. William Rees, and if this did not sufficiently identify him, his grandfather's name would be added e.g. William Rees Lewis, and so on. So William Rees, William Rees Lewis and William Rees Lewis Thomas might all be the same person. Women's names were constructed in a similar way using the father's name and they would not therefore change their names on marriage. Before the seventeenth century the word ap (Welsh - son) was sometimes placed between the names giving William ap Rees while for women it was ferch giving, for example, Gwenllian ferch Rees ap Lewis. Occasionally a nickname such as *Goch* (red) or *Llwyd* (holy or grey) might also be added. More commonly fychan (junior) was used when father and son had the same name e.g. Rees fychan ap Rees.

Rev. Gwilym Thomas (1870-1964)
This photograph is included courtesy of Dr. David Williams. who is descended from a sister of Evan James.
The written memories of Rev. Gwilym Thomas have shed light on many aspects of life and work as well as the appearance of the local area in the decades prior to the sinking of Bargoed Colliery. Perhaps some readers of this work were present when, as recorded by the headteacher in the school log book in October 1958, he spoke to the pupils of Bargoed Infants' School telling them that he remembered the school being built.

The photographs that appear on the next two pages illustrate how the local area has changed in recent decades as most traces of the coal industry have gone.

Below: Bargoed and Gilfach from the north in 1977 (photograph by Terry McCarthy).

Opposite: Bargoed and Gilfach from the south 30 years later (photograph, from a balloon, by Brian Jarrett).

Two images associated with Bargoed's iconic Emporium.

SAVE WHILE YOU SPEND!

The EMPORIUM
PURCHASING CLUB

Our Club enables you to Purchase Goods at
CASH PRICES
from over thirty-three well stocked Departments
offering the Keenest Value obtainable.

All Prices marked in Plain Figures and
no Poundage Charged.
NO OTHER CLUB OFFERS YOU THESE ADVANTAGES.

BARGOED
————TELEPHONE 41.————

Call or send a Post Card and our Agent will supply you with full particulars

CHAPTER 2
GEOLOGICAL AND GEOGRAPHICAL CONTEXT

Location of Bargoed and Gilfach:

In global terms the urban area of Bargoed and Gilfach is located at latitude 51.68°N, longitude 3.22°W, and its National Grid position is ST 151995. Thus it is in the southern part of Great Britain, approximately 150 miles west of London. In its South Wales context, the urban area of Bargoed and Gilfach is approximately 17 miles north of Cardiff, on the northern side of the Bristol Channel and on the west (Glamorganshire) bank of the River Rhymney, south of its confluence with the Bargoed-Rhymney river. The earliest development, at Pontaberbargoed, was close to this confluence, but the *modern* urban area lies on higher land, part of the south eastern flank of Gelligaer Common. The latter upland rises to the north and forms part of the northern section of the South Wales coal basin, outcropping approximately 10 miles north of Bargoed, and forms part of the Brecon Beacons escarpment, which is some 15 miles to the north. Bargoed and Gilfach lie to the west of the main railway route from Cardiff to Rhymney, and formerly there were junctions with lines southwards to Newport and up the Darran Valley for Dowlais and Brecon. In relation to the modern road network, until 2008 Bargoed and Gilfach lay astride the A469 on its route between Cardiff and Rhymney Bridge, but with the opening of the Bargoed by-pass (Angel Way) it now lies to the west of this road. To the north of Bargoed there are cross roads, with one route climbing up to Aberbargoed and Bedwellty and the other heading up the Darran Valley to Fochriw and Dowlais.

Site of Bargoed and Gilfach:

The site (i.e. the nature of the land on which it is built) of Pontaberbargoed differed from that of the later main development of Bargoed and Gilfach in that it lay on the valley floor at about 525 feet O.D. (over datum - above sea level) close to the confluence of the Rhymney and Bargoed-Rhymney rivers. This site, relatively flat though flanked by steep valley sides, was probably chosen because it had access to water for both human and animal consumption and disposal of waste products. It also offered potential for water power, which for most of the nineteenth century was harnessed to power a woollen mill. However, being so close to rivers whose régimes (or patterns of flow) could fluctuate widely from trickle to flood on both a seasonal and daily basis, it would have been vulnerable to inundation. The site of the post 1850s settlement is on a downward slope from north to south so provides a major pre-requisite for habitation, that is, good, natural drainage for run-off water. Little, if any, of the settlement lies on the narrow valley floor, access being denied initially by the presence of the main railway line and later by the development of the

17

colliery which dominated Bargoed between 1901 and 1977. Today, following reclamation, the lower part of the valley is occupied by Angel Way and a Country Park. Most of the modern settlement was built on higher land to the west and south of the steep valley sides. To the west, the land slopes up towards the Common, rising from 630 feet in Bargoed to 1220 feet at Cefn Gelligaer. From Heolddu, the highest point of the settlement overlooking the Darran Valley at 869 feet, the land slopes gently southwards to Gilfach at 591 feet. Initially, this relatively high but sloping site provided the essentials for human life: water, drainage and the means of disposing of effluent waste. The many small streams rising on the Common fringes provided these functions in the very early days of local urban development. By the twentieth century large scale water supply and interrelated drainage and sewerage systems were necessary and duly provided, but at considerable cost consequential of the nature of the terrain on which the township was being built.

Geological History:

Bargoed and Gilfach's development owed much to the geology of the site, which was built directly upon rocks formed during Carboniferous times some 359 - 299 million years ago (correctly termed Before Present and abbreviated to B.P.). It is likely these rocks were formed when the tectonic plate on which the area is carried (European plate – before it 'joined' with the Asian plate) was located near the equator in an environment possibly not dissimilar to the present-day Amazonian basin. Previous to the Carboniferous period the area had been submerged forming part of a continental shelf fed by rivers flowing across and eroding a land surface providing a range of deposits which formed the sandstones, mudstone and shales of Mid Wales. During the Devonian period, (418 - 359 million years ago) Bargoed and Gilfach lay on the coastal plain of an area where hot desert conditions prevailed, wherein flash floods carried erosion debris and laid down the distinctive red rocks characterising the Brecon Beacons only 15 miles north of Bargoed. Later, during the early (Lower) Carboniferous (also termed Dinantian), this desert landscape was invaded by shallow tropical seas where major coral reefs developed to form the limestone which subsequently weathered to create caves and caverns now characteristic of the area north of Rhymney. Distant tectonic uplift linked with the beginnings of the Variscan Earth Movements (also Hercynian or Amorican orogeny), led to the area becoming a huge river basin fed by rivers flowing from an upland area to the north. This extensive plain was affected by further mild tectonic activity and was subject to periodic submergence beneath and emergence from shallow estuarine waters.

In this latter environment, on the dry land surface there was a luxuriant vegetation cover dominated by primitive plants, notably giant fern-like species, of which the contemporary maiden-hair ferns from Australasia are descendants. This formed the basis for the coal measures of the Westphalian series (314 – 308 million years ago), sequences of rock deposits, which became the catalysts for Bargoed and Gilfach's nineteenth and early twentieth century growth. Coal measures comprise layers of clays; remnants of the primaeval soils, coal seams formed from buried trees during a period of forest growth (several thousand years usually) and a coarse sandstone laid when the sea invaded the forest areas, covering them with sand and silt. After a period of time renewed tectonic activity would uplift the area and another sequence began. In the Rhymney Valley two series of coal measures can be identified: Lower (incorporating the Middle) and Upper and both are represented in the Bargoed and Gilfach area. The Lower Coal Measures buried deep beneath Bargoed and Gilfach (at least 2100 feet), range from eleven feet thick economically viable coal seams to thin black lines in the rock strata. Overlying the Lower Coal Measures is a series of sand or grit stones, known locally as the Pennant Grits, which are truly part of the Upper Coal Measures. In the Bargoed and Gilfach area only one significant seam existed in the Upper Coal Measures, the relatively thin Brithdir seam, which is near or even outcropping at the surface in many places. The Pennant Grits became very important building stones from which much of Bargoed and Gilfach was constructed, at least until cheaper brick became available in the second decade of the twentieth century. Church Street and Heolddu Road are just two examples of local streets with terraced houses built of local Pennant stone.

In late Carboniferous times (approximately) 300 million years ago, the climax of a major plate collision south and east of 'South Wales', linked with the Variscan orogeny, ended the period of coal formation. A consequence of these events and its associated uplift resulted in the folding and faulting of the coal measures to form the basin structure characteristic of the South Wales coalfield; Bargoed and Gilfach being located just to the north of the point the basin is at its deepest. However, later tectonic activity (probably associated with the formation of the Alps), led to the re-activation of many faults which hampered mining operations in South Wales collieries. In the Cardiff - Vale of Glamorgan area there is evidence of younger rocks than those beneath Bargoed, but whether the conditions which caused their formation prevailed here too, is not known for certain, as there is no trace of them or later rock successions. However, interpretations of the way rivers have developed and sculptured the land have led some geologists to suggest that there could have been younger rocks overlying Bargoed's site - chalk being a strong contender, but subsequent denudation mainly by marine erosion has removed all trace of its presence.

Geomorphological Development:

Geomorphological processes, (shaping of the land by weathering and erosion processes) have dominated over the past few million years and shaped the rocks which form the area around Bargoed and Gilfach. Two major processes have operated, with collectively a profound effect on the landscape of the area:

Rivers have eroded the land surface creating the general pattern of valleys displayed.

This development has been punctuated by the occurrence of a number of glacial epochs.

Earth scientists who have studied the South Wales area accept the hypothesis that many of the local rivers, including the Rhymney, developed on a land surface that was tilted; highest to the north, lowest in the south. Rivers formed upon this surface, flowing generally north to south, eroding valleys as they proceeded to a sea somewhere to the south – a proto Bristol Channel? It is uncertain of what rocks this surface was composed, but the notion that it was chalk, laid down during the Cretaceous period (145 – 65 million years ago) is widely accepted. However, it is evident that all trace of this chalk in South Wales was eroded away long before the first glaciers appeared (Pleistocene period 1.8 million years ago) but these rivers had established a distinct pattern of parallel drainage, fed by small tributaries flowing from the adjoining slopes. This pattern was distinguished by its discordance with the earlier rock structures now exposed, as the rivers crossed the folds and troughs (anticlines and synclines) formed during the Variscan and Alpine (during the Cenozoic era, from 65 million years ago to the present) orogenies. Such drainage is not uncommon and has been termed 'superimposed'. By the beginning of the Pleistocene era, the drainage system was well established, but over the next 1.8 million years it was to be substantially modified.

The origins of glacial events are uncertain, but research suggests that the European plate (upon which Bargoed and Gilfach are located) had moved north from its equatorial location of the Carboniferous period to a latitude not very different from the present. During the Pleistocene epoch there seem to have been four major advances and retreats of ice, termed glacial and interglacial events. Only the two latest series of events appear to have left an imprint on the local landscape, but each took a different form and created different landscapes.

The glaciations took two forms; namely ice sheets and valley glaciers. The former affected the area at least once, notably during the Wolstonian or third advance of the ice (approximately 200,000 to 130,000 years ago). The source of the ice for the local area was the central Welsh uplands, which in turn was part of the Irish Sea ice sheet. Its erosive powers seem to have been relatively weak, because as the ice sheets probably extended little further than the north Somerset coast, they were melting rather than eroding. Notwithstanding this, signs of ice sheet erosion have been observed and recorded in the Rhymney Valley. These ice sheets were transporting huge quantities of rock debris, much of which was deposited from the decaying ice on to the surface beneath. This debris, (ground moraine, till or boulder clay) covers most of the land surface in the Bargoed environs, smoothing-out much of the preceding surface. In the surrounding area there is evidence of ice transportation in the form of rock fragments (erratics) randomly distributed over the surface, notably pieces of Old Red Sandstone or Millstone Grit, of varying sizes, whose origins can be traced to the Brecon Beacons and perhaps beyond.

Valley glaciers were the main instruments of denudation during the fourth or Devensian advance (110, 000 – 12,000 years ago, with the main extent about 18,000 years ago). These glaciers flowing either from ice fields over the Brecon Beacons, or the larger Cambrian Mountains ice sheet, had a greater impact on the landscape, despite their being less extensive than the ice sheets. As they flowed down the pre-existing river valleys their erosive power was concentrated, so both overdeepening and straightening them and accentuating their characteristics, clearly evident in the Rhymney Valley in the vicinity of Bargoed and Gilfach. The steep valley sides overlooking Pontaberbargoed are a product of the overdeepening, as are those overlooking Angel Way. The site of Bargoed and Gilfach is at the top of this steep slope, on a form of bench, which in Switzerland might be termed an 'alp', a feature which extends southwards towards lower Gilfach, at which point it is lost in the slightly different landscape of the Pengam area. This also demonstrates the influence of the rocks, for where there are resistant rocks such as Pennant Grits, higher ground and steeper slopes result, but less resistant coal measure rocks tend not to support steep slopes.

Furthermore, some geographers have propounded the idea that a number of the pre-glacial river courses were significantly altered by the presence of ice; the unusual course of the lower Rhymney has attracted such a hypothesis. The course of the lower part of the Darran valley could also be the result of glacial modification – the glacier taking a 'short cut' to the Rhymney Valley rather than proceeding down a possible pre-glacial course, the Cylla valley.

Both during the erosion process and weathering, especially by frost action, of exposed valley sides, large quantities of debris or moraine were produced. When the glaciers began to melt (a process which took many centuries) moraine was deposited on the valley floor and sides, often forming an undulating landscape. In places, though not in Bargoed and Gilfach, this was sometimes shaped into other landforms. Nevertheless, it has been suggested that a relatively unusual depositional landform – a medial moraine, has been identified at the northern end of Bargoed railway viaduct. Such features form where two valley glaciers join, as they did at the confluence of the Rhymney and Darran valleys, and some of the debris that fell onto the sides of the glacier as it flowed down the valley remains in the space left at the point of meeting. This landform proved to be of use to the railway builders.

The transition from glacial to 'normal' conditions, which occurred at the end of the Wolstonian era, as well as the most recent glacial event, was marked by periglacial or tundra conditions. During such times winters were marked by snowfall and deeply frozen soil and subsoil, but summers, being warmer, saw the formation of large amounts of melt water, much of which saturated the upper, defrosted layers of soil and subsoil. In some areas the abundant melt water eroded new valleys, some of which were abandoned, but evidence of such action in the Bargoed and Gilfach area is lacking, though there are possibilities in the Caerphilly basin. It is possible that some of the river diversions, including that cited above, were contributed to by the vast energy of the summer melt water.

The saturated soil and subsoil referred to could have been a significant agent in moulding the valley sides. In immediate post glacial times slopes might have been much steeper than now, but the slow down-slope movement of sodden soil etc. (solifluction) rounded-off the lower slopes in particular. Furthermore, other parts of the Rhymney Valley, such as Troedrhiwfuwch and New Tredegar a few miles north of Bargoed, show evidence of landslides, many of which originated during these periglacial conditions.

When in post glacial times the rivers resumed their work, it was in overdeepened valleys with steep, often unstable sides. Landslides, as indicated above, have been a significant agent of land sculpture and it is feasible that valley sides in the Bargoed and Gilfach area could have been similarly affected. The régime of the River Rhymney is such that following heavy rain, water, unable to soak into the generally impervious rock, flows into the river causing flows to increase rapidly resulting in floods. Then the river's erosive capabilities are maximised and debris and even man-made structures are removed from the banks or main channel. The river has shown its power on many occasions, notably in December 1979.

However, during this period a new denudational agent, man, appeared. Until 1800, man's influence on the physical landscape in the Bargoed and Gilfach area had been slight, but after that date it became increasingly evident, profoundly altering what nature created. The river was channelled initially during construction of Bargoed Colliery 1897-1903, as well as being partly covered over. Following the closure of the colliery in 1977, the valley floor was briefly given the opportunity to revert to nature, but in 1994 Bargoed Colliery Reclamation Scheme began, part of which was the straightening and culverting of the river that was completed in April 1995. Subsequently, the area was covered with colliery waste from Bargoed tip and sculptured in readiness for construction of a new road system (Angel Way) which was eventually completed in September 2009. Man's impact was not restricted to the river: valley sides were changed in a number of ways as they were excavated for rock for building purposes, used for construction of railway lines or as dumping grounds for spoil from the coal mines.

Weather and Climate:

Climatologists place Bargoed and Gilfach in the North West European Maritime climate zone characterised by cool, moist winters and warm, moist summers. As precise climatic data for the local area is not available, Meteorological Office data relating to the village of Cilfynydd 7.7 miles to the south west in the Taff Valley can be considered. However, while Cilfynydd has some physical characteristics in common with Bargoed and Gilfach such as its altitude of 636 feet, it lies on the eastern or windward side of its valley, while Bargoed and Gilfach are on the leeward or sheltered side of the Rhymney

Valley. Further quantitative indication may be derived from maps in the Glamorgan County History, which relate to a different time period for calculation of averages, but it is suggested the differences are minor. Interpreted, these maps show Bargoed to have the following averages:

Temps °C Jan (min)	Temps °C Jan (max)	Temps °C July (min)	Temps °C July (max)	Days of frost	Rainfall (mm)
1.3	6.5	11.7	20.3	44	1400 (55 inches)

Bargoed and Gilfach benefit from relatively low altitude and shelter from Senghenydd mountain especially when the wind and weather is coming from the prevailing west or south westerly direction. The relative configuration of relief and rain-bearing wind generates a minor föhn-like modification thus temperatures are slightly higher and rainfall a little lower than those experienced in Cilfynydd or, more locally, Ystrad Mynach. The data indicates that January is the coldest month on average, and July the warmest while frost is most frequent during the winter months of December, January and February. Rain falls on about 190 days in an average year, with October to January being the wettest and April to July the driest. During an average year there are 6 – 8 days with snow and approximately 1,450 hours of sunshine.

Even data such as this is generalised, as our own experience will tell. The aforementioned föhn effect provides Bargoed and Gilfach with less rain than many surrounding areas, as might be observed by the way clouds from the south west break-up over the Nelson basin, not re-forming again until they pass well to the north of Bargoed and Gilfach. Furthermore, the data shows averages, but reports in *Merthyr Express* as well as our memories highlight many extreme weather conditions, such as the hot weather and severe drought of 1976, heavy snows of 1909, 1947, 1963, 1982 and 2010, and exceptional rainfall events as occurred in 1903, 1908, 1910 and 1979. It also hides local, microclimatic variations such as the lower level of the snow line in Gilfach compared with Heolddu in Bargoed, or the greater incidence of rainfall north from Gilfach, both concomitant with the increasing height of the land that reduces temperatures and results in greater cloud formation and more rain. Also very localised is the occurrence of fog. Radiation fog, associated with high pressure, cloudless skies and low temperatures, affects the lower parts adjoining the river in all seasons apart from the summer. However, orographic fog, associated with warm or occluded frontal conditions bringing low cloud, affects the higher parts of Bargoed in any season, and is usually accompanied by rain.

'Climate change' is an emotive concept exercising many minds at present, but as suggested in the foregoing account, there is abundant evidence from the geological record that the Bargoed and Gilfach area has experienced considerable changes in climatic conditions over time, from tropical, to equatorial, to temperate, to polar and so on. Most of these changes can be explained acceptably by reference to the hypothesis of 'Plate Tectonics'. However, the causes of the glacial events are less clear; some suggest they were a product of terrestrial environmental changes, notably major and cataclysmic volcanic eruptions, others cite a combination of solar fluctuations caused by sunspots or variations in the Earth's rotation or tilt.

On a historical time scale there is evidence of a number of 'climate changes' since the end of the last glacial advance, about 10,000 years ago. Analysis of pollens from lake beds in South Wales suggests that prior to 3,000 years ago temperatures were warmer than today but after that average temperatures declined and rainfall possibly increased. Temperatures increased during the Roman period, reaching a maximum, probably higher than today, during the thirteenth century A.D. A century later temperatures began to fall, leading to the so-called 'Little Ice Age' of the sixteenth to early nineteenth centuries. These fluctuations, identified from a wide range of sources, continued through the twentieth century, and have been considered evidence for the dynamism of both weather and climate, even if their causes are still uncertain and speculative.

It is short-term climatic changes which have generated most controversy, especially since 1987, when notions such as 'Global Warming' entered the political arena. Positive evidence for such warming, either scientific or anecdotal, in the Bargoed and Gilfach area is non-existent. Anecdotal evidence such as *we don't have the winters we used to*, or *summers are better now than in the past*, are very subjective and usually do not stand-up to scrutiny. Scientific evidence is clouded by the paucity of reliable data and allegations that the statistical manipulation of the data and derived conclusions is biased. So is our climate changing? Yes, history shows it has. Is it a result of 'Global Warming? *That* is the crux of the debate. Therefore, if you are reading this in 2111, perhaps you could tell us!

Soils and Vegetation:

Both soils and vegetation in the Bargoed area are relatively young, having formed after the disappearance of the valley glaciers around 10,000 years ago. It is likely that a continuous soil and vegetation cover was not established until around 9,000 years ago on a surface of glacial and periglacial debris, not long before men first wandered through the area. Both soils and vegetation seem to have benefited from slightly warmer conditions than today, thus it is likely, and supported by pollen evidence, that the area was covered by deciduous woodland e.g. oak, etc. However, around 3,000 years ago the climate cooled, for reasons unknown, and rainfall increased. As a result of a combination of early man's initial forest clearance, grazing animals and the cooler, damp conditions, peat bog and moorland grasses replaced the woodland on the plateau surface forming Gelligaer Common. Woodland, especially oak wood, survived on the relatively untouched, better drained parts of the valley floor and sides, although the thin, acid soils on valley-side slopes inclined to stunt tree growth, consequently durmast oak tended to dominate. In wetter areas of the valley floor, alder and perhaps willow existed too.

Most of the area is covered by glacial drift. This forms much of the soil, most noticeably on the lower slopes, particularly towards Gilfach, as any local gardener will testify. The soils are generally wet, heavy and cold, and because of the rock from which they were derived, are rather acid and not good growing media for crops. Although cultivation has proceeded and improved such soils somewhat, these areas are predominantly pastoral with the principal crop being hay for winter feed. Potentially more fertile, but in very limited supply, are fluvial soils, commonly known as silt and generally restricted to the valley floor. Their value has been diminished by relatively frequent flooding and subsequent water logging, and since the mid nineteenth century much has been covered by local mining activity so they contribute little to the agricultural potential of the area.

On Gelligaer Common, boulder clays are often covered by blanket bog. On land that is not waterlogged the coarse moorland grasses are broken down slowly to form a rather acid soil. When dried, this soil can be of use, but still tends to levels of acidity plants do not like, thus is left as permanent 'rough' pasture. The peat bogs are uncultivable, unless the moorland is deep ploughed and drained, as seen in the areas afforested with conifers in the 1950s. However, apart from limited potential for forestry, the peat bog areas can form part of the summer grazing lands for livestock from farms on the lower, more sheltered and fertile land. The latter, where the land is better drained, either naturally or with man's help, have been cultivated within recent times for a small range of crops, such as oats and potatoes, besides providing winter pasture for grazing animals.

Today natural woodland is limited to the valley sides, but seems to be expanding in extent as industry declines, along with its voracious appetite for timber. Trees are beginning to form relatively dense cover along the banks of the Rhymney river in the Country Park extending from south Bargoed to Pengam bridge. Oak, horse chestnut, alder, silver birch, are but four of the species to be noted today. The site of old Pontaberbargoed and the lower Darran valley is also surrounded by relatively luxuriant tree cover, which extends almost continuously to Deri. Another narrow avenue of woodland can also be seen alongside the railway lines between Gilfach and Pengam, something which causes some operational problems for trains during the leaf fall season. The trees surrounding Lewis School Pengam, planted during the late 1920s to compensate the school for loss of land to the *New Road* from Gilfach to Ystrad Mynach, are just one example of the many stretches of woodland that, like much of the vegetation in Bargoed and Gilfach, is not natural or even native, but the product of man's interference.

Conclusions:

To fully appreciate the way Bargoed and Gilfach has developed demands an understanding of the physical context. Geology, geomorphology, weather and climate as well as soils and vegetation have all played a significant part in shaping the valley, offering the potential that man grasped so readily in the latter part of the nineteenth century and continues to the present. Man has altered the landscape radically, but what nature achieved prior to the arrival of homo sapiens is still clearly recognisable in the landscape and, whether mankind likes it or not, still determines where buildings are built or route ways laid, hence the importance of the physical context to an understanding of activities, past, present and future. Indeed it is, perhaps salutary to consider that the events described in this chapter extended over a period of 500 million years, and the next chapter covers over 5,000 years while the rest of the book deals with events which for the most part, took place only over the past 200 years.

A photograph of Bargoed and Gilfach taken October 2011 by Brian Jarrett.

CHAPTER 3
FROM PREHISTORIC TIMES TO THE LATER MEDIEVAL PERIOD

The local area in prehistoric times

By about 5000 B.C. a moist, oceanic warm Atlantic climatic phase was established in Britain and most of the land was covered by dense forests rich in food plants and abundant fauna for the skilled hunter-gatherers of the Mesolithic (Middle Stone Age) period to exploit. Farming had first reached Europe around 6500 B.C. spreading west from the Middle East, and was introduced into the British Isles c.4000 B.C. during the Neolithic (New Stone Age) period. Forests were burned or felled as land was cleared for farming and new communities. The Neolithic people used any available hard stone to make polished stone axes for felling trees and digging the land. The first evidence of human occupation in what is now the Bargoed and Gilfach area amounts to a few isolated finds such as the stone axehead from this period appearing in the National Museum's Archaeology Database as record 55962.

The introduction and subsequent expansion of farming occurred against a background of further climatic change so that by c.3000 B.C. the climate became drier and more Continental with more frequent and wider extremes of heat and cold. The farming pattern would probably have been a combination of crops and animals, but still supplemented by hunting and gathering. The growing population was scattered across the landscape in small groups with individual family holdings in cleared areas in the forest. In some parts of Britain there are remains of monumental Neolithic tombs constructed for the collective burial of the dead, each containing scores of burials probably accumulated over hundreds of years, but there is little evidence of these people in the local area. Evidence of settlement sites from the Neolithic and Early Bronze Age is a matter of chance finds of pottery or other objects (such as the hoard of four bronze axes found at Pont Caradog [north of Heolddu] and, in recent years, metal-detectors' finds of axes in surrounding areas) and the probability is that purely domestic sites would have consisted of small groups of lightly constructed buildings compatible with a semi-nomadic lifestyle. The practice of forming decorative cup-shaped hollows in stone probably belonged to the Early Bronze Age and, in 1925, archaeologist Sir Mortimer Wheeler was able to identify some fifty cup-marks on Maen Catwg (about half a mile north west of Gelligaer Village) but nowadays there is no trace of the previously reported connecting channel between some of the cups.

It is believed that the transition from the Neolithic to the Bronze Age in Britain coincided with the appearance of a class of hand-made beaker often found in graves of a distinctive character, such as the cist burial in the farmyard at Llancaiach Isaf which contained the remains of a child aged about six years.

Bronze Age people are primarily evidenced by their burials and most of the numerous round cairns and barrows on the higher ground are burial places belonging to the period between c.1700 and c.1200 B.C. and point to a substantial population. This assumes that Bronze Age peoples buried their dead in the area in which they lived, an assumption supported by the occasional finds of bronze axes and the recent find of a pottery sherd in a ditch system at Llancaiach Fawr. Any attempt to estimate population would be guesswork as the burials that remain represent many generations while the proportion of the population receiving ceremonial burial as well as the number of destroyed burials remain unknown. The population of Britain in the Bronze Age may have totalled only 250,000 but it has been held that the distribution of distinctive finds such as socketed axes provide early evidence of later tribal areas. Such remains tend to cluster on the semi-permeable soils, avoid steep hillsides, and show a preference for high ground which would have provided large areas of moorland grazing together with relatively easy movement along the ridges.

During the Middle Bronze Age (c.1450 – 900 B.C.) in Wales the distinctive burial traditions of the Early Bronze Age were in decline and only scant domestic evidence has been found. It has been argued that the apparent decline of the upland barrow cemeteries in the Middle Bronze Age reflects the beginning of a shift in population towards the main river valleys and coastal plains. Human activity (deforestation and other interference by man and his animals) and climatic change were responsible for the deterioration of upland pastures and cultivated fields and that resulted in the exploitation of the previously heavily-forested valleys. The change from a warmer to a wetter and cooler climatic phase encouraged the formation of the blanket peat which now covers the moorland above Bargoed and Gilfach on land previously deprived of its forest cover during the Neolithic and early Bronze Ages. Dendrochronological evidence from bog oaks excavated in Ireland reveals very narrow rings indicating limited tree growth in certain periods. One such period started in 1159 B.C. and lasted for eighteen consecutive years. The most obvious cause of growth restriction over such a long period is that conditions got colder or wetter, or both colder and wetter, and there was little or no sunlight. Recent research into volcanic activity at the time revealed these events coincided with eruption of Iceland's super-volcano Hekla while others argue that the massive dust veil that smothered our planet was caused by a comet travelling near the earth's atmosphere. Whatever the cause, it is difficult to appreciate the catastrophic effect of such conditions on the Bronze Age peoples who would not have been able to store food for any length of time to meet their needs when their crops failed and soil eroded away. Archaeological evidence from similarly affected areas in the Scottish Highlands and on Salisbury Plain, point to abandonment having taken place over a very short period of time. The lack of evidence of settlements from the late Bronze Age could point to a catastrophic breakdown in society in the period caused by over-population, over-cultivation of the land and extreme climatic deterioration and archaeologists have suggested that this time of turmoil and strife gave rise to a warrior elite. However, after a lengthy period of poor climatic conditions a gradual improvement occurred and by c.600 B.C. conditions were much as we are experiencing today.

The writings of archaeologists such as Robert Bewley show that generally Iron Age Britain is characterised by its settlements and not, as in the major part of the Bronze Age, by its burials. There are remains of small fortified homesteads and larger hill-forts in areas towards the coastal plain such as Llantrisant, but the fact that no such remains have been found in the area around Bargoed and Gilfach may be because the remains of any small homesteads have been ploughed out. However, there is also evidence that much of the population of Wales survived with little change since the Middle Bronze Age and that there was a considerable delay in the spread of hill-fort building in both south and north-west Wales.

The farmers of Iron Age Britain were highly skilled but pastoralism would have been more common on the poor soils of the uplands in the vicinity of Bargoed and Gilfach. Where conditions were suitable, cereals were grown and formed an important part of the people's diet. The use of iron implements and more efficient farming methods resulted in production of a food surplus and it has been estimated that the population of Britain grew from 250,000 in the Bronze Age to 1,000,000 in the Iron Age.

What we know of Iron Age people is gleaned from the often biased accounts of Roman writers who regarded them as hard drinking and ferocious warriors as well as clever craftspeople with a rich oral tradition. They had a strict hierarchy with powerful religious leaders, the Druids, who besides being a trained group of priests also had an important role in maintaining tribal law.

The Bronze Age had witnessed the beginnings of the areas of the later tribes and by the Iron Age strong regional and tribal identities had developed. Today's Bargoed and Gilfach lie within the tribal territory of the Silures which Ray Howell suggests covered an area bounded by the rivers Wye and Tywi. Although both the Roman writer and historian, Cornelius Tacitus, and epigraphical evidence from Caerwent refer to the name Silures there is no evidence to confirm that it was the name used by the tribe themselves.

The Roman impact on the local area

There was diplomatic contact between Rome and some of the British tribes in the century following the invasions of Julius Caesar and by the time of the Claudian invasion in A.D. 43 the invaders could have relied on the support of at least some British tribes. The invading army under Aulus Plautius, consisting of four legions plus auxiliaries, probably exceeded 40,000 men. The account of the Roman invasion in Tacitus' *Annals* begins in the last years of Claudius (late in A.D. 47) and, although it was written many years later (c. A.D. 100) and for a Roman readership, it gives an insight into Silurian society and the Silures' fierce resistance to the invaders. From this it can be deduced that between A.D. 48 and 78 most Roman offensive campaigns were directed at what is now

Wales and, specifically at certain tribes within it. In the first Annual Caerleon Lecture, Professor W. H. Manning discussed how P. Ostorius Scapula, who arrived as governor in A.D. 47, followed up actions in the West Midlands and probably Flintshire, by embarking on a series of campaigns against the Silures and the Ordovices, the two major tribes in Wales, both of whom may have been under the command of Caradog (also Caratacus, Caractacus or Caradoc). Contrary to what some local people think (probably because a bridge over Bargoed-Rhymney river north of Bargoed is known as Pont Caradog), Caradog was not a local man: he was one of the sons of Cunobelinus the chief of the Catuvellauni tribe who were based on modern-day Colchester. Caradog had unsuccessfully led resistance to the Roman invasion force in A.D. 43 before moving west with what remained of his forces to find willing allies in the Silures. In response to the Romans' extreme military pressure on the Silurian territory which had become the focus of opposition to the invasion, Caradog moved with his forces to join up with the Ordovices in Mid Wales. There, in A.D. 51, they were defeated in battle and Caradog and his family were eventually taken as prisoners to Rome. Whereas this defeat may have broken the Ordovices, the Silures were another matter. They seemed to become more aggressive and began a period of highly effective guerrilla warfare that lasted for about quarter of a century and resulted in heavy Roman casualties. In *The Annals* Tacitus remarked that *the Silures were turned neither by brutality nor by clemency from pursuing war and required the encampment of legions to keep them down*, so painting a picture of groups of soldiers constructing forts and foraging a short distance from major concentrations of troops based at existing forts. Late in summer A.D. 52 the Silures were successful against a legion (probably XX *Valeria*) and for the next twenty five years or so, under successive governorships, Roman military campaigns were somewhat spasmodic and for about a decade after the Boudican rebellion (in A.D. 60) Roman policy with regard to Britain remained at a near standstill.

The civil war which followed Nero's suicide in A.D. 68 resulted in the emergence of Vespasian as emperor in A.D. 69 and the end of the Julio-Claudian dynasty. The accession of Vespasian who had commanded *Legio ll Augusta* in the invasion army, saw the adoption of a much firmer policy towards Britain that may have had the conquest of Britain as a whole as its aim.

It was not until the governorship of Julius Frontinus (A.D. 74-78) that the attack on Wales was resumed and Tacitus covered this period with an extremely brief statement that Frontinus overcame the Silures, surmounting not only their valour but the physical difficulties of their land. In so doing he established a network of closely spaced auxiliary forts (each housing 500 or 1000 men) linked by roads and based on the legionary fortress of *Isca* at Caerleon, as by then the old legionary fortress at Usk may well have become partly derelict. It should be noted that about 50 forts ultimately covered Wales and by A.D. 78 some 30,000 troops were stationed either in Wales or on its borders. It is believed that the Glamorgan forts including the first, earth and timber, fort at

Gelligaer (but excluding that at Cardiff and possibly Neath and some of the marching camps which probably date from earlier campaigns) were constructed at this time.

The pattern of garrisons set up in the territory of the Silures reflects the Roman method of controlling areas with difficult terrain by splitting the tribes into small units which could be more easily supervised and so prevented from regrouping their forces. In Britain the frontier regions were manned by auxiliary units and the legions were not expected to carry out routine patrol and policing duties, while the auxiliary forts were linked by roads and within a day's march of each other. Some forts were sited on estuaries for ease of supply by sea while inland forts were often at strategic valley junctions or, as in the case of Gelligaer, on lonely upland roads to monitor the passage of supplies and discourage insurrection by the Silures.

The Roman army of occupation would have had a profound impact on the local population, not least in terms of confiscation and exploitation of tribal land. In the immediate post-conquest period, the Silures were treated as defeated people and their land declared forfeit, as the Roman army made huge demands on food supplies and raw materials.

During the reign of the Emperor Trajan there appears to have been a policy decision to rebuild forts in stone and this resulted in the construction of a second fort at Gelligaer. Three fragmentary inscriptions for the site point to a construction date between A.D. 103 and 111. This fort, approximately 128 yards square and covering about 3.5 acres, constructed adjacent to the earlier installation, had massive defences and would have provided accommodation for a 500-strong infantry unit.

It has long been assumed that the fort lay on the main route from Cardiff to Y Gaer at Brecon but there remains little trace of what must have been a comprehensive network of main and subsidiary Roman roads. Apart from a few sections which consisted of pitching and kerbs, it appears that the roads in this locality were not paved but surfaced with a mix of gravel and sand or small stones. The surviving sections on Cefn Gelligaer suggest that the road rarely consisted of more than a single thin layer of metalling. Such roads across the Welsh uplands enabled Roman soldiers to be rapidly deployed achieving progress of 25 miles a day even in inclement weather so saving manpower as garrisons could be spaced further apart. This would have deterred any Silures from taking up arms.

In a 1968 article in *Archaeologia Cambrensis*, R. W. Davies considers the duty of the commanding officer to bring his troops out for exercises. Evidence from eight forts in Wales confirms that troops had been taken out into the *territorium* of the unit to build practice-camps. These camps were small, often less than 100 feet square, earthworks thrown up by soldiers as part of their training, and are frequently found in the vicinity of forts. They reproduce the essential features of marching camps (constructed to protect the encampments of an army on campaign), having carefully rounded corners and protected gateways, and serve as a reminder that the garrisons could be ordered into the field at any time and would be required to know how to construct marching-camps even under the most taxing conditions. The area enclosed by such practice camps is much too small to be of any practical use.

The five such camps identified on Gelligaer Common were all within a short march of the fort at Gelligaer and not far from a Roman road. Four of the practice camps are located in an area known as Fforest Gwladys, whilst the siting of one at Heolddu Uchaf may be significant in that it has been suggested it could also have served as a signalling station.

The only fixed point for the history of the Romans at Gelligaer and surrounding area is provided by fragmentary inscriptions which mention Emperor Trajan's fifth consulship (A.D. 103-112). From the limited work carried out to date it appears that there were periods of occupation (either full or partial), abandonment and rebuilding of the fort and metal detector finds in recent years point to a Roman presence in the area until the late fourth century. It should be noted, however, that evidence from the three hundred or so letters and documents (written on wooden tablets) discovered at the fort of *Vindolanda* on Hadrian's Wall indicates that garrisons may often have been considerably under-strength and that the Roman army, by means of efficient communications and good roads, was able to dominate large areas by only occupying key strategic points with minimal resources.

There is no way of knowing what the attitude of the defeated Silures may have been towards the Romans but after such a fierce and protracted guerrilla war lingering hostility seems inevitable especially as the tribe would have become impoverished. There must also have been considerable mistrust on the part of the Romans as it was not until the earlier part of the second century, almost half a century after the conquest, that the Silures were granted a form of local government and a *civitas* capital set up at *Venta Silurum* (Caerwent). This system allowed a range of local government functions to be devolved back to the tribe and implemented by the tribal elite and it has been held that the mechanisms put in place by the *civitas* enabled tribal identity to survive and develop through the later Romano-British period. The establishment of *civitas* capitals was considered vital to the process of romanisation but the siting of *Venta Silurum* on the coastal belt and close to the Second Augustan Legion at Caerleon may owe much to Roman convenience and security concerns and casts grave doubts on the extent to which romanisation extended into the uplands. There is growing evidence that many communities in the uplands continued to follow traditional practices throughout the Roman occupation. The uplands had good mineral resources and pockets of arable land, but little else to plunder by Romans who regarded war as an investment from which they could earn good returns.

By the late third century, when the stone wall surrounding *Venta Silurum* was probably constructed, increasing seaborne attacks by Irish, Saxon and Frankish raiders brought about a re-organisation of Roman forces in Britain and resulted in the fort at Cardiff being rebuilt, to eventually replace Caerleon as the military centre of this region. The exact date of the ending of legionary occupation at Caerleon is not known but there is evidence that people continued to live there during the fourth century and beyond. At Caerwent the basilica was demolished in the mid fourth century but finds of late fourth century coins point to a Roman presence in the area for some time afterwards even though the town itself was in decline and becoming a ruin.

Some recent research is presented in Ray Howell's *Searching for the Silures, an Iron Age Tribe in South-East Wales* (Tempus Publishing Limited, Stroud, 2006) and sheds further light on the Roman impact on this part of Wales.

The traditional date for the end of Roman rule in Britain is A.D. 410 when Emperor Honorius issued a *rescript* renouncing responsibility for Britain and instructing local authorities to look after their own affairs. Whilst the military and Roman administrators will have left these shores, some soldiers and their dependents as well as veterans remained and, in some places, continued to occupy former Roman installations. No evidence of re-occupation has been found at Gelligaer but early archaeologists may have failed to spot it as they did in other sites excavated in Victorian and Edwardian times. The transition into the early medieval period, with increasing evidence from some areas that hillforts were re-occupied, points to a return to a pre-conquest lifestyle and traditions, and it has been argued that, particularly in the uplands, dynastic systems were directly related to the pre-Roman past.

Christianity

The influence of Christianity had been growing in Britain throughout the later Roman period and was to become an important factor in early medieval society in Wales and this era is often referred to as the *Age of the Saints* because the holy men and women who led the church were figures of power. One of the most important of these saints, and one closely linked to this area, was Catwg (also Cadoc, Cadog or Cadocus) who, according to *Vita Sancti Cadoci* (his Latin life) was the son of Gwynllyw Filwr, ruler of Gwynllwg, and Gwladys (also Gwladus or Gladis). Catwg's mother was said to be the most eminent of the many daughters of Brychan who ruled over Brycheiniog. In the late twelfth century Giraldus Cambrensis referred to Brychan as a *nobly born and powerful ruler* and adds that *the British histories testified that he had four and twenty daughters, all of whom, dedicated from their youth to religious observances, happily ended their lives in sanctity.* Catwg was probably born in the late fifth or early sixth century and, at a young age, he was sent to be educated under Meuthius (a scholar of great repute who was also known as Tatheus) at Caerwent. After some twelve years there, Catwg grew up to be a great leader and was renowned for his wisdom and learning as well as his piety and missionary zeal and he was often referred to as Catwg Ddoeth (Catwg the Wise). Catwg and his followers travelled widely, founding numerous places of worship in Wales, Ireland, Scotland and Brittany as well as the great monastery at Nantcarfan (Llancarfan) in the Vale of Glamorgan. It is said that he persuaded his parents to take vows of celibacy and they eventually parted in monastic fashion: his father founded a monastery at Newport which bore his name (now corrupted to St. Woollos) while his mother founded a religious community at Fforest Gwladys (now known as Capel Gwladys) on Gelligaer Common.

In later life, Catwg found the management of the large establishment at Llancarfan too much for him and so he nominated Elli, a favourite disciple, as his successor and departed *in a cloud* to a place called Beneventum, the whereabouts of which is unknown. On his arrival there he was elected abbot over the large community of monks and set about organising the repair of the settlement and its defences which were in ruins. He was subsequently made bishop but soon afterwards was to suffer martyrdom at the hands of Saxon invaders c.A.D. 570. The extent of the influence of the early church locally can be gauged from the Llandaff charters that refer to some 36 *monasteries* and 38 *churches* in south east Wales in the sixth century.

The Tegernacus stone, as it was in a field opposite Capel Brithdir, with its Latin inscription.

The Roman practice of roadside burial continued into this period and inscribed grave marker stones, often in the form of large undressed boulders, have been found in a wide range of locations besides Roman roads, tracks and ridgeway routes. Such stones are usually inscribed with the Latin formula *hic iacit* (meaning here lies) and a fine example is the Tegernacus Stone which formerly stood near Capel Brithdir and is now in the custody of the National Museum of Wales. Its rough surface bears a Latin inscription vertically down the face in four lines which translates as *Tegernacus, son of Marti(us), lies here*. For centuries such inscriptions have been dismissed as the clumsy scrawling of a semi-literate society but such inscribed stones/memorials are now increasingly regarded as clear evidence of a highly literate society committing their thoughts to stone.

By the seventh century the cross had become the symbol of Christianity and developed from the plain incised crosses (such as that on the slab with incised ring-cross found at Capel Gwladys in 1906 and now in Gelligaer parish church) to more elaborate crosses with dots or rings in the angles. A stone slab with incised crosses was discovered built into a wall at Capel Brithdir when, in 1960, the more modern chapel on an older site was being demolished and it is now in Bargoed's St. Gwladys' Church (a later dedication opened in 1876 as part of the parish of Gelligaer until a separate parish was created in 1904).

Medieval period

Little historical evidence remains from the Early Medieval period but the Book of Llandaff (which survives primarily in a twelfth century document) provides what purports to be a chronological list of rulers in Gwent and Glywysing, the main kingdoms to emerge in the Silurian region. Archaeologically, traces of secular domestic occupation from this period are extremely rare and the perishable nature of many objects made from materials such as wood and leather has resulted in poor survival of evidence. In 1936, Lady Aileen Fox excavated platform houses at Dinas Noddfa on Gelligaer Common but was unable to date them. Similar houses exist at nine other sites on the Common and when Lady Fox excavated the Graig Spyddyd site in 1938 it produced stratified potsherds indicating occupation in the Medieval period with a likely terminal date for occupation in the first half of the fourteenth century.

This photograph by Arthur Wright (© Winding House CCBC Museums and Heritage Service) was taken when the Gelligaer fort was excavated in the early twentieth century

CHAPTER 4
FARMS AND FARMING

Introduction

The landscape of the early medieval period - and for a very long period prior to this - must have been enclosed farms on the mountain slopes bordering the open moorland, the communal grazing of the mountaintops. The fact that archaeological relics have been found only on our mountaintops does not suggest that this was man's only habited area in the pre-history periods, simply that evidence of early occupation of the mountainsides and valleys would have been obliterated by continuous farming and extensive and consecutive developments on the valley floors. Gradual clearance of the forested mountainsides would have increased the farmed area so that farms extended to the valley floors (and onto the communal moorland) certainly well before the thirteenth century, and the agricultural lifestyle in a rural landscape changed little over centuries.

The landscape of the local area today reflects changes which have occurred during the last 150 years and the development of industry and the growth of the town itself which is discussed later. This chapter looks at the farms which made up the area.

We will look (albeit briefly) not just at the farms themselves, their extent and where possible the types of farming, the crops grown and animals kept, but also the farming families, the owners and/or occupiers. We will see how many of the farming families were related, not just within this area but across the wider parish. Indeed, some old established farming families are still represented on the farms today.

For clarity and consistency, modern day place and farm names have been used (except in *italics*). Personal names may present a problem as the peoples of Gelligaer parish did not start using surnames till the eighteenth century (see Chapter 1 for a brief explanation of patronymic naming), but an effort has been made to write these in as consistent and unambiguous a manner as possible. Acres have been used as the measurement of land and money shown in £.s.d. – see appendix for conversion tables.

The first thing to note is that early deeds describe the farm holdings as being *in a place called Kelache Vargoyd*. The name *Gilfach Fargoed* today is associated with the large old property (the R.A.F.A. Club) to the south of the town of Bargoed, but originally it is believed that it was the general place name for the lands to the west of the Rhymney river between Pontaberbargoed and the bridge at Pengam; the holdings which have been called Pencaedrain, Heolddu, Pandy, Gilfach Fargoed Fawr, Gilfach Fargoed Fach and Gwerthonor.

The Bargoed–Gilfach area formed the northern section of Hengoed Hamlet in Gelligaer parish, which itself was (with Merthyr Tydfil parish) the northern section of the Manor of Senghennydd, called Uwch Caiach or Senghennydd Supra (Upper Senghennydd). The Lordship of Senghennydd, part of the Lordship of Glamorgan, was taken over by the Normans at the end of the eleventh century and consisted of three administrative areas; Uwch Caiach in the north, Is Caiach, also called Senghennydd Subtus or Lower Senghennydd between the Caiach stream and Caerphilly Mountain, and Cibwr stretching southward to the Bristol Channel.

Little is known of the day-to-day life of the early people of the area but certainly it would have been based mainly on subsistence farming. By the mid fifteenth century, however, we have written records of a well-established and organised system of administration and land ownership with a hierarchy of land owners. Although the records were written in Latin and later, English, the local people would have spoken Welsh. Within these records there is further evidence that there was an organised administration dating back to at least the administrative changes inaugurated by Edward I in 1283 and even the times of the Welsh princes. This was then incorporated into the Norman Manorial Lordship system outlined above. More definitive control of the organised administration and record keeping came after the struggle for the English throne, which was effectively decided when Henry Tudor (VII) won the Battle of Bosworth, 1485. We do not know how the Tudors directly affected the lives of the people of the area - although Jasper Tudor (Henry's uncle) gave a gift of bells to the parish church at Gelligaer – but it is probable that the written records relating to Gelligaer parish which survive with regularity from the 1540s within the Senghennydd Manorial records are a result of the 1536 and 1543 Acts of Union enacted by Henry VIII (Laws in Wales Acts, 1535 and 1542, repealed 1993 and 1995). It is only from this time that we have more specific and consistent information on the Bargoed-Gilfach farms and their owners and occupiers.

Most of the farmers of the local area had rights (mainly grazing) on Gelligaer and Merthyr Common – and also owed duties and payments to the Lord of the Manor of Senghennydd in return. Manorial land rents and issues were managed by the Lord's agents in the court leet, held in May and October at Caerphilly. Landowners were obliged to attend to pay chief rents on their properties; payments similar to a modern ground rent although paid by men whom we would think of as the land owner. These payments continued until abolished in the 1925 Law of Property Act and were then redeemed in Senghennydd Manor in 1935 when the farmers of the area paid the equivalent of 20 years chief rent; Mrs Lewis Jenkins of Heolddu Uchaf for example, paid 3s 5d, while Mrs Sarah Thomas of Pencaedrain paid 2d (the latter payment may have been the final amount of the lump sum payable).

Alongside the chief rent, landowners also paid cymortha, a payment which survived since at least the time of the Welsh princes. Despite the lack of written evidence for the earlier period, there must have been a well-organised system of land ownership and administration in the area which developed after the Roman occupation or co-existed with it and was a continuation of an existing system based on the Welsh tribes. Unfortunately, Hengoed hamlet is the only one of the Gelligaer hamlets for which no evidence of payment of cymortha survives.

Another custom was the payment of heriot following the death of a landowner and the introduction of his heir into the Court rolls, commonly the *best beast* but sometimes commuted to a money payment. Thus we find, for example, heriot paid after the deaths of Edward Phillips of Pencaedrain and William Davies of Gwerthonor in 1884, Jenkin Jenkins of Heolddu Isaf in 1899 and Lewis Philip Edwards of Gilfach Fargoed Farm (as owner of Llan Isaf Farm, Bedlinog) in 1913.

Management of the Common was another feature of the leet court; matters such as the appointment of constables for the parish and of haywards, the managers of the common land. William Thomas of Pont Aberbargoed, for example, was both constable of Gelligaer parish and one of the four or five haywards from sometime prior to 1877 until 1891 when he was succeeded by his son, David, who continued in these positions into the twentieth century (although in 1886 the family had moved to Tir Ferch Gronow Farm, Brithdir hamlet).

The leet also dealt with encroachments on the Common and records of the Marquesses of Bute reveal such encroachments on the mountaintops of the Bargoed-Gilfach area which date from at least the sixteenth century.

It is the use of such manorial records, together with nationally generated records such as hearth taxes, land taxes, tithe and census records as well as the local and personal records, church records, electoral rolls, estate records, deeds and wills, which have provided the information for this chapter. It must be noted, however, that relevant quotations in the text below are from the calendars of estate deeds, particularly those of the Llancaiach, Dynevor and Hanbury estates, and not from the deeds themselves. Wills in particular are useful as they provide information about families and relationships and bequests of animals, money or household items which reflect the type of farming and the wealth of the person who died. Their major disadvantage is that they seldom mention property, especially the major family holding (and often the stock belonging to it) because inheritance of this would have been dealt with through other documents such as an entail or part of a nuptial settlement.

The farms, Heolddu and Gilfach Fargoed as well as Pont Aberbargoed (the area or the Pandy?) were all important enough to be depicted on the 1799 Yates map of Glamorgan – old maps being a further source of information.

A further source which has been used is Professor T. V. Davies' book, *The Farms and Farmers of Senghennydd Lordship, part 2, Gelligaer Parish*, where Professor Davies uses Bute Estate records in the National Library, starting with the 1449 manorial rental (the earliest surviving list of payments of chief rents which also gives us the owners of the lands at the time) and attempts to identify all the Gelligaer and Merthyr parish farms by linking them to the 1540 and subsequent rentals.

It is not intended that the use of the word *estate* in this chapter should conjure up an image of a landowner and lifestyle such as that portrayed in Downton Abbey on contemporary television. Nevertheless, there were groups of properties which, although not covering huge areas, can be described as *estates* in the Bargoed-Gilfach (and Gelligaer parish) areas, and originally these were owned by the Lewis and Pritchard (Llancaiach) families. It is these two families who had become the most important landowners - and people – in Gelligaer parish, although discussion of land owners and ownership should not be confined to just this small area as many of the owners either lived in or possessed holdings or pieces of land both in other parts of Gelligaer parish and in neighbouring parishes.

The Gelligaer parish estates have never been as large or as valuable as those of elsewhere and a feature of the landownership was that until the eighteenth century the owners themselves lived locally and mainly confined their activities to Uwch Caiach. Gradually however, the wealthier families of Gelligaer married into more important and wealthier families, mainly from the Vale of Glamorgan, the Plymouth, St. Fagan's Estate, the Carnes of Nash and the Mansel Talbots; other landowners, such as the Butes and the Hanburys of Pontypool, acquired land in the Parish in later years,

No discussion of the history of farms would be complete without reference to the tithe map and schedule which gives a snapshot of each at the start of the Victorian era and Table 1 shows some of the information which is available. One interesting feature is the high proportion of arable land at this time, over 162 acres out of a total of 833, nearly 20%, yet today a negligible area of land is cultivated on the remaining farmed area. It is probable that this would have been a mixture of root crops and corn – the latter milled locally.

Names (mainly Welsh) were given to each field and comparison of these names with ones on earlier deeds and records suggests that the field names are much older than the farm names themselves. These field names have been used in the discussion of farms below to identify and link properties at different periods but are also of interest in describing various features and land use; Graig Cradog at Heolddu Uchaf, for example, reinforces the idea that someone named Cradog had been important in the area at one time; the name *mynydd* is given to fields on a few farms and these are usually large pasture fields adjoining the mountain or Common, for example, waun y mynydd, 16½ acres at Gilfach Fargoed Fawr and three fields at Pencaedrain and two at Gwerthonor Ganol called cae mynydd. Waun y bara and cae bara at Heolddu Uchaf and Pencaedrain suggest corn crops (but without indicating when such crops were grown in these particular fields) while cae rye grass at Heolddu Uchaf and cae vetches at Heolddu Isaf (again, no indication of when these crops had been grown) signify that local farmers were aware of agricultural improvements. Cae odyn at Pencaedrain may refer to a lime kiln while the mill at Gilfach Fargoed

Fawr relates to the water mill there. The tramroad in a field at Gilfach Fargoed Fach and cae level at Gwerthonor Ganol indicate that mining had begun by this time.

As shown on the extract from the tithe map, opposite, roads or tracks were delineated. A main route appears to come from the north, from Pont Caradog and the Bargoed-Rhymney valley and then runs between Pencaedrain and the Heolddu lands (rhiw caradog?), continuing southward over the common to the farms to the west and south. Tracks lead off this route to all the farms mentioned here and also link to the east, to Bedwellty parish via Pont Aberbargoed and Pont Aberpengam. A portent of the future was the tramroad within Gilfach Fargoed Fach and the track leading from cae level (within Gwerthonor Ganol) to the access track of Gwerthonor Isaf Farm.

Table 1 INFORMATION FROM THE TITHE MAP AND SCHEDULE 1841

Farm Name	Owner	Occupier	Tithe	Acres
Pencaedrain	Llancaiach Estate	Edward Phillips	£4 13s 11d	63½
Heolddu Uchaf	Harry, Edmund, Richard and Harry Lewis	Harry Lewis	£9 15s 0d	176½
Heolddu Isaf	Francis McDonnell	Harry Lewis	£8 4s 11d	115
Pandy	Alexander Waddington	Edward James	2s 4d	2
Gilfach Fargoed Fawr	Capel Hanbury Leigh	Thomas Morgan	£14 7s 2d	223½
Gilfach Fargoed Fawr	Capel Hanbury Leigh	Himself (woodland)		60
Gilfach Fargoed Fach	Lewis Williams and William Howells	William Williams	£2 4s 6d	32
Gilfach Fargoed Fach	as above	Joshua Fletcher Hanson	£2 8s 5d	29½
Gwerthonor Ganol	William Davies	Himself	£8 6s 8d	131
Gwerthonor Isaf and Tir y Bont	Charity land	Lewis Jenkins	£8 3s 3d	135½

Farm Name	Area acres	Arable and approx %	Meadow	Pasture & Brake	Wood Land
Pencaedrain	63½	9½ (15%)	36½	16	--
Heolddu Uchaf	176½	23 (13%)	23	75½ + 54*	
Heolddu Isaf	115	17 (15%)	23	71**	--
Gilfach Fargoed Fawr	223½	58½ (26%)	58	106	
Gilfach Fargoed Fach	32	4½ (14%)	13	13½	--
Gilfach Fargoed Fach	29½	18½ (63%)	--	8	--
Gwerthonor Ganol	131	30 (23%)	34	63	--
Gwerthonor Isaf and Tir y Bont	135½	30½ (22.5%)	39	49	2+14

*Includes 54 acres of steep sparsely wooded land falling down to Bargoed-Rhymney River.
** Includes 27 acres of pasture and woodland down to Rhymney River.

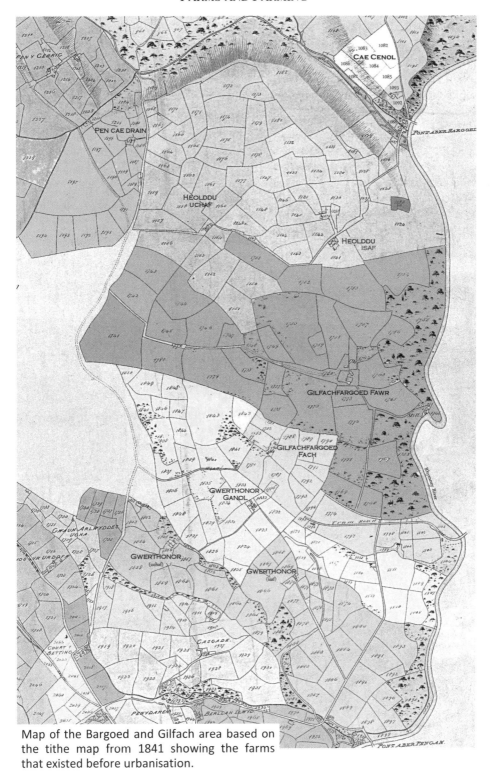

Map of the Bargoed and Gilfach area based on the tithe map from 1841 showing the farms that existed before urbanisation.

Certainly it was the case that the influx of people and the industrialisation over the next decades, changed not only the landscape, where farmland was built on or developed for industry, but also influenced the change from largely subsistence farming. Farmers responded to the changes by producing more fresh milk and food for the local market, and the railways meant that they also had easier access to seeds, medicines and new ideas from further afield.

The tithe and contemporary census material demonstrate that there had been local (but mainly agriculture-related) industries in the pre-industrial era in Gelligaer parish. In addition to the Pandy and the Gilfach Fargoed Mill, there were the corn and grist mills near Deri and Ystrad Mynach for example, and blacksmiths at Ystrad Mynach and Bedlinog. Coal had long been extracted on a small scale in the area but industrialists were now moving in; Alexander Waddington and Joshua Fletcher Hanson, for example as mentioned in Table 1. The main industry in the pre industrial era, however, was farming and the farms of the area will be discussed in turn below.

Pencaedrain

Pencaedrain Farm lies to the north-west of the town of Bargoed. It was shown in the 1841 tithe schedule as a 63 acre farm, owned by the heirs of the Llancaiach estate. The earliest evidence of Pencaedrain, when it was part of a much larger property called *Pen Rhiw Cradock*, is found in 1539 when it was acquired by the Pritchard family. The purchase deeds state:

Bargain and Sale for 26s 8d, 27ᵗʰ June 1539
Gllm ap Jevan ap Llewelyn, parson of Bedwas husbandman, to Dafydd ap Thomas ap Jevan Traharon of Gelligaer yeoman;
Part of a messuage and lands called Terre pen rue Cradock; in lordship of Senghennydd Supra in Gelligaer.

and later,

Bargain and Sale for 40 shillings, 6 Oct. 1539;
Crisle verch William Bydrys of St. George's, widow, to Dafydd ap Richerde of Gelligaer, gent., Part of Pene Rewe Cradok
Appointment of Jenkin D[avi]d ap Ho[ell] as attorney for Crisle verch William.

Jenkin David ap Howell, Dafydd ap Richard's cousin, lived in the nearby property that was to become Heolddu and the early history of Pencaedrain is also linked to that of Heolddu and included in discussion of that farm, below.

From this time, the 1540s, the two properties, Pen Rhiw Cradog and Pencaedrain remained separate. Pencaedrain is the holding to the west of *Rhiw Cradock*, bounded in the north by Penygarreg farm and in the south by open land, Gelligaer and Merthyr Common, with the fields falling down towards the Bargoed-Rhymney river and Groesfaen Farm.

In the 1540 Senghennydd manorial survey Pencaedrain is identified as the tenement owned by Dafydd ap Richard paying chief rent of 10½d to the Lord of the Manor. The tenant of the property was Llewellyn Howell who was also shown as the tenant of neighbouring *Pen Rue Cradock*. In a tax return of 1545 we find *Richard Llen Hullyl* (son of Llewelyn Howell) *paying 1d*, and in the survey of 1570 it is Richard Llewellyn Howell who is shown as tenant of both farms. The owner of Pencaedrain was then Dafydd ap Richard's son, Edward ap Richarde (later to become Edward Prichard as the surname became established) and in his 1578 marriage settlement (he married Ann Lewis, daughter of Thomas Lewis of the Van) one of the properties involved is identified as *one tenement in Gelligaer in tenure of Richard Llen howell at the yearly rent of 40 shillings* - Pencaedrain Farm.

By the time of the 1630 rental the property had passed to Edward Prichard's son David, and the tenant was Thomas Rosser John. David Pritchard had a son, Edward, who had no surviving sons and the 1670 manorial survey shows David Jenkins and John Whitwick esqs. (husbands to Mary Prichard and Jane Prichard, the heirs to the Llancaiach estate) as the owners of Pencaedrain. David Jenkins was heir to the Hensol estate which by the end of the eighteenth century, mainly by reason of lack of male heirs, had become part of the Mathews of Castell y Mynach estate, the Talbots and finally, when William Talbot was created Lord, the Dynevor estate. Dynevor estate records therefore give information about their half of the Llancaiach estate and thus, Pencaedrain. Jane and John Whitwick's share was later sold to the Richards family of Cardiff.

The tenant in 1670 was Morgan ap Morgan who is also identified as having paid 12d in a tax of 1660 after the restoration of Charles II, and as paying hearth tax on one hearth in 1666 and 1671. The name also appears in the court records of the Great Sessions at Cardiff in autumn 1648 where he was *bailed* for a very high sum for an offence described as *matters of treason*:

William Howell Lewis of Merthir	*recognisances: £100;*
Morgan Morgan of Kelligare	*recognisances: £100;*
John Prichard of Whitchurch	*recognisances: £100.*

Professor T. V. Davies has identified William Howell Lewis as a leading dissenter in Merthyr Tydfil parish at that time and John Prichard of Whitchurch is almost certainly the brother of Edward Prichard, the owner of Llancaiach estate. It is therefore possible that Morgan Morgan of Gelligaer is Morgan ap Morgan of Pencaedrain. Unfortunately we do not know the outcome of the case.

The next information we have about Pencaedrain comes in a 1701 Llancaiach estate survey where the farm is identified as a 20 (Welsh) acre farm tenanted by Mary Morgan under a 17 year lease for £6 p.a. which was granted on 11 September 1696. The measurement here is the local or Welsh acre known as the Llathblethin measure, about 2½ standard or modern acres (approximately 50 acres), thus the farm appears to be less than the 60+ acres recorded later. By the early 1740s the Llancaiach estate had changed from using the local acre to the standard acre and a field by field estate survey had been carried out by the late 1750s, although the detailed data for Gelligaer appears not to have survived. The acreage was then recorded as 63¾ acres. The annual rent had remained unchanged for almost 100 years but was now almost doubled to £11, although also including an initial payment.

The 1776 estate survey shows that on 6 November 1714 William Lewis of Heolddu had taken out the lease on Pencaedrain for the term of three lives, his own, that of his daughter, Mary, and Charles Rogers his son-in-law. The Lewis family had by that time built Heolddu into an estate that included the entire northern tip of Hengoed hamlet - except Pencaedrain - but including what had been the other half of the original property of Pen Rhiw Cradock. William Lewis and his heirs continued as leaseholders until 1780. The Senghennydd rentals for this period show that between 1747 and at least 1765 Thomas Harry was tenant on the other half of the holding and then William Lewis took over the tenancy in 1778, both paying 4d chief rent.

In April 1780 a new lease was granted to William Lewis of Gelligaer, yeoman. The lease was for 99 years or 3 lives (of William Lewis, his son Lewis aged 15 and daughter Mary, aged 18) at an annual rent of £11 for *A messuage and appurtenances, and tenement of lands called Pen cae'r Drain (63¾acres); in Gelligaer* (timber and mineral rights were reserved).

William Lewis is a very common name in Gelligaer parish and it has not been possible to identify with any certainty which William Lewis this is. Records of taxes show the property as being occupied by William Rosser between 1783 and 1796; the land for tax purposes was valued at £4 10s so he paid a land tax of 13s 6d p.a. and window tax on 4 windows in 1786 and on 6 windows in 1795. A number of different tenants, James Davies, Henry Lewis and Evan Moses then occupied Pencaedrain until James Phillips took over the lease in 1804 and remained as tenant at least until the time of the end of the land tax returns in 1831.

The tithe apportionment shows that Pencaedrain was occupied by Edward Phillips. John Phillips (25, farmer), William (25, a carpenter) and Mary Powell (25, John's sister) and their 10 month son, David, together with William Phillips (20, carpenter), Daniel Jones (20, carpenter) and William Phillips (25, tiler) were enumerated there in 1841. The Phillips family were at Pencaedrain in 1851. Edward's wife, Jane, had died in June 1850 but he lived there with his 6 daughters aged between 2 and 15, John Price, farm labourer and Cecilia Lewis, general servant. Edward remained at Pencaedrain until at least 1881. In 1861 and 1871 three of his daughters and two man servants lived with him, but by 1881, 33 year old Adelaide was the only daughter left at home and Louisa Jones (6), Evan Evans (59) and Thomas Parry (13) and Elizabeth Morgan (14) were also at Pencaedrain.

Pencaedrain would appear to be untouched by the burgeoning industrialisation and urbanisation to the south, however receipts exist which show that Thomas Lewis of Clwydtrawscae Farm (near Bedlinog) bought coal from Pencaedrain Colliery, for example, paying 11s for 10 cwt on 14 September 1915 and 5s 6d for 5 cwt on 21 June 1916. Prior to this, receipts demonstrate that during the 1880s Thomas Lewis had bought coal from the Wingfield

Colliery in adjacent Penygarreg Farm. Nevertheless, Pencaedrain is the only one of the farms studied to continue as a farming unit in its entirety.

Heolddu

The lands of Heolddu are no longer farmed and today, Bargoed Golf Club, Heolddu farmhouse, yard and gardens, houses, shops, public houses, schools, playing fields (the entire north-western section of Bargoed town) covers the land once occupied by the farms of Heolddu Uchaf and Heolddu Isaf - although the area of the Graig still exists very much as it was in 1841, when it was described as *Graig Fawr, pasture and brake*.

In 1841 Heolddu is shown as two farms, Heolddu Isaf (Lower Heolddu) being 115 acres and Heolddu Uchaf (Upper Heolddu) 176 acres. However it had only been divided in 1839. Throughout the eighteenth and early nineteenth centuries it had been a single farm of almost 300 acres, a holding which had been consolidated during the seventeenth century from many smaller farms, some of which had themselves been split off from a larger property by 1540.

T.V. Davies speculates that Heolddu was leased to Llewelyn ap Jevan Fychan ap Jevan ap Madoc in 1426 and that Dafydd ap Howell acquired the property around 1450. We know his son Jenkin David ap Howell, whose descendants continued to live there into the eighteenth century, bought the southern part of Heolddu in 1533, and that he was already the tenant there.

29 August 25 Henry VIII (1533)
(1)   William ap Phelip and Thomas ap Phelip.
(2)   Jankin David ap Howell.
Grant and Confirmation.
One tenement of land with its appurts which he had of Phelip Gwilim ap Jeuan ap Myric lying in the Lordship of Senghenith Supra in the parish of Kelligaer in a place called Kilvach Vargoed in length from the river called Romney thence coming to the place called Gwain Roduy, in breadth from the water called Nant Frode, from thence to a place called foose Lae held in the tenure of the aforesaid Jankin David ap Howell.

In the 1540 Senghennydd Manor survey, five holdings have been identified as the constituent parts of what became known as Heolddu: *Thomas William Gough for a tenement now in tenure Lln ap Hoell paying 6d, Lln ap Jevan ap Hoell for a tenement now in tenure of Rs Deo paying 15d, and Jenkyn dd ap Hoell for three tenements paying 47d*. These five tenements or properties (paying a total of 68d chief rent) extended over land rising from the River Rhymney to flatter land on the mountaintop to the east of Pencaedrain Farm, and between Groesfaen Farm in the north and Gilfach Fargoed Fawr in the south. They are identified as Pen Rhiw Cradog, Pen y Graig Ddu and three other holdings - which later formed Heolddu. The name itself does not appear to have been used at this date, although for convenience, it is described as such within this chapter. Documents show that not all of the land of the last three holdings was incorporated into Heolddu; a small portion became incorporated into Gilfach Fargoed Fawr and part of it is the Pandy at Pont Aberbargoed.

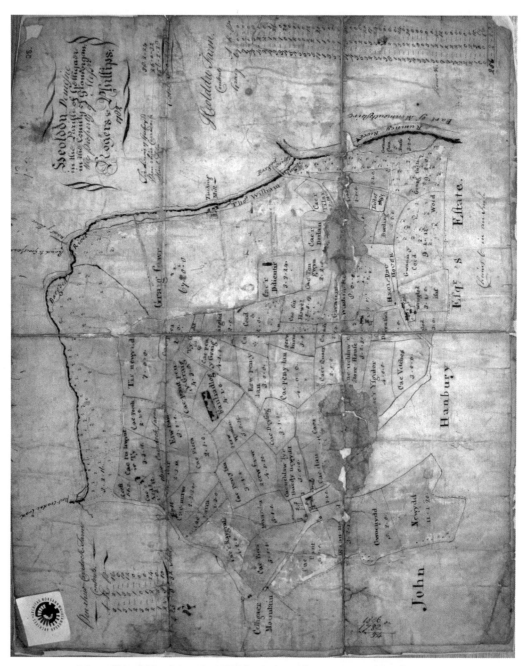

Map of Heolddu drawn in 1782 (courtesy Glamorgan Archives).

The first of these five properties was Pen Rhiw Cradog, the name perhaps referring to the property's position at the top of the track leading from Pont Cradog, the bridge over the Bargoed-Rhymney River to the west of Groesfaen village. The holding is shown on a 1782 map of Heolddu (see page 46) as nine fields totalling 25 acres adjacent to the Nant Bargoed and Pencaedrain Farm. As detailed above, deeds of 1539 relating to Pencaedrain describe it as *Part of Pene Rewe Cradok* (although there is no mention of Thomas William Gough in those deeds) and the same family (Llewelyn ap Howell and his son, Richard) leased both properties until after 1570. In the Manorial rental of 1570 Pen Rhiw Cradog is identified by the record *Thomas ap Thomas holds a tenement formerly Thomas William Goghe in the tenure of Richard Lln Hoell pays 6 pence*. Thomas ap Thomas may be the son of Thomas William Gough although this is not certain and in the 1630 Manor rental the property is recorded as *Thomas Arnold for a tenement called tir pen rhiw gradocke pays 6d.*

Pen y Graig Ddu, the second of the five properties, is identified in the 1570 survey by the record *Lewis Lln holds a tenement formerly Lln ap Jevan ap Howell now in the tenure of Lewis Thomas pays 15 pence*, and in 1630 by *Thomas Arnold for a tenement called tir pen y graig ddy pays 15 pence*. The property is not depicted on the 1782 map of Heolddu but there are fields named cae pant, pen y graig and cae pen y graig just to the east of Pen Rhiw Cradog which may be the site of Pen y Graig Ddu, although the precise extent of its boundaries cannot be confirmed.

Thomas Arnold who owned both Pen Rhiw Cradog and Pen y Graig Ddu in 1630 can be identified as the oldest son of Arnold William Lewis, the brother of Edmund William Lewis of Gilfach Fargoed. Arnold William Lewis had purchased other parts of what became Heolddu. The inventory associated with his 1626 Will gives an idea of the livestock kept on the farm: 5 oxen: £8 6s 8d; 9 kine and calves: £12; 6 kine: £6; 4 steers of 3 year old: £2 13s 4d; 2 steers of 2 year old: 20s 0d; 4 heifers of 2 year old: 40s 0d; 4 yearling beasts: £1 6s 8d; 3 head of horses: £4; 5 head of swine and pigs: 10s. 0d; 120 head of sheep: £48; 60 lambs: £5; household stuff: £10, a total of £100 16s 8d.

About 30 head of cattle and 180 sheep and lambs. Note also that the work animals were oxen and not horses. His son, Thomas Arnold, inherited the main property and is referred to in several documents. A deed of 1620 reveals that his wife was Elizabeth Thomas, the daughter of Lewis Thomas of Bedwellty and he is named as a trustee in a 1615 nuptial settlement when his sister Isabel married William Llewelyn of Gilfachmaen Uchaf (near Trelewis) and Troed y Rhiw Gymrwg (south of Troedyrhiw in the Taff Valley, Merthyr Tydfil parish). In addition to owning Pen Rhiw Cradog and Pen y Graig Ddu, Thomas Arnold also leased about 50 acres of land from the Lord of the Manor, Lord Pembroke, bordering on Nant Bargoed-Rhymney for 14 shillings and two hens. This was Graig ddu and the 1782 map of Heolddu shows Graig Fawr (Graig Ddu) extending over the 67 acres of the steep wooded area running to the north and east of Pen y Graig Ddu and down to the Bargoed-Rhymney and Rhymney rivers. Thomas Arnold therefore farmed the whole of the north-eastern corner of Hengoed hamlet. He also had a lease from the Manor on about 60 acres of Tir Evan Colly (now called Coly Uchaf, a farm just north of present day Bedlinog).

Thomas Arnold died about 1658/9 and was succeeded by his wife and children. Over the next 40 years land was slowly sold to their neighbours Lewis William Lewis and his son William Lewis. The 1670 Manorial survey shows Lewis William (ap Lewis) owned Pen Rhyw Gradock which was leased to Lewis Thomas Arnold, while Thomas Arnold's wife Elizabeth Thomas was shown as still owning Pen y Graig Ddy.

Lewis William Lewis died in early 1772 and in his will he mentions *the Lands called Teere Pen y graige purchased of Rowland Thomas and Elizabeth Thomas his mother, and all the meadow which I hadd and purchased of Thomas Arnold*. The 1688 nuptial settlement of his son, William Lewis, mentions these lands as fields *called y ddwy Erw vawr, yr Erw ver, yr Erw vanall, Cae Tir Newidd, Cae Picca, y ddwy Erw Wynnon and Cae pen y Can, Erw'r brest, Cae'r Scibor ddy and y Coedcae bach, Cae'r Coed, Cae'r arredd ycha, Cae'r arredd yssa, y vanhaddlog vawr, Cae'r pant, y ddoy gae newydd, y Cae ty hwnt yr Ty and Ballia'r Scibor*. Some of these fields can be identified with Heolddu field names used 150 years later.

Even Graig Ddu, the leased Manor land, became part of Heolddu. A new lease was granted 11 May 1678, to Thomas Arnold's children. However in June 1698, the land was sold to William Lewis of Heolddu, although Eleanor Thomas, one of Thomas Arnold's daughters continued as the tenant.

In relation to the third item on the original 1540 rental, on the death of Jenkin Dafydd ap Howell, the three tenements were divided between his three sons, Morgan, John and William Jenkin.

John's portion was described in a deed of 1563:

one parcel of land called Tyre Phillipp Gwillim and of and in one close of land called Kaer Frood Genel and of and in one fulling mill in one acre of land to the said Mill adjoining and with watercources stone bridges and weirs next and adjoining to the bridge of Abergutt with appurtenances by mears and bounds well known.

It consists of the land to the south of the property bordering Nant Ffrwd and the Pandy or fulling mill to the north and in 1588 this land to the south was sold to Arnold William Lewis (mentioned above):

(1) John Jenkin of Kelligaer co Glam. gent
(2) Arnold William of Kelligare co. Glam. gent.
Grant and Confirmation
All that messuage or tenement lying in Kelligaer with all messuages, buildings, gardens, land, meadows, pasture, wood, waste, rents, reversions and services, lying between the R. Rompne on the east, Nant y ffroode on the south, land of William ap Ieuan Moris and land of Lewis Jenkin on the West and land of David Lewis on the North.

A series of deeds from 1590 then shows that this portion of the property was subsequently sold to William Jevan of Eglwysilan and then in 1618 it was bought by Sir William Lewis of Gilfach Fargoed Fawr. The tithe map and schedule reveals that these are the Gilfach Fargoed Fawr fields to the north of Nant Ffrwd, one of which is Cae Shan Shinkin, or John Jenkin's field (and was referred to as such in relation to his charity by Edward Lewis in his will in 1715).

There is less direct evidence to show exactly what happened to William and Morgan Jenkin's portions but in the 1630 Manor rental we find: *Sir William Lewis knight for one tenement late the landes of William Jenkine and John Jenkine pays 11d, John Lewis dio price for one tenement late the landes of Morgan Jenkine pays 11d, William Lewis Jenkine for part of the landes and tenement of William Jenkine and Morgan Jenkine pays 12d, Thomas Arnold for part of the landes and tenement of John Jenkine and Morgan Jenkine pays 9d, Jenkine Thomas ap Thomas for part of the landes and tenement of John Jenkine aforesaid:4d.* A total of 47 pence chief rent as in 1540.

The first entry refers to the lands which became part of Gilfach Fargoed Fawr and the last entry is the Pandy or fulling mill, in 1630 owned by the owner of Gwaelod y Brithdir, the farm on the northern bank of Nant Bargoed.

John Lewis Dio Price sold at least part of his property to William Lewis Jenkin in 1629 as shown by the following deed – the earliest deed in the Heolddu archive.

..., for £58
John. Lewis of Gelligaer, yeoman, & wife Johane, and Lewis John of Aberdare, yeoman, to Wm. Lewis Jenkine of Gelligaer, yeoman
Two closes called y dduy Kae Crunnon (Cae'r Crunnon, 1148), one other close called y Kae pickae (1157 /1165 /1173), one other close Kae y Valhen (1128), one other close of land called y duy errow hirrion (Ddw Erw Hirion, 1133) all containing together 8 welsh acres of the measure called llath llethine; also six score and 4 yards of land of the measure aforesaid in a close called Kae Kenoll; all in the parish of Gelligaer; adj. S. to the highway called yr howle ddy N. & W. on the lands of Tho. Arnold, and E. on lands of Wm. Lewis and on other lands of said Lewis John All formerly parcel of the tenement called Tyre Kilvache vargoed.

Most of these field names were still in use in the mid nineteenth century and are recorded on the tithe map and schedule (numbers in brackets above). Of particular interest is the reference to *yr heol ddu*, (the black road) the earliest known reference to the highway from which the farm took its name. *Ddu* is a common appendage to names in this specific locality; the steep rocky slopes above the Bargoed-Rhymney River were called Graig Ddu and the farm above them Pen y Graig Ddu. Reference to the tithe map shows that the fields of Heolddu Isaf and Heolddu Uchaf straddled the track leading from the east, from Pont Aberbargoed westward, passing both farm homesteads and joining rhiw Cradog as described above.

William Lewis Jenkin died in November 1652 and extracts from his will read:

... Item I do devise give and bequeath unto my loving wife Isabell Lewis the one half of one messuage or dwelling house, the one half of my barn, the one half of my kine houses the one half of my stables together with the moytie or one half of the land which I had and received of my father Lewis Jenkin and my mother Alson Lewis ... Item ... unto my sayd wife Isabell Lewis one parcel of land which I of late had and purchased of John Lewis and Juhan his wife and Lewis John ... and after her decease unto my son Lewis William and his right heyres forever Item I do give and bequeath unto my sayd Wife six kine, one mare and two colts......... and all the sheepes and lambes ... Item I give and bequeath unto my daughter Alson William five oxen, tenne kine and fiftie head of sheepes of all sorte Item I give and bequeath unto my natural brother Thomas Lewis one colt of three years old. Item I give and bequeath unto my nephew William Rees one cow Item I give and bequeath unto my nephew William Meredith two lambes. Item I give and bequeath unto Meredith Rees six lambes to be equally divided between his three other children that were begotten of the body of my neece Elizabeth Phillip. Item I give and bequeath unto Phillip Prosser of Bedwellty twelve lambes to be equally divided between his sixe children begotten of the body of my niece Margaret Phillip. Item I give and bequeath unto Margaret William one heyffer of one year old. Item I give and bequeath unto my grand child Rachell William one heyffir of one year old. Item I give and bequeath unto my sonne Thomas William all the sheepes and lambes that are in the custody of William Edmund Item I do give devise and bequeath unto my son and heir Lewis William all the rest of my lands, goods, cattles and chattels not before bequeathed ... Item There is due unto me of these persons under named as follows first upon Phillip Evan one pound Item Upon Anthonie William one pound Item upon Thomas John howell of Merthyr one pound and fifteen shillings, Item upon John Lewis five pounds thyrteene shillings and four pence. Item upon the sayd John Lewis one pound and two shillings more upon the aforesayd John Lewis three pounds. Item upon Edmund Morgan Matthews four pounds and tenne Shillings Item upon Margaret Evan two pounds and four shillings...

This illustrates the livestock on his property and his wealth – and also that he belonged to a wealthy family, which means that many members left wills - useful for local and family historians! These wills reveal that family members had been buying property around present day Bedlinog which on their deaths without heirs came to Lewis Wm Lewis.

In the Manor survey of 1670 the properties are listed as: *Lewis William Lewis for part of a tenement called Tir Morgan Jenkin and John Jenkin pays 9d., Edw. Lewis Esq. for the Rest of the said tenement pays 11d, Lewis John for a tenement late the lands of Morgan Jenkin parte whereof in his own tenure pays 6d, the rest in the tenure of Lewis William pays 5d, Lewis William Lewis for a tenement late the lands of William Jenkin and Morgan Jenkin pays 12d, Elizabeth Thomas for one acre of the said tenement 4d.*

Lewis William Lewis also owned the lands formerly owned by Thomas Arnold. The former died in 1671/2 and left a will which mentions many of his properties, their rents, as well as family relationships. He left £80 to his daughter Isabel, and £60 to daughter Alice to be paid, £20 pa for seven years, out of the rents of his *lands houses and mill with same leased within the Hamlett of Garthkind,* any amounts above £20 to be given to his son, Thomas Lewis.

Item ... unto my daughter Isabell Lewis six kine foure steers of foure year old appeece one newe greate Chest which in the Chamber over the halle and fifty head of sheepe of all sorte. Item ... unto my daughter Alice Lewis six kine fowre steeres of foure yeare ould apeece one newe great gest fifty sheepe of all sortes. Item ... unto my sonne Thomas Lewis fifty head of sheepe of all sorte and two oxen which is with Lewis William of Penallty. Item ... more unto my daughter Isabell Lewis one Bay mare which I bought of Thomas William and one brassen pott, one brassen pann the lest of the three great panns. Item ... unto my sonne William Lewis fifty head of sheepe of all sorte one Bedstead which is in the chamber over the hall which I hadd from my father the best which is in that roome, one great pann the bigest which I have in my house and alsoe I doe give him all the Loose plankes which is in my house att home and he not to to expell or move them from the place where they are nowe during the naturall liffe of his mother. Item ... more unto my sonne Thomas Lewis one Redd mare the best of the two mares. Item ... unto Morgan Mredith one yearlinge heyffor. Item ... unto William Watkin one yearlinge heyfer. Item ... unto Howell Evan one sheepe. Item ... unto Rowland Evan brother unto the said Howell one sheepe. Item ... Thomas William Rees one sheepe and to his sister Ragell William Rees one sheepe. Item ... unto William Mredith one yearlinge heyffer. Item ... unto Abraham Gabriel one sheepe. Item I give unto William Rees Lewis fifty shillings. Item for all the rest and residue of all my goods ... not before bequeathed I give and bequeath unto Gwenllian my wedded wieffe for and during the terme of her widowhood (although if she remarries he bequeaths more household goods to his children) *Item ... unto my said wieffe all the lands which I hadd and purchased of Richard Rowland together with all the messuage and Lands called Pen y kay maure nowe in the tenure and occupation of John Griffith and the Lands called Teere Penn y graige in as large and ample manner I hadd and purchased the same of Rowland Thomas and Elizabeth Thomas his mother ... Item I doe give and devise unto my wedded wieffe all the meadow which I hadd and purchased of Thomas Arnold now in my tenure and occupation ....*

As well as illustrating the wealth of his farm stock and household goods, the will (unusually) gives a little information about his real estate (although not of his main property, Heolddu, which would have been left to his eldest son,

51

William). In addition to the lands inherited from his grandfather and uncles he also owned farms near Trelewis (Pen Cae Mawr and Pen y Graig), as well as the land from Thomas Arnold as had been indicated in the 1670 survey.

In 1668 William Lewis married Amie the daughter of Thomas Morgan of Cefn Carn in Eglwysilan. His marriage settlement gives a very detailed inventory of his properties which confirms much of how Heolddu was put together. Also mentioned are the farmlands that became Bedlinog Isaf on which the village of Bedlinog stands today and the farm just to the north today called Coly Isaf, and Pen Cae Mawr which is today being quarried by the Hanson company. By buying small parcels of land over three generations the family had nearly completed the consolidation of the northern section of the Hengoed hamlet into a single farm; they had another forty acres just to the south. This had of course been helped by the fact that the family's younger sons seem to have died relatively young and without issue thus keeping most properties in a single line.

The Heolddu deeds show that the expansion had not yet finished. In 1690 William Lewis added more land to Heolddu when he bought the rest of the farmland of John Lewis Dio Price from John's grandson, John Lewis for £100,

> Lewis Thomas, yeoman, & wife Mary, and Jn. Lewis, yeoman all of Monithystloyne (co.Mon) to Wm. Lewis
>
> A messuage, barn, cowhouse, garden, orchard, curtilage and 5 closes called y Waine Dan y Tuy, Cae Dychllaw yr Tuy, Cae kenol, Cae Ton wyne (1130) and Cae Sir Howell (1134), adj.on all sides the lands of Wm. Lewis, formerly called Tir John Lewis (9 acres of Welsh measure), in Gelligaer

The two numbered fields are identified with Heolddu fields in the 1840 Tithe schedule.

In 1698 William Lewis purchased the final part of Heolddu when as mentioned earlier he bought Graig Ddu, about 60 acres of steep land which separated Heolddu from the banks of Bargoed-Rhymney and Rhymney Rivers. William Lewis now owned virtually all the land north of Gilfach Fargoed Fawr up to the banks of Nant Bargoed, about 290 acres. His mother, Gwenllian William, died in 1709 and in addition to several personal family bequests her will shows that she left all *houses lands & Adifices & buildings commonly called Tir clawr Ystrad...purchased of my sister Law Blanch Lewis ...,* - yet more land for William.

William Lewis died in September 1720 but the only lands mentioned in his will are Clawr Ystrad, land upon which Ystrad Mynach has been built – although by that time the land had passed out of the hands of the Heolddu family. A plaque on the altar floor of Gelligaer church records William Lewis' death on 15 September 1720 aged 59, and the death of his wife Amy on 4 January 1741 aged 84. Heolddu passed into the hands of their two daughters, Mary and Elizabeth.

Mary, William Lewis' elder daughter, had married David Miles of Llandevall in Monmouthshire (Gwent). He died in 1733 and the half share descended to their three daughters Mary, wife of Charles Rogers of Pontypool, Elizabeth Edwards, widow, and Barbara Miles. The farm continued to be owned by the family. In 1807 William Rogers of Pontnewydd, Monmouthshire, Mary's grandson, leased the property to Thomas Williams. Then in 1824 great great grandson Charles Thomas Edwards of Pontypool sold the family's half share to Thomas Williams for £300, however there was also a mortgage of £850 on the farm. Thomas Williams was the owner of Gilfach Fargoed Fach and as will be seen below his father had leased Gilfach Fargoed Fawr in 1749. Thomas Williams died in 1834 leaving a very detailed will which describes him as being of Heolddu of which he says:

> *… all that farm and lands called Heol Thu in the parish of Gellygare and all my right title and interest in the same to my nephews David Davies of pen y van in the parish of Monythusloyne to my nephew Richard Lewis of the parish of Bedwellty to my nephew Edmund Lewis of the same parish to my nephew Harry Lewis of the parish of Aberystwyth to my nephew John Lewis of the same parish and to my nephew Harry Lewis of Croes Vane in the parish of Gellygare between them share and share alike for ever.*

He does not indicate that he had only a half interest in the property, but this was the case, and we find that two of the nephews (David Davies and John Lewis) sold their one twelfth shares to Harry Lewis of Groesfaen in 1836.

Elizabeth, the younger daughter of William and Amy Lewis married John Waters, shown as a Gelligaer freeholder in 1752, when the couple lived at Heolddu. In the diary of William Thomas[1] we find,

> *27 May 1763 was buried in Gellygare or Risga Mr John Waters and his wife in the same grave, lately of Risca, but now of pen yr heolddu her house and land in the parish of Gellygaer they were near 70 yrs of age each of them and dyed both from the fever within few hours the one to the other, She a member of the Church of England and he a papist, their daughter the only child they had is the wife of Mr Philip late of gellygear now of Risga, she was one of the Morgans of Ru Biena.*

Gelligaer parish registers supports this and there is a plaque in the church recording that Elizabeth died 22 May 1763 aged 72. As a Catholic, John Waters should not have been buried there, and although he may have been, there is no record that he was. The ownership of their half of Heolddu passed to their daughter, Amy, who lived in Risca with her husband Charles Phillips; both died in 1775 and ownership passed to their son William Phillips. He took out a mortgage for £650 in 1801 and the farm subsequently passed to Francis McDonnell of Usk but there are no deeds to show when or how.

---

[1] A school master in the Vale of Glamorgan with roots in Gelligaer parish, his diaries 1762-1795 edited by R. W. T. Denning from a complete transcript by J. B. Davies and G. H. Rhys, is published by South Wales Record Society

In 1838 Francis McDonnell of Usk owner of one half share of Heolddu, and Henry, Richard, Henry and Edmund Lewis, joint owners of the other half share, wished to go their separate ways and agreed to divide the property. To do this fairly, it was decided that a surveyor should be asked to divide the farm into two parts of equal value. Once this had been done, to ensure complete impartiality, the two owners would draw lots to see who would have each part. The report was presented on 4 January 1839; Henry, Richard, Henry and Edmund Lewis received the northern and western section, the 176 acres of Heolddu Uchaf while Francis McDonnell received 115 acres, Heolddu Isaf with fields going down to the banks of the River Rhymney.

It could not be known then that Bargoed was to be build on Heolddu Isaf. However for Francis McDonnell Esq. an Usk solicitor, Heolddu Isaf was probably an investment in the burgeoning industry of the area, whereas the Lewis family were farmers. Harry Lewis, one of the owners, who had been farming at Groesfaen, became the farmer of both Heolddu Uchaf and Isaf, although by 1851 he was only farming Heolddu Uchaf, living there with two of his sons and a daughter. Harry died in 1856, and in 1861 the farm was occupied by his widow and the three children, all unmarried. Subsequently the farm was taken over by Harry's son-in-law, Lewis Jenkins, daughter Jane's husband, and the family remain the owners today although most of the land is occupied by Bargoed Golf Club. Lydric Jenkins, descendant of the original *Jenkins* of Heolddu still lives there with his family, and he recounts how his great grand father's mother, Jane, was the daughter of Harry Lewis. He described how the family ran a coal level on the property and, indeed, existing receipts for 1893 and 1894 show Thomas Lewis of Clwydtrawscae Farm bought 10 cwt of small coal (2s) on a monthly basis from Heolddu Colliery. Mr Jenkins tells of how his grandmother's father (surname, Jeremiah) was killed in the level after a roof collapse left him trapped with timber across his arm and of how his grandfather closed the entrance to the mine.

Meanwhile, by 1851 Heolddu Isaf was also occupied by a Lewis Jenkin – although there is no evidence that this was the same Lewis Jenkin who occupied Heolddu Uchaf. This Lewis was a 67 year old widower who had been born in Llanfabon and lived at Heolddu Isaf with his son and two daughters. His son David took over the farm which subsequently disappeared under a section of the town of Bargoed.

The Pandy, Cloth mill or Factory

North east of Heolddu, on the banks of the Bargoed-Rhymney was the Pandy. Pandy is Welsh for a Cloth Mill, also known as a fulling or tucking mill and later as factory. There has been a pandy associated with approximately 2½ acres of land adjacent to Pont Aberbargoed (the bridge at the mouth of the Bargoed-Rhymney), since at least the fifteenth century. It was sited in the valley below Heolddu, on the south side of the Bargoed-Rhymney River. In a list of Senghennydd Manor properties dating from about 1450, one of the entries for the chief rents reads *terre pandde 3d*. It is probable that this was the

Aberbargoed Mill, and certainly later surveys reveal that the chief rent on the Aberbargoed Pandy and one Welsh acre of Land (equivalent to 2½ acres) was 4d.

Nothing more of the property is known until 1563 when a deed shows that Morgan Jenkin David ap Howell sold some lands, including a fulling mill, to his brother, John:

> ... and in one fulling mill in one acre of land to the said Mill adjoining and with watercources stone bridges and weirs next and adjoining to the bridge of Abergutt with appurtenances by mears and bounds well known.

Abergutt is perhaps mistake for Aber[bar]goed, the scribe being unfamiliar with Welsh. The deed also tells us that a bridge over the Bargoed-Rhymney River had been built prior to 1563. This can be identified in the Senghennydd manor survey of 1540 as part of three tenements owned by Jenkyn Dafydd ap Howell. By the 1570 Senghennydd survey these lands were owned by Morgan Jenkyn, John Jenkyn and William Jankyn but with no specific mention of the mill. In the 1630 survey it is recorded as *Jenkine Thomas ap Thomas for part of the landes and tenement of John Jenkine pays 4d*. Jenkin Thomas ap Thomas owned Gwaelod y Brithdir the farm on the northern bank of the Bargoed-Rhymney river. The 1670 survey records the property as *Elizabeth Thomas for one acre pays 4 pence,* although there is no specific mention of the mill, the chief rent of 4 pence for a single acre indicates that it was more than just farmland. Elizabeth was the widow of Thomas Arnold who had leased the steep slopes rising from behind the mill as has been mentioned above.

In his 1690 will, Edmund Lewis of Cefn y Brithdir (a farm on the mountain to the north of the Pandy), says

> ... I doe give and devise ... , the Tucking Mill and one acre of land, more or less, which I purchased of Lewis Arnold now in the tenure of Lewis Prosser, ... unto my well beloved wife Blanch Lewis for and during the term of her naturall life, and from affter her decease unto Thomas Lewis, my nephew, my brother Thomas his son ... .

This is the first reference to the Prosser family who ran the mill for the next 120 years. A witness in a 1693 nuptial settlement relating to a neighbouring farm was William Prosser, a tucker – someone who works in a cloth mill. The mill is next mentioned in the 1724 will of William George, another nephew of Edmund Lewis, who wrote ... *Item I give unto Thomas my son one Tucer mill and Tucker house one acer of land in as large as the same now is in the possession of Edmund William to have and to hold to him his heires and assignes forever.*

The Edmund William mention here was Edmund William Prosser probably the son of the William Prosser of the 1693 nuptial settlement. People's names can be complicated at this time as it was the period when families were adopting surnames. Edmund William Prosser died sometime in 1752 as his widow, Catherine Prosser, was granted probate of his will in December of that year. Catherine Prosser continued at the mill to at least 1778. She is named in land tax returns from the 1760s. She was succeeded by her son John, and then in 1792, by his son, Harry Prosser, who remained at the mill until 1802 when the association of the Prosser family with the mill appears to have ended. Land tax records show that Rev. Charles Williams paid the taxes in 1803, Lewis Henry in 1804 – 05 and Lewis Lewis in 1806.

In 1818 the mill was leased for 30 years at £30 per year to Evan James, a weaver, and the lease detailed a messuage and *wollen manufactory* called Pont Aberbargoed. It included a covenant that the lessee would have free use of *one double carding machine, 2 spinning jacks, 1 reel, 8 weavers harness, screwpins, castings of a turning Lathe.* Evan James further covenanted to keep the buildings, wares, watercourses and waterwheels in good repair and also to give up these and listed properties except *the Boilers for dyeing, iron furnaces and working tools ... which shall be considered the property of the said Evan Williams.* Land tax records show Evan James as tenant at Pont Aberbargoed between 1819 and 1825. His first wife died in 1824 and in December 1826 he remarried, his new wife being Elizabeth Williams, widow of Lewis Williams of Ffos yr Hebog (a farm on the mountain, west of Deri) where they lived until at least 1831. One of Evan James' younger sons, also Evan, became famous as the author of the words of the Welsh national anthem, but it was Evan's eldest son, Edward, who took over the tenancy of the mill – or *factory*, the origin of the name of the road running alongside the Bargoed-Rhymney river from the north – Factory Road.

The owner, Thomas William, died in 1782 and ownership passed to his wife Sarah, and then, from 1795, to Evan Williams, their eldest son who farmed in Abercarn in nearby Mynyddislwyn parish. Although he paid taxes on the Pandy property between 1808 and 1818, it was probably leased. In 1823 the Williams family sold the Mill and several other properties to Benjamin Waddington Esq. of Llanover House.

Both the 1839 Senghennydd rental (still 4d) and the 1841 tithe schedule show the owner as Alexander Waddington Esq. while the occupier of the pandy, a cottage and just over 2 acres was still Edward James who paid 2s 4d tithe. Edward, described as a wool weaver, lived with his wife, Mary and five children (the eldest, David, described as a shoemaker), two wool weavers, a wool spinner and a female servant. By the time of the 1851 census, Edward was described as a hand-loom weaver employing three men, and the other occupants of the mill were his wife, youngest daughter, a niece (18) and nephew (7) and male servants described as a fuller and two hand-loom weavers as well as a female general servant. Edward still lived there in 1861 with his wife, his 17 year old grandson, Gwilym, a woollen weaver, as well as Elizabeth Rees, a woollen spinner and Mary Hall, a house servant. By 1871 Edward, described as a retired flannel manufacturer, was living in Fleur de Lys. There is further reference to this mill in Chapter 6.

Today the memory of this early industry in the hamlet is kept alive by the public house, the Old Mill which is situated close to the site of the Pandy.

Gilfach Fargoed Fawr

Southward from the Pandy and Heolddu lay the dominating property in the area, Gilfach Fargoed Fawr. In 1841 this was a 223 acre farm with an additional 43 acres of woodland, a mill and a grand seventeenth century house (some of which still survives as the R.A.F.A. club). Its origins can be traced to an entry in the 1540 Senghennydd manor survey that reads simply *William Lewis for a tenement pays 24 pence*. According to the genealogies, William Lewys or William Lewis ychan was the son of Lewis Vaughan junior the son of Lewis Vaughan senior of Merthyr, an illegitimate son of Sir Roger Vaughan of Tretower in Breconshire. A series of deeds in the Hanbury collection relates to this family although to exactly which property is uncertain. The earliest dates from 1475 and concerns William Lewis' grandfather. .

1475 - 20 May, 15 Edward IV
(1)   Phillip ap Thomas ap Howell bach of Kellygaer.
(2)   Lewis Vaghan ap Rogger and Agnes daughter of Richard Cradoc his wife
Grant: of all those tenements lands, rents and services, meadows, woods, pasture and feedings with their appurtenances situate in Supra Kayagh in parishes of Merthyr and Kelligaer in the Lordship of Syenge Genyth which he lately had of the gift and enfeoffment of Roger Vaghan knight.

However the first mention of Gilfach Fargoed from which both Gilfach and Bargoed could be considered to take their names comes in a deed of 1485 which mention *a tenement ... in the Lordship of Senghenith and parish of Kelligaer there lying called Kylvachvargott which was formerly of Sir Lewis Moell.* Sir Lewis Moell would not have been a knight, the 'Sir' was simply honorific. A deed of 1520 gives more detail describing *a tenement of land arable, meadow wood and waste with all its appurtenances lying in the parish of Kelligaer in the Lordship of Senghenith in a place there called Kelach Vargoyd that is to say in breadth between river called Nant y ffrwd on the one part and a river called Nant Seis on the other part and in length between river called Rymeny on the one head and a stone called y Llaych Vawr Arybryn y Linpan on the other head.*

The physical features which bounded the property were also included in a number of other fifteenth and sixteenth century deeds and, although the streams Nant ffrwd (both Nant and ffrwd also mean stream!) and Nant Seis have disappeared and are now probably no more than drains, their probable course can be discerned from old maps. However Llech fawr ar y bryn Linpan(?) (large slate on the hill ....) has not been located. It is uncertain how exactly these early deeds relate to William Lewis ychan alias William Lewis Vaughan. Although his ancestors used Vaughan as a surname William Lewis had gone back to his Welsh roots and used the traditional patronymic naming. There is nothing to indicate that he was a person of particular importance or wealth despite his being recorded in the old Welsh genealogies.

A 1554 deed, probably a nuptial settlement, shows *his wife to be Elizabeth ferch Jeuan ap Rhys ychan* and *mentions all those lands and tenements, feedings, pastures, wood and underwood with the mill and all appurtenances lying in the parish of Kelligare and lordship of Senghenith and are called teir Sir Lewis moel and tir vach Jeuan david ichan in the place called Kylach Vargoyd.* These holdings, as *terre Sir Lewys Meille* and *terre Jevan ap Dafydd ichan or Vaughan* confirm the Vaughan's involvement in the properties from at least the last quarter of the fifteenth century. Sometime after 1570 an incident took place that led to this family feuding with the other main family of Gelligaer Parish, the Prichards of Llancaiach Fawr. Edward Prichard accused Edmond William (the son of William Lewis ychan) of abducting his sister Jane, and forcing her to marry him; Edmund William claimed that it was an elopement. However the fact Jane Prichard died within a few months of the marriage obviously caused great bitterness. The outcome of the case in the Court of Star Chamber is unknown, but later cases between 1594 and 1614 demonstrate that there was continuous feuding between the two families. Records of the Star Chamber show that there were a number of allegations of assault, including one at Gelligaer Church and one involving the legality of Ffair y Waun, the market or fair on the mountaintop east of Merthyr.

It is not known when Edmund William succeeded his father but he appears to have been an aggressive man who was perhaps not above breaking the law. In 1578 he married, Jenet, the daughter of David Thomas of Merthyr Tydfil. After Jenet's death Edmond married Elizabeth the widow of Edward Lewis Rees of Llancaiach Isaf. By the time of his death in about 1614 he had built up a considerable estate in Gelligaer which included not only an expanded Gilfach Fargoed Fawr but also Gwerthonor Isaf and Uchaf as well as many other farms throughout Gelligaer.

In the process of building up his estate, Edmund William had also bought two properties from Sir William Lewis of the Van and this connection was consolidated in 1611 when Edmund's younger daughter, Ann, married William Lewis, the second son of Sir Edward Lewis. The marriage settlement combined the Gelligaer estate of Edmund William, described as being Gilfach Fargoed Fawr, Groesvaen and *two and twentie messuages tenements and divers parcells of lands*, with the Gelligaer estate of Sir Edward Lewis made up of *thirteen messuages, 13 barns, 13 gardens, 50 acres of land, 200 acres of meadow, 200 acres of pasture, 100 acres of wood, 300 acres of furse and heath, with appurts … £500 and lands.*

His will, written in 1614 proves that he was a wealthy man with connections to major families in Glamorgan, his daughter, Mary, having married into the Stradling family and Ann (as above) married into the family of Lewis the Van. Extracts read:

> *… I therefore give and bequeath unto Elizabeth my saide wife fower and twentie kyne and a Bull, six oxen, a hundred of sheepe and a standing Bedstead now being within the lower chamber over the Brewhouse and a feather bed togeather with the furniture belonging to the same. Item … to Philipp[a], the daughter of John Stradling the somme of 100 markes when*

she shall accomplish the age of fifteen yeres And yf she be at that tyme married or els within three months after her marryage. If Philippa died before reaching the age of fifteen, the money was to be given to her mother, Mary my daughter and wife to the said John Stradling, Item I give and bequeath to William my reputed sonne and the sonne of one Jane Stradling the somme of £50 of lawfull money of England ... Item I give and bequeath to Edward Williams my brother the somme of 20 shillings.....

It is interesting to note he thought his granddaughter might be married by the time she was 15. Edmund William then bequeathed half of five acres he owned in Monmouthshire to Mary and her family (it would appear that William and Anne owned the other half) before continuing,

Item I give and bequeath to the sayed Mary 100 sheep ... Item I give and bequeath 13s. 4d. of lawfull money of England towards the building and erecting of the Bridge called pont kylla near the Church of Kelligare ...

Probate was granted in 1620 although it can be noted that no deeds survive relating to Edmund William after 1614, and that in 1617 it was his son-in-law, William Lewis who was buying land adjacent to Gilfach Fargoed Fawr.

As described above, Ann William and Sir William Lewis' marriage created a major estate. In addition to his Gelligaer estate, Sir William Lewis owned land in Aberdare and Llanwonno Parishes, and G. T. Clark gives his income in 1645 as £400 pa. He later built Gilfach Fargoed House (the R.A.F.A. Club now the only remains of a subsequent large farmhouse which was built on the site), an imposing manor house which Elizabeth Parkinson in *The Glamorgan Hearth Tax Assessment of 1670* lists as an eleven hearth house, a major building indeed when we consider that she only identifies three houses in the whole of this area of upland Glamorgan – Gilfach Fargoed Fawr, Van, Caerphilly and Llanbradach Fawr – as having over 10 hearths (the remaining 50 large houses and manor houses being in the lowland area of the county). In Hengoed hamlet at that time there were 21 houses paying tax on one hearth, two on two hearths, two on three hearths – and Gilfach Fargoed Fawr; However, neither the estate created by the 1611 wedding, nor the marriage itself, continued intact. Lady Anne died in early 1664 (having separated from her husband in 1649) and Sir William Lewis died in December of the same year; his personal property and stock appraised as *His Wearing Apparel: £13/6/8; 12 Oxen: £24; 27 Kine: £40; 3 Bulls: £3 10 Steers of 3 years old: £10; 10 Heyfers of ye same age: £10; 16 Beasts of five years old: £8; 13 Calves: £3/5/0; 2 Riding horses: £5; 4 Labouring horses: £5; 5 young horses: £3/6/8; 67 sheep: £8/7/6; pigges and poultrie £1/14/0; one silver beere bowle: £1; some graine of all sorts: £25; household stuff and implements: £60; implements of husbandry; £1/10/0; implements in the house: £5; 7 acres of wheat in the ground: £7; Studie and bookes: £2; 1 Chattle Lease: £20;   Total: £256/19/10.*

A very large sum at that time. Gilfach Fargoed Fawr and its estate was inherited by their eldest son, Edward Lewis. An article by G. Buick in *Gelligaer, Vol. XVI* details the wrangling over the estate by Sir William Lewis' five sons which resulted not only in the estate being confiscated for a while but also the youngest son spending some time in the Fleet prison for debtors in London. Gilfach Fargoed Fawr became the property of the fourth son Charles but the wrangle over money and property continued. He died intestate in 1701 when his personal effects and livestock, including *all the horses much decayed,* were valued at the relatively small sum of £73 9s – particularly when compared to his father's estate just 40 years previously. Because Charles' son, also Edward, was only ten years old, it was his widow, Elizabeth, who initially took over Gilfach Fargoed Fawr and the estate. Edward later disposed of some of the property by establishing the charity which – amongst other legacies - founded Lewis School Pengam. His will of 1715 gives much information relating to the Bargoed – Gilfach area, as well as some of the other landowners there. Extracts read:

... to my Cozen John Morris ... ALL my Capitall Messuage Milne and Desmesne Lands now in mine or my said Mothers Possession called Kilvach Vargoad and also the Revercion of the Messuage Lands and Tenements of my Uncle George Lewis Expectant upon his Death which is in his or his under tenants possession in the said parish of Kellygare ... SUBJECT nevertheless to the payment of Two Hundred pounds apiece to his daughters Mary and Elizabeth and Sarah ... AND upon this further Condicion of paying the sume of ten pounds yearly (£5 twice a year) to such of the poor of the said parish of Kelleygare as do not receive Comon Almes And such as the said John Morris and his Heires and the respective Minister Church Wardens of the said Parish Church and Overseer of the poor of the Hamlets I give and Devise to William Lewis of Pen yr Hewl Dee, Mr William Mathews of LlanKayach, Mr William Lewis of Goor Thonar, Mr Lewis William of Kayr Lleyr Gwelt, Mr Edmond Llewellin Garthgoned and Mr William Thomas Lewis of Bedlynog and the said John Morris of Cliffords Inne London Gent ... ALL those Messuages or Tenements in the possession of Henry Isaac, And all that Messuage or tenement in the possession of Rowland Thomas ... That they in the first place out of the profitts of the Wood and premises build a School near the Church of the value of fforty pounds And also every Year after the Building of the said School That my said Trustees pay to a School Master yearly out of the rents and profitts of the said premises the sume of ten pounds per annum, and likewise That my said Trustees lay out ffifteen pounds Yearly for Coats and Caps for ffifteen poor Boys of the said parish to be taught by the said Master to Read write and cast Accompt, and the rest of the profitts for the improving that Charity for the use of the said Master and Boys ... I give and Devise to the said William Lewis, William Mathews, Lewis William, Lewis William, Edmond Llewellin, William Thomas Lewis and John Morris ... ALL that Messuage or Tenement in the possession of John Evan with the Lands thereto belonging commonly called John Jenkins Lands and the house and Lands in the possession of Lewis William commonly called Goor Thonar Ugha That my said Trustees pay yearly to the poor of the said Parish the profitts of the said

last mencioned premises AND I do hereby appoint That such person as Shall enjoy my Estate at Kilvach Vargoad Shall always be one of the Trustees of all these my Charities.

Edward Lewis also bequeathed to his trustees the income of *Good Thonar Isha And Tier a pont* to pay for the preaching of sermons at Bedwellty and Mynyddislwyn churches, and *Crosvain Isha and the house and Lands late in the possession of Rees William Giles* (Tir Trosnant Farm) to provide five pounds to buy bread for the poor of the parish of Bedwellty to be distributed on Sunday mornings and the remainder of this income towards the placing out of apprentices. He also wrote ... *I give to my Uncle George Lewis One Guinea, to my cozen Mr Edmond Lewis of Hendee and his children five shillings apiece,* and bequeathed the residue of his estate to his cousin John Morris and his heirs. This included his coal pits, lime kilns, limestone and lands in Merthyr Tydfil parish, although his mother was to receive all income from these during her lifetime; his mother also received all of his personal effects. Edward died in 1729 and the men named in his will are found in the subsequent list of trustees for the charity in the same year.

However all this was on hold till the death of his mother who had an interest in the estate during her lifetime. Elizabeth Lewis, his mother, was a wealthy woman of great standing in the area and her entry in the burial register at Gelligaer church was *Madam Elizabeth Lewis buried 20 Feb 1739.* Although much of the estate had already been disposed of under the terms of Edwards's will she still left property, as well as not insubstantial sums of money to various relations (some of whom had also benefited under her son's will) and bequests to all servants, those hired yearly and by the day, and to her friends including Mrs Waters her neighbour at Heolddu Farm.

When he succeeded to the estate, John Morris undertook a survey of Gilfach Fargoed Fawr and the title of the resultant plan was *A Mapp of the Capitall Mansion and Lands called Kilvach Vargoed belonging to Mr John Morris of London, Gent., lying in the Parish of Kelligare in the County of Glamorgan containing 265 ac 1rd 18po surveyed by William Downing 1729.* Professor T. V. Davies compares this 1729 Estate Map with the 1846 Tithe Map, and notes that the property had not changed in overall area during the period, although the wooded area alongside the Rhymney river, comprising 46 acres in 1846, was not a part of the above mentioned 265 acres. He also makes a comparison of the fields of Gilfach Fargoed Fawr in 1729 and 1846, and, where the 1729 ones are distinct enough to be read, says that they are the same as in the 1846 Tithe Schedule.

John Morris' inheritance of the entire estate (the manor and lands, the mill and lands and the other holdings) however, was challenged by Edmund Lewis of Hendai Farm (first cousin to Edward Lewis) who claimed that the estate was entailed and as the senior male member of the family it should come to him. The dispute continued until John Morris died in October 1747 when his will stated that he was of Clifford's Inn, London and that he lived in Christchurch,

Surrey. Probate was granted to Robert Morris, son and one of the executors, in December 1747 and the Manorial rental for that year shows Robert Morrice at Gilfach Fargoed Fawr.

Thus the Lewis Gelligaer and Monmouthshire properties were in separate ownership although Joseph Morris, John's other son, seems to have had further involvement with Gilfach Fargoed Fawr, leasing the farm to Edmond William George in 1749 for 21 years at £30 a year. He then sold Gilfach Fargoed Fawr and the remainder of the Gelligaer Estate (excluding the Charity lands) to Capel Hanbury of Pontypool in 1751. At the time of the sale, the annual rental of the entire estate was £68 1s 4d, with Gilfach Fargoed mansion, farm and mill leased at £30. By 1782 the estate's annual value was £91 5s 8d, although the 1803 rent roll records this at £206 5s (and valued for sale at this time at £211 7s); the rent for Gilfach Fargoed Fawr in 1803 was £80, rising to £105 in 1811.

The 1756 manorial rental shows that Edmund William George the tenant installed by Joseph Morris remained there. Edmond William George was the youngest son of William George of Cefn y Brithdir Farm and a member of one of the more affluent families in Gelligaer parish at the time. In 1753 he purchased Maerdy Bach farm, west of Deri. In 1766 he acquired Gilfach Fargoed Fach and appears to have moved there and sub-let Gilfach Fargoed Fawr to Harry Lewis. Edmund William George (alias Edmund Williams) died in 1771 and his properties passed to his wife, Ann, and his two sons, William Williams and Thomas Williams. The land tax returns show the family paying tax on both Gilfach Fargoed Fawr and Fach in the period 1783 to 1806, but Thomas Williams, having acquired half of Heolddu Farm in about 1801 moved there in 1806.

The next tenant at Gilfach Fargoed Fawr was William Edwards who leased the farm sometime in 1808 before being succeeded by William Morgan who was the tenant from 1808 until 1830 and made some repairs there. He paid £2 5s for the carrying and labour of a *dozen* of lime (3s 9d at the kiln) in December 1808 (repaid at the summer rental) and records also show a £15 allowance for hedging and 15s for 600 house tiles (2s 6d per hundred). His will of 1839 (probate 1849) informs us that he had built four houses in Bedwellty parish (profits to go to his second son, Edward), that he had three daughters, Margaret, Mary and Rachel, to all of whom he left £30 and that the remainder of his estate was to go to his oldest son, Thomas Morgan. William Morgan died in September 1844 and his inventory, appraised in February 1845 by Edward Phillips and Harry Lewis further illustrated his wealth, for example, his wearing apparel valued at £5 9s, cottages by lease at £20 each £180. His funeral expenses amounted to £10.

William's son, Thomas Morgan had taken over the tenancy of Gilfach Fargoed Fawr in 1830; his wife, Mary was the grand daughter and sole beneficiary of Lewis Williams of Penfidyfedw (Brithdir hamlet). The 1841 census showed Thomas and Mary at the farm with their three children, William Morgan (previous tenant) and Jenkin Jenkins, both 65 and *independent* and three male and two female servants. At this time the farm was described in the tithe schedule as a 270 acre holding. By 1851, David Phillips, his wife and three sons together with three male and two female servants lived at and worked the farm and David Phillips was enumerated there in 1861 with his wife, two older sons and two daughters.

The Hanbury family remained the owners of the entire estate after 1751 and that included Gilfach Fargoed Fawr mansion and mill and lands. As part of the exercise of mapping their entire estate, their mid-eighteenth century land agents, John Aram, and his son of the same name, surveyed and mapped the entire Gilfach Fargoed estate which shows the land they owned at the time. The family's interest in the area also extended to what have become known as the Charity Lands, and as directed by Edward Lewis' will, the owner was always represented (chairman) on the Board of Trustees of the Gelligaer charity. The family later benefited as coal mines, houses and business and public properties covered the majority of the holding of Gilfach Fargoed Fawr, both as part of the development of the town itself and then with G.U.D.C.'s Gilfach Bargoed estate of the 1960s and 1970s. The Hanbury family still own the fields to the west of the town adjoining the Common.

Gilfach Fargoed Fach /Gwerthonor Ganol

South of Gilfach Fargoed Fawr are Gilfach Fargoed Fach and Gwerthonor Ganol. Both were typical of most of the farms within the old parish of Gelligaer. They were the farms of yeomen farmers, farmers who owned and lived on their own farms, although by 1841 only Gwerthonor Ganol in the Bargoed and Gilfach area was strictly speaking a yeoman farm.

Gilfach Fargoed Fach (small) like Gilfach Fargoed Fawr (large) took its name from the area of Gilfach Fargoed in which both farms lie. The farms appear to have no connection aside from their names. Gilfach Fargoed Fach can be traced back to lands shown in the Senghennydd manor survey of 1540 as owned by Mathew Howell. From deeds of that time it is known that his wife was Margaret ferch Llewelyn, but little else is known of them. 30 years later the farm is shown as owned by *William Mathewe Hoell, yeoman,* undoubtedly the son of Mathew Howell.

Gwerthonor Ganol can be traced back to lands owned in 1540 by Jevan Jevan Traherne ap Meuric who also owned Gwerthonor, a farm to the south. Gwerthonor Ganol however appears to have been acquired at some date by William Mathew Howell. Possibly in the 1580s as it is then that his name first appears in national tax lists. These tax lists suggest that he died early in the seventeenth century since by 1609 his name was replaced by that of his son Richard William Mathew.

The Senghennydd manor survey of 1630 shows that Richard William Mathew owned Gilfach Fargoed Fach and another son Edmund William Mathew owned Gwerthonor Ganol. Richard William Mathew died in 1640 and his Will written in April 1640 tells us a little about farming and family at Gilfach Fargoed Fach at the time:

.... I geve and bequeath unto my daughter Katherin one poyse of wooll and one bushell of oatemell. Item I geve and bequeath unto my daughter Margarett one Brasse little crocke and two acres of oate which I have sowed upon her lande. Item I geve and bequeath more to my daughter Katherin foure stakes of oates according to the measure used in Cardiffe to be payed by me executor in the moneth of October next. Item I geve and bequeath unto my daughter Gwenllian foure stakes of oates of the like measure to be payed in October aforesayd and ... unto my sonne in lawe Morgan James ... all my wheat nowe growinge oats and barley alsoe groweinge ... deliver unto Richard Rowland, John Rowland and Walter Rowland my grandchildren the cows sheepe lambs oxen horses and heyffers which they had from theire father: first my true intent and meaninge is that the sayd Richard Rowland shall have three kine 13 heade of sheepe 7 lamps one heyffer of one yere ould and 2 oxen to be delivered unto him att all Saints next, ...

He goes on to make similar bequests to his two other grandsons and his granddaughter Jane Rowland. The Will shows that oats, wheat and barley had been sown at the farm by April and (probably in addition to other stock on his farm which will have been given to his main heir) he was holding 12 cows, 52 sheep, 28 lambs, 3 one-year-old heifers, a horse and 8 oxen for his grandchildren under their father's will; ownership of this number of oxen, in particular underlines the fact that this was quite a large holding.

It appears to have been his grandson Richard Rowland who inherited Gilfach Fargoed Fach. Richard's will of 1660 shows his eldest son was William and in 1670 William Richard was shown as owner of Gilfach Fargoed Fach. But the survey also indicates that it is a smaller farm (approximately 50 acres less than that owned by his great great great grandfather Mathew Howell in 1540) as his father had sold part of the farm, Tir Lewis y Gwlad, to Lewis William Lewis of Heolddu.

There is little information about Gilfach Fargoed Fach during the next 70 years. Although there are no surviving deeds for the property, there is a schedule of deeds relating to it - but this was not drawn up until the early twentieth century and is not very detailed and attempts at using this schedule to identify Gilfach Fargoed Fach in the early eighteenth century cannot be verified.

The next positive identity of the property comes in Senghennydd manor rentals from around 1750, showing the property to be owned and occupied by William Richard Rowland. The names used suggest some family connection back to 1670 but whether or not this is the case is not known. According to Gelligaer Church Parish register, William Richard Rowland was buried in February 1761 and Senghennydd Manor court leet records indicates his heir was his niece Ann Edmund spinster.

The next surviving manorial rental, that of 1765, shows that Gilfach Fargoed Fach (recorded by this name for the first time) was owned and occupied by

Edmund William George, tenant of Gilfach Fargoed Fawr. How he comes to be owner is not known. His wife's name was Ann but she appears to have been Ann Lewis not Ann Edmund. As mentioned earlier, people of Gelligaer began to adopt surnames in the eighteenth century and Edmund William George became Edmund Williams. He was buried at Gelligaer Church on 11 March 1771 but left no Will. Administration was granted to Ann Williams his widow and she was listed as the freeholder in 1771. In 1781 she settled Gilfach Fargoed Fach on her younger son, Thomas Williams; Maerdy Bach (west of Deri) had already been settled on her elder son William Williams. A plaque in Gelligaer church records that Ann Williams died aged 89 on 7 October 1808, William, died aged 76 in 1825 and Thomas, aged 72 in 1834.

Land tax returns show that between 1786 and 1800, Thomas Williams farmed both Gilfach Fargoed Fach and Gilfach Fargoed Fawr. However by 1801 his attention had turned to Heolddu. The returns show that he paid the tax on Gilfach Fargoed Fach until 1808 after which it was tenanted; between 1809 - 1816 it was paid by William Waters, in hand until Rees Rees became tenant, 1819-27 and then occupied by William Evans between 1819 and 1831 when the land tax records end. Thomas Williams meanwhile lived at Heolddu where he died in 1834. As neither Thomas Williams nor his brother William had heirs, Gilfach Fargoed Fach passed to the children of a cousin who lived in Mynyddislwyn parish (at least two members of Gelligaer Historical Society are descended from this Mynyddislwyn family).

By 1841, at the time of the Gelligaer tithe map and schedule, Lewis Williams and William Howells were shown as the owners of Gilfach Fargoed Fach. The farm was leased in two parts perhaps indicative of the future. Thirty one acres were let to William Williams, a farmer, (and coincidently the ancestor of another Gelligaer Historical Society member) who was enumerated in Gilfach Fargoed Fach homestead in 1841 with his wife Ann, four children, a servant and Elizabeth Lewis, *independent*, and his family continued to live there during much of the nineteenth century. At the time of the 1851 census he, his wife, two of the children named in 1841 and a further two of their children lived there with a niece and a male servant but by 1861 it was the home of his son, Jabes and his wife, daughter and an agricultural labourer; William Williams, his unmarried son, John and servants were at nearby Gwerthonor Farm. At this time there were about six other families living somewhere on the lands of Gilfach Fargoed Fach, all of these involved in mining activities.

The other twenty nine acres in 1841 were let to Joshua Fletcher Hanson named as the proprietor of Gilfach Fargoed Colliery in the 1842 Employment Commission Report on Children in Mines and Factories. It is interesting to note that in the Report, Jabes Williams, the eldest son of William Williams who farmed the other half of Gilfach Fargoed Fach was a 15 year old *hitcher*, one of seven aged thirteen to eighteen working at Gilfach Fargoed Colliery; there were also fifty adults and twelve children under thirteen years old. Within Hanson's portion of the land were two small areas where there were *cottages and gardens*, possibly for men working at the colliery. A tram road ran through the property and the 1870 Ordnance Survey Map shows Gilfach Colliery sited at the end of this tram road. This heralded the future for the Gilfach Fargoed Fach land, most of which gradually succumbed to industry and urbanisation.

As mentioned above, in 1630 Gwerthonor Ganol was owned by Edmund William Mathew. There is no indication of when he died, but Gwerthonor Ganol had passed to his daughter Ann as shown by the 1654 will of Rees William Evan.

> *... Item I doe devise give and bequeath unto my loving wife Anne Edmund the moytie or one halfe of all the lands houses barnes stables cowhouses and edifices ... as I had and purchased the same of my father-in-law Edmond William Mathew. ... unto my sonne and heyre William Rees the other moytie or one halfe of the sayd lands, mansion house barnes etc ... and to his heyres for ever conditionally that my aforesayd sonne and heyre William Rees shall and will marrie by the consent of his mother Anne Edmond, his unkle Thomas William Evan and his cousin Evan Thomas,.*

The inventory that accompanied the will shows that Rees William Evan left 6 oxen, 1 bull of 2 year old, 23 other cattle of various sorts, 3 horses, 75 sheep and all kind grain corn and fodder valued at £10. The total value of his stock was £88. The will and inventory not only indicate that Rees William Evan was quite a wealthy man, with large numbers of livestock but also show details of his family relationships and the importance of an *approved* marriage. Did son William want to marry someone his father disapproved of, or, as is more probable, was the attitude in the will a normal one for property holders at the time? William Rees's son as *right heir* would have inherited the property in the event that William did marry someone who was not *approved*, but this latter event does not appear to have occurred because Anne Edmund and her son, William Rees continued to be listed as taxpayers in Hengoed hamlet in the 1660s and 1670s. The Senghennydd Manor survey of 1670 shows William Rees and Anne Edmund as owners and they pay hearth tax on 1 hearth.

It is difficult to follow the farms in the period 1670 to 1750 but it is probable that William Rees William was followed at Gwerthonor by his son Lewis William Rees who died in 1737 and was in turn succeeded by his son William Lewis. However these are some of the commonest names in the area and it is difficult to be certain.

The Senghennydd Manor rentals from 1750 show the farm as being owned and occupied by William Lewis. The manorial court leet of 5 April 1771 records that William Lewis of *the Cwm, Gelligaer* sold property to James Davies the younger (although the reference to *the Cwm* here cannot be explained) who is possibly James Davies of Pen-y-Garreg. Land tax records show that Gwerthonor Ganol was owned by James Davies in 1790, and in 1791 and 1792 was part-owned by James Davies and (his son) Lewis Davies. Lewis Davies had married Catherine Lewis, the daughter of William Lewis of

Bedlwyn Farm (Ystrad Mynach) so his father may have settled the property on him then as James did not die until 1823.

The Senghennydd Manor records also show that sometime in the 1780s James Davies had acquired *Tir Lewis y Gwlad* from Charles Phillips, one of the owners of Heolddu. This property can be identified as part of the original Gilfach Fargoed Fach that had been sold to the Heolddu family in the mid seventeenth century. The name *Lewis y Gwlad* (Lewis' land – William Lewis owned Heolddu) is first recorded on the 1782 Map of Heolddu. There is no indication of the precise location of the land, although it is recorded as being 38 acres 2 rods 24 poles but the 1841 tithe map shows field 1843 in Gwerthonor Ganol as *Waun Lewis y Gwaydd* and it is therefore probable that the holding consisted of this and adjacent fields, part of north-west Gwerthonor Ganol.

When Lewis Davies died in May 1818 aged 55 the farm passed to his son William Davies. The Davies family had been members of Hengoed Baptist Church since at least the early eighteenth century, and Lewis was buried in the graveyard at Hengoed. His will, in which he refers to himself as a yeoman, was proved 1 June 1818 with probate being granted to William Davies described as farmer, the term yeoman was disappearing. In 1837 William Davies leased 2 coal mines lying beneath the farms known as Gwerthonor and Tyr Lewis y Gwaidd for 47 years to *Rosser Thomas of Gelligaer, coal proprietor, Thomas Wedlake of Pilgwenlly near Newport co. Mon., coal shipper, Lewis Thomas of Bedwellty co. Mon. coal proprietor, Thomas Powell of the Gaer in St. Wollas co. Mon., esq. and Thomas Protheroe of St. Wollas esq.* The rent was £326 0s. 10d. a year. and there was a royalty of 10d. on every ton of large coal mined and 3d. on every ton of small coal, and 1d. a ton was to be paid as a way leave over the farm lands.

The 1841 census shows William Davis on the farm with his wife Mary, their three children and a male and female servant. He, his wife, a daughter and his mother were also enumerated there in 1851 but by 1861 he was retired and living at Gwerthonor Cottage with his wife and a servant. The name Gwerthonor Ganol still appears on the modern OS map although much of the farm land has now disappeared.

Gwerthonor

Professor T. V. Davies writes of three farms covering these lands: *the three holdings Gwrthonog, Gwrthonog Ucha and Gwrthonog Issa are difficult to disentangle in the 16th and 17th century Rentals, although the information for these three is clear in the 18th century Rentals and in the 1846 Tithe Schedule.*

The first mention of the name Gwerthonor, as *Tir ir Gwohothne*, occurs in a deed of 1545, but the problem lies in the fact that much land in this area came into the hands of the Lewis of the Van estate and it is difficult to identify specific pieces of land. With the marriage of William Lewis, the second son of Sir Edward Lewis of the Van, to Anne, daughter of Edmund William Lewis of Gilfach Fargoed Fawr in 1611, all this land became part of the Gilfach Fargoed estate and continued as such for the next century. In his Will of 1715 Edward Lewis, who gave Groesfaen Farm to fund a school which later became Lewis School, Pengam, gave Gwerthonor Uchaf to a charity that was *to pay yearly to the poor of the Parish the proffitts* of the farm, and Gwerthonor Isaf to a charity *to procure and Elect one good learned and Orthodox Divine of the Church of England to preach two Sermons on Sunday at the end of every three weeks the one in the morning at the parish Church of Bedwellty and the other in the afternoon at the parish Church of Mynyddislwyn.* These charities still exist today and co-incidentally, Lewis School Pengam is built on former farmland of Gwerthonor Isaf.

Over 135 acres of Gwerthonor Isaf and Tir y Bont were rented from the Lewis Charity trustees by Lewis Jenkins in 1841, and Rosser Thomas and Thomas Lewis also rented a portion of the property. Their section was a tramroad and waste, a foundry and waste and a croft, waste and garden with a track leading to the main roads which ran west-eastward towards Pont Aberpengam and also to the north. The charity's trustees also kept 14 acres of woodland in hand. Much of Tir y Bont became the site of Lewis Boys Pengam school buildings and grounds in 1853, while the central sections of Gwerthonor Ganol and Isaf were incorporated into the village of Gilfach.

Conclusion

The town of Bargoed became a centre for the local farming community. For example, Heolddu Uchaf had hosted the Gelligaer, Llanfabon and Merthyr Ploughing and Hedging Society match in 1894 and did so again - but with far more spectators - in 1957. It was also the first venue when the Gelligaer and District Sheep Shearing Society moved their annual matches from Bedlinog in 1953. By 1959 however, the Shearing Match, now a much bigger event, with a gymkhana and sheepdog trials, was attracting greater numbers of competitors and members of the public and moved to Bargoed Park.

The remnants of some of the farms mentioned above still surround Bargoed and Gilfach; Pencaedrain remains in its entirety. Farms and their owners have also left their legacy in the names of roads and buildings in the town; to name just a few, Heolddu, Gwerthonor, McDonnell and Hanbury Roads, Hanbury Road Chapel, Heolddu Comprehensive School and the Hanbury, Capel, Old Mill, Gwerthonor and McDonnell hotels and public houses.

CHAPTER 5
GOVERNMENT AND POLITICS

National government at Westminster

Wales has been represented in Westminster since the sixteenth century Act of Union and, from then until the nineteenth century, the area that became Bargoed and Gilfach was on the eastern edge of Glamorgan County, a constituency represented by one Member of Parliament (M.P.). During these three centuries, voters (40 shilling freeholders) had few chances of exercising their right to vote as, especially because of the excessive costs of a contest, all but four of the county elections before 1832 (those of 1734, 1745, 1756 and 1820) were uncontested. The majority of M.P.s, whether elected or returned unopposed, belonging to landed families with substantial estates and influence in Glamorgan's fertile and prosperous regions and saw the County seat as a symbol of their power and prestige. Local issues were rarely discussed in Parliament before the nineteenth century. It is questionable whether or not voters living in the Bargoed and Gilfach area had much influence or interest in national government and politics. According to the 1820 Caerphilly Poll Book fifty one men qualified as 40 shilling freeholders in Gelligaer parish and so would have been able to vote in the 1820 County election when Sir Christopher Cole defeated John Edwards of Rheola and Hon. William Booth Grey.

Social and economic change in the country from the late eighteenth century onwards was reflected in political life with extension of the franchise and redistribution of constituencies. After 1832, Glamorgan County was represented by two M.P.s elected by a wider electorate including copyholders, leaseholders and some tenants at will. The following table based on a Glamorgan Electoral Register 1845-1846 in the custody of Bargoed Library, shows the men able to vote through their interests in local land.

Glamorgan Electoral Register 1845/6			
Elector	Abode	Property qualification	Property address
William Davies	Gwerthonor	Freehold Farm	Gwerthonor
Harry Lewis Harries	Aberystruth, Mons	Freehold house and land	Heolddu
William Howell	Pontycynon, Llanwonno	Freehold colliery	Gilfach Fargoed
Isaac Hughes	Near Pentwynmawr, Mons	Annuity on land	Tyr y Bont and Gwerthonor Isha
Lewis Jenkins	Heolddu	Land as Occupier	Heolddu
William Jones	Myrtle Gr. Bedwellty	Annuity on land	Tyr y Bont and Gwerthonor Isha
Capel Hanbury Leigh	Pontypool Park, Mons	Freehold land	Gilfach Fargoed Fawr
Edward Lewis	Dregog, Bedwellty	Freehold land	
Henry Lewis	Heolddu	Freehold land	Joint owners of Heolddu
Richard Lewis	Bedwellty, Mons	Freehold land	
Francis McDonnell	Plas Newydd	Freehold land	Hengoed
Thomas Morgan	Gilfach Fargoed	Occupier of land	Gilfach Fargoed
Edward Phillips	Pencaedrain	Leasehold land	Pencaedrain
Rosser Thomas	Pontaberpengam, Bedwellty	Land as occupier	Hengoed
Alexander Joseph Waddington	Usk, Mons	Freehold factory and houses	Hengoed
Lewis Williams	Parish of Mynyddislwyn	Freehold land	Gilfach Fargoed Fach

It is clear that local people were aware of Chartist activities as on Thursday 31 October 1839 Chartist leaders Zephaniah Williams and William Jones were at Pontaberbargoed warning people to be prepared and ready to follow their leaders and the following day, delegates from nearby Fleur-de-Lys and Maesycwmmer attended the meeting at Coach and Horses in Blackwood. The movement failed in the short term but five of their six aims were eventually achieved.

Christopher Rice Mansel Talbot of Margam, a member of the landed gentry, had a long political career as a County M.P., surviving challenges from industrial and professional interests as well as 1832 (and later) reform of Parliament. Male workers and tenants in the expanding communities of Bargoed and Gilfach were enfranchised by legislation of 1867 and 1884 and safeguarded from bribery and corruption by secret ballot (after 1872) and the Corrupt Practices Act of 1883.

Glamorgan was represented by two wealthy Liberal M.P.s prior to 1885 but neither landowner Talbot, representing the party's aristocratic Whig branch, nor industrialist Vivian, representing its Radical branch, had any real interest in or understanding of the problems of working class voters. In 1885, consequent upon the rapid population growth in its industrial north, Glamorgan county was divided into five single-member constituencies. The emerging communities of Bargoed and Gilfach became part of East Glamorgan, a constituency in which mining was the largest single occupation. Its first M.P. was the nonconformist, Radical middle-class Alfred Thomas (knighted 1902 and raised to peerage as Lord Pontypridd 1912), a loyal Gladstonian Liberal who held the seat until 1910, when he was succeeded by Allen Clement Edwards (1910-1918), a Liberal barrister especially interested in Trade Union cases. As he retained the seat until it ceased to exist on further redistribution of seats in 1918 he was the sitting M.P. not only when, in 1911, M.P.s first received the salary that helped break the monopoly of the rich in Westminster but also for the duration of World War I.

In 1918 Glamorgan County became seven single-member Parliamentary Divisions and from then to the present Bargoed and Gilfach has been part of Caerphilly Division and represented by Labour M.P.s. The constituency name and boundary have seen small changes in the intervening decades. The constituency's first three Labour M.P.s, Alfred Onions (1918-1921), Morgan Jones (1921-1939) and Ness Edwards (1939-1968), each served until their respective deaths. Alfred Onions, on the right wing of the Labour Party, had gained experience in local government as a member of Monmouthshire County Council including a term as chairman. Both Alfred Onions and Ness Edwards had worked in the coal mining industry and served fellow workers, the former as Treasurer of South Wales Miners Federation (S.W.M.F. and popularly known as the Fed) and the latter as Miners' Agent. Alfred Onions did not attain any high office in Westminster but Ness Edwards was Postmaster-General 1950-51. By way of contrast, local man Morgan Jones started his working life as a teacher but, as a conscientious objector during World War I, he was deprived of his post and imprisoned. He became an underground colliery labourer when he was refused reinstatement in his profession on the conclusion of the war. He became a member of the I.L.P. (Independent Labour Party) and gained political experience as a councillor. After entering Parliament in 1921 he served two terms as Parliamentary Secretary, Board of Education (January – October 1924 and June 1929 – October 1931).

Although Britain was a democracy, only 2/5 of its adult population was enfranchised at the turn of the century. Most men over 21 were able to vote before the end of the nineteenth century and those excluded then were enfranchised in 1918. At the same time, especially as a result of Suffragette

Morgan Jones who taught in Bargoed and was M.P. for Caerphilly 1921-39.

activities coupled with the responsible way in which women worked during World War I, some women over 30 years of age secured the right to vote in parliamentary elections. On the eve of World War I, Mrs Clark, who with her husband, accountant Arthur Iorwerth Clark, had recently moved into the area from Cardiff, was secretary of Bargoed and District branch of the non-militant National Union of Women's Suffrage Societies. It is not clear how active this group was in the Bargoed and Gilfach area but nationally the movement went far to raise public perception of women and the reality of their life. Women over 21 were enfranchised in 1928 and the franchise was further extended in 1969 when the voting age was reduced to 18. To date the local area has never had a female M.P. but some local women such as Hettie Jones played an active role in local politics in the inter-war era.

Election campaigns of the eighteenth and early nineteenth century depended on personal persuasion. Over the years, electoral campaigns adapted to the constantly growing electorate and embraced the widening range of appropriate contemporary methods. There were organised party campaigns, on the streets and in the local newspapers (with the increase in literacy) in the later nineteenth and early twentieth century. Since then, campaigners have made use of the ever-expanding technology available, including radio, television and internet, and transport by rail, road and air, as well as more intellectual arguments and sophisticated techniques. Perhaps the most interesting election campaign in Caerphilly constituency was that of the July 1968 by-election when Plaid Cymru, with local candidate, Dr. Phil Williams, and an intensive campaign, presented a very strong challenge to the successful Labour candidate, A. T.

(Fred) Evans, another local man, which turned a Labour majority of 21,148 into one of only 1874. The constituency has continued to dally with Plaid Cymru in national and local politics but, to date, it has never had a Plaid Cymru M.P..

The educational and economic background of the constituency's Labour M.P.s since 1968 reflect extension of educational opportunities and contraction in the local mining industry. Local miner's son, Fred Evans (1968-79) was one of the new type of Labour M.P.. Having graduated from University College, Cardiff he entered the teaching profession and, on election to Westminster, was headmaster of the prestigious Lewis School, Pengam. Ednyfed Hudson Davies, a lecturer and broadcaster who served as Labour M.P. for Conway 1966-1970, defected to the new Social Democratic Party while representing Caerphilly constituency ((1979-1983). He did not contest the Caerphilly seat as the Liberal side of the party fielded a candidate in 1983 and Ron Davies was elected. As M.P., Ron Davies (1983-2001) became Labour's Welsh Secretary until following a well-documented *moment of madness*, he lost the job and eventually quit the party in 2004. Since then he has re-entered the political scene as an elected County Councillor who is currently Caerphilly County Borough's Cabinet Member for Regeneration and Planning. The present M.P., Wayne David (first elected in 2001), was Parliamentary Under Secretary of State in the Welsh Office between October 2008 and May 2010, and is currently Shadow Minister for Europe. Unlike earlier M.P.s such as Alfred Onions who was in his mid 50s when elected, both Ron Davies and Wayne David entered Parliament while young enough to serve parliamentary apprenticeships before gaining senior Ministerial rank with responsibilities in the wider political context.

Recent developments

In recent decades residents of Bargoed and Gilfach have been represented in and had their lives shaped by the dictates of two democratic bodies far more recent in origin than the Westminster Parliament, namely European Parliament and Welsh Assembly Government, (now Welsh Government). Another new feature has been the use of referenda to decide on some issues. The first referendum in Wales was that on Sunday opening while the first UK wide referendum was that of 1975 to determine whether or not Britain should remain part of what was then called the Common Market. Since then referenda have been used on devolution issues.

Alfred Thomas had fought unsuccessfully in the Commons for a measure of autonomy for Wales: in 1890 he pressed for the creation of a Secretaryship of State for Wales, and in 1892 his National Institutions (Wales) bill aimed to establish a National Council, a separate Education Department, Local Government Board and National Museum in Wales. Welsh national feeling and heightened awareness of Welsh culture (especially of the Welsh language) has grown since then. The Welsh Office of the Ministry of Housing and Local Government was established in the 1950s and its sphere of authority progressively expanded and, in 1964 the office of Secretary of State for Wales was created. Referenda of 1979 and 1997 returned first a *No* and then a *Yes* verdict on devolution for Wales. Ron Davies became Caerphilly's first Assembly Member (AM) serving from 1999 to his resignation in 2003, and since then Jeff Cuthbert has represented the constituency. Standing as a Plaid Cymru candidate Ron Davies came second to Jeff Cuthbert in the May 2011 election. It is to be hoped that the Welsh Government (a parliament in all but name after enhanced-law-making powers gained in the March 2011 referendum) elected May 2011, will repay the trust of voters by implementing dynamic policies to improve the life of the people of Bargoed and Gilfach as well as the rest of Wales.

Local Government

For generations of local people from the sixteenth century to 1974 local government was administered through the county, Glamorgan, and the parish, Gelligaer. Justices of the Peace (JPs) drawn from the county's landed gentry families like Prichard of Llancaiach Fawr and Thomas of Llanbradach Fawr, exercised administrative and judicial control of the counties through Quarter and Petty Sessions from the sixteenth century to the later nineteenth century while parishes operated on a civil level to deliver statutory provision for matters such as poverty and roads as well as ensuring law and order. This system served the pre-industrial rural society for several centuries but it was unable to cope with more complex local matters arising in the new industrial urban society. Nineteenth century legislation superimposed a national system of locally-elected bodies, and Merthyr Tydfil Poor Law Union, Highways Board and Local Board of Health (the latter to become a Sanitary District in the 1870s) became responsible for matters relating to poverty and public health in Gelligaer parish, including the Bargoed and Gilfach communities.

Experience quickly showed the Sanitary Districts were often no more able than the parishes to cope with their responsibilities, therefore in 1888 and 1894 Parliament passed two Local Government Acts, totally reforming the structure of local government. The 1888 Act formalised the Counties, forming democratically elected councils including Glamorgan, mainly to administer law and order (judicial matters continued to be administered through the Lord Lieutenant), emergency services, roads and education. The new Glamorgan County Council met in 1889 with 88 members, comprising 22 Aldermen (elected from among the councillors by fellow councillors, aldermen were abolished under the Local Government Act of 1972) and 66 Councillors. At first the two separate small communities in Bargoed and Gilfach were part of a much larger area but as they grew they had their own representatives and County Councillors D. S. Jones and Rev. Daniel Leyshon Evans are just two of the men who served Bargoed and Gilfach in the early decades of the twentieth century. By 1939, when Glamorgan County Council celebrated its Golden Jubilee, Bargoed and Gilfach, represented by Councillor (later Alderman) William John Kedward, had changed dramatically as the small village communities had become bustling urban areas. Gelligaer and Rhigos Rural District Council, a second tier of local government, came into being in 1894, replacing the former Rural Sanitary District, and took responsibility for matters such as water supply, sewage disposal, refuse collection, local roads and footpaths, local planning powers and recreation grounds. The rapid urbanisation in Gelligaer parish, especially in the Bargoed and Gilfach areas, outpaced the powers of a Rural District Council and so the District was divided in 1908, when Rhigos joined Neath RDC and Gelligaer Urban District Council (G.U.D.C.) was created. This latter body had to meet the challenges of administering the rapidly emerging communities of Bargoed and Gilfach. The post 1894 civil parish, a form of community council, was in reality a listening board and advisory body for County and District Councils.

In 1896 Hengoed was preferred to Bargoed for the new local Council Offices. The location of the Council Offices came to the fore again when G.U.D.C. was formed but Hengoed prevailed probably as its rail links served the district better than those of Bargoed. By the late 1920s when G.U.D.C. established its Electricity Department Bargoed was the main business and retail centre in its district and the council took steps to secure suitable land near the Fire Station to move its various departments from Hengoed to Bargoed. However, the strong body of opinion in favour of remaining in Hengoed won the day and the offices remained in Hengoed.

During the second half of the twentieth century local government in Wales has undergone two major reorganisations, both resulting in including communities on both sides of the Rhymney river in the same county, something that had been done earlier by bodies such as Rhymney Valley Water Board. The idea had been mooted more than once in the early twentieth century: in 1904 when considering the advantages of one large sewer instead of one on each side of the valley and again in 1910 with the Joint Rhymney Valley Councils.

Under the two-tier system of County and District Councils that came into being in 1974, the local area was administered by Rhymney Valley District Council (R.V.D.C.), the easternmost of the six second-tier districts in Mid Glamorgan county. That system was replaced by Unitary Authorities in 1996, since when Bargoed and Gilfach have been administered by Caerphilly County Borough Council. The third tier of local government then was the Community Council. In both 1972 and 1996, a Bargoed Town Council was set-up to replace the former parish council functions. Bargoed Town Council with responsibilities like those of a parish council and its four wards (Aberbargoed, Bargoed, Gilfach and Park) originated after the 1985 Boundary Commission

Local nonconformists and politics

In the later nineteenth and early twentieth century nonconformist clergy across the country were eager to serve their communities by securing election to locally-elected bodies. Rev. Harri Edwards and Rev. Daniel Leyshon Evans are just two local nonconformist clergy who served the Bargoed and Gilfach communities with distinction in the first two decades of the twentieth century.

From time to time the clergy and diaconate of the local nonconformist chapels influenced their congregations in politics as well as in moral and spiritual matters. In 1920, the local press reported that a deacon in one of the local Welsh chapels had asked voters among the congregation not to support local licensee Jenkin Morgan in the County Council election. It is not clear whether or not this affected the result (Morgan Jones polled 2,223 votes to Jenkin Morgan's 1,649).

Local Liberalism

The late nineteenth century Welsh Liberal-nonconformist tradition in which incomers to the area like headmaster J. Sylvan Evans had grown up, appealed to some local middle and working class voters and its strength in the decades prior to World War II owed much to the influence of nonconformist ministers and deacons. As it was primarily concerned with issues such as Disestablishment of the Church and securing representation on Gelligaer School Board and similar bodies rather than getting to the root of social and economic grievances, it failed to retain working class voters in the face of the growth of socialism. In Autumn 1923 local Liberals responded to the enfranchisement of women by forming a local women's branch, the elected officers of which included wives of notable local Liberals such as A. S. Williams (councillor and businessman), T. M. Cule (bank manager) and J. Sylvan Evans (headmaster). Their inaugural lecture on current politics was delivered at Bargoed Workmen's Hall. Liberalism dwindled locally as some four years later, following a meeting presided over by J. Sylvan Evans, at Berni's Cafe Trafalgar Square, a local Liberal branch was formed with a new Women's Branch a few weeks later. They gained strength with five well-attended fortnightly lectures in the Workmen's Institute and a visit by Jack Jones of Blaengarw, a former miner's agent who had recently joined the Liberal party. In his speech on Liberal coal and power policy delivered in the Workmen's Institute, he refuted accusations from Arthur J. Cook in *The Miner* by saying he neither advocated new unions nor betrayed workers, while in reference to Cook's £600 p.a. salary he confirmed he was not in receipt of a high salary from Liberal funds. He saw Liberal policy as a practical solution to the coal problem when coalowners were closing pits and rendering men idle. Liberalism did not disappear from the local area and although Liberals did not contest the parliamentary seat in the mid twentieth century they have done so in more recent elections.

The local Labour movement

By the early twentieth century the Labour Party had made an impact in some Glamorgan constituencies, but the local area did not have a Labour M.P. until 1918. While nonconformist pastors and diaconates had encouraged working class support for the Liberal Party, the miners' union (S.W.M.F.) performed a similar role for the Labour Party and, from 1923 onwards, Labour dominated the local power-bases until it met a challenge from Plaid Cymru in the later decades of the twentieth century. In March 1923, when members of the local Labour party assembled at Bargoed Workmen's Institute to present Morgan

Jones with a wedding present, Moses C. Price and Morgan Jones spoke about the developments in the Labour party in the local area over the previous decade and a half. In the first decade of the twentieth century, the local Labour Party was an insignificant little group that was sneered at and treated with contumely and contempt as notable local citizens in Bargoed and Gilfach did not recognise their worth. Over the years local supporters sacrificed much for their principles and the local Labour Party grew in strength and improved its organisation. It arranged for speakers to visit the area and address members at venues such as the Workmen's Institute, it organised debates and, like local Liberals, it set up a local Women's Section in the 1920s. While men such as W. H. Hopkins and T. D. Matthews played key roles in local Labour politics, their wives were enthusiastic workers in the Women's Section.

Born in Aberdare, Morgan Walter Phillips (1902-1963) moved to Bargoed while he was young. He left school at the age of twelve to work in the colliery. Aged 18, he became a member of Caerphilly Divisional Labour Party, and served as secretary of the party in Bargoed 1923-1925. When in 1926 he won a two year scholarship at Central Labour College in London, he was chairman of Bargoed Steam Coal Colliery Lodge of S.W.M.F. (a position he held 1924-1926), Vice Chairman of Local Canteen Committee and member of Glamorgan Agricultural Wages Board. After completing his two year course in economic and social subjects Morgan Phillips gained experience in local government in Fulham and from 1937 he served at party headquarters, Transport House, where his abilities were recognised and he rose to become general secretary in 1960. Sadly he suffered a stroke and retired from that post in 1961 and died in 1963. The family link with politics and the Labour party continued: his widow became a life peer in 1964, his daughter, Gwyneth, and son-in-law, John Dunwoody, became Members of Parliament, and his granddaughter, Tamsin, a member of the Welsh Assembly Government.

Local Conservatives

The local newspapers show that, although the party did not make any significant impact on the local political scene, the Conservative party had some support in Bargoed and Gilfach in the inter-war era and, in common with the Liberal and Labour parties of the time, they had Men's and Women's branches, meeting regularly and sending delegates to Party Conferences.

Local Plaid Cymru

In the last half century or so local voters have flirted with Plaid Cymru in national and local politics. The Labour Party lost control of Caerphilly County Borough Council in 1999 and, at the present time (2011), it is run by a Plaid-led coalition but no Plaid Cymru candidate was returned for Bargoed and Gilfach wards.

Philip James Stradling Williams (1939—2003)

No book about Bargoed and Gilfach would be complete without mention of Phil Williams, who although born in Tredegar, was brought up in Bargoed and educated at Lewis School Pengam before going to Clare College, Cambridge. His achievements as a physicist are too numerous to itemise but suffice it to say he was recognised as a world authority in his field. He applied his huge intellectual ability to politics, and was largely responsible for the metamorphosis of Plaid Cymru, the party he joined in 1960, from a cultural movement into an effective political party. His remarkable campaign, that decimated Labour's majority in Caerphilly's 1968 by-election, attracted much attention. Following his election as one of the list members for the south east region in Wales' National Assembly in 1999 he applied his critical analytical mind to sources of government expenditure in Wales. Although identified in *Welsh Academy Encyclopaedia of Wales* (John Davies, Nigel Jenkins, Menna Baines and Peredur I. Lynch) as *physicist and politician*, Phil's abilities and interests were not confined to those fields: he also excelled as a saxophone player, scholar of Russian literature and researcher of the Welsh contribution to science, and he was, as the compilers of that volume concluded, *without doubt, the ablest Welshman of his generation.*

Clerk to G.U.D.C.

When in 1920, the post of clerk to G.U.D.C. fell vacant on the resignation of Frank T. James after many years of faithful service to the council (and its predecessor), it was open to qualified solicitors who did not hold any other public appointment and subject to three months notice on either side. There were nine applicants for the post including two Bargoed men, John Evans of 2 Capel Street, a well-known and highly esteemed Bargoed solicitor (who won on the third round of voting) and solicitor L. Arnold Williams (who was knocked out in the second round of voting). In 1920 John Evans was considered well-equipped for the post: not only was he an experienced solicitor but he was also well-acquainted with the work through his years of service as deputy clerk to Caerphilly U.D.C.. The post involved daily attendance at the Council Offices, attendance at all council meetings and committees and police court prosecutions, as well as doing all the council's conveyancing and High Court, Parliamentary and Quarter Sessions work. His salary was £600 pa and the Council would provide the office staff. On being appointed clerk, John Evans thanked the council for the confidence they placed in him and, as he was following in the steps of a man honoured by G.U.D.C. and whose opinions had been relied on, he faced a difficult task, but, he hoped that, with the assistance of the staff, he would carry out his duties successfully, faithfully and impartially. At the same meeting G.U.D.C. thanked Frank T. James for long and faithful service as it was the last meeting that he would attend. The current office staff was retained: John R. Hughes (at a salary of £209 p.a., and he was allowed to keep his position as registrar of marriages), J. R. Rowlands (salary £208 p.a.) and I. I. Thomas (salary £98 p.a.).

Many changes took place in the decades that followed but space does not permit further description and discussion of other personnel and the nature of their work. Suffice it to say that, having adapted in line with changing demands and facilities, the number of people involved and the nature of the work is very different today from that of the days of either Frank T. James or John Evans.

Some local councillors

It is not possible to name all the men and women who have made their mark in the local council over the years but it would not be invidious to mention the following who have served over decades.

Born in Llantrisant Jonathan Williams (1838-1904) was a collier's son who, through his own ability and hard work, became a successful businessman and highly respected public figure. Moving to Bargoed in the 1870s with his second wife and the children of his first and second marriages, Colliery Proprietor Jonathan Williams soon became closely associated with various local bodies including Calfaria Chapel, and Gelligaer School Board, as well as the local council and bench of magistrates. According to his obituary in *Merthyr Express* he was regarded as a solicitor-general for Bargoed whose words of advice would live on as Bargoed continued to develop.

Shopkeeper and Postman Edward Lewis (1846-1926) had grown up in the local area. He served on the local Boards and the Councils that superseded them, as well as on the influential Bargoed Chamber of Trade. Such was the importance of the role he played in public life that he was referred to as the *General Looker-After of Bargoed*.

It was not unusual for Nonconformist clergy to seek election to serve their local community and, in the first two decades of the twentieth century, Rev. Harri Edwards (of Hanbury Road Baptist) and Rev. Daniel Leyshon Evans (of Calfaria Independent) played important roles in local public life. Other notable local councillors in the decades prior to World War II included Samuel Carter, Gus Jones and A. S. Williams (son of Jonathan Williams mentioned above). In the first half of the twentieth century these men and their fellow-councillors faced a challenging task in helping to mould the local area at a crucial time in its development.

Today many local people have vivid memories of local councillors such as William John Kedward, O.B.E., J.P. and Kenneth Graham Turner. The former served for many years as a Glamorgan County Councillor. He was chairman of that council in the late 1950s and elected as a county alderman a few years later. The latter was chairman of G.U.D.C. 1969-1970 and during that year one of his many duties was to attend the investiture of the Prince of Wales at Caernarvon Castle. Bill Coleman belonged to the next generation of local councillors and is well-known as the long-serving chairman of Heolddu Comprehensive School governing body until his retirement in 2010.

Currently Bargoed and Gilfach are represented on Caerphilly County Borough Council by Councillors Harry Andrews, M.B.E., David Carter, Tudor

Davies and Dianne Price. All four belong to the Labour Party and the first-named represents Gilfach Ward while the other three represent Bargoed Ward.

Greater Bargoed Partnership

Communities First is a Welsh Government programme targeting Wales' more deprived areas. Greater Bargoed Communities First Partnership, covering Bargoed and Gilfach Wards (as well as Aberbargoed) is made up of representatives of community groups and residents.

Conclusion

Since the 1960s, gradually at first and then gaining pace, the enthusiasm shown by leaders and voters in the earlier twentieth century has given way to a growing lack of public faith in mainstream politics. In Bargoed and Gilfach, as in the rest of the country, falling turnout to vote in elections reflects cynicism and disillusionment that, from time to time (and most recently in the case of the 2009 parliamentary expenses row), has been reinforced with a measure of anger and disgust.

SS, SATURDAY, APRIL 14, 1923

GELLYGAER COUNCIL.

MINISTRY OF HEALTH AND THE WELFARE COMMITTEE.

DIRECT LABOUR VERSUS WORK BY CONTRACT.

A meeting of the Gellygaer Council took place on Tuesday evening, when Mr. J. H. Charles, J.P., presided. There were also present Messrs. Wm. Griffiths, E. Jenkins, Wm. Hammond, C. A. M. Cattermole, T. John, Rev. Gilbert Williams, John Phillips, W. J. Meredith, J. Hill, A. S. Williams, J. Penry Williams, Capt. Ridge, Gus Jones, John Edwards, and E. T. Morgan, together with Messrs. J. Evans (clerk), F. Reed (surveyor), J. Brown (inspector), H. McNaul (electrical engineer), C. J. Samuel (accountant), and Pugh Jones Williams (architect).

PERSONAL.—The Chairman at the outset congratulated those who had been returned as members of the Council. They were, however, sorry that Mr. Edgar Jenkins had not been successful in the election. Mr. Jenkins, he said, had been a very useful member, and he hoped he would soon be back with them once more. The Council also regretted that Mr. Sydney Jones was unable to offer himself for re-election, owing to ill-health. They all wished him a speedy and complete recovery.

WELFARE SCHEME.—The Clerk reported that he had received a communication from the Ministry of Health regarding the proposal to hand over the Bargoed Park to the Miners' Welfare Committee. The Ministry stated that the Council were not legally competent to hand over any open space they possessed, neither could they hand the park to the conveyancer so that it could be handed to the committee. Under the Public Health Act the Council could provide all that the committee were out to provide, and could make charge, if necessary, for the provision of such facilities. The Welfare Committee could then be represented on the management committee should they so desire. The Clerk also said that he had again communicated with the Ministry asking them to receive a deputation on the matter, but he had received a reply to the effect that no useful purpose would be served by the deputation going to London.—Mr. Gus

end and after holidays. He did not like the remark of the Surveyor in regard to his own men, and he would like to know when, and where, they had been at all stringent on the contractors. In fact, it was the other way about. They had given the scavenging of 30 houses above Bargoed by contract some time ago, and they found that the work had not been done for 18 months, although the contractors had been paid all the time. When an epidemic broke out in the street they had to pay to get the back lanes cleared.—Mr. F. Read (the Surveyor) said he could not take the responsibility for the figures placed before them that evening, as he had not been able to go into the matter on account of pressure of work.—Mr. Hill then proceeded, and said they could not discuss the matter any further until they had the figures they had asked for. The Council could not move in the dark. The scavenging in Bargoed under the present system was as well done as in any other town, and if there was any economy or want of supervision, it was not the fault of direct labour, but the fault of the department responsible for the oversight of the work. The contractors in some cases had to recoup themselves by hauling stones; they had to be given extra work to enable them to make the thing pay.—The Chairman said it was clear that Mr. Hill was right. They had not had the estimates which they asked for, and the Surveyor could not even confirm the figures presented to them by the Accountant.—Mr. A. S. Williams: Then how did the Surveyor arrive at the figures to enable him to make the rate?—The Chairman: They were based on last year.—Mr. Williams: He would not put down a figure, unless he thought that amount was going to be spent.—The Chairman: I am as anxious to reduce the rate as anybody, but we have not had even the correct cost of last year.—Mr. Hill: I move that we get the correct estimate by next year.—Mr. A. S. Williams: If we can save this money, we ought to do it now, and I move we have the figures by the next Council meeting.—The Accountant said he could vouch for the accuracy of all the figures submitted, with the exception of those from the time sheet.—Mr. A. S. Williams's motion was eventually adopted.

HOUSING.—It was decided, on account of the inability of the contractor to pro-

Political report in Merthyr Express. Note the detail included in local newspapers at that time.

CHAPTER 6
ECONOMIC ACTIVITY

Primary or Extractive Industries.

Secondary or Manufacturing Industries.

Tertiary or Service Industries.

The economy of Bargoed and Gilfach has never achieved anything approaching the textbook balance with all three forms of production present in equal balance. Nevertheless, for about seven decades (1900–1969) it was a hive of industry when the coal industry was dominant, generating relatively high levels of prosperity for many inhabitants and this chapter considers not only the nature of and changes in the main economic activities, but also outlines what happened, when and why.

Primary or Extractive Industries

Primary or Extractive industries involve the exploitation of natural resources, usually from the land, and encompass all forms of agriculture, forestry, quarrying, mining and fishing. Apart from fishing, they have all long existed in the Bargoed and Gilfach area on an organised basis.

Agriculture

Farms and farming are considered in another chapter. Consequently, little will be added, simply reiterating that farming was the dominant activity in the area until the late nineteenth century. It was never a particularly prosperous activity locally, as climate, soils and topography in the mid Rhymney valley are generally unhelpful to the farmer, even on those occasions in history when a market for produce existed nearby. Most farmers worked hill farms, producing sheep, a few cattle and horses for sale, fodder for the animals, especially as winter feed and a range of coarse grains (oats mainly), vegetables and animal products for the family. There was rarely a surplus for sale, but what existed remained within the local community. However, although farming followed the traditional patterns, some farmers were endeavouring to improve their stock and methods as exemplified by a *Merthyr Express* advertisement in 1900, indicating that Maerdy farm (between Bargoed and Deri) had pedigree Hereford beef cattle for sale, an improvement on the indigenous Welsh Black cattle for meat production. Overall, agriculture did not share in the prosperity brought by the coal industry, but some benefits accrued, especially for those who owned land and leased mineral rights.

Forestry

Forestry was practiced locally on a small scale, usually as a side-line for local farmers. Half a century ago, it was suggested in *The Gelligaer Story*, that woodlands in the nearby Darran valley were exploited for production of charcoal for the Heads of the Valleys' iron industry in the early nineteenth century, ceasing when coke, produced from the abundant local coal measures proved more efficient for large-scale smelting of iron. The respite was short, for in the late nineteenth century, colliery development and provision of homes for those who came to work in the coal industry, caused demand for timber to soar, consequently most woodland was decimated.

Evidence of systematic commercial timber production is found in two sources. Arthur Wright's *History of Lewis' School* (1929), quotes from the accounts of the Trustees of Lewis' Charity School in 1818 (when the school was still in Gelligaer): *In the same year the woods were felled and the timber sold by public auction ... and the price £200.* Which woods are being referred to is uncertain, but they may have been their farms in the Groesfaen area and/or Gwerthonor Uchaf and Isha farms, although the last two named were not part of the School Charity. He continued, stating in 1825 *... timber was now seen to be a likely source of revenue if well-managed and the trustees made an appointment which was new, i.e. a Woodward, whose duty was ... to see that the timber was kept in good order, thinned out and felled when necessary.* In 1833 Wright reported: *... the revenues had consisted mainly of the rentals of the various farms and of the proceeds of felling the timber in the copses on the Grossvane* (Groesfaen – in the Darran Valley) *farms ... cash derived from the sale of timber ... amounted to this date to over £1,000 ...* However, by 1833 the Trustees realised that even greater revenues to support the school could be derived from leasing mineral rights to the coal lying beneath their estates. In his personal memoir, Rev. Gwilym Thomas recalled that during the 1870s the Darran Valley area of Bargoed *was well wooded and at that time much timber was cut.* Much of this timber, he stated, was taken to Bargoed's railway goods yards from where it was transported, probably to places where coal mining was established and demand greater.

In the past 30 years there has been a noticeable return of natural woodland, but little of this has been developed commercially. It is feasible that in the future, the coniferous tree plantations planted on and covering the sides of the Darran valley, might be exploited commercially, but the scale of such operations is likely to be small.

Quarrying

The fact that many of the buildings and structures in Bargoed and Gilfach are stone-built indicates the existence of local quarries. Initially, quarrying for stone for local farms and some public works, such as churches and chapels, would have been a small scale activity leaving little long term trace on the landscape. The demand for building stone increased with the growth of new industries and of population to serve in them. However, evidence for quarrying on the Glamorgan bank of the Rhymney is scant. The 1901 edition of the Ordnance Survey (O.S.) 1:2500 plan, shows two quarries (one described as an *old quarry*) in Gilfach Fargoed, neither of which appeared on the 1873 edition. *The South Wales Coal Annual* (1914 edition) refers *to Gwerthonor Quarry, Gilfach near Bargoed*, suggesting the quarry was owned by Price and Smith, who employed *a commercial manager/officer*. A photograph caption in a volume of James' *History of Bargoed and Gilfach in Pictures*, suggests stone from this quarry was used locally, including construction of the Presbyterian Chapel in Commercial Street. Neither the quarry (closed by 1927) nor that chapel exist today but the cliff-like rock exposures behind Gilfach Bowling Green show where it had been. Another quarry features on the 1998 edition of the O.S. 1:25,000 plan on the west bank of the Rhymney and was formerly visible in the grounds of Lewis School Pengam, between the B4254 road and river. Quite when this quarry was operational has not been determined. The O.S. plans show there were several quarries on the Monmouthshire bank of the Rhymney, all of which might have supplied some stone for buildings in Bargoed and Gilfach. One, overlooking the site of Britannia Colliery, known as *Gilfach Quarry* was worked by the Rhymney Iron Company, like that in Gilfach Fargoed. This quarry probably opened in 1890, later became part of Powell Duffryn Associated Collieries Company and was closed by 1956. However, a photograph of a railway wagon produced by the Gloster Wagon Company prior to a Railway Clearing House Regulation of 1887, bears the legend *J. C. Gilvach Quarry, Pengam. No. 1* and registered by the Great Western Railway. Did this quarry open earlier than 1890? And who was *J. C.*?

Stone quarrying provided some employment in the local area, as demonstrated in the 1881 census, when ten men claimed to work in quarries but it is not clear where they worked. Stone for construction and road repairs was brought into the area by train, and, according to reports in *Merthyr Express* unloading was carried out at both Bargoed and Pengam station goods yards.

Coal-mining

The pre-eminent primary industry in the local area was undoubtedly coal mining. Arthur Wright's quotation from the 1833 Trustees' meeting, shows a recognition that the future prosperity of the Trusteeship, and the area in general, lay in the exploitation of coal seams underlying their property. Furthermore, it suggests a pit already existed on the land of Gwerthonor Uchaf. The coal industry came to dominate and shape most aspects of local economic, social and political life in the beginning of the twentieth century, several decades after the industry developed in other parts of the South Wales coalfield.

It seems there were no commercial coal mines operating in the Bargoed and Gilfach area before 1833 as neither the 1829 edition of the O.S. "One Inch" map relating to the area nor Gelligaer parish tithe map of 1841, show any collieries in the local area. However it is likely that small scale mining of outcropping coal seams by local farmers and others existed and had done so for many centuries, but it hardly constituted commercial production. Although the tithe map reveals an absence of local collieries, it shows a *Tram Road* in Gilfach, which later maps indicate, served a coal level as discussed in the chapter on Transport.

Additional to Wright's reference from the Trusteeship meeting in 1833, is a reference to a mine in Gilfach. An October 1837 lease agreement from William Davies, owner of Gwerthonor-ganol farm, refers to a coal mine lying beneath the farm known as *Gwerthonor*. The Royal Commission on Children Working in Mines, 1842, visited Gilfach Fargoed Colliery (Gilfach Fargoed Fach) in 1841/42. The Report stated the colliery was owned by Joshua Fletcher Hanson Esq., who with his contractor, employed 69 persons in the pit, twelve of whom were under thirteen years of age. Perplexing is where this work force came from, as there were very few buildings apart from farms, in the immediate Gilfach area and few more in Bargoed. One boy said he lived in *Cwmgelly* (?), while others presumably came from the more densely populated areas a couple of miles distant around Fleur-de-Lys and Gelligaer. The colliery, an adit mine (known locally as a level or drift), was basically a sloping tunnel from the surface giving access to the Mynyddislwyn Seam which was very near the surface in this location. Commercial production benefited from the colliery's links, via a bridge over the Rhymney, with the Rumney Tramroad, to secure access to Rhymney Iron Works and Newport Docks, both potential markets for their coal.

This level had a chequered history, involving several changes in ownership, including: Phillips Brothers (1858), Cope & Latch (1858–1860s) and Price & Evans (1878-1881). The latter 'failed' in 1881 and the colliery closed only to be subsequently purchased by W. G. Cartwright and reopened sometime after 1883. The Welsh Coal Mines web site suggested that in 1890 the colliery was redeveloped by Cartwright's executors, by sinking a *pair of pits* and a *tunnel was driven from near the mouth of the level to the top of the pit*. In 1894 it had 206 employees, while tables compiled in 1896 by Joseph S. Martin (Her Majesty's Inspector for the South-Western District) show 168 employees. Figures of coal production published in *Merthyr Express* (Gelligaer Parish section of the Merthyr Union Assessment Committee for rating), showed in 1903/04 Gilfach level, Messrs. Cartwright's, produced 27,618 tons, a decrease of 16,988 tons from that recorded in 1902/03. In 1909/10 production there had declined further to 12,678 tons and by 1915 the site was abandoned.

It is possible that a further three levels also worked the Mynyddislwyn seam in the Gilfach area, though details are sparse and rely mainly on tables produced by Olbris Davies (*Gelligaer*, Volume V). Confusingly one is known as *Gilfach Bargoed (Drift)* which existed from about 1871. The Welsh Coal Mines web site suggests this level was owned by William Davies in 1879-80, while in 1881-82 ownership was in the hands of M. H. Jones, by whom it was put into liquidation in 1883. Thereafter, there is no further mention of its existence, however, it could be the *Old Coal Level* shown a few yards west of Gilfach quarry on the 1901 O.S. Plan. Secondly, there was *Union Level*, which Olbris Davies suggested was active, at least, between 1843 and 1855, but the Welsh Coal Mines web site suggests it was abandoned in 1873. It continues, quoting a *South Wales Daily News* report of its reopening in 1890, reinforced by reference to this pit on the 1901 O.S. Plan. The aforementioned web site suggests that *Union Level* was operated by T. W. Watkins between 1916 and 1925, when it was finally abandoned. A third mine, located east of the Rhymney Railway's main line, is referred to on both 1875 and 1900 maps produced (based on O.S. plans) by R. A. Cooke, as *Cartwright's Gilfach Colliery*. Record of its opening date is unknown, but Cooke's researches suggest a closure date of 1915/16.

Three other collieries worked the Mynyddislwyn seam in the Bargoed area, close to where it outcropped. The smallest was Heolddu Ucha Drift, whose existence is alluded to in a leasing document dated 1842. Olbris Davies lists it in 1893, while Joseph S. Martin reported in 1896, it was owned by L. Jenkins, employing three workers. Under the terms of an agreement made 28 July 1920 between Lewis Jenkins and John Capel Hanbury, Lewis Jenkins held a lease of minerals under part of Gilfach Fargoed. Only weeks later, Heolddu Colliery Company Limited was formed 25 September 1920. Its directors were brothers Arthur Sydney Williams of Hendre, Hillside Park and Christopher James Williams, Caerffynon, farmer Lewis Jenkins of Heolddu Uchaf and mining engineer Edward Prosser Jones of Bryngwyn House, Pontypool. A. S. Williams, well-known in the community through his work as a councillor, was the permanent chairman, and like his brother he was a colliery agent. In 1920 Lewis Jenkins was the majority shareholder as the Company purchased his interest in return for 700 fully paid ordinary shares. By 1924 100 of Lewis Jenkins' shares had passed to Edward Prosser Jones. The following year saw further change as the Williams brothers and Lewis Jenkins were no longer shareholders: their shares had passed to Lydric and Mrs Gwendoline Jenkins of Heolddu Uchaf. Details of the operation of this Company are unclear and its dissolution was announced in London Gazette, 28 May 1929.

The history of the Wingfield Collieries is similarly complex. A colliery known as *Wingfield* is mentioned as bringing coal for transhipment to sidings on the Darran Branch of the Rhymney Railway soon after the latter's opening in 1864, but it does not appear in Olbris Davies' table prior to 1871. A *Merthyr Express* article (1875) ascribed ownership of the colliery to *Messrs. Bevan and Price*, while in 1884 *Western Mail* stated it belonged to Bevan & Davies. Between 1887 and 1891 (perhaps earlier) it became known as South Wingfield Pit. The colliery achieved its peak in 1881 when 85,141 tons of coal were raised, but it was abandoned in 1891, whereupon, its machinery was advertised for sale in *Western Mail*. Close to the latter, was a second, smaller Wingfield pit, known initially as the Maerdy Colliery (1874-81), after the farm nearby and tabulated as such in 1881 by Olbris Davies. It became known as North Wingfield between 1882 and 1892 and in 1889 produced 34,955 tons of coal. The Welsh Coal Mines Forum (A. Williams, 2006) suggested it was abandoned, exhausted, with its owners bankrupt in December 1892 and in 1893 *Western Mail* advertised sale of its machinery.

So ended the history of commercial exploitation of the Mynyddislwyn coal seam. Increased knowledge of the geology of the coalfield, aided by the careful mapping of coal seam outcrops and study of the stratigraphical record as revealed by sinking shafts, it became evident there were even greater riches deeper down. First of the deeper seams worked locally was the Brithdir Seam, which like the Mynyddislwyn seam was part of the Upper Coal Measures series. It dipped or tilted in a southerly direction, so that beneath Bargoed, it lay at 198 yards below the surface and 312 yards at Pengam. Greater capital investment was required to establish collieries to reach such depths and consequently exploitation of this seam, basically bituminous house coal, demanded greater resources than most of the individuals who worked the earlier pits could realise.

What the O.S. plan of 1901 named as *Gilfach Pit*, was the first of two collieries to tap the Brithdir seam locally. Its early history is unclear, but the Welsh Coal Mines web site, says it was sunk initially by Messrs. Cope & Latch during the 1860s, but the Inspector of Mines list for 1880 shows it to have been owned by Messrs. Price & Evans, also owners of the older Gilfach Colliery (level). However, Olbris Davies suggests the pit was actually sunk by the Rhymney Coal & Iron Company in 1874, while Cooke, ascribes ownership to the Rhymney Coal & Iron Company by 1886, remaining so until the latter company was taken over by the Powell Duffryn Steam Coal Co. in 1920. During Rhymney Coal & Iron Company ownership, the pit was linked underground with the company's Darran Colliery, a fortuitous development as it allowed some survivors to escape from and rescuers to enter the Darran Colliery following a fatal explosion in 1909. In Joseph S. Martin's 1896 list of mines, Rhymney Coal & Iron Company is shown as employing 85 men, increasing to 363 in 1908, though declining later, with 285 in 1918 and 281 in 1923. Production figures are scarce, but *Merthyr Express* reported in 1904 that 16,406 tons were produced, a reflection of the pit being idle in the previous year, but a figure of 115,541 tons in 1909/10; a 'normal year', gives a more realistic impression of production levels.

As with most collieries in south Wales, Gilfach suffered its share of industrial unrest, notably a strike in 1902-1903 which lasted for almost two years. The stoppage undoubtedly caused the colliers and their families considerable hardship, but they were supported by many community events, including concerts given by a male voice choir comprising striking miners. Miners were supported by the local community in similar ways in later strikes, notably that of 1926. Problems of another sort affected the colliery in 1909 when the G.U.D.C. Surveyor accepted liability on behalf of the Council for a leak in the colliery pond in *consequence of the construction of the Council's main sewer near by*. Closure came in 1932, though the pit remained in use as a pumping station until 1963, when the site was finally cleared, ultimately for housing development (Andrews Close).

A shaft of 18 feet diameter and 600 feet deep, within the Bargoed colliery complex, known as the House coal or Brithdir Pit, also reached the Brithdir seam. This shaft was on the Monmouthshire bank of the River Rhymney, albeit culverted at this point, but was an integral part of Bargoed Colliery whose

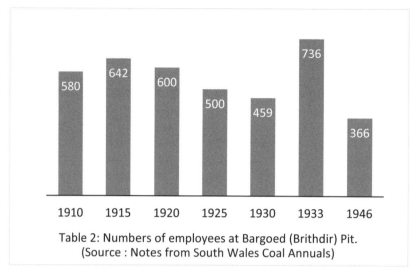

Table 2: Numbers of employees at Bargoed (Brithdir) Pit.
(Source : Notes from South Wales Coal Annuals)

buildings straddled the river. In December 1903 *Merthyr Express* reported: *Coal was raised for the first time at the Brithdir House Coal Pit of the Powell Duffryn Co., on Monday.* In 1918, it was reported as producing household and coking coal, a proportion of which was blended with the colliery's steam coal production for particular markets. According to a Powell Duffryn Steam Coal Co. handbook published about 1928, it produced *coal known as White Rose, a bituminous coal; the small coal is used almost entirely for coking purposes at the Company's coke ovens. White Rose Large coal is recommended for household purposes, and although not a first grade coal, finds a steady market in view of its moderate price. It is extensively used for China Clay drying.* Later, it suggests that *White Rose Cobbles is mainly suited for domestic purposes.*

It was a very wet colliery and electric centrifugal pumps pumped about 65,700 gallons of water per hour from the workings. Manpower fluctuated as suggested in Table 2. The 1930s saw both manpower and output (280,000 tons in 1934) fluctuate, generally declining slowly. Production ceased in 1949, but it continued to operate as a training pit for several years, at least until 1966, when this function was transferred to Britannia colliery.

During the latter part of the nineteenth century the Powell Duffryn Steam Coal Co. saw the middle section of the Rhymney Valley, south of its fast developing existing operation in New Tredegar (acquired in 1864), as an area of huge potential for steam coal production from the Lower Coal Measures. Geological surveys had, by that time, proved the Lower Coal Measures lying at about 1200 feet below the surface in New Tredegar, dipped gently southwards to reach a maximum depth in Bedwas of 2300 feet and was broken by few significant faults. Progressively the Powell Duffryn Steam Coal Co. purchased mineral rights for a continuous area extending for seven miles from just south of Rhymney to Penallta Junction (west of Ystrad Mynach), an area of 10,647 acres. Exploitation and management of mining these coal resources was placed in the capable hands of Edmund Mills Hann, a mining engineer trained in Durham, Yorkshire and South Wales, recruited by the Powell Duffryn Steam Coal Co. in 1879 to manage New Tredegar and White Rose collieries. He became manager of all Powell Duffryn Steam Coal Co. collieries in 1883, was the driving force behind development of the East and West Elliot Collieries between 1883 and 1890 and solved serious water problems in East Elliot with *one of the finest installations of underground steam pumps to be seen in mines at that time ...* wrote Leslie Shore (*Gelligaer* Vol. XVII).

Further expansion of the Company's operations was initiated by directors Graeme Ogilvie (died 1897) and Joseph Shaw and managed by E. M. Hann, the first stage being sinking a new colliery on the floor of the Rhymney Valley near Bargoed. Planning began in 1894, based on a company preference for a narrow valley floor site bisected by the river, but one which could be linked relatively easily with the existing railway network. Sinking started in April 1897 and, according to *Merthyr Express*, was undertaken by New Tredegar contractors, J. Piggott & Son and their band of experienced sinkers. The latter, working in arduous conditions using heavy chisels and picks, reached the first targeted, commercially productive seam, the Ras Las Nine Foot seam (actually about 3 feet 8 inches thick) in November 1901, at a depth of 1875 feet in the South Shaft. To mark this, a first, ceremonial load of coal was raised, but the colliery was not fully operational until November 1903, when Sir Alfred Thomas, M.P. formally started the engines to wind up the first four trams of coal from the South Pit. The second shaft to be completed was the North, which reached the Ras Las seam at a depth of 2105 feet, while the third and last shaft, the Brithdir shaft was completed in 1903, as indicated previously. The steam coal shafts were 21 feet in diameter and lined with brickwork nine inches thick.

Although the shafts were located on the Monmouthshire bank of the river, the new colliery was officially referred to by Powell Duffryn Steam Coal Co. as Bargoed (Glamorgan) Colliery, for much of the surface infrastructure, lay within Glamorganshire. Leslie Shore, wrote that Hann *specified, selected and purchased colliery equipment equal to, or even better than the best used in the European coal indus*try, adding the *colliery was representative of the best of enterprising engineering in Britain in the first decade of the twentieth century.* The impact of Bargoed colliery on the Powell Duffryn Steam Coal Co. (besides some other contemporary developments overseen by E. M. Hann) was summarised by Shore ... *with the advantageous trade conditions, efficiently engineered and well maintained collieries, dedicated colliery managers and officials and the toil of miners, the Company's fortunes were turned around.* The colliery became a major attraction for a wide range of visitors, including Society of Belgian Engineers (1904), Students from County Schools in Ebbw Vale area (1904), sixty delegates from the Associated Chambers of Commerce meeting in Cardiff travelling in a special train with chairman Lord Brassey and Lord Glantawe (1908), representatives from the National Union of Conservative

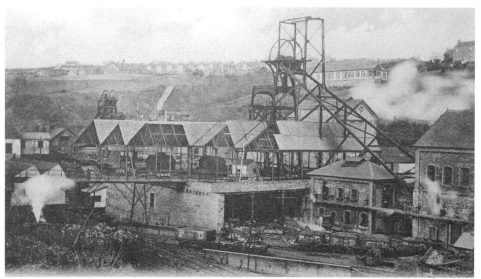

This photograph from the Terry McCarthy Collection shows Bargoed Colliery around 1906, the shafts and, to the rear, the beginnings of the tip. The construction of Bargoed Tip, for decades an unsightly local landmark consisting of hundreds of thousands of tons of debris, was started in August 1905. Constructed on the Continental System in popular use in Belgium and Germany, it was the only one of its kind in Britain. In August 1927 it was estimated that it consisted of 2,500,000 tons and about 100,000 tons was being added to the tip annually.

Associations, accompanied by Mr. Bonar Law (1908), Chancellor of the Exchequer, David Lloyd George (1909) and the Duchess of Kent (1949).

During the period 1897-1904 hardly a week passed without *Merthyr Express* reporting something new being added to the colliery's inventory. Reg Malpas, corresponding in the Welsh Coal Mines Forum, reported in 1911 gas-engine motors powered centrifugal pumps raising 34,000 gallons of water per hour from a depth of 1,620 feet to keep the workings dry. The South Pit winding engine, the main shaft for raising coal, was powered by a Thornewill & Warham four-cylinder compound engine, one of the earliest applications of this sort of engine. The cages raised and lowered by this engine had two decks, each capable of carrying two loaded trams (one tram held 5 tons 12 cwts of coal), which could be loaded and unloaded simultaneously, so that 400 tons of coal could be raised in an hour. To assist maximisation of winding speed, the cages ran along steel rails attached to the sides of the shaft. Ventilation was essential, with air being forced down the North Pit shaft by a Walker fan, which could produce 400,000 cubic feet of air per minute. Primary haulage was performed by electrical power, one of the first applications of this technology in South Wales, but compressed air was used for subsidiary haulage, face conveying and pumping. In subsequent years this equipment was progressively added to, with a washery being an invaluable addition in 1908, while in 1922 a power station was constructed at the south end of the site to provide power for

This 1949 photograph, courtesy of Nita Smith, shows Duchess of Kent with, on the left, G. D. Corfield (Area General Manager) and, on the right, Nita's father, James Campbell, Manager of Bargoed Colliery.

many more operations in Bargoed and other Powell Duffryn Steam Coal Co. pits in South Wales.

The new colliery quickly became a source of great pride for those working there, as Merthyr Express reported (January 1904): *In order to celebrate the completion of the new collieries of the Powell Duffryn Company at Bargoed, the whole of the enginemen and others employed on the pit surface sat down to dinner at the Hanbury Arms Hotel, Bargoed, on Wednesday evening. Upwards of 60 persons were present. Mr. S. Chester gave 'Success to the Bargoed Collieries'. He referred to the rapid change of scene at Bargoed during the few years since the Powell Duffryn Co. commenced operations. By their speculation and outlay employment was now found for a large number of hands, and there would still be many more in the future. When he looked back over the last six years he saw what a transformation had taken place. Where the pits now stood was then a field. He referred to the sinking of the colliery and the fact during that hazardous work there had not been a fatal accident ... They had fitted the place out with the best and most modern machinery, and the general arrangement of the whole work which made the colliery to be recognised as the finest in South Wales spoke volumes for the engineering staff.....*

Overall, Bargoed colliery was a major investment and cost between £300,000 and £350,000 to develop (in modern prices and according to which measure is employed, the equivalent of £24.1million - £28.1 million [retail price index] or £130 million - £152 million [average earnings]), sums which could be borne only by a large company with a good record of profitability, able to raise large sums in the London Stock Exchange. The prospects for the colliery seemed good, having secured mineral rights to 2,450 acres of coal, leased from ten different landowners, the largest being the Marquess of Bute and Lord Tredegar. Completion (1904) of the principal rail outlet, the Rhymney Railway Bargoed Pits branch, plus a link with the Brecon & Merthyr Railway ensured all was ready for full scale production to begin.

A most important prerequisite for the commencement of coal production was assembly of a workforce. In 1901 Bargoed and Gilfach had a population of 4,453, but by 1905 this had increased rapidly to over 10,000 in response to the new employment opportunities and relatively high wages available at the colliery. While some of those who worked in the pit were from the indigenous local population, the majority were immigrants from a range of places including declining coal mining and iron producing areas in adjoining South Wales Valleys, Somerset and the Forest of Dean and economically depressed agricultural regions of Wales and south west England. Anecdotal evidence has it that at least one family came because the father had read about Bargoed's promising job prospects in the magazine *Tit-bits* (a mass circulation commercial publication with emphasis on human-interest stories). The influx of English people soon meant that Welsh was replaced by English as the majority language, both at work and in the home, and this language issue is further discussed in Chapter 15. Marking the end of the strikes afflicting the coal industry in the Aberdare and Rhondda Valleys, but not the Rhymney Valley, the editor of *Merthyr Express* in December 1910, wrote implying that Bargoed Colliery had benefited from the migration of miners, even from strike-bound Powell Duffryn Steam Coal Co. collieries in the Aberaman area, to the more 'peaceful' working environment offered in Bargoed. This inflow of people also had major ramifications for provision of such of a range of facilities including housing, public utilities, services, schools and law and order with which the local authorities and other providers, were hardly able to cope.

Date	No. of employees	Production (tons)
1908	2,040	295,772
1910	1,943	289,621
1915	2,700	
1920	2,300	
1925	2,500	
1930	1,153	
1934	1,220	400,000
1947	1,048	
1949		363,000
1955	1,177	252,300
1961	792	198,609
1977	360	

Table 3: Numbers of employees, and production at Bargoed Pit.
(Source: South Wales Coal Annual, *Merthyr Express*, various websites).

During the succeeding years, employment in Bargoed colliery fluctuated, as indicated in Table 3. Numbers of men working at the colliery varied with production figures, which in turn was determined by the state of the coal trade and the degree of mechanisation. Prior to World War I, the coal trade was expanding to meet growing demands for coal, especially South Wales steam coal, by both merchant marine and naval services, a trade to which Bargoed Colliery contributed large amounts of coal. However, World War I heralded significant changes in technology, much of which was based on petroleum. Steam raising on ships switched to more convenient oil fuel, while a transport revolution on land (and later in the air) powered by internal combustion engines, began to replace railways and animal (mainly horse) power as significant movers of people and goods. Furthermore, development of electricity from larger, albeit mostly coal fired power stations, as a major source of power was embraced by the new industries. Older coal using industries declined so further reducing the declining market for coal. These trends gathered momentum in the post-war era and coal production, even for large efficient collieries like Bargoed, continued to fall as markets contracted. Large companies like Powell Duffryn Steam Coal Co. attempted to maintain competitiveness by introducing more machinery into collieries, but the task often proved beyond their means to fund, thus their market share declined regardless. Bargoed Colliery was capable of some mechanisation, hence the maintenance of relatively high production levels despite considerable falls in the numbers employed. Even though Nationalisation brought some new capital expenditure to Bargoed, competitiveness continued to wane to the point that by 1977, exploitation of its still considerable coal resources was deemed economically unviable so the colliery closed.

Powell Duffryn Steam Coal Co. handbook (circa 1928) indicates that Bargoed Colliery produced a wide range of coals for various different markets. There was Powell Duffryn Large Steam Coal – screened over bars 1⅛ inches apart and this class of coal it stated, is *world renowned, and is regularly purchased, year after year, for use by the Admiralty, Great Western, Southern and L.M.S. Railways for locomotive purposes; by the principal shipping lines, such as P.& O., Royal Mail Lines, Union Castle ... etc.; and by the leading railway and shipping companies overseas. It has been shipped to places as far afield as Newcastle (New South Wales), and is principally and regularly exported to France, Italy, Northern Africa, India, South America, and Atlantic coaling stations and depots.* Bargoed coal, besides being on the Admiralty List, was considered to be free burning and particularly suited for locomotive use. The Colliery's Rhymney Valley Washed Steam Coals came in three varieties: nuts (+ ¾ inches), beans (⅜ to ¾ inches), duff (under ⅜ inches). The first was described as a *high efficiency coal suited for electricity and similar works and for bunkering steamers of good natural or forced draught. Contracts ... regularly obtained for the Metropolitan Asylums Board, Metropolitan Water Board, War Office, Admiralty etc.* Apart from general steam-raising, beans were considered suitable for electricity generating stations, as was duff, indeed the Powell Duffryn Steam Coal Co. used it in their own power station in Bargoed. However, it was particularly commended as part of a blend for coking purposes. These washed coals were often blended with similar coals from Company pits in the Aberdare valley, much of which was exported to both France and South America. Much of Bargoed Colliery's production was used in the manufacture of coal products in the Bargoed complex, as described in the 'Manufacturing' section, below.

During the first decade of its working life, Bargoed Colliery's workforce achieved recognition by setting records for coal production during a shift. In December 1908 the colliery broke the world record for production when a ten hour shift produced 3,562 tons of coal, but four months later in April 1909, this record was surpassed when 4,020 tons were raised.

Despite the record breaking, its modern construction and operation and the relative prosperity of its miners, Bargoed was not immune from the industrial unrest afflicting the South Wales Coalfield during the early twentieth century. Until 1947, coal mining was based on private capital. Initially, mines were operated by the individuals owning them, who having invested their own money and effort were determined to secure a return on their investment. Threats of strikes and strike action were taken as personal insults and usually elicited a ruthless response. Resentment developed amongst the workforce, not helped by fluctuations in market returns, leading to cuts in wages and men laid off with little regard for the hardship caused; Thomas Powell being a prime example. In this volatile environment labourers tried organising themselves to pressurise mine owners into accepting terms benefiting their workforce. The owners saw this as a threat to their profits, upon which they depended for income and future investment. To counter such perceived threats, in 1873 the coal owners formed the South Wales Coal Owners' Association, with delegated powers to negotiate settlements on behalf of its members. Soon after, Parliament, through the Sliding Scale Committee, required wage levels of South Wales miners to be related to the price of coal.

As Bargoed Colliery exemplifies, the cost of establishing a new colliery was considerable and necessitated establishment of limited liability colliery companies, able to raise starting capital by selling shares. The success of so doing was determined by the anticipated prospects for the enterprise, often measured by past profitability. To recompense those investing their money in the company, shareholders were promised a yearly dividend related to profits made by the business. In those days, institutional shareholders were few, most being individuals for whom the investment and dividends constituted their pension, thus the company felt obliged to protect their interests above all else. Powell Duffryn Steam Coal Co. could not have sunk Bargoed Colliery without these investors, thus any perceived threat to their profit was seen as a threat to the company's future well-being, especially in such a highly competitive market, for although the coal owners worked in association, competition for the available trade was fierce.

Notwithstanding the perceptions of and pressures on coal owners, miners felt conditions of work and wages were unsatisfactory and their cavalier treatment by many owners stoked their resentment. Action often led to unemployment as owners countered by hiring replacement labourers. This led to the formation of unions, but until the Fed was founded in 1898, there was no single union in the coalfield, thus concerted action proved difficult. Initially, the Fed was the product of a combination of Welsh Nonconformist and Liberal traditions, as espoused by its founder, William Abraham, M.P., (Mabon), and the failure of a significant strike/lock out in 1898 against the *Sliding Scale*.

The dawn of the twentieth century saw new forces working in the miners' union, spearheaded by young radicals with a political agenda, influenced by the tenets of socialism. Like their leaders, (regarded increasingly as 'reactionary' – opined Mr. George Kenshole, architect, at the opening of Aberbargoed hospital in 1909), they strove to improve the lot of working miners, by securing such advantages as better conditions, insurance for medical assistance, compensation for injury or death at work and improved educational opportunities. Some of these aims were acceded to by more liberal-minded coal company managers, notably E. M. Hann, who recognised that supporting mining communities would be beneficial in the longer run, hence the company's contributions to Aberbargoed Hospital, Miners' Institutes, Mines Rescue Service and local cultural activities. However, the 'young bloods' aimed to change the political system, perceiving the established, capitalist system as 'selfish' and against the interests of the majority. Companies like Powell Duffryn Steam Coal Co. were anathema and to be rid of, by nationalising them. Soon after affiliating with the new Labour Party in 1908, they ousted the 'old guard' led by Mabon and began their challenge for political power. On a local level this was achieved by the end of World War I, and continuing at least until the new Millennium, but nationally they had to wait until 1945.

Views on both sides became entrenched and, hindsight suggests they lived and worked in 'parallel universes', unable or unwilling to recognise the symbiotic nature of their relationship (that they depended on each other). Coal owners failed to recognise or ignored the resentment their actions generated, while miners and their unions failed or did not wish to acknowledge the financial pressures on the part of owners and their managers. Reports of strikes in contemporary newspapers were frequent, with hardly a week passing in the first decade of the twentieth century without a report of a stoppage somewhere or another. Some of the causes seem now to have been very trivial, even contrived, but others are more understandable. However, the consequences of the clashes between two uncompromising parties were dire, adversely affecting both miners and their families, and shareholders. As history tends to be written by the 'victors', and undeniably the socialist politics proclaimed by the Fed prevailed in the area from the 1920s, perhaps it is time to re-evaluate the charge that P.D. stood for 'poverty and death'. It takes two sides to make a conflict, and while Powell Duffryn Steam Coal Co. (locally) has been deemed wholly blameworthy in the past, a balanced examination of events, might consider the role of the Fed in causing social and economic hardship to its members, as its leadership strove to further its political goals.

The South Wales Federation of Miners, formed its first lodge in Bargoed Colliery in May 1902. In 1903 it gave notice of action against the employment of non union workmen in the pit. This seems to have failed, but the question re-emerged the following year when the Fed expressed concern at the number of non-unionists working in the Rhymney Valley and gave notice of strike action. Once again there was no action, beyond a house-to-house canvass, which, it was reported, led to further recruitment so the 'problem' passed. However, this issue re-emerged as shown in Table 4. Bargoed was not affected by the major and violent strike called in the Rhondda and Cynon Valleys in 1910, despite efforts by Fed zealots. *Recorder*, commenting in *Merthyr Express* after one meeting in December 1910, suggested large numbers of those present were aged 14-16 years and it was they who expressed most enthusiasm for joining the strike. Though sympathetic, older married family men resisted the call and carried the day. The newspaper's editor suggested a consequence of this was the movement of a number of miners to Bargoed from the strife-ridden areas.

Date of stoppage	Duration (if known)	Cause (if stated)
1906	10 days	Employment of non-unionist labour
1909	A few days	Unknown
1912	5 weeks	National strike
1913		Non-unionism question
1914	11 days	Use of defective lamps
1920	7 days	Daytime removal of props.
1921	3 months	National strike – mines re-privatised, wage reduction
1926	7 months	General strike – further reduction in wages
1931	?	?
1969	10 days	Support strike in Derbyshire
1972	7 weeks	National strike – wage claim
1974	4 weeks	National strike – wage claim

Table 4 – summary of stoppages known to have affected Bargoed Colliery.
(Various sources – *Merthyr Express*, South Wales Coal Annual 1933, South Wales Federation website, etc.)

The summary suggests that apart from two short-lived strikes on local matters, Bargoed Colliery seems to have avoided all but the national stoppages shown above. That of 1921, was triggered by the return of coal mines to the companies, following their 'nationalisation' (Fed policy) in 1916 and non acceptance by the owners of wage increases given by a 'generous' government. A Royal Commission suggested nationalisation of coal production (and railways) might be a solution to these issues, but, to the union's chagrin, the government did not accept this. The 1926 strike was a disaster for the industry, although Bargoed Colliery resumed work soon after it ended with little change in production. In 1943 the Fed became part of a National Union of Mineworkers, but despite achieving its goal of nationalisation in 1947, strikes continued, with a particular 'flurry' between 1969 and 1974. These related to national wage claims, although Bargoed was one of a small number of pits which joined a strike of Derbyshire miners in 1969.

In 1946, the Labour government under Clement Attlee, passed an Act nationalising the coal industry and establishing the National Coal Board. Bargoed Colliery was placed in South Western Division No. 5 (Rhymney) Area, Group No.2. Ray Lawrence writing in *The South Wales Coalfield Directory*, Vol. 2 (1998 edition) suggested Bargoed *after nationalisation in 1947 .... continued to grow in terms of size and production*. In 1949 the N.C.B. announced *the pit had 34.5 million tons of coal, enough to allow for up to 80 years of work*. Such optimism proved short-lived, as N.C.B. strategic planning concentrated large investment resources on other collieries, including Ogilvie in the Darran Valley, consequently Bargoed slowly declined. Loss of the coke ovens to Nantgarw in 1958 was a major blow, but with the sixties came the era of *cheap oil*, and, later, North Sea gas, which together contributed to the N.C.B.'s escalating deficit as the market for its coal declined. Bargoed, like many in South Wales, was a high cost pit as its workable seams were not considered suitable for modern, mechanised and efficient mining. Exacerbating this realisation were strikes in 1972 and 1974, consequently in June 1977 and ironically under a Labour government, Bargoed Colliery closed.

For almost four years the site remained semi-derelict, until in 1981 full scale demolition occurred. In 1982, the last train departed from the Bargoed Pits branch, thus ending an era. In 1994-95 the site of Bargoed Colliery was obliterated, when a large proportion of the waste tip on the Monmouthshire side of the river, was used to landscape the colliery site and prepare for construction of the long-awaited Bargoed by-pass, Angel Way, which is mentioned in the chapter on Transport. Travelling along this road today, it is difficult to imagine that it passes over what was the economic and social heart of Bargoed and Gilfach, leaving the casual observer to wonder just what sustained the town seen on the valley side above. While the colliery was not the reason for Bargoed's establishment, it was the spur to its rapid growth in the years between 1900 and 1914, and it made the Bargoed and Gilfach of today and, for that, the colliery's contribution should be remembered.

Secondary or Manufacturing Industries:

These are industries which assemble raw materials and change them into something more useful and valuable. In a balanced economy such industries should occupy a relatively high proportion of the employed population. However, Bargoed past and present has not had a balanced economy and manufacturing has not been a major component of its wealth creation. Consequently, when its major primary industry declined, there was little alternative employment in the immediate area, leaving many working people to commute to work outside the local area, or move to other areas.

Before 1900 there were a small number of manufacturing industries locally, mostly corn and textile mills processing the products of local agriculture. The corn-grinding mill near the confluence of the Rhymney and Bargoed-Rhymney rivers in Pontaberbargoed may have existed for some five hundred years. It was an undershot water mill, fed by the Bargoed-Rhymney river, and discharged into the Rhymney, which some claimed (Bryn H. Rees, Gelligaer, Vol. 9) was unique in so doing. The mill produced oatmeal from locally grown grain which was dried on the premises. *The Gelligaer Story*, in an unsourced comment states: *a very advanced system to roast the grain existed, and accounted for the fine quality of the oatmeal which made it famous throughout the principality and far beyond the border.* Rees intimates that *at this mill, Lord Bute (then Lord Cardiff) raised the toll upon the corn of the district.* However, the mill was not owned by Lord Bute but by the owner of Gwaelod-y-Brithdir, the farm on which it stood. It was working in the first quarter of the nineteenth century as it was mentioned by Evan James in his poems about his youth in the second decade of the century. It is marked on the O.S. plan for 1873 when it may have still been working, but neither the mill, nor its leats appear on the 1901 edition. The mill was demolished but its name lived on in *Old Mill Hotel* at the junction of the main road (A469) and that to Aberbargoed Hill (B4511). However, the present public house of that name replaced an earlier *Old Mill Inn*, located on the opposite side of the road (Bridge Street), behind which and almost beneath the Rhymney Railway viaduct, stood the mill. In unpublished reminiscences Rev. Gwilym Thomas recalled that this older inn, owned by the last miller, Daniel Lewis, also brewed its own *Home Brewed Ale*.

Study of both O.S. 'One inch' (1829) and tithe (1841) maps shows the presence of another corn mill in Gilfach. The O.S. map labels it *Woods Mill*, whereas the tithe map does not name it. By the time the 1873 O.S. plan was surveyed all trace of the mill seems to have disappeared, possibly beneath the junction of the Brecon & Merthyr and Rhymney Railways.

Upstream from the corn mill in Pontaberbargoed, at the side of Factory Road, was another mill, which produced woollen textiles. Rees suggests that one of its doorways bore the date *1704*, supporting the contention that this was an 'old established factory', while *The Gelligaer Story* suggests *there are records of a tucking or fulling mill at Bargoed in 1713*. However, there is evidence that it was operating in the sixteenth century, and it is likely that it was working for at least a century before that. Like the corn mill, it was water powered, but it is likely to have employed more people and thus earned the sobriquet *the factory*, still recalled in the name *Factory Road* given to the A469 between the viaduct and the *Puzzle House*. The 'factory' is referred to in a number of census returns: in 1851, it was occupied by Edward James, a handloom weaver who held a lease on the mill, and employed two other handloom weavers and a fuller, while, a decade later he was described as a woollen manufacturer employing a weaver and a spinner. In 1881 the occupier, William Thomas, was described as a *flannel manufacturer*, employing nine men, three boys and five women. Rees indicates in later years Edward James (brother of Evan James, composer of *Hen Wlad fy Nhadau*) owned the factory, however, an item published in *Merthyr Express* (23/06/1900) refers to a Mr. M. James (presumably Morgan James):

Those interested in home industry generally, and the inhabitants of Bargoed in particular, will be pleased to hear of the success which follows Mr M. James, The Factory, in connection with the Welsh Industry Association. At a meeting of the promoters, held at the London residence of Lady Aberdare, on the 30th ult., a letter was directed to be sent to Mr James intimating that a large quantity of flannel, &c., sent by him, and manufactured at his factory, had been purchased by H.R.H. the Prince of Wales. This augers well for future success, and we extend our congratulations to Mr James upon having attained such prominence, which is a proof of superiority.

However, *Merthyr Express* (December 1902) contained an advertisement for *The Important Sale of a Valuable Freehold Woollen Factory, Land and Premises*, placed by Mr. Seth Phillips, auctioneer, which provides some interesting details:

Auction at the Old Mill Hotel, Bargoed, on Thursday, December 18th, 1902 at 3.30 o'clock ... Freehold Woollen Factory Land and premises, viz: Lot 1 – All that Woollen Factory, land and premises known as Bargoed Factory situate at Bargoed, ... having the following accommodation, viz: - First floor carding room; second floor, spinning room; third floor weaving room. A dwelling house used as a dipping room, press house and a dye-house; a coach house and stable with sorting room above, a large shed for storing wool, coal house and large water wheel. ... The above Properties being in the centre of the rapidly growing town of Bargoed, and within a short distance of both railway stations, afford a good opportunity to capitalists and others for investment. The Factory is an exceptionally good one, and well placed for water power and a well-established business is being carried on thereat, by Mr. Morgan James, the tenant, who has been in occupation for many years ... Merthyr Express contains no reference to the outcome of this sale, but Rees stated *Early this century (twentieth) it closed down*, and probably Ifor Coggan (Fochriw website) correctly concluded *...improved communications and new inventions brought overwhelming competition from Yorkshire and resulted in the decline of the local woollen industry* as the reasons for its closure. Later the premises were used as a common lodging house as suggested in a reminiscence by David Edwards (*Merthyr Express*, April 1920). Writing in 1991, George Thompson suggested it was destroyed in a fire and that is confirmed by a report in *Merthyr Express* June 1924. Rees noted that the James family also owned the flannel mill at Maesycwmmer, which continued to operate until the 1950s. James of Maesycwmmer Mill, a partner in Lewis & James one of the pioneer providers of bus services to and from Bargoed, who later sold his business to British Electric Traction and became a director, is mentioned in the chapter on Transport.

Census returns also indicate the presence of other small scale manufacturing premises, namely shoe making, dressmaking and a smithy. In 1851 two shoemakers are recorded at the Croft, along with a dressmaker, but in 1861, just one cordwainer (shoemaker) is recorded there. The 1861 census records the presence of a blacksmith at Bargoed Station Inn (forerunner of the Junction Hotel).

While the beginning of the twentieth century seems to have marked the demise of traditional manufacturing activities, it also heralded the beginnings of a major industrial complex in conjunction with the development by Powell Duffryn Steam Coal Co. of Bargoed colliery. Basic to these plans was installation of coke ovens, which Powell Duffryn Steam Coal Co. records suggest were operating by 1908. Reg Malpas (Welsh Coal Mines web site) wrote that in 1911 one hundred Koppers regenerative by-product coke ovens were operating to the north of the main colliery buildings, as shown on the O.S. Plan of 1921. Powell Duffryn Steam Coal Co. handbook of 1928 indicates that a further fifty ovens of the Still Type had been added, to the south. Together these 150 ovens produced 260,000 tons of coke and the handbook reported a further fifty were in course of construction. At nationalisation in 1947, there were 86 Still coke-ovens operating on the site, which the N.C.B. replaced with new ovens between 1949 and 51. However, competition from coke production at new integrated iron and steel works, along with a change in N.C.B. policy to one of centralising coke production at new facilities, notably Nantgarw, led to the closure of Bargoed's 86 coke ovens in 1958.

Type	Size	Potential use	Location of markets
Foundry coke	Large size – hand picked	Cupola work & foundries	Throughout England & Wales, H.M. Dockyards
Furnace coke	Medium	Blast furnaces	South Wales & Midlands
Coke screenings	1 - 1½ inches	Central heating, greenhouses, bakehouse ovens etc.	
Coke peas	⅝ - 1 inch	Smiths' forges, central heating	
Coke breeze	Under ⅝ inch	Boilers with forced draught	Bargoed Power Station

Table 5 – Range of coke produced and markets in Bargoed. (P.D. Handbook, 1928)

Coke was manufactured from a mixture of small coals supplied by Bargoed's Steam and Bituminous pits, which was first treated by washing by the Froth Floatation process and then carried by aerial ropeway to the ovens. Screening (grading by size) provided a range of cokes as outlined in Table 5:

During the coking process the volatile coals release large quantities of gas, with a hydrogen content of 57%. In 1911 Malpas says about half the gas produced was used to heat the ovens and a high proportion of the rest was used in gas engines which were used on the colliery site to power the winding gear, generation of electricity and steam raising for other colliery machinery. A small amount was sold to the Rhymney & Aber Valleys Gas & Water Co. to supplement its own small gas-making plant, in supplying sufficient gas to meet the demands from the expanding local population.

After 1908 Powell Duffryn Steam Coal Company began to utilise the gas, saturated with tar, benzole and ammonia, for a wide range of chemicals. First stage in the process was to pass the gas through condensers, after which crude tar and ammoniacal liquor was deposited, separated and taken to other plants for further refining. Then the remaining gases were treated further, to produce motor benzole and grades of solvent naphtha, besides coal gas which was passed to on-site gas holders for distribution to households and industries in the Rhymney Valley. Meanwhile, the ammoniacal liquors were distilled, treated with sulphuric acid to make sulphate of ammonia, an important general fertilizer. The crude tar was further refined to produce creosote oil, creosote or naphthalene salts, anthracene, pitch and refined tar. In connection with the latter, in conjunction with Western Trinidad Lake Asphalt Co., Ltd., a plant was erected in 1925 at Bargoed to manufacture what has become known as 'Tarmac'. A large proportion of these products was despatched by rail, often in tank wagons, to all parts of Great Britain, and many were used in further chemical processing to make a wide range of products including wood preservatives, paints and pharmaceuticals.

From the beginning electricity was generated on the Bargoed Colliery site for colliery use. Three gas engines powered generators, which together produced about 4000 kilowatts of electricity, used both in Bargoed and other Powell Duffryn Steam Coal Co. Collieries linked by overhead power-lines. A new power station was inaugurated in 1922, claimed as the first of its type in the world (continuous operation using high temperature and high pressure steam) and its success led to similar power stations being commissioned in the U.S.A. and Continental Europe. Steam was raised by a combination of Rhymney Valley Washed Duff, Coke Breeze fed into furnaces by mechanical stokers, and surplus coke oven gas. The turbo-generators were capable of producing 33,000 kilowatts of electricity, most of which was used by Powell Duffryn Steam Coal Co. installations in south east Wales. There was no further development of Bargoed Power Station as, in 1948, the N.C.B., its new owners, opted to co-operate with the recently nationalised British Electricity Authority (custodians of the National Grid, established in 1926 and completed in 1937). While demand for electricity in collieries was increasing, the number of collieries needing that power was falling, so Bargoed Power Station became increasingly redundant. Closure of the colliery in 1977 also saw the end for the power station and by 1980 the site had been cleared, the characteristic wooden cooling towers being blown-up one Saturday lunchtime about 1980.

The closure of the Bargoed Colliery complex ended the era of secondary production in the local area. However, anecdotal evidence suggests a small foundry existed in Bargoed until *recently*, which produced amongst other things, colliery tokens. Sadly Bargoed and Gilfach did not directly benefit from the provision of government or local authority factory units, unlike neighbouring Aberbargoed, Britannia and Tir-y-berth, consequently, in recent

This photograph (courtesy of Terry McCarthy Collection/Powell Duffryn Co.) of Bargoed Power Station is taken from a Powell Duffryn publication of the late 1920s, and shows the electricity generating station they built in 1922, primarily to serve the increasing electrical power needs of their own collieries, but they also sold power to Gelligaer Urban District Council for domestic use in the middle Rhymney Valley. The power station ceased production when the colliery closed in 1977.

years, local people have generally had to travel out of the area for work in manufacturing.

Tertiary or Service Industries:

This category of industries embraces a wide range of activities which produce no tangible product but aim to improve the lives and well-being of their users. Most service outlets are relatively small both in size and numbers employed, but are very numerous and tend to be gregarious, from time immemorial congregating in settlements, ranging from villages to enormous megalopoli, according to the size of the potential market and number, size and specialism in services. Service providers show great variety, but might be divided into those that provide statutory services and those that provide general services. The former are provided either directly by a government body, such as a Job Centre, or more usually delegated to a local authority as in the case of schools and roads, while the latter, provided by private or corporate bodies, include retail outlets, construction and places of worship. Both ranges can be subdivided into myriad subcategories and some services are provided by both types of provider, sometimes contemporaneously.

In this history of Bargoed and Gilfach, many aspects of the service industry such as transport, education, churches and chapels, retailing, public houses and hotels, cafés and sports clubs are considered in other chapters so, what follows attempts to avoid repetition and summarises the rest. The significance of services in the local economy should not be underestimated as it is likely that the numbers of people working in services during Bargoed's heyday was probably little short of the number employed in the area's collieries, but unlike that workforce their disparate nature prevented them forming an effective political force. Although they did not express it as such, the relationship between those working in the service industries and those in coal mining or associated industries was symbiotic. The service sector has survived the disappearance of the area's primary and secondary industries, commonly considered the backbone of the community.

Services supplied by local authorities

The elected bodies that administered statutory services provided in the local area from the sixteenth century to the present day are discussed in Chapter 5 (Government and Politics). Care of the poor and road maintenance were administered through the parish (Gelligaer) from the sixteenth century until Merthyr Tydfil Poor Law Union (in 1834) and Glamorgan Highway Board (in 1844) were created to take responsibility for the poor and roads respectively. From the mid nineteenth century onwards, concern about the state of the country's new urban areas and their potential for disease and insurrection led to legislation establishing local Boards of Health (later to become Sanitary Districts) with responsibility and powers for public health matters while county police forces helped ensure law and order. As society's needs grew increasingly complex a wider range of statutory services was administered through local councils created by legislation from 1888 onwards and by other government agencies.

General Post Office

Probably the first national service to arrive was the General Post Office. Initially, the local area was served from older communities, such as Merthyr Tydfil while nineteenth century letters from the Antipodes to Ysgwyddgwyn (Deri) came via Blackwood. Its first local postman, David Edwards, told a *Merthyr Express* interviewer in 1920, that he had started work about 1890. He lived in Aberbargoed, but his twice daily deliveries encompassed Bargoed, Deri and all farms in between, plus a further midday delivery in Bargoed town, all undertaken on foot. The first post office was in the Quarry Arms, Aberbargoed, of which his father was licensee, until being removed to The Croft, at the bottom of Station Road, Bargoed, under Edward Lewis, postmaster for twenty years. In April 1904 *Merthyr Express* indicated that the main post office was to be moved to Hanbury Road, by then the town's centre, but this proved optimistic and was repudiated in a letter from the postmaster himself. However, the O.S. Plan, published 1921 shows the post office to be in Lower Wood Street, opposite Trafalgar Square. Sometime later, post 1945, the post office moved to its present position on Under Cardiff Road. Meanwhile more pillar boxes were requested (erection of one in Heolddu Road was reported in the *Merthyr Express* in 1903) and eventually obtained as business developed, so that by 1920 Mr. Edwards recalled there were twelve postmen in Bargoed.

McDonnell Road Post Office was opened to serve the residents in the new inter-war Heolddu housing developments.

Gilfach was initially served by Pengam, (its address was Gilfach, Pengam around 1900) but *Merthyr Express* (April 1904) reported that Bargoed Chamber of Trade member: *Mr. J. Davies moved that the postal authorities be appealed to attach Gilfach to the Bargoed Post Office and not Pengam as at present. ... They would have far greater facilities by being attached to Bargoed than to Pengam.* Supported by the Council, success was achieved and it became a sub-post office of Bargoed, with an appropriate amendment in its address. While Gilfach lost its sub-post office in 2008, Bargoed retains a post office but it is no longer a head office, with collections and deliveries being based at Hengoed.

Telephone

As early as December 1902, *Merthyr Express* reporting the introduction of telephone lines in the Rhymney Valley, including Bargoed, regretted there were 'difficulties' in making trunk calls through the equipment put in place. The Chamber of Trade was exercised on several occasions by the reluctance of the railway companies to install telephone lines and publish their numbers, but at that time, the railways had their own telephone system, so were reluctant to pay towards another. Reminiscences by Edward Lewis, postmaster (*Cardiff Times*, 1914 – republished in *Gelligaer* Volume XIV) stated that in 1914, there were ninety phones linked to the exchange, as well as telegraph lines. Over the decades the telephone became increasingly a regular part of daily life and work and by the later part of the twentieth century, there was a line in most local businesses and homes and in recent years the ubiquitous mobile phone has become a necessity for many people.

Police

When Glamorgan Constabulary was established in 1841 the local area was a sparsely populated rural area in which everyone knew everyone else and there was little to concern the constabulary. Anecdotal evidence suggests that Bargoed's first policeman, P.C. Olway Boobyer, arrived in the area in 1879. His presence in Bargoed is recorded in the 1881 census and he remained in Bargoed for the rest of his career. Until 1904, there was no police station in Bargoed, but meetings of parish and district councils and Chamber of Trade articulate concerns about there being only two constables stationed in Bargoed, plus a lack of a police station in what was a rapidly growing town, *Merthyr Express* 11 July 1903 reported *The Chairman* [of Bargoed Chamber of Trade] *... drew attention to the police accommodation at Bargoed. He said there was no police station, neither had the authorities sent the second constable to the district, as was sanctioned by the Joint Standing Committee. With so many new people coming in this was greatly needed. When a person was arrested he had to be conveyed to Caerphilly. This requisitioned the services of one man, thus leaving over 5,000 people in the care of only one officer. ...* In February 1904, the lack of cell accommodation was again a cause of concern for the Chamber:

Mr. H. Paul drew attention to the need of police cell accommodation at Bargoed. He pointed out that although it was understood the standing joint committee of the county had purchased the Hanbury Villa, some time ago, no apparent effort was made to convert the building into use. Meanwhile there was a great and increasing need of cells in the district. At present, if a prisoner was arrested late at night, a man must remain with him at the constable's house, or he would have to be conveyed to Caerphilly.

On 9 April 1904, the Merthyr Express reported: *During this week Police Sergeant Nicholls and his staff have been removed into their new quarters hitherto known as Hanbury Villa. ... With the characteristic slow methods of the Glamorgan County Council, it may yet be a few years before the station is complete, meanwhile the rougher element of the district becomes uncontrollable in the absence of a lock-up.* The building and its extension, was provided with cells and live-in accommodation for an inspector. In 1920, there were twelve policemen stationed in Bargoed, a number that increased to twenty nine during the 1980s, decreasing thereafter to eight in 2011, as a result of financial cuts and, latterly, the opening of a fully equipped custody unit in Ystrad Mynach in December 2006.

An advertisement in *Merthyr Express* (April 1904) relating to the sale of leaseholds of properties in Gilfach, suggests that 1 Maesygraig Street, had sitting *respectable tenants* and it was occupied by Glamorgan Constabulary. It is unlikely it was a police station, but it could have been a house owned by the Constabulary for renting out to policemen (and family) working in the district. Police houses existed in Bargoed and Gilfach until relatively recently, with two in Cardiff Road and a further two in Gwerthonor Road. *Merthyr Express* reported in October 1904, *John Hopkins, ex-police officer of the Glamorgan Force, will undertake any private enquiries at Bargoed or the Rhymney Valley. Rents and debts collected. Address, 4 High Street, Bargoed. Phone , P.O. 8.* It is of note that Mr. Hopkins had a telephone!

Over the decades local police have had to deal with a range of work as evidenced in the columns of the local press. In the inter-war era, they were also active in the social life of the area, especially in connection with Bargoed Rugby Club.

Police Court

As might be intimated, Bargoed was a lively place, especially on Saturday nights! The police were busy, a situation exacerbated by the lack of a magistrates' court nearer than Caerphilly. No sooner had the Chamber of Trade achieved success in getting a police station than it began to campaign for a court, as expressed in its October 1904 meeting when: *Mr. W. Harris moved that the Chamber support the application of the District Council for a police court for the valley. For his part he should like to see it at Bargoed, although the train conveniences would probably suit Hengoed best.* Much to the annoyance of Bargoed's worthies, Hengoed was preferred by the authorities,

This drawing of Bargoed Police Court by T. J. Raymond Berrow appeared in a pre World War I town directory. Costing Glamorgan County Council £2,300, the building was the work of contractors Messrs W. Williams and Sons of Bargoed and New Tredegar and was based on designs by George Kenshole, M.S.A. The Court was needed because of the rapid growth of the local community. The building in late Renaissance style, housed a Court-Room 45 feet by 27 feet with a semi-circular ceiling, as well as waiting and witness rooms, and magistrates' room at the rear of the Bench, and it was joined to the Police Station cells. The imposing front elevation is of Portland stone with dressings of the windows and doors of the same material. The carving work was by Tom Jones of Cardiff. The roof was constructed of steel covered by slates from Cornwall. Internally, the joinery is of oak and the Bench and magistrates' room are panelled in oak, while the floor is of wood block. At the time of construction it was heated throughout with the low pressure system and was electrically lighted. It could seat about 150 people.

gaining its court in 1908. However, such was the pressure on the courts consequential of the expanding population that in July 1910 *Merthyr Express* reported construction of Bargoed's Police court had commenced. The first cases were heard 8 December 1911 and sittings continued thereafter until 1997, when Bargoed Magistrates court was amongst those court houses closed as part of a rationalisation of court facilities. Happily, the Bargoed Court House was listed and survives to this day, but of the future ...?

Fire

For centuries, local inhabitants coped with emergencies and hazards in their rural community as and when required, but that changed following social and economic developments coupled with government legislation from the later nineteenth century onwards. Since then the local area has been served by many effective firemen and its Fire Station has occupied at least three different sites in the area. As Gelligaer parish in general and the Bargoed and Gilfach communities in particular grew increasingly congested in the early twentieth

This photograph, belonging to Lawrence Brobyn, shows the first Fire Station in Bargoed. It is likely that it was constructed in the Brigade's early years following the Hanbury estate's offer to sell to the Council the freeholds of various areas of land for a range of purposes including a Fire Station. It was at the south end of Hanbury Road, opposite Hanbury Hotel. The fire-fighting appliances were housed in a garage elsewhere. When it was replaced by a new Fire Station in Gilfach Street, this building was converted for use as an Infant Welfare Centre.

century so the local council's responsibilities for fire fighting and rescue assumed greater importance. In May 1903 at a District Council meeting it was announced *In the event of Fire - The G.R.D.C. have, during the last few days, affixed two water hydrants at Bargoed. ... In the case of fire, the nearest hose available is in the neighbouring parishes of Bedwellty at New Tredegar, or at Caerphilly town ...* The Chamber of Trade in April 1904 acknowledged this, but *Mr. George Barnett drew attention to the fact that only two hydrants were fixed in Bargoed, and these at such points as to make them practically useless for many parts of the town in the event of fire.* Soon after at a District Council meeting: *Mr. D. Hopkins on hearing another letter read from the same body asking that more hydrants should be fixed at Bargoed, and that the Council should provide a hose and reel ... They should try and get a fire engine like the one they had in Rhymney.* Following the next Chamber of Trade meeting *It was reported by the chairman that the G.D.C. had granted half a dozen new hydrants for Bargoed.* An outcome of all this discussion was the formation of the volunteer fire brigade in 1905

Rules and regulations of the Gelligaer U.D.C. Fire Brigade, 1909 (UDG/C/26 in Glamorgan Archives) and reports in *Merthyr Express* shed light on Gelligaer Urban District Council Fire Brigade from its establishment in 1908 to 1941. Prior to 1924 it was led by a Captain and divided into nine Corps, of which Bargoed Corps, with 19 members, was the biggest, reflecting its responsibility for the largest and most congested urban area in Gelligaer. There was no fire station until January 1909, when it was reported a *new fire station was opened in Hanbury Road*. George Thompson wrote *the fire brigade occupied a building opposite the intersection of Greenfield Street,* and continued saying, *the terraced house was totally unsuitable for such an important utility ... in the upper rooms, quarters for staff and, at ground level, a room barely allowing space to house the small fire engine. At the rear of the station, a cellar provided stabling for the powerful horses which were kept in readiness, in turn, to draw the engine whenever an emergency arose.* This was followed by a graphic description of the protracted process of responding to a call-out, including such details as harnessing the horses to the engine. The shortcomings of the local fire service were evident in two pre-war fires in Bargoed shopping centre described in Chapter 13 Retail.

In the early and mid 1920s, G.U.D.C. aimed to make its Fire Brigade more efficient and professional. During 1923 they concentrated on acquiring up-to-date fire-fighting equipment and suitable premises for a fire station. Before the end of the year the council applied for a £8,000 loan to enable them to buy the fire engine and acquire a former motor garage in Gilfach Street (a site later occupied by Oldway House, and, at the time of writing, by Oldway Health Centre). The Brigade's move into the new Fire Station started a long association between the Fire Service and Gilfach Street. In 1924 attention turned to ensuring the Brigade was manned by suitable personnel. *Merthyr Express* 5 July 1924 carried an advertisement for the post of full-time Chief Officer of the Fire Brigade that sheds some light on the nature of the job. They sought a man with previous experience of a Brigade equipped with modern appliances and a thorough knowledge of petrol motor fire engines with turbine pumps. This post, carrying a salary of £390 p.a. plus a house, was tenable on a month's notice on either side. T. H. Mather was appointed and he served locally until, in 1928, he was appointed Controller of Brigade at East Ham, and he was replaced by P. J. Moody. Chief Officers Mather and Moody continued to modernise the Brigade in line with contemporary legislation and local needs. It was a difficult task as, although the Brigade served a largely rural area with poor roads, it also had to deal with the problems of Bargoed's congested town centre and its large buildings such as Emporium, Bon Marche and Royal Hotel.

In 1941 it became part of the National Fire Service, a single fire service in Great Britain designed to meet the wartime emergency before local fire fighting functions, equipment, premises and personnel were transferred to the newly-created Glamorgan Fire Service on 1 April 1948. Glamorgan's Chief Fire Officers' Annual Reports to Glamorgan Fire Service Committee provide an insight into the operation of this Service showing that it faced numerous difficulties in its early years, especially because of the poor state of the inherited equipment and premises, the grim post-war economic situation and the difficult terrain, particularly in industrial communities such as Bargoed and Gilfach, within the large area under its jurisdiction.

It is not clear where this photograph, belonging to Menna Hughes, was taken but it shows her paternal grandfather, Evan While of South Street, in his uniform as a part time fireman. He served as a Fireman for about fifteen years and attained the rank of Sergeant. Following an accident suffered during the course of his full time employment as a contractor underground at Bargoed Colliery in 1926, the Fire Service presented him with a wheelchair. He died in 1929.

The photograph below, belonging to Robert Lee, shows his maternal grandfather, George Davies (3rd from left standing) and his mother's uncle, Ben While, (1st from left seated) older son of Evan While (shown in the other photograph). The only other person identified to date is

Sam Parry (2nd left standing). It is likely that these men were miners, and joined as Volunteers with family and friends, a sign of the comradeship that was a feature of the contemporary community. Undoubtedly, local people would have been impressed to see members of the local fire brigade in their smart uniform parade through the town. It is not clear how often they did this, but *Merthyr Express* 26 May 1923 reported on one such parade when, on the previous Wednesday they had raised £6 1s (£6.05) when they paraded in aid of Widows and Orphans Fund.

When Glamorgan County Fire Service was formed, P. J. Moody was appointed Station Officer in charge of Gelligaer and Caerphilly Units, a post he held until his retirement October 1950, and, before the end of 1950, Merthyr-born George Clive Warren was appointed Station Officer Bargoed Fire Station.

Firemen serving in Bargoed and Gilfach worked in a difficult area. The post-war Glamorgan Fire Service identified Bargoed and Gilfach as one of their high risk (D risk) communities, especially because of Bargoed's congested shopping centre, the local collieries and by-product plant, while the surrounding rural area served by the station included some steep inclines and difficult communications. Sub-Officer Evan Owens was just one of a number of Bargoed Firemen named in the Chief Fire Officers' Annual Reports to Glamorgan Fire Service Committee: he received the Chief Officer's Commendation in recognition of outstanding behaviour in a difficult situation in a house fire in Bristol Terrace on 29 January 1954 when, with little regard for personal safety as the fire had spread rapidly from ground to first floor, he attempted to rescue a young boy.

It was reported in *Merthyr Express* June 4 1947 that initially, the County's Chief Fire Officer found serious problems with the Bargoed Fire Alarm System comprising three loop circuits and 21 alarm boxes to provide a means of communication between the isolated areas of G.U.D.C. and Bargoed Fire Station. He found that maintenance was a serious drain on manpower as it took an average of six man hours per week to test each fire alarm box. He questioned its usefulness as the number of genuine fire calls received over the system was small in comparison with the number of malicious false calls. The system had deteriorated as maintenance and repair had been neglected during the war years. As a result he recommended that six of the alarm boxes should be replaced by G.P.O. telephone boxes, and the remainder of the system should be disestablished.

The Gilfach Street Fire Station, in common with many contemporary Fire Stations in the county, left much to be desired when transferred to Glamorgan Fire Service, but repairs and essential maintenance kept it in commission until the effects of subsidence on the rear of the building forced the Service to make a special case to the Home Office to replace it. The new three-bay station in William Street was ready for operational purposes 14 September 1966 and remains in use to the present day, while, due to its dangerous condition, the Gilfach Street Fire Station was demolished.

Glamorgan Fire Service's last year was the busiest in its quarter century history because of the number of fires in the periods of dry weather at the beginning and the end of the year, together with the number of false alarms, particularly of malicious false alarms. In the year ending 31 March 1973, Bargoed Fire Station dealt with 223 fires, far more than any other year since 1948, and it had 44 malicious false alarms. Local government reorganisation in 1974 and 1996 brought changes in the fire service. Glamorgan Fire Service ceased to exist and the local area was served by Mid Glamorgan Fire Service from 1974 to 1996. In 1996 Mid Glamorgan Fire Service merged with the services of South Glamorgan and Gwent to form South Wales Fire Service and that was renamed South Wales Fire and Rescue Service in 2004. Although Bargoed Fire Station was threatened with closure in the late 1990s, the matter was raised in the House of Commons in 1999, and the facility survived. At present it is equipped with one pump and seventeen personnel.

Ambulance

According to a town Directory of 1911, there was a successful Ambulance Brigade in Aberbargoed with Richard Evans of 6 Francis Street as its secretary. The same source noted that local police had access to the ambulance (presumably a comparatively recent purchase by G.U.D.C.) housed in Bargoed Fire Station. Sources do not shed much light on the way in which the local ambulance service developed but anecdotal evidence confirms that the partnership between the fire and ambulance services continued to the mid century. By the second half of the twentieth century the ambulance service, operating independently of the fire service, was based in a station in John Street but before the end of the century a new larger modern ambulance station was constructed on the valley floor in north Bargoed.

St. John Ambulance Brigade played an important role in assisting local doctors in the early decades of the twentieth century, and it remains active locally to the present day. Cancer Lifeline Upper Rhymney Valley (New CLURV) is a voluntary organisation based in Bargoed. By offering door-to-door transport for patients (accompanied by a family member or friend) to and from hospital for treatments and appointments it relieves them of the stress associated with travelling by ambulance, public transport or private car. A self funding organisation, it relies on fund-raising and donations to continue operating.

Water Supply and Disposal of Sewage

For centuries the small rural population had fresh, clean water from local springs but they were totally inadequate to meet the unprecedented demand for water in the expanding Bargoed and Gilfach communities of the early twentieth century. Local people faced problems with the quality and quantity of water and water supply and disposal of sewage figured among the most pressing matters facing the local council in the early twentieth century. A letter in *Merthyr Express* (February 1902), from Shoni, summarises the situation, relating to the *disgraceful state of things at Bargoed .... I wonder if they* (District Council) *are aware that the filth of the place* being *tipped about fifty yards above a spring of water here, and a good many people are bound to carry water from this spring for their domestic use.* Bargoed was provided with its first piped water supply soon after the formation in 1877 of the Bargoed Gas & Water Company, which in 1898 was absorbed into the Rhymney & Aber Valley Gas & Water Co. By 1900 this supply could not cope with the demands of the rapidly growing population and for the ensuing twenty years an adequate and reliable supply of water was a matter of great debate, but until 1921, there was little agreement.

In 1902 the County Medical Officer of Health indicated; *The most urgent requirements of this district are: (1) the sewerage of Gilfach, Bargoed ... (2) the provision of an adequate supply of water for the places named. For the latter the District Council's Medical Officer reported in 1903: Referring to water supply, Dr. Jones says, that as the construction of reservoirs at Blaen Rhymney, is proceeding rapidly, he hoped shortly to be able to report that the district has an ample supply of water of good quality.* Later that year in a Chamber of Trade meeting: *Mr. Paul drew attention to the apparent determination of the Water Company not to connect streets and houses with their service. About 18 months ago application was made to the company to connect certain houses in West-street. They have not done so, but had placed a stand pipe at the end of the street ... The Chairman, in reply said that weather permitting the company would be able to fill the new reservoir at Rhymney Bridge before the end of the present year. When this was accomplished, there should be no difficulty about water.* In 1904 complaints were published concerning interruptions to the water supply: *Sir, - As a resident in Hanbury-road, Bargoed, I beg to call attention of the Aber Gas and Water Co. to the way the water is stopped. ... On Saturday last the water was turned off at nine and remained so until after five o'clock in the evening. Some warning should certainly be given, and as a workman I must enter my protest in this matter. Coming home from my work mid-day, I had to remain indoors, and could not obtain water to wash myself or do any domestic work.* At a ratepayers' meeting later that year *Merthyr Express* reported: *... Rev. Harri Edwards (Parish councillor) also spoke, after which a resolution was moved ... and adopted, protesting against the cutting off the water supply, and to ask that a new water main should be laid from Deri to Bargoed to ensure a more regular supply. Also water supplied to Bargoed should be properly filtered.* Even Gelligaer Parish Council voiced its concerns, resolving *to ask the District Council by whose authority the houses in North-street were occupied before being supplied with water. ... also resolved to ask the district Council to use all pressure possible to compel the Rhymney & Aber Valley Gas & Water Co. to give a better supply of water.* Complaints seem to have abated thereafter, but in 1910 a *Merthyr Express* editorial returned to the issue: *Local authorities in the Rhymney Valley are today faced with several big problems. Owing to the sinking of new pits the population is increasing at a rapid rate, and considerable difficulty is being experienced in keeping pace with the growth. Several conferences have of late been held to discuss the question of water supply ...* The discussions referred to related to the formation of a water board, and as *The Gelligaer Story* states agreement was difficult to obtain.

In 1911 a Bill seeking powers to acquire Rhymney Valley Gas & Water Co., set-up a Water Board and build a reservoir at Taf Fechan, north of Merthyr Tydfil, encountered strong objections and the Bill failed. Not until 1921, was such a Bill passed by Parliament. 1928 saw the completion of Taf Fechan reservoir and the trunk mains linking it with the Rhymney Valley, and so those who lived and worked in Bargoed and Gilfach began to enjoy the water supply they craved. By that time population growth had ceased, thus this supply has proved adequate for local needs, apart from a short period during the 1976 drought. After that Welsh Water, successor to Taf Fechan Water Supply Board, constructed a mains link with the River Wye near Monmouth to minimise the risks of a recurrence of such a break in supply.

The County Medical Officer's report, referred to above, also highlighted the priority of an effective sewage disposal system. A letter to *Merthyr Express* (1900) illustrates the problem in Bargoed: ... *Instead of a proper drainage for every house, carried through the proper pipes, buckets are substituted, and a man sent round. He is supposed to come every week, but it is generally twice monthly, to collect the refuse, and carries through the town to a field a little way off.* In his report, the Medical Officer reassured the Council: *During the present year the sewerage of Gilfach, Bargoed, ... will be carried out. The contracts for sewering ... Bargoed and Gilfach have been let.* The Surveyor prepared plans showing the line of the proposed sewer to be laid and reported that the contractor, finding it difficult to get housing for his workmen, wanted to erect a temporary hut for them. In May 1903, Dr. W. W. Jones, Medical Officer to Gelligaer District Council, reported: *When the works are completed, there will have been provided for some years to come, adequate sewerage and sewage disposal systems for the whole of the large villages in the area.* Furthermore, justifying the expenditure he stated: *Enteric fever was principally prevalent in ... Bargoed ward, and prompted by defective sanitary conditions.* The District Council's Surveyor reported in August: ... *sewage tanks at Tirphil and Gilfach are now being completed, ... a great deal of damage is done to them, owing to no one at present being at these places to take charge and look after the same.* In November Dr. Jones reported: *Five cases of diphtheria occurred at Bargoed, where sanitary conditions are not at all satisfactory during the transition between the bucket and water-closet system. Greenfield-street is most unsatisfactory.* At the same meeting the Surveyor stated: ... *all connections have now been made to the main sewers in the lanes at the rear of Greenfield-street and Francis-street ... I am glad to state that the main sewers at Bargoed and Gilfach have worked very satisfactorily during the recent heavy rainstorms, although a great amount of surface water had to be dealt with, in consequence of the street gullies being stopped, and the water being turned into the sewers. I may also mention that some evil disposed persons have been attempting to block up the main sewers by depositing large stones and a quantity of turf in some of the manholes.* Evidently, then as now, not everyone in the area was acting for the common good.

For the next few years, sewerage issues seem to have been off the agenda, but in July 1909 at a G.U.D.C. meeting: *Another letter from the County Authority drew attention to the unsatisfactory state of the sewage works at Bargoed. The Surveyor said that originally the works were intended to provide for a population of 5,000, and there is now a population of over 8,000. If there was much delay in making the proposed main sewer he did not know what would become of the parish. – The Clerk said there would be a conference on Friday on the subject of the main sewer.* As usual, agreement was difficult to achieve, for in a G.U.D.C. meeting (December 1910), rival sewerage schemes were discussed. Sewerage seemed to have focussed minds more readily than water supply, consequently The Rhymney Valley Sewerage Board Act, 1912 was passed, permitting construction of a main sewer from Rhymney to St. Mellons, where an outfall works was to be constructed. Apart from branch sewer connections, this system served all the needs of the local area until the 1990s, when parts of the system in the Bargoed area needed renewal.

Refuse collection and disposal

Linked with sewerage was the matter of refuse collection and disposal. Initially, this was undertaken by *scavengers*, contractors who tendered for the work annually. Many were the complaints about the quality of their work, but counter complaints also arose, as outlined in the following exchange between the Chamber of Trade and District Council: *complaining of the way in which the scavenging was being done ... suggesting that an extra man from within the area be engaged, as the work was now being done very late in the morning'.* The Surveyor retorted: *'some complain that he comes too early. ... The officers report that the work is being satisfactorily done.* He continued saying: *several Bargoed people have told me that they feel sorry for the scavenger ... he has to scavenge some rows twice, because the people won't put out their buckets in time.* Ultimately, the Council took over these duties directly, a situation which prevailed until the 1980s, when, government policy required R.V.D.C. to put such duties out to tender.

Recreation Ground

Public Health matters were at the heart of the demands for a recreation ground locally. In July 1903: *... a meeting of the ratepayers of Bargoed district was held to consider the question of securing a recreation ground for the district. ... The Chairman explained the urgency of such a claim, as plots of land were being used up all over the place, and shortly there would be no suitable spot available for recreation purposes.* It was moved that: *the Parish Council apply to the Hanbury Leigh estate to grant the people a plot of land for recreational purposes.* Negotiations followed and Bargoed Park was established. In 1907 the Parish Council reported the installation of seats in the Park, however, Thompson suggests that this recreational area: *was a retreat for the elderly, and also provided grazing for cattle belonging to neighbouring dairy farmers. Surrounded by a high fence, the Park was not a popular resort.* He mentioned the presence of swings, so there was some provision for play and during the summer months, carnivals were held, involving large numbers of local people, young and old. In 1937 an outdoor swimming pool was built, proving a popular summertime facility, until replaced by an indoor pool as part of the Heolddu Leisure Centre, opened in 1974. At some time, too, the Park was provided with a cinder running track and grandstand, which was used for athletics meetings, including a few international events, as well as becoming home ground for Bargoed Rugby Club.

Gas

Somerset-born John Knight (1840-1920) arrived in Bargoed in 1877. He was the first person to manufacture gas in Bargoed and was responsible for the first gas and water main in the town. During a career that spanned some four decades he served as Under Manager and later Manager of the local gas works before retiring from the employ of Rhymney and Aber Gas and Water Company. Outside his work he was a lifelong supporter of Liberal politics, a staunch Baptist who was a founder and trustee of Hanbury Road English Baptist Church, as well as being highly respected as a fine historian with a remarkable memory. When the local population grew, demand for gas outstripped the capability of Rhymney & Aber Valleys Gas & Water Company's small gas-making plant (built 1877) on the valley floor below the Junction Hotel. The Company was able to ensure sufficient gas to meet the increased needs by purchasing some of the surplus produced at Bargoed Colliery's Coke Ovens. Writing in Australia in 1991, George Thompson referred to the gasometer towering over cottages and river about 1920 as well as the gas lamps and the lamplighter who *disturbed the morning solitude, as with a long pole on his shoulder*, he *cycled from gas lamp to gas lamp, extinguishing the flaring jets he had kindled the previous evening*. By the later 1920s as an increasing number of local housewives were cooking with gas, gas cookery lectures were announced in the pages of the local press.

Electricity

When in 1908 electricity was first introduced locally by Rhymney Valley and General Electric Supply Company it was confined to properties in Hanbury Road, High Street and Hillside Park. After the end of World War I, G.U.D.C. acquired the works at Bargoed for £5,528 and, as demand increased rapidly, the Council planned a progressive scheme that before the end of the 1920s earned them many plaudits. In 1920 the Electricity Commissioners sanctioned the plans and the following year the extensions started with the use of direct labour. By 1927, having expanded from a mere two miles of mains to forty miles in the district, G.U.D.C. provided an admirable public service making a substantial profit. Credit for this was due to engineer H. H. McNaul A.M.I.E.E., and the Electricity Committee, chaired by W. J. Meredith of Bargoed.

The Electricity Committee's decision to rent the large corner block (excluding the ground floor) on Bargoed's Trafalgar Square for a new electricity department, reflected the fact that by that time Bargoed was recognized as the main business and retail centre within the district. By Spring 1927 the fully equipped showrooms had all the newest electrical devices on display as well as the staff to carry out any installation work required and the Manageress, Miss Burrows, was soon very busy as housewives were interested in the variety of labour-saving devices for hire and purchase.

While local housewives of the 1920s and 30s may have looked at the labour-saving electrically-powered domestic equipment in the showroom most of them knew they could not afford such luxuries and they continued to struggle with their time-consuming and heavy domestic duties. However, in the post World War II era the situation was different as not only did the equipment become more reliable and cheaper but the majority of households had more disposable income and by the 1960s the majority of local homes had such equipment to help them with cleaning, laundry and cooking. As a result housewives finding their housework could be done more quickly and easily were more likely to seek paid employment outside the home.

The remaining statutory service in the area, education, is considered in another chapter. It is interesting to note that by the time Bargoed was established, a school existed in Pengam – Lewis' School, supported by the Lewis Trust. The first state school was the Board School founded in Factory Road in 1873. Thereafter, as population grew, so did the demand for a range of new facilities. Organisation of education changed through the twentieth century and coupled with declining population provision was reviewed, rationalised and parts renewed. To date the newest school in Bargoed and Gilfach is Lewis School, Pengam, the comprehensive successor to that first local school.

One educational feature of Bargoed's life deserving of mention is the Settlement in Cardiff Road. Founded in 1933, this organisation provided educational self-help for the community, especially the unemployed. Its activities branched out into library (1935) and advice services, besides being a venue for a number of clubs and societies, including Gelligaer Historical Society from 1961 until 1979. In 1969 the library functions became the responsibility of Glamorgan County Council, who in 1972 opened a purpose-built library in Hanbury Road, where it remained until 2009. As part of the regeneration scheme, it was transferred to St. Gwladys' Church Hall until 2011, while Hanbury Road Baptist Chapel, the planned permanent replacement, was converted. The advice function was formalised under the aegis of Citizens Advice Bureau (mid 1960s) and moved to the redundant Co-op building in Hanbury Road in 1980. The Settlement is now used mainly for Chamber of Trade and Bargoed Town Council meetings.

The non-statutory services take a wide variety of forms, many of which are considered in other chapters. The importance of these service activities cannot be underestimated in terms of the income they generated and how they made people's lives 'better'. In Pontaberbargoed, in pre Rhymney Railway days, Gwilym Thomas suggested the Old Mill Inn was the social centre of the community, but the chapel and smithy provided additional support to a society which was almost self-sufficient. As Bargoed, and later Gilfach emerged and grew, self-sufficiency declined and services became more significant in the inhabitants' lives, consequently both the range and number of services increased, especially after sinking Bargoed Colliery began in 1897.

In the post-1858 era, some of the most important services locally were the hotels. During the Edwardian decade, most local hotels became important

This photograph from the Terry McCarthy Collection shows Hanbury Road, between 1904 and 1908. Development of the town was rapid during the Edwardian period. Prior to 1900 most shops were on the east side of Hanbury Road, but as the photograph shows after 1904 the western side was redeveloped for retail outlets. Also prominent is Bargoed's first bank, opened by the London & Provincial Bank in 1904. The bank became part of Barclays in 1917 and they still occupy the building. Noteworthy, too, is that there is only one wheeled form of transport shown, that being a pony and trap.

meeting places where house auctions and inquests as well as meetings of a wide range of local clubs and organisations were held. Most of these establishments survive, although some have been renamed. The range of cafés, particularly those opened by Italian immigrants, were meeting places where alcohol was not served. One of the earliest was the Hanbury Café, meeting place for the Liberal & Labour Association and Debating Society. Also mentioned in *Merthyr Express* are Pritchard's Restaurant and, in the New Hall complex, the Ballroom Café and a businessmen's restaurant. Meeting places of a different sort included the New Hall, which included a theatre/cinema, meeting hall and a ballroom and a Roller Skating Rink which featured in an advertisement in the *Merthyr Express* (11/12/1909). George Thompson wrote that the latter had closed by 1920 and though dilapidated, was used as a market hall. Other formal centres of entertainment were the cinemas, of which Bargoed had three by the publication date of the 1921 O.S. plan; the Palace and New Hall being opened in 1910.

The chapels and churches in Bargoed and Gilfach were not only centres of spiritual guidance but also major centres of entertainment, Although St. Gwladys' Church was one of the earliest ecclesiastical buildings in the town (1876), it was preceded (1874 – first Calfaria chapel) and outnumbered by nonconformist chapels in some of which the services were conducted in the Welsh language until well into the twentieth century. Other denominations also appeared; the Salvation Army Corps was established in 1902, while in 1916 the Independent Chapel in Usk Street was sold and became St. Peter's Roman Catholic Church. All saw social activities as an integral part of their pastoral responsibilities, with music and choirs being the most common activities.

With development of Bargoed Colliery and its concomitant population growth, during Edwardian times the town rapidly became a major service centre, with the retail trade at its core. Anecdotally, Bargoed was said to have had over 200 businesses in the 1920s, most of having been set-up in the Edwardian period; e.g. Roath Furnishing, The Emporium (its characteristic tower's clock being supplied and erected in 1912, courtesy of Gus Jones), Bon Marché, and Gus Jones' – perhaps the only survivor from this era. George Thompson suggests Woolworth opened a store in Upper High Street in the 1920s. They moved premises to a newly constructed building located on the site of New Hall, destroyed by fire 6 February 1958, but it closed at the end of 2009, when its parent company became insolvent. Closure of Woolworth, marked a nadir point for Bargoed's shopping centre, a decline which began in the 1950s and continued remorselessly through the last quarter of the twentieth century. Many long-established shops disappeared to be replaced by a motley range of charity shops, cut-price stores, card shops, hair dressers and fast food outlets. It is ironic, economically and politically, that the regeneration of Bargoed is being based on a supermarket, usually regarded as the destroyer of small town shopping.

Gilfach, developed as a smaller, yet significant service centre, with, it has been suggested, over ninety retail outlets in its heyday. In 2011, there are as few as ten shops, plus the 'village store' that is New Bridge garage (formerly Llewelyn's). The village still has two hotels, the church of St. Margaret's and a chapel, a Workman's club and the Y.M.C.A., but it is a shadow of its previous existence.

Significant in the early growth of Bargoed was the introduction of banking facilities. London & Provincial Bank (now Barclays) opened its branch in 1904, closely followed by Lloyds Bank, with the Midland Bank branch, now HSBC, coming later. A range of other professional services was also established in the town; solicitors, accountants, dentist, doctors, and by 1904, a photographer, H. D. Riden.

Overall, for a relatively short period Bargoed and Gilfach were vibrant and prosperous communities, thanks to the industries (coal mining and associated manufacturing) and services. Decline accompanied the demise of the coal-based industry, for which there was no short, or seemingly, long term alternative. Apart from those service industries which survive, local job opportunities are few, and so a large proportion of the working population now commute to work, by train (using the new park and ride facility) or car, to manufactories located outside Bargoed and Gilfach or to major service centres such as Cardiff and Ystrad Mynach. Therefore, it seems that the likely future for Bargoed and Gilfach is as dormitory communities, with their own limited range of services, hopefully provided by Morrisons and a revitalised Bargoed town centre, set in an increasingly pleasant, semi-rural landscape.

CHAPTER 7
TRANSPORT

Roads

The Ordnance Survey map of 1829 and Gelligaer parish tithe map of 1841, the first accurate and detailed maps of the area, show that there were few roads of any description in the area of present day Bargoed and Gilfach before the mid nineteenth century. The local 'roads', like those in other parts of the South Wales Valleys, had probably existed for centuries linking farms with one another and with local markets such as Caerphilly. Little more than unmetalled tracks and, in most cases, unsuitable for wheeled vehicles, they were essentially fair-weather roads, as during wet weather, notably during the winter months, they would have been impassable for much of the time. A large proportion of goods transported along such route ways was carried by pack animals, travois-like sledges drawn by draught stock or, infrequently, a wheeled cart. The evidence of early wills suggests that oxen were more common than horse as draught animals in the local area. People movements were predominantly by foot, although some of the relatively better-off might have ridden on horseback.

The 1829 map shows that the bridges across the river Rhymney at Pontaberbargoed in the north and Pontaberpengam in the south were important local route foci. Not only did several routes from different directions converge near the bridges but they also gave local farmers and craftsmen access to the slightly better road running along the Bedwellty ridge in Monmouthshire. By 1829, these river crossings also gave access to the Rumney Tramroad, operating between Rhymney and Newport and capable of carrying relatively large quantities of goods, including coal, which was being mined in a small way locally.

The cross roads near Pontaberbargoed bridge was the meeting of routes from all directions. The routes from the north (Cefn Brithdir) and the Darran Valley converged with those from the west, south and east. Significantly, the presence of the mill on Bargoed-Rhymney river upstream from the bridge offered the potential of more traffic in the form of woollen textiles. The route to the Heolddu area continued west across Gelligaer Common to join the 'main' road through the area, Anthony Bacon's reconstructed (1767) Roman road (Heol Adam) that carried iron wares from Dowlais to Cardiff prior to the opening of the Glamorganshire Canal (1798). It is possible that local farmers used this route to transport produce for sale in the growing urban markets of the Merthyr 'metalopolis'. Meeting the aforementioned road to Heolddu was another from Pontaberpengam to the south, a track which also served Gilfach Fargoed Fawr, then one of the larger farms in the area. From Pontaberpengam, a route extended westwards, joining that from Pontaberbargoed, at Tir-yr-bont, before continuing to Gelligaer, then still the main settlement in the parish. At Gelligaer, it also joined Bacon's updated road, the principal route to the south.

This track also served a number of local farms besides linking with other moorland tracks. How much traffic such routes handled is impossible to gauge, but as the population density of the area around Bargoed–Gilfach was low, it is probable traffic levels were also sparse.

The tithe map of 1841 shows a similar pattern of routes to those of the 1820s, with a few variations. Apparently absent is the continuation of the track past Gilfach Fargoed Fawr to that from Heolddu, which the Ordnance Survey map of 1829 suggested provided a continuous link between the two bridges mentioned previously. More significant, though not a road, is the reference to *Tram Road* in what became Gilfach, which extended, seemingly, from the middle of a field, eastwards towards the Rhymney river, which it crossed by a bridge to reach the Monmouthshire bank of the river. Reference to later maps, notably the Ordnance Survey 1:2500 plan of 1873, suggests this tram road served a number of coal workings (some abandoned by 1873), including Gilfach Colliery (also known as Gilfach Level) and crossed the Rhymney, which later maps show, enabled it to link with the Rumney Tramroad. According to the tithe award, the farm, Gilfach Fargoed Fach, owned by Lewis Williams and William Howells, was let in two units, 31 acres to William Williams (who according to the 1841 census lived at Gilfach Fargoed Fach) and 29 acres to Joshua Fletcher Hanson. Joshua Fletcher Hanson, owner of the tram road running through the property and, as noted in the previous chapter, proprietor of Gilfach Fargoed Colliery.

Basically, there is little difference between the route ways shown on the two map sheets. And why should there be? Apart from the suggestion of small scale coal working locally nothing had changed and demand for improved and more routes had not emerged. The only new route, the tram road, was built to serve one purpose, carriage of locally mined coal and possibly quarried stone, which the pre-existing farm tracks were probably incapable of carrying.

Ordnance Survey 1:2500 plans published in 1873 show few changes to the pattern of routes described above, though it might be inferred that the tracks described earlier were being delineated as roads, though most would have remained unmetalled. Perhaps the biggest change is that streets, lined with houses, had appeared in what we now call Bargoed. Anecdotal evidence has it that some residential properties in Bristol Terrace pre-dated the arrival of the Rhymney Railway (1858), but not by much and they may have been nothing more than temporary accommodation for navvies working on railway construction. Its location was obviously guided by the presence of a railway boundary and was developed on land owned by the railway company, which would have been clearly marked when the railway route was surveyed in 1853. It is unlikely that the residential streets of Bristol Terrace, High Street, Hanbury Road and Wingfield (later Heolddu) Road and Church Street were metalled, nor were they considered as through routes to anywhere other than the immediate locality and they were private roads, not paid for by a local authority.

Gilfach, in 1873, displays little or no development, although the track from Pontaberpengam seems to hint at the present day pattern in places. The 'main' route focuses upon Gwerthonor Place, which had not been built when the earlier maps were surveyed, before continuing to Gilfach Fargoed Fawr. Interestingly, this 'main' route is still traceable as a back lane, from what is now Gwerthonor Road, as is much of the continuation to Gilfach Fargoed Fawr

To the north of Pontaberbargoed, there appear to have been developments. Correspondence between the Rhymney Railway and a tenant farmer dated 1858, refers to *the Parish Road* (identified on earlier maps as that heading north from Pontaberbargoed). Parish responsibility for certain roads started in the sixteenth century but road improvements by parishes were usually very slow and riven by arguments as to who should pay. The County Highway Board (established 1844) helped and might have been an agent promoting improvements to roads such as those from Pontlottyn to Tirphil in 1865 and Deri to Bargoed, via Groesfaen in 1875. It is likely that these were macadamised roads and thus better able to withstand the rigours of the weather and traffic. After the Local Government Act, 1888, management of roads become the responsibility of the newly defined Councils, but improvements were slow to emerge.

The 1901 edition of the Ordnance Survey 1:2500 plan shows a rather different picture. Many more streets are apparent, but more significantly, some of these streets have been linked forming an apparently continuous route way through Bargoed to Gilfach, which joins the old track to Pontaberpengam or Pengam (Glan-y-Nant) as it was known by that time. It is likely the track had been upgraded to some extent, and along with the other streets, including Hanbury Road, Gilfach Street, Park Place and Gwerthonor Place, was probably metalled. Indeed photographic images from the first decade of the twentieth century suggest these roads were metalled, as were many of the other streets in Bargoed and Gilfach. However, though macadamised, these roads and streets had not been sealed with tar, thus they were vulnerable to extremes of weather as witnessed when in October 1903 storm run-off caused serious damage to Heolddu Road and High Street, both metalled roads, forming gullies between over twelve inches deep, while the debris was deposited over the road near the station, as described in chapter 9.

During the first decade of the twentieth century, the state of the thoroughfares in Bargoed was causing concern. Many of the older streets, such as Bristol Terrace, Church Street and Wingfield Road were subject of particular criticism in local council meetings in the early years of the twentieth century. Bristol Terrace was so bad that hauliers using the street to access the Rhymney Railway goods yard (opened 1902) at its northern end, went on strike in September 1904 to encourage improvement of this roadway. Apart from the matter of funding such improvements, there were problems arising out of the ownership of many roads. Bristol Terrace was a private road, owned partly by the Rhymney Railway and partly by *Colonel McDonnell's Trustees*, with neither being inclined to spend money. In November 1902 the Council began the drawn-out process of obtaining a Private Act under the terms of the Private Street Improvement Act to take responsibility for this and other private roads in the area. Improvements had not taken place by September 1906, when there were further complaints, to which the railway company responded, blaming the damage on the greatly increased traffic using the road, notably that carrying building materials and stone for road metalling. At a meeting in 1902 the road to the schools in Bargoed was described as being in *deplorable condition* and *almost impassable*, to which the Council Surveyor added that *in some parts children were up to their knees in mud.*

In the first decade of the twentieth century the Council was under pressure, especially from the local Chambers of Trade, to improve roadways as urban growth increased demand for a wider range of services, most of which required roads for local access, deliveries and collections of goods, even if rail provided the main form of longer distance transport. For Bargoed, apart from the issues of upgrading neglected private roads, the need for improvement to three bridges dominated local spending:

- Over the Rhymney in Pontaberbargoed – in January 1903 negotiations began between Gelligaer & Rhigos and Bedwellty Rural District Councils to rebuild this bridge. Not until late 1904 was there agreement between the two councils and reconstruction could begin.

- Over the Rhymney Railway at Bargoed station – subject of a Bargoed Chamber of Trade meeting in November 1903 when the Council and Rhymney Railway were encouraged to widen the bridge spanning the railway line at the south end of the station to meet the requirements of *modern traffic*. Ever reactive to complaints from this influential quarter, the Council entered negotiations with the railway company over funding. The bridge was reported to have been completed in 1906, the earlier masonry structure being replaced by a steel girder bridge which itself was removed in 2007 as part of the Angel Way project. However, in 1909-10 complaints were expressed about the rough nature of the limestone blocks used by the railway company to surface the road over the bridge. At a parish council meeting the surface was said to be cruel to the animals pulling heavy carts over the bridge. Furthermore, the bridge's road surface was also cited as being responsible for tyre damage to the buses which had commenced services through Bargoed. Again the railway company was unwilling to do anything about it, stating, while they were responsible for the bridge, the road surface was the County Council's concern.

- Over a *swamp* in the vicinity of the Hanbury Hotel – reported in July 1904 was a call from the Bargoed Chamber of Trade to improve the bridge and road by filling in the *swamp* in this location. The Rural District Council's surveyor attended and agreed to raise the matter with the Council who would undertake the work.

Both Gelligaer Parish and Rural District Council were assailed by demands for a range of improvements including street lighting, removal of obstructions, street naming and house numbering, as well as concerns for safety such as the problem of speeding cyclists raised in a Parish Council meeting in June 1904, a matter that was redirected to the local police. While it was accepted that new roads were important to the development of the district (one priority being a road from Pengam to Hengoed) it was set against vociferous concerns expressed in public meetings about the high rates being demanded by the Council. Furthermore, during consultations with Gelligaer Parish Council relating to the application for Gelligaer to secure Urban District status, it was pointed out that the rateable value of railways would be reduced in an Urban District, thus there would be *less money available for urgent road improvements.*

In many respects the local authorities were being overwhelmed by such demands as road improvements consequential of rapid population growth, so it is little wonder their solutions were more reactive than proactive. Nevertheless, a start was being made, as indicated in *Merthyr Express* references to the award of contracts for cartage of road stone delivered to Bargoed and Pengam stations for use in Bargoed town and Gilfach respectively, while in September 1904, the District Council authorised purchase of their first steam roller. However, that was to be shared with other parts of the district as evidenced by a statement in a District Council meeting in May 1906, when it was stated, *as a matter of priority, that when the steamroller had finished its work in Tirphil it should go to Bargoed and Gilfach to assist in the improvement of roads and streets.*

Meanwhile, this period also saw Gilfach acquiring new streets, whose houses provided accommodation for those working in places such as Gilfach Pit. Significantly, this period saw the beginnings of a new road to Bargoed, for *Merthyr Express* reported in August 1903, the Council's Surveyor's recommendations for such a road had been adopted in a meeting of the District Council by linking some of the new streets to form a continuous route way. Ultimately, this road paralleled the old track to Gilfach Fargoed Fawr, following a new line marked by Park Place, Commercial Street and Gwerthonor Place. The latter made a junction with the old track from Pontaberpengam, which by 1905 had become Gwerthonor Road and was developed for housing. Contemporary photographic evidence indicates all these thoroughfares were metalled.

By the publication in 1921 of a revised O.S. 1:2500 plan, the pattern of roads and streets resembled that existing prior to construction of Angel Way in 2005, with one significant exception. The plans show that the number of streets in Bargoed and Gilfach had considerably increased to provide access to the large number of dwellings built to meet the enormous increase in the area's population between 1900 and 1914. The main road between Bargoed and Gilfach (later A469) had evolved by linking Hanbury Road and Gilfach Street with Park Place, Commercial Street and Gwerthonor Place. However, a proposal made in a meeting of G.U.D.C. for a new road from Pengam to Ystrad

This photograph courtesy Winding House CCBC Museums and Heritage Service Collection shows The New Bridge, Gilfach under construction, c1926 - the bridge was built to carry a new, much needed and long planned main road. linking Bargoed with Ystrad Mynach. As shown it was a reinforced concrete structure, one of the first of its type in the Rhymney Valley. The locomotive (an unidentified G.W.R. 56xx on a Rhymney Valley shunting turn) is on the Bargoed Pits branch, built in 1904, to connect the Bargoed colliery complex with the Rhymney Railway main line (seen to the left) so giving access to Cardiff Docks, the British railways network and thus its markets.

Mynach in abeyance since 1910 was implemented and extended from 1920, as a new road from Gilfach to Ystrad Mynach. This road required a new bridge over the Rhymney Railway (R.R.) at the south end of Gilfach and passage through the grounds of Lewis School Pengam. The bridge, still known locally as *New Bridge*, was eventually built jointly with the Great Western Railway (G.W.R) (R.R. amalgamated with the G.W.R. in April 1922) and was one of the first reinforced concrete structures on transport facilities in the Rhymney Valley. The road opened for traffic in 1926, enabling Gwerthonor Road to become a quiet, residential, back road, until the dangers posed by traffic using the road as a by-pass for Pengam traffic lights necessitated its closure at the road bridge in the 1980s, thus ending the road's life as a through-route.

Photographic evidence suggests that the period following the Great War saw most roads in the area being sealed with tar or tar macadam. There were exceptions, notably side streets, some of which waited many more years for all-weather surfaces. This process was encouraged by an increase in motorised, vehicular traffic, which demanded better surfaces than those general in the first decade of the twentieth century, especially when the pneumatic tyre became commonplace, requiring surfaces which would not break-up following their passage.

Generally, the inter war period was one of consolidation and *Merthyr Express* reported on three such schemes undertaken by G.U.D.C. in 1937. In cooperation with Glamorgan County Council and Ministry of Transport, G.U.D.C. undertook work to ease a dangerous bend at Puzzle House corner on the Bargoed-Brithdir road (A469): the river was culverted and a new river bridge was constructed ten yards from the old Dyffryn bridge which was demolished. They also improved road safety within the built-up area by getting rid of the bottleneck near Royal Hotel, Bargoed, which *Merthyr Express* described as *a boon to motorists*, and widening the road at the top of Gilfach Street, so removing what the newspaper described as *a death trap*. At the same time it expressed hopes that the local council would *tackle Bargoed Viaduct and introduce a two way traffic system as at Hengoed Viaduct to satisfy pedestrians and motorists* – eventually, in the 1960s, they did.

Apart from some relatively small-scale developments in conjunction with the development of housing estates such as The Drive, Gilfach in the 1920s, the Heolddu Estates in the 1920s and 1950s and the Gilfach Fargoed Estate (known locally as *The Site*) in the 1970s little was added to the road network until the Angel Way development. The latter was an integral part of the plans to restore Bargoed colliery site, first proposed in the 1980s. The road's formation was laid out during the 1990s, as part of the removal of Bargoed tip and reclamation of the colliery site, but construction did not begin until 2005, with completion in November 2008. This new road is an essential part of the scheme to regenerate the local area, but for many it functions as a handy by-pass to the built-up area of Bargoed and Gilfach, thus facilitating the re-designation of some of Bargoed's roads as one-way streets to reduce the traffic problems that blighted business hours in Hanbury Road and High Street for the last quarter of the last century.

Road Transport

Prior to the 1860s, road transport was small scale and relatively local. The principal form of goods transport was pack horses, usually operating in teams according to transport demands. They seem not to have worked to any sort of schedule and there is little recorded about their ownership and operation. There is evidence that man-powered wheel barrows were used for iron traffic along Bacon's road, but it is likely that some goods were transported on 'A' framed hurdles dragged by a horse, like the travois attributed to American Plains Indians. Early road transport made little use of vehicles, with animals driven to market 'on the hoof' while people often walked long distances to conduct their business, look for employment, or simply visit family. Only a very few rode on horse back and even fewer would have used wheeled transport.

There is anecdotal evidence that even during the Victorian period, carriers offered long distance road transport from the valley, to places that included London. Occasional references in railway histories suggest the operation of *vans* in various parts of south Wales, but the first substantive evidence of such vehicular operations in the Bargoed area is in a photograph from the National Museum of Wales collection, which shows a *van* named *Gwalia* hauled by four horses belonging to one A.R. Williams of Bargoed offering removal services. Records of such activities seem to be few, explained perhaps by the carriers being small, one-man or family businesses, which were neither registered companies nor did they need to be licensed, but they existed and are recalled by a few members of the community.

By the late nineteenth century, a large proportion of road transport involved delivery and collection of goods from the railway stations. In his personal reminiscences Rev. Gwilym Thomas recalled that during the 1870s the Darran valley area of Bargoed was well wooded and many of the trees were felled for timber. He observed that the *heavy wood – trunks – was hauled to the railway station in timber lorries drawn by horses, but small logs ... were carried on panniers on the backs of donkeys and mules.* This, besides the problems referred to earlier, involving hauliers carrying building materials and road stone from the railway goods yard in Bristol Terrace, suggests the roads had an important delivery and collection function to perform in conjunction with rail transport. Similar traffic emanated from Pengam station including Council contracts to deliver road stone to Gilfach.

Local road goods transport seems to have an importance of its own and not just for distributing and collecting goods moved by rail. Two accidents reported in *Merthyr Express* serve to exemplify the nature of such traffic. The first, in 1902, reports a fatal accident in Gilfach, involving a collision between a fruiterer's cart from Newbridge and a little girl. The second, much less serious, reports an incident in 1903 involving one of two brewery drays en route from Rhondda Brewery to Bargoed across Gelligaer Common, near the gate to the Common at Heolddu. In neither case was the carriage linked with the railways, at least directly. Interestingly, in 1909 a *Merthyr Express* correspondent regretted the absence of carriers' carts in the district for delivery of parcels and the like.

The report that at a Gelligaer District Council meeting in 1910 a letter was read from a Bargoed firm respecting the dangerous state of the roadway past their premises, and stating that a traction engine ran into the next premises confirms both the condition of Bargoed's roads and the fact that mechanical transport was beginning to replace horse power on the roads. This trend accelerated during the inter war period, when many ex-servicemen, trained to use and maintain vehicles powered by internal combustion engines purchased former military lorries for comparatively low prices and set-up road haulage operations. Most were small scale and unrecorded transport businesses, but a photograph in Paul James' Bargoed and Gilfach in Pictures, Volume II, shows one such vehicle which was owned by Dickenson, a garage in Under Cardiff Road, and driven by ex-serviceman William Jones. The impact of such operations was such that by the 1930s they were serious competitors for some of the more profitable trade carried hitherto by the railway companies. Such competition was deemed 'unfair' by the railways, in that these road operators were free of most of the legal constraints afflicting the railways. They did not have to publish their rates, were not 'common carriers' so could pick and chose what they were prepared to carry and paid very little for the roads they used and demanded improvements for. The railways paid considerable sums annually in council rates, so were effectively subsidising their competition. As early as 1900 *Merthyr Express* reported the R.R. was paying £13,300 in rates on each of its stations in Gelligaer Parish. This is less valid today, as there are more legal constraints on road transport, while those relating to the railways have been reduced.

Until 1909, passenger traffic on the roads was limited and private. Cycles had appeared before this date, and there are references to the first motor cars in the newspapers. Some of the better off had carriages, but they were few. The nearest thing to public transport was the 'brake'; basically a horse-drawn cart fitted with crude seats.

Non railway public transport began in October 1909, as reported in *Merthyr Express*, when three 19-seat Clarkson steam buses operated by the Road Motor Service Company of Bargoed began a service from Deri to Maesycwmmer via Bargoed. There were problems, notably the road surface on the railway bridge at Bargoed which damaged the tyres, but also the circuitous route, necessitated by the valley being *without a main road northward of Ystrad Mynach.* The *Merthyr Express* reporter extolled the advantages of a bus service for Bargoed's growth as a shopping centre and encouraged the addition of further routes to places such as Blackwood and Gelligaer to enhance such development.

How long this service operated is unclear, as steam buses were not known for their reliability. In May 1914 (or July 1915, depending on source) South Wales Transport began operations in the Rhymney Valley with a route from Caerphilly to Bargoed. Withdrawn in May 1917 and its buses sold to the army, South Wales Transport left the Rhymney Valley to concentrate its operations in Swansea, citing as their reasons poor roads in the area together with threatened competition from local authorities who wished to operate and control bus services. G.U.D.C. applied to introduce its own bus services in 1919 with effect from 1921 but cost and Ministry of Transport resistance thwarted this. Before its next and successful attempt in 1928 Bargoed had become the centre for at least five private services, besides municipal services operated by Caerphilly U.D.C. (1922) and West Monmouthshire Omnibus Board (Bedwellty and Mynyddislwyn U.D.C. – 1926). These included Imperial of Abercynon (1921) and Aberdare Motor Services (1924) who introduced services from Bargoed to Nelson, Pontypridd, and Aberdare, which along with the Valley Motor Services (1922) route Bargoed to Rhymney Bridge and Dowlais, became part of Red and

White Services between 1924 and 1937. The Bargoed – Ystrad Mynach route attracted four private operators, besides Caerphilly U.D.C., one of which, Lewis and James also operated a Bargoed – Deri service and in 1926 planned a Bargoed – New Tredegar and Markham service via Aberbargoed hill.

Local authorities became more keen to control public bus services during the 1920s, with Caerphilly U.D.C. and West Mon being in the vanguard. The latter took over the Lewis and James routes in its area, though not those between Bargoed and Deri and Bargoed to Newport via Caerphilly, which became part of Western Welsh in 1933 when Lewis and James sold out to this company. West Mon., having ousted Lewis and James from many of its routes, introduced the latter's planned service from Bargoed to Markham via Aberbargoed hill, notable for gradients as steep as 1 in 4.7, the steepest worked by a regular bus service in Great Britain. The difficulties presented were such that special buses were used and one supplier, Saurer, even highlighted the fact in its vehicle advertising. Services ceased in 1963, when the service was re-routed. The severe gradients on the hill were eased following closure of the railway line whose bridge caused the steepest gradient.

G.U.D.C. secured an Act to operate bus services in 1921, but was unable to implement the powers granted until 1928, when it became the last South Wales local authority to operate bus services. Their first route was Bargoed to Ystrad Mynach via Gelligaer quickly followed by services from its centre of operations in Bargoed to Deri, Pontlottyn, Nelson and Bedlinog. In all cases they operated in competition with pre-existing private companies, two of which – Amber Motor Services and Ystrad Saloon Services – sold out to the Council in 1929. Several of the small private companies, amalgamated with larger firms, which could compete with the G.U.D.C. operations, while also permitting some rationalisation of competing services. In 1931 G.U.D.C. bus services operated from Bargoed to Blackwood (in conjunction with West Mon.) and extended their Pontlottyn service to Rhymney Bridge. The pattern of services established by this time remained virtually unchanged, apart from adjustments to the service timetables, until 1968 when the Rhymney Bridge service became a joint operation with Bedwas & Machen U.D.C., Red & White and Western Welsh.

G.U.D.C. bus services were made possible by raising an additional 3d on the rates, but early results were disappointing. Significant improvements came with reorganisation, led by the appointment of Mr. E. B. Blainey as General Manager, who lived in Gwerthonor Road, Gilfach from 1933 until his death in 1946 (coincidently in the same house in which the writer lived for 30 years). He brought many innovations, including introducing the first diesel engined vehicles in any South Wales municipal service, that enabled G.U.D.C. bus services to operate at a profit – an unusual occurrence amongst South Wales municipal operations! At first (in 1928) the main G.U.D.C. bus depot was in Maes-y-Graig Street Gilfach but in 1929 it moved to Aeron Place where it remained until a new depot was opened in Tir-y-berth in 1952.

Local government re-organisation in 1974 had a major effect on bus operations: the three municipal authorities forming Rhymney Valley District Council merged their bus fleets, while West Mon. became Islwyn Borough Transport. R.V.D.C. operations were significantly affected by de-regulation of bus services in 1986, when it became Inter Valley Link Limited, a company with which the council had informal links. The new company introduced a range of new routes, including the first Bargoed to Cardiff service (X38), besides a Saturdays only service from Bargoed to London! However, new services emerged challenging the former municipal operator, notably Harris Coaches, whose limited, but local objectives have enabled them to maintain a number of services centred on Bargoed until the present time, many in conjunction with other operators. Inter Valley Link Limited struggled in the highly competitive bus service market, eventually selling out to National Welsh Omnibus Services in 1989. Islwyn Borough Transport also became a private company, but not until after the demise of Islwyn Borough itself and continued to serve Bargoed until it was sold to Stagecoach in 2009. Thus the era of the municipals ended.

Meanwhile, the private bus companies, Red & White Services and Western Welsh, through purchase and amalgamation with some of the smaller private operators in the local area also saw changes. Red and White Services sold their operation to the British Transport Commission in 1948 and became part of the National Bus Company in 1969. Western Welsh, formed in 1929 as a subsidiary company of British Electric Traction (Mr. James of Lewis and James had become a director of B.E.T.), also took over the Great Western Railway's bus services in south Wales. B.E.T. resisted state ownership until 1967 when it sold its interests to what became (in 1969) the National Bus Company. In 1978 N.B.C. merged the Red & White and B.E.T. operations in Wales to form National Welsh. For Bargoed one significant change was the inclusion of Bargoed on an Aberdare – London coach service operated briefly by National Express. National Welsh was bought-out by its management in 1987, but declining profitability, despite rationalisation and introduction of the innovative Bustler services, led in 1992 to its being placed in receivership. Ownership for the ensuing five years was in the hands of Western Travel, who traded as Red and White, until in 1997 the Stagecoach Group took over Western Travel and operated as Stagecoach South Wales. Today Stagecoach, dominate operations into Bargoed, its only rivals being Harris' and Glamorgan Buses, the latter having taken over the unremunerative and truncated route 38 Bargoed – Pontypridd service in 2009.

June 2011 witnessed a significant change in bus operations in Bargoed with the opening of the new, purpose-built bus station. Since bus services began, Trafalgar Square, Bargoed has been the main bus terminus. In the 1980s the triangular area forming the square (!), was modified to provide three parallel bays, so removing buses from all but Hanbury Road, and offering a better turnaround point. The new location close to the railway station provides a more realistic transport interchange than the arrangements which hitherto prevailed, although many potential passengers are deterred by the many steps linking the bus station with the main shopping street. To some extent this reflects the enforced change in attitudes towards transport facilities in the area. Traditionally, and G.U.D.C. was no exception, socialist local authorities desired to control transport, but until 1948 the railways were owned by private companies, to whom the councils were antipathetic, so they resisted any moves towards transport integration, to protect their own bus interests. Even after the nationalisation of the railways, local authorities paid lip service to integration, primarily because they could not control the railways as they could bus services. De-regulation of bus services and privatisation of railways has removed such philosophical barriers to public convenience and thus integration is now both acceptable and encouraged, especially in these environmentally aware times.

Road transport in the area has benefited from private hire businesses, for both coaches and taxis. These catered not only for the proverbial Sunday School or School Outing, but also for contract work, especially the transport of colliers to more distant pits and school children who lived more than two miles from their schools. Only one initially Bargoed-based coach company exists today, that being Cled Williams Coaches now of Fleur-de-Lys, but originally based in Maes-y-Graig Street, Gilfach. Bus services and even contract hire seems to be in decline as the population at large prefers ownership and use of private cars. However, while car owners and non car owners alike recognise the convenience of car transport, demand for taxis has grown in recent years. At present two Bargoed-based firms (Bargoed Taxis and Bee Line) are listed on the web, but many others in neighbouring areas serve local people for shopping, airport transfers and for those opting not to use their cars for evenings out.

Railways

In 1854 the Rhymney Railway's incorporation by Act of Parliament heralded irrevocable physical, economic, social and cultural changes to the landscape and people of Bargoed and Gilfach. Indeed, it could be said that this Act of Parliament was instrumental in creating today's urban area by setting in motion a series of developments that saw the eclipse of the hamlet of Pontaberbargoed and its replacement by a town with a population of over 13,900 at its peak in 1921.

The first tentative steps towards building a railway in the Rhymney Valley were seen in the 1840s, but a combination of low demand, the presence of a tramroad linking Rhymney with Newport and a clash of railway politics involving the Marquess of Bute and the Taff Vale Railway Company curtailed further action. The main demand for a railway came from the iron works at Rhymney. This complex was built on land leased from the Bute Estates, but the Rumney Tramroad which served the works was built on the Monmouthshire side of the valley and terminated in Newport, a rival to the Bute owned Cardiff Docks. The tramroad was old technology and increasingly unsuited to the demands imposed on transport facilities in the 1840s. Furthermore, between

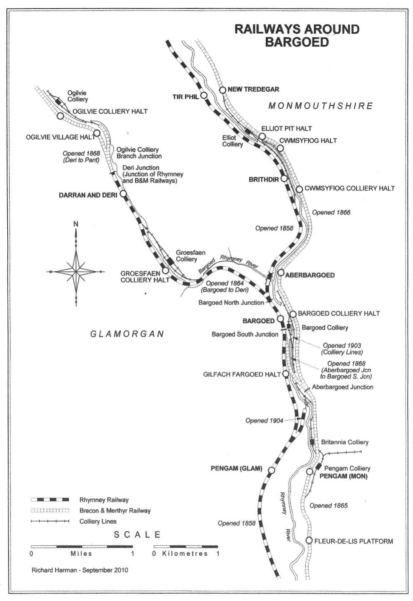

RAILWAYS AROUND BARGOED

Richard Harman - September 2010

Rhymney and the docks at Newport, with the exception of some small coal mines in the Fleur-de-Lys–Maesycwmmer area and tinplate works near Machen there were few opportunities for intermediate traffic, as most of the valley's small population relied on the low productivity, agricultural activities traditional in the upland area.

However, seeing developments in the Taff and Cynon valleys, plus the desire by the Third Marquess of Bute's Trustees to realise more from their assets, especially in the Rhymney Valley, more plans were produced for a rail link. Parliament rejected the first Bill in 1853, but ultimately, the Rhymney

Railway Act was passed on 24 July 1854, empowering the new company to build a line, shown on the map above, from Rhymney to Hengoed, where it was to join the Newport, Abergavenny and Hereford Railway, then being extended westwards from Pontypool to Quakers Yard. Using a section of the N.A. & H.R. route from Hengoed to Llancaiach, the R.R. intended reaching its real goal, Cardiff Docks, over the T.V.R. branch line to Cilfynydd, thence over the T.V.R. main line to Cardiff. Parliament rejected this part of the Bill, whereupon the R.R. revised its plans, obtaining an Amendment Act in 1855, to continue from Hengoed to Caerphilly, through the Nantgarw gap to join the T.V.R. at Walnut Tree Junction (now known as Taffs Well). The link with the T.V.R. proved a major operating headache for both railways, consequently the R.R. returned to Parliament in 1864, to secure the Rhymney Railway (Cardiff & Caerphilly) Act, authorising construction of a line giving them access to Cardiff Docks independent of the T.V.R., which was completed in 1871. Bargoed and Gilfach were not mentioned specifically in the first Act, but the plans showed that in the vicinity of Pont Aberbargoed *(sic)*, there was to be a junction for branch line to Bute-owned collieries in the Ysgwyddgwyn (Deri) area.

The consulting engineer for the project was Joseph Cubitt, while the resident engineer was G. Smithson, both known to the Bute Trustees. The Bute links were strengthened as W. S. Clark, the Bute mineral agent, was given responsibility for generating the capital to fund the line by selling shares (£30,000 worth were purchased by Lady Bute, the second Marquess' widow) and John Boyle, a Trustee, was appointed Chairman of the Company, a role he fulfilled until he retired in 1898. Furthermore, one source (Kidner, R.W.) suggests that the ceremonial cutting of the first sod, *took place on 4 November 1854, on the Marquis of Bute's property near Bargoed,* though the exact location has not been identified.

The construction of the main line was undertaken by a contractor named Mr. Wythes. Much of the line was constructed along a shelf on the hillside, but the 'gap' created by the Bargoed-Rhymney river, near Pontaberbargoed required a viaduct. Designed by Cubitt, it was built of rubble masonry and comprised seven arches of 30 feet span, with length of 357 feet and a maximum height of 70 feet. The deck was 30 feet wide and of sufficient strength to carry a double track, though for most of the line, the width of the permanent way was 18 feet, only sufficient for a single track.

The viaduct took two years to complete, but the engineer's reports foreshadow the issue of the name the R.R. was to apply to the area. In his reports of August 1855 he refers to *Aber-Bargoed* viaduct, but a year later he wrote of *Pont Aber-Bargoed* viaduct, while in his 1857 report it had become *Bargoed* Viaduct. In the same report, Cubitt informed the Board of Directors that *the permanent way is now laid from Rhymney all along the original line, and down to the point at which the N.A.&H.R. line intersects* (Hengoed). In the Director's report it states that *sidings to the collieries are being put in and stations (planned with the utmost regard to economy) are being erected upon*

This photograph from the Terry McCarthy Collection, shows Bargoed Viaduct c1905 - built 1857 to carry the Rhymney Railway main line over the Darran Valley. Beneath the arches can be seen some of the buildings which constituted Pontaberbargoed. The fields beneath the viaduct were used for fairs and the first travelling cinema. Beyond the row of houses (Bridge Street) the roof line of the Old Mill Hotel and next to it the first Post Office. The road on the right side of the photograph is that linking Deri with Bargoed.

this portion of line .... However, Lieutenant Colonel W. Yolland, the Board of Trade Inspector, who visited the line in February 1858 commented that *no permanent station buildings have yet been erected, and the temporary structures are not yet all on the ground.* This, plus the unfinished nature of the signalling system, led him to recommend a one month postponement of the line's opening. The Directors reported later that the line opened for mineral traffic on 25 February 1858, and for passengers on 31 March 1858.

In August 1857, the Directors announced that a number of stations were to be opened including the two in the local area at *Pont-aber-bargoed* and *Pont-aber-pengam*. However, Lieutenant Colonel Yolland's report referred to them as *Bargoed* and *Pengam*. Neither was a name in local use, but both became the names by which these settlements are known up to and including the present day, thus Bargoed and Pengam were literally put on the map by the R.R. This event was referred to in a letter written in 1860 by Mary James (wife of Edward James) to her daughter in Australia and quoted verbatim – *Since the Rhymney Railway is opened this place (Pontaberbargoed) have had the name cut shorter and so is Pengam these being the Stations called at,* while Bryn Rees reports that *when the R.R. was constructed, they named the station 'Bargoed'.* This he regarded as an *apt choice* suggesting that was the name of the river which joined the Rhymney at Pontaberbargoed. He added that *Deri is another instance where the name was derived from the railway station.* None of this explains why the change was made, but the author's flippant suggestion several

131

years ago, quoted in more recently published work, was that the financially straitened R.R. looking for ways to reduce expenditure, economised by producing station name boards that required a reduced number of letters to be painted!

Another commonly used local place nickname could have railway origins. Gwerthonor Road, Gilfach has long been known locally as *the Shant*. The origin seemed a mystery, until, one local resident mentioned he had heard it was named after a field where navvies building the R.R. about 1856-1857, constructed a series of huts, forming a *shanty town*, shortened to *shant*. Although, Gwerthonor Road was not developed until 40 years later, the name was probably recalled and mischievously applied to the road where many of the more well-to-do residents of Gilfach lived. Later, in 1903/4 and in response to local demand, the R.R. built a footpath alongside its tracks linking Pengam station and Gwerthonor Road, so providing another thoroughfare given a local nickname; the *Black Path*.

The location of Bargoed station was determined by two main factors:

- being single track, the R.R. had to be divided into a number of sections, separated by loops enabling trains from opposite directions to pass each other safely. The lengths of such sections were usually determined by the needs of the signalling technology used at the time, but were approximately two miles long. Pengam was one passing place, Bargoed was the next. As trains had to pass, it was normal to provide a station at such points.

- Bargoed was planned to be a junction. The first prospectus of late 1853 shows a branch up the Darran Valley was planned, starting from what became Bargoed. Financially drained by constructing its main line in 1858, the R.R. secured additional powers to defer building this line, nevertheless Bargoed station was built.

Appropriately, Bargoed station was built roughly mid way between the hamlet of Pontaberbargoed and a 'new' development that many local people say was called Charlestown, comprising part of Bristol Terrace. The station had two platforms, a stone-built booking hall, waiting room and a wooden footbridge. Initially, there were only two passenger workings per day to and from Cardiff, but before the end of April 1858 this had been increased to three per day each way, adequate for a population of only 351 in 1851. As Table 6, below, shows, by 1891, when the population was approximately 3,000, there were seven trains a day to and from Cardiff. Most of the traffic passing through Bargoed was goods and minerals, the majority serving the iron works at Rhymney and Pontlottyn. Initially, coal traffic grew more slowly than anticipated, but as new collieries developed further north in the Rhymney Valley, so traffic increased.

The Bargoed and Gilfach area provided little coal for the R.R. to transport in its early years. One colliery, a small drift at Gilfach owned by Messrs. Cope &

Latch proposed to construct for themselves a branch from their pit to the R.R., but required accommodation at the junction. This, Cubitt advised in a letter to the directors in 1857, should be provided by the Company. Interestingly, the plan for this showed the R.R. line as a double track, but at that time it was being built as a single line and remained so for 30 years. It is possible that some of the other small, local pits sent coal to Bargoed station's goods yards for loading, but the colliery siding built in Gilfach remained the only local one linked to the main line for over 40 years. Although unclear on maps, there might have been a link from these sidings to Cartwright's Pit between the railway and the river, while in 1873 a shaft mine was developed alongside the sidings, so confirming the significance of the rail link and adding to the coal traffic originating locally.

In 1859, it was reported to the R.R. directors that the Brecon and Merthyr Tydfil Junction Railway planned an extension to the Rhymney Valley to join the R.R. at Bargoed, despite not having started building its first line from Brecon to Merthyr. In 1861 Parliament agreed to its construction, but on condition that it agreed to join the R.R. Bargoed branch just north of Ysgwyddgwyn and use R.R. metals to reach Bargoed. Legal restrictions involving other railway companies in the Dowlais area slowed the B.&M.R. advance towards Bargoed. In 1863 by acquiring the Rumney Tramroad in process of expensive conversion to railway standards, it secured the access to a Bristol Channel port (Newport) it craved. To reach this isolated part of its system, the B.& M.R. sought and obtained powers to construct a link from the R.R. main line south of Bargoed. In August 1863 the R.R. began work on their Bargoed branch as shown on the map *Railways around Bargoed*, opening it for traffic in August 1865, so giving a number of collieries in, what the R.R. called the Deri area, access to Cardiff Docks and thus adding to R.R. revenue. Soon after opening and approximately three quarters of a mile north of the branch junction (Bargoed North), a siding was provided at the terminus of a tramway from Wingfield Pit to transport its coal production.

Having fulfilled most of its legal requirements the B.& M.R. commenced working traffic from Brecon through to Bargoed (renamed Bargoed Junction) in September 1868 and, as the map shows, thence over the new connection at Bargoed South Junction to its Rhymney Branch and Newport. In the meantime, the B.& M.R., in financial as well as legal difficulty, gave the R.R. lucrative running rights to Fochriw Colliery, over its tracks. Two return passenger services daily were provided by the B.& M.R. initially, soon to increase to three, as shown in Table 6. Goods traffic was sparse, as the R.R. carried most of the mineral traffic from Fochriw southwards, while to the north in 1902 only four up goods train paths and three down were timetabled from Bargoed.

For the next 20 years there was little change in the Bargoed area. The R.R. half yearly accounts show no capital expenditure in the area during this period, but traffic was increasing slowly as new, larger collieries were sunk between Pontlottyn and Brithdir. This increase more than off-set the declining traffic from Rhymney Iron Works, as the diseconomies of the latter's location away from sources of iron ore and dependence on expensive imported ores reduced its ability to compete with newer plant elsewhere in the United Kingdom. After the works closed in 1891 the R.R. depended on coal for its staple traffic.

During this period, Bargoed witnessed one tragic occurrence. In August 1874 an R.R. mineral train, comprising engine and tender, brake van and 41 loaded wagons left Fochriw Colliery junction on a routine trip. As Captain Tyler, reported to the Railway Department, Board of Trade; *after leaving that station (Fochriw), the train gradually acquired speed, on a gradient of about 1 in 40 , until the servants of the Company became powerless to control it; and finally after passing through the Bargoed Junction, and travelling little more than five and a half miles, it came into collision, at very high speed, with an engine and nine empty wagons of a coal train, on a curve on the south of that junction. ... The engine-driver and fireman of the runaway train were both killed...* Less serious, was an incident earlier in 1874, when a wagon carrying hay on a goods train bound for Rhymney, was noted to be on fire passing Pengam. The driver continued to Bargoed Junction, where the fire was extinguished, but not before it spread to Gilfach Bargoed wood, doing *much damage,* said the *Western Mail* report.

By 1886 traffic, especially coal traffic, on the single track main line exceeded line capacity, consequently the R.R. began the process to double their line from Ystrad Mynach to Pontlottyn. Preparatory work between Pengam and Bargoed Junction included widening three under bridges in Gilfach (the join between the old and new can still be seen under the arches) and alterations to sidings for Gilfach Pits. Being on a loop, the infrastructure at Bargoed Junction station required less change, although a number of new sidings were laid in 1892, mostly to extend the down side goods yard, besides providing a new refuge or relief siding south of the station (where a mineral train could be shunted to allow other traffic to pass). Much of this work also necessitated amendments to signalling arrangements which involved erecting two new signal cabins. The doubling of the main line was finally approved for use by the inspector in 1892, but it was not until 1909 that the branch to Deri was doubled.

The 1890s also coincided with growth in population and passenger traffic, consequently, as soon as the doubling of the main line was complete, capital began to be spent on improvements to passenger facilities. Pengam station was an early candidate, with plans approved in late 1893 for the shelter on 'up' platform to be enhanced by the addition of a urinal, ladies waiting room and W.C.. A major redevelopment of Bargoed Junction station was completed in 1900, when the 'up' platform was converted into an island, enabling cross platform connections between 'up' B.& M.R. and R.R. trains. *Merthyr Express* reported the 40 year old wooden footbridge was replaced during 1900 *and various other improvements were wrought to make the station more worthy of a growing town like Bargoed.* Additional sidings were laid just to the north of Bargoed North Junction (Bargoed New Goods Yard) mainly, the Board Meeting minutes state, *for the loading and unloading of building materials and other heavy articles*, which in 1902 benefited from the provision of a weighbridge. In addition, as the Board Meetings minutes suggest, extensions and improvements were sanctioned and built in the 'old' goods yard adjacent to the 'down' main line. Alterations again had to be made to the signalling.

However, modernisation at Bargoed was not finished, as following an inspection of the Railway in 1903 by the directors, further improvements to Bargoed Junction station were considered a priority. A new, reliable water supply was the prime need and quickly approved. In 1906, and in conjunction with the District Council, they replaced the road bridge at the south end of the station by a wider, steel girder structure capable of meeting the increasing demands of road traffic. Contemporaneously, the R.R. announced plans to enhance the facilities at Bargoed Junction station (renamed Bargoed and Aberbargoed in June 1905 – no saving of letters and paint on those sign boards!). These included enlargement of station buildings, provision of verandas and repositioning of the main booking office on a bridge from which stairs led down to the platforms. These considerable improvements were completed by 1906-07 and remained unaltered until rationalisation of station facilities in 1970.

It is evident that in the first quarter of the twentieth century Bargoed's station had become one of the most important on the R.R. system, as suggested in the following extract from *Merthyr Express* in August 1921: *Mr W.C. Parish who has been station master at the Bargoed R.R. station since 1910 has been promoted to the position of station master at Cardiff ... He will be succeeded at Bargoed by Mr John Boobyer, station master Caerphilly ...* This implies that a posting to Bargoed was a promotion over one at Caerphilly. Interestingly, Mr. Boobyer, hailed from Bargoed, son of the first policeman in the town. Bargoed station had become very busy during this period, as shown in another, rather unflattering article in *Merthyr Express* from 1909, written by someone using the nom de plume *Giraldus the Lesser*: *...* (the) *party proceeded up the hill to the Bargoed railway station to take their tickets for Rhymney: for it had been resolved not to proceed thither on foot, but to make acquaintance of this famous railway system. And here the party met with very much discomfort, for the station was crowded with "all sorts and conditions of men", women and children. Many had imbibed too freely from the cask and bottle; the air was polluted with the smell of coarse spirits; women were laden and hindered with packages of provisions often with babies and young children – often looking more like slaves and drudges than women – whilst their lords and masters, who are so enthusiastic for the rights of labour and fair treatment for themselves, stood at their ease and smoked, and expectorated, and cursed, and laughed, and sang. ... this was the usual state of things on Saturdays at this place, and that many fights and such riotous conduct frequently occurred there.* In January 1921 *Merthyr Express* reported: *Bargoed station showed record bookings during the Christmas holidays. Estimated 10,000 people visited. Special trains cleared backlogs.*

That these changes were beneficial and reflected the growing demand of an expanding and more prosperous population is indicated in the Table 6 below. In general it demonstrates increases in numbers and frequency of R.R. trains timetabled between Rhymney Bridge and Cardiff Parade, as well as B.& M.R. services to Brecon and Newport:

From Bargoed	Numbers of trains per day			
	1858	1895	1910	1924
To Rhymney/Rhymney Bridge (up)	3	7	15	22
To Cardiff (down)	3	8	15	21
To Brecon (up)		3	3	4
To Newport (down)		3	5	4

Table 6 – Numbers of scheduled weekday passenger trains from Bargoed.

Inevitably, these figures do not tell the whole story. Following pressure from G.U.D.C. and Bargoed Chamber of Trade, there were, in addition, a number of Saturday-only services that had the dual function of bringing more people to Bargoed's shops and helping those desiring to visit Cardiff's shops, sports venues and leisure attractions, all of which were gaining popularity in the early twentieth century. Furthermore, there were a number of services specifically for colliers, especially as larger, more modern collieries were attracting labour from older settlements where collieries or, as in Rhymney, iron works were closing. These figures also show nothing of the 'through carriages' which the R.R. operated in conjunction with the London and North Western Railway (whose Merthyr Tydfil to Abergavenny route it joined at Rhymney Bridge after 1871). In the 1880s many 'R.R. local' trains were worked through to Abergavenny, but of greater interest were the L.& N.W.R. carriages attached to the first morning train from Cardiff which worked through to Liverpool and Manchester. At its height (1897) these services could comprise up to four coaches; one each for Liverpool and Manchester, and two to Crewe for which until 1907, the L.& N.W.R. paid the R.R. a subsidy. After that the number of through carriages declined, finally ceasing in 1916, casualties of the war, and never restored.

In 1908 the R.R. introduced, what it termed 'motor trains' on some of its off-peak services. These were based on a small locomotive and integrated coach, which could work in either direction, without a need for uncoupling at the terminus. In 1910 two 'down' trains were worked by one of these units and five 'up' trains – though most of the latter started from Bargoed, having connected with a normal train from Cardiff. These operations did not last long, as the locomotive was *officially* deemed unsuitable for hauling more than one trailer coach (Mr. J. J. Best a former R.R. locoman interviewed in 1982 suggested one driver, Tommy Lloyd, regularly managed up to four trailers on workmen's trains!) and they were replaced with normal locomotive-hauled trains. However, one notable survivor of the motor train experiment was the opening, in 1908, of Gilfach Halt, a short distance to the south of Bargoed Station. It was

This photograph from the Terry McCarthy Collection shows Bargoed station c1910-1912. The photograph shows an 'up' train, Rhymney Railway Steam Rail Motor No.1 waiting to depart. The station was, by this time in its final Rhymney Railway form, having been reconstructed three times since 1900, to meet rapidly increasing patronage. The Motor Trains were relatively short-lived, but their operation led to the opening of Gilfach Halt. In the background the incomplete clock tower of the Emporium, is visible and the presence of scaffolding could suggest installation of the clock was imminent, which occurred, thanks to Gus Jones' in 1912.

built in response to local 'agitation', when Gilfach's population had grown to the point where even a small station could be justified to the R.R. management. The halt comprised a short platform, extended in 1911, and was unstaffed. Initially, no shelter was provided, but local pressure resulted in one being provided about 1910. Local pressure especially from the Chamber of Commerce at this time, however, failed to convince the R.R. of the desirability of a goods station in Gilfach.

Not everyone was satisfied with these improvements, arguing they should have gone further. Two items in the press were very critical of R.R. services and passenger coaches: *...Mr Jones said the coaches were cold and "absolutely unfit" for one travelling for a long distance. Apart from being cold, added the speaker, they were not very clean, and were often overcrowded. They ought to take up the matter in real earnest and get other bodies to do likewise, so as to get the company to improve the service. (Mr Jones expressed the sentiments of most of the passengers on the line.) (Merthyr Express, 1920)* while someone writing as *Y Cymro: Complaints regarding the state of things on the Rhymney Railway are to be heard at every hand and I must agree there is room for complaint. The carriages are filthy, draughty, unheated and badly lit, the seats* *are without cushions and are like cattle trucks, which reminds me of riding in state in France during the war.*

Another serious complaint is that they have no regard for running trains to the scheduled time. On Tuesday the 4.07pm. train from Cardiff to Hengoed arrived at Caerphilly at 4.45 pm., whilst again in the evening the 8.35 pm. from Cardiff was another quarter of an hour late. ... It is time Caerphilly District Council took this matter up again with the Railway Company and endeavoured to have a general improvement because at the present travelling on the Rhymney is enough to put years on anyone, whilst it is no wonder influenza is about so much when they are in such traps as so-called passenger carriages. (Caerphilly Journal 1921)

These critics had a point. Contemporary (1920) photographs show passenger rolling stock to be shabby and comprised many six-wheeled vehicles of nineteenth century design, which though provided with electric lights lacked heating apparatus. Until 1919 foot warmers were the only form of heating provided in R.R. trains, though after then steam heating equipment was fitted to all new and more modern bogie carriages, a task completed by the G.W.R. by 1924. Unlike many companies R.R. third class carriages, even those built in 1920, had wooden slatted seats rather than upholstery (as did all workmen's carriages, which also had neither lights nor heat), though seats in first and second class coaches were upholstered. In fairness to the R.R., when World War I broke out, the company was implementing a policy of modernisation of both motive power and rolling stock, but in 1915 it was placed under the control of the Railway Executive (government control, 1915-20) which stopped all non essential new construction and minimised maintenance of existing stock. Not until 1919 was the R.R. authorised to purchase new stock (delivered in 1920). Thus the R.R. was being pilloried, particularly by antipathetic local councils, for policies imposed on it by an outside agency (R.E.), over which it had little control.

The B.& M.R. was no better and possibly worse, but having been a musical hall joke for so long, few took it too seriously. In 1920 *Merthyr Express* reported: *So far as the Brecon and Merthyr Railway was concerned (this is the line which says a wag, is mentioned in the Bible, in Genesis), ...they had effected some improvement. So far as cleanliness was concerned, however, there was room for further improvement. It would also be well to have the coaches water-tight ... in train the other day, and to his discomfiture found water dripping in from the roof. 'You wanted an umbrella inside', added the complainant.*

Throughout this period goods traffic continued to flourish, notably on the R.R. mainline. In the 1895 working timetable 19 'up' and 20 'down' goods train paths are shown. Three were L.& N.W.R. through services and one was a 'pick-up train', which the timetable stated was *to call at all stations and sidings when required.* It was the latter that delivered general goods to the goods yards adjoining most stations for local consumption. The rest, were connected with coal traffic, linking places (mostly collieries) such as Fochriw, New Tredegar, Rhymney, Nantybwch (L.& N.W.R.), besides others en route, with Cardiff Docks. One 'up' path was shown as being for *Rhymney iron ore and goods*, but as iron ore traffic ceased in 1891, it was probably a general goods train. R.R. coal traffic was significantly increased with the opening in 1904 of the Bargoed Pits branch, the last major local railway development. As shown on the map *Railways around Bargoed* the branch diverged from the main line north of Pengam, serving an extensive array of sidings at the Bargoed Colliery complex. Although coal was the principal traffic, later traffic also included a range of chemical products, as well as coke from the plants established alongside the colliery. Groesfaen (1906) and Ogilvie (1923), new colliery developments in the Darran valley enhanced R.R. revenues further; both benefiting from pre-existing rail links; indeed *Merthyr Express* in 1921 praised *the foresight of Mr E. A. Prosser, the General Manager of the Rhymney Railway Company has already provided an outlet for the conveyance of coal to Cardiff, new sidings and duplicate lines having been laid down wherever possible.*

Like its passenger traffic, B.& M.R. goods traffic was comparatively small. In 1902 their working timetable showed only four paths through Bargoed, one of which was a through train between Brecon and Newport, while another worked between Bassaleg and Pantywaun. The 'Bargoed Branch Goods', also worked to Pantywaen, while the fourth served Fochriw colliery. The B.& M.R. too, was linked to Bargoed colliery, but the latter's owners, Powell Duffryn Steam Coal Company Limited, preferred their coal to be exported through Cardiff Docks, thus the R.R. took the lion's share of the available traffic.

By 1924 mineral train operations had changed (1913 on the R.R.). Only eight goods train paths were timetabled, four of which were operated by the London Midland & Scottish Railway (successor to L.& N.W.R. following 'Grouping' in 1923). Mineral trains were under the supervision of a controller, based in Cardiff, and in contact with the docks, collieries and signal boxes by telephone. Locomotives and guards' vans were allocated a target denoting the time of departure from their parent base; usually a locomotive shed or goods yard to some specified point. Having arrived at the latter, it would undertake whatever duties control required of it, including mineral or goods train working or shunting duties, which, if all went smoothly, was completed within allotted hours and returning back to the starting point. In 1924, sixteen target numbers were allocated to workings through and at Bargoed, while a further four related to shunting locomotives in the area. Two targets were allotted to Bargoed Pits Branch, which with that in the Darran valley, was carrying considerable traffic. The main line especially north of Bargoed, was characterised by declining traffic as progressively the older collieries closed. In 1932 Gilfach, the last local old mine, closed, the traffic from which, like those north of Bargoed, was not replaced.

In 1933 the L.M.& S.R. and G.W.R. in the face of declining traffic and need for economies concentrated all freight traffic between Abergavenny and Cardiff on the former N. A. & H.R. (G.W.R. after 1863) route via Pontypool Road and Newport. As a result timetabled paths for these trains from Rhymney Bridge ceased, ending an arrangement dating from the 1870s. G.W.R. Rhymney Valley passenger trains continued to work to Rhymney Bridge and local traffic was exchanged there. The only through workings, thereafter were excursions from the Rhymney Valley (including Bargoed) to Blackpool for the illuminations or to Edinburgh for rugby internationals. Eventually, in 1953, the line between Rhymney and Rhymney Bridge was closed to all traffic, even to the aforementioned special traffic.

Following the Railways Act, 1921, when Britain's railways were grouped into four large companies, from April 1922 the R.R. and B.& M.R. became part of an enlarged Great Western Railway. In 1924 the G.W.R. made two changes affecting Bargoed. The summer timetable saw the introduction of two new trains from Cardiff Parade (former R.R. station) to Aberystwyth and Pontsticill Junction respectively, which were routed via the R.R. to Bargoed Junction and

Bargoed – Goods traffic figures included with Pengam after 1926	1923	1929	1930	1933
Staff employed	36	24	20	18
Passenger tickets issued	423,778	175,749	169,085	128,238
Season tickets issued	458	769	639	681
Parcels forwarded	n/a			
General goods forwarded (tons)	4,274			
Coal & coke received (tons)	1,013			
Other minerals received (tons)	8,685			
General goods received (tons)	13,342			
Trucks of livestock handled	130			
Total carted tonnage.	4,502			
Pengam – Includes figures from Gilfach Fargoed Halt.				
Staff employed	n/a	n/a	n/a	n/a
Passenger tickets issued	139,116	76,993	71,958	59,119
Season tickets issued	274	592	540	533
Parcels forwarded	16,632	18,093	21,929	32,575
General goods forwarded (tons)	307	6,297	5,593	4,248
Coal & coke received (tons)	451	1,180	1,303	384
Other minerals received (tons)	12,729	12,879	10,643	5,332
General goods received (tons)	3,651	43,063	45,607	32,030
Trucks of livestock handled	2	81	40	2
Total carted tonnage.	n/a	n/a	n/a	n/a

Table 7 – G.W.R. Official Traffic returns from Bargoed and Pengam stations, 1923–1933.

thence over the B.& M.R. to Pontsticill Junction and beyond. Neither service lasted long, but for a short time they added further credence to the R.R. station name board's invitation to passengers to change for *Brecon Merthyr and Cambrian Railways*. Secondly the station was renamed, becoming *Bargoed* again.

Of greater significance was the rationalisation in 1928 of facilities in Cardiff. A short link allowed R.R. trains to be diverted from Parade station, to the former T.V.R. Queen Street station. This gave access to routes to Penarth and Barry, which should have pleased Caerphilly Urban District Council, who in 1920 pointed out that *the Rhymney Valley was the only valley in Glamorgan which did not have any direct access to the seaside*. In addition, R.R. line trains from Bargoed connected with G.W.R main line services, offering a better link than the slower and less frequent B.&M.R. trains to Newport.

The period 1919–1939 began optimistically, but post Great War political and economic forces brought conflict and decline to the area's industry and people, from which local railways were not immune, as Table 7 demonstrates.

The inclusion of Bargoed's traffic with Pengam's reflects changes in the organisation of G.W.R. goods traffic. In almost all categories the trend is down, even when data for the two stations is combined after 1926. The trend is explained by both economic decline and significant competition from motorised road transport for goods and passenger traffic with small transport businesses operated by ex-servicemen using war surplus lorries and a 3d rate was levied on G.U.D.C. ratepayers, including G.W.R., to establish bus services. It is unsurprising, therefore, that the more profitable forms of goods traffic were lost to road transport and that ticket sales declined in the face of bus competition. The latter is reflected in the decline in the numbers of passenger services during the 1930s, shown in Table 8 below:

From Bargoed	No. trains per day		
	1924	1935	1944
To Rhymney/Rhymney Bridge (up)	22	17	13
To Cardiff (down)	21	19	14
To Brecon (up)	4	4	n/a
To Newport (down)	4	4	n/a

Table 8 – numbers of scheduled weekday passenger trains from Bargoed.

Wartime restrictions imposed on the railways by the Railway Executive (1939-1947) mainly account for further reductions in services during the 1940s but as the figures in Table 8 are based on the public timetable, they do not show the increase in workmen's trains, including daily workings to the Royal Ordnance Factory at Glascoed. After the end of the Second World War services returned to something like normal, but once again the economic and political climate had changed.

Nationalisation of coal mines in 1947 and railways in 1948 did nothing to stave off the decline. Older collieries closed, while some of the larger mines were modernised and for a few years produced economically viable quantities of coal for the railways to transport. Many of the traditional overseas markets were lost during and after the war, when foreign customers found more secure, cheaper alternative supplies, or were lost to competition from petroleum products, thus the good times did not last long. North of Bargoed, closure of Elliott Colliery at New Tredegar (1967) saw the end of large scale coal production in the upper Rhymney Valley. Some coal-based traffic continued over the R.R. main line to Tirphil for the so-called *McLaren Dump*, but that line was closed by 1976. In the Darran valley, despite modernisation, first Groesfaen (1968) then Ogilvie (1975) ceased production with the branch from Bargoed North Junction closing in 1978. General goods traffic to the sidings in Bargoed ceased in 1963, but some traffic continued beyond Bargoed to Rhymney, before that too closed in the 1980s. Part of the latter was reactivated in the late 1990s by the privatised freight company English, Welsh and Scottish Railways (E.W.S.), as a short-lived experiment, for tin plate traffic from Ebbw Vale.

Bargoed Colliery continued to supply diminishing quantities of coal to the Bargoed Pits branch, and when the colliery closed in 1977 the mine was the only functioning part of a complex which had produced chemical feedstocks, tar and even coal-based petroleum in its day. Once site clearance work had been completed the last train departed the branch in 1982 watched by only two people. So ended coal production and its transport in Bargoed and Gilfach.

Steam locomotion continued unchallenged on the declining number of goods and mineral trains until 1963 when the first of what became known as the Class 37 diesel locomotives arrived. In 1965 all steam workings through Bargoed ended when diesel locomotives took over workings to Ogilvie and Groesfaen collieries as well as operating on the Bargoed Pits branch. However, steam trains have returned to Bargoed on two occasions, in 1991 and 2001, when well-patronised special trains worked from Cardiff to Rhymney and back.

Passenger services fared somewhat differently. A major change was wrought in autumn 1953 when the passenger timetable in the Cardiff Valleys was comprehensively revised as *an interval service*. Rhymney Valley services, did not benefit as much as other routes, and was described as *not very regular* by one writer (R.W. Kidner) and *approximately hourly* by another (R.C. Riley). This was not the last change affecting passenger services through Bargoed for in 1958 British Railways introduced diesel multiple units in place of steam trains, comprising coaches provided by the G.W.R. to replace the much derided R.R. vehicles, on regular Cardiff to Rhymney services. In general, services were neither accelerated nor improved and football extras or Sunday excursions continued to be steam hauled until the early 1960s. At the end of 1962 passenger services ceased on the former B.& M.R., Newport to Brecon route, in advance of closures recommended by Dr. Beeching in his report (The Reshaping of British Railways, published in 1963).

As Table 9 shows, for the next twenty or so years passenger services through Bargoed slowly declined, reaching a nadir point in 1983:

From Bargoed	Number of trains per day					
	1961	1964	1983	1994	2003	2011
To Rhymney (up)	26	24	13	18	18	18
To Cardiff (down)	28	24	16	27	28	49
To Brecon (up)	3	-	-	-	-	-
To Newport (down)	3	-	-	-	-	-

Table 9 – Numbers of scheduled weekday passenger trains from Bargoed.

In 1970 rationalisation of services led to Bargoed station being reduced to a single platform, while the 1900-built island platform lost its buildings and was effectively demolished. Contemporaneously, the line from Bargoed to Rhymney and the branch to Ogilvie colliery were singled, as part of a major rationalisation of track and signalling in the station area, following the earlier withdrawal of all goods facilities.

Ironically, the improvements shown after 1983 were primarily a product of the Transport Act of 1985 which required de-regulation of bus services as from October 1986. The latter also discouraged councils from operating their own bus services and, with limited exceptions, prevented them subsidising bus services. Many councils, including those through which the Rhymney Valley line passed, used funds released to subsidise railway services, encouraged by the emerging environmental lobby's campaigns against internal combustion engine powered road transport. By 1986 councils' names (Mid Glamorgan C.C. on the Rhymney Valley pocket timetable) were appearing on marketing material produced by Valley Lines, a marketing subsidiary of the Regional Rail sector which took over day-to-day control of local services in the South Wales Valleys in 1982.

The additional funding that accompanied these changes also led to the introduction of a second generation of diesel multiple units marketed initially as 'Sprinters', besides the start of major investment in new signalling and track works to allow increased train speeds and services accelerated to levels not previously achieved, as demonstrated in Table 10 below:

From Bargoed	Journey times in minutes			
	1895	1924	1986	2003
To Cardiff	60	56	49	41
To Rhymney	24	24	17	14

Table 10 – Journey times of scheduled weekday passenger trains from Bargoed.

In the 1990s railway organisation became more complex as privatisation loomed. Valley Lines (Cardiff Railways Company was the parent operator) became part of the Wales and West division of Regional Wales in 1992 to become, in 1995, part of the Prism franchise, which in turn was bought out by National Express. In 2001, Cardiff Railways became part of the redefined National Express franchise, Wales and Borders Trains. This lasted until December 2003 when Arriva Trains Wales' bid for the franchise was preferred and accepted. In 2010, Arriva became part of Deutsche Bahn, (German Railways Group). The Arriva Trains Wales bid contained an undertaking to increase train frequency, a promise that has been partly fulfilled, as shown in Table 10, but increasing the frequency of services to Rhymney from Bargoed awaits further track and signalling work.

Until 2006 both Valley Lines and Arriva Trains Wales found it difficult to improve service frequency because of shortage of trains. As a stop-gap, one which lasted for ten years, two peak hour and rugby international day services comprised a set of corridor coaches, hauled by a diesel locomotive. This operation had the effect of giving Bargoed and the Rhymney Valley services celebrity status as railway enthusiasts flocked to the line to sample these services. When such operations finally ceased in December 2006 Arriva Trains Wales sponsored a Gala Day during which most of the frequent four coach trains were full to capacity with many passengers cheerfully standing throughout their journeys!

Subject to fluctuations caused partly by the vicissitudes of the economy following these enhancements ticket sales have increased from Pengam, but not from either Bargoed or Gilfach, as Table 11 suggests:

	Annual ticket sales	
	2004/05	2008/09
Bargoed	148,448	135,000
Gilfach	8,997	2,394
Pengam	375,000	476,000

Table 11 – Annual ticket sales for passenger services in the study area.

Comparisons with ticket sales collected by the G.W.R. shown in Table 7 and those shown in Table 11 are interesting. Ticket sales have increased at both Bargoed and Pengam stations, Pengam's by the larger proportion, possibly because of the availability of Park and Ride facilities at the latter, provided jointly by the railway company and Caerphilly County Borough Council. It remains to be seen whether the opening in 2010 of Park and Ride facilities at Bargoed, along with the relocated bus station will have a similar effect.

To cater for the enhanced services, Bargoed station's island platform was reinstated in July 2001 along with the necessary rearrangements to signalling and track. A new footbridge and lifts for disabled access were installed to connect the two platforms, together with a new entrance on the High Street side of the road bridge and a passenger shelter on the new 'up' platform. As part of the Angel Way project, Bargoed station environment has been altered significantly: in 2008 the 1906 road bridge was replaced by a short 'tunnel' over which a new roundabout and bus station were built. Surviving all this change has been the station building on the 'down' platform, which probably dates from the opening of the station in 1858, in which a ticket issuing franchise operates alongside a local taxi firm.

After over 150 years of service Bargoed station still survives and, indeed, thrives. The passing mineral traffic might have gone and the goods yards no longer handle wares for sale in Hanbury Road's shops, but the station now has the best passenger service to and from Cardiff it has ever had, a service that is planned to be enhanced before the end of Arriva Trains Wales' present franchise in 2015. Hopefully, this optimistic outlook for the station might be reflected in a revival of the fortunes of the town which bears the name given by the directors of the R.R. in 1858 and which it still shares.

Bargoed Station looking North. (courtesy of Terry McCarthy)
It was the building of this station that started the growth of Bargoed and gave it its name.

CHAPTER 8
PEOPLE AND HOMES

For centuries, the land that became Bargoed and Gilfach was a sparsely-populated rural area in which most people earned a living from farming and rural industries. The majority of people enumerated in the local area in 1841 and 1851 farmed the land discussed in Chapter 4 while a few worked in Pontaberbargoed's corn mill or woollen textile factory near the confluence of the rivers Rhymney and Bargoed-Rhymney, and a small minority was dependent upon small-scale coal enterprises operating locally in the early Victorian era. This general picture is confirmed in the parish tithe award and in the description by Bryn H. Rees that appears in *Gelligaer* Volume 9 1972. The pace of life was generally unhurried in what, since the later eighteenth century, was a fairly thriving rural community producing food for subsistence and for sale to the rapidly growing iron communities at the heads of the valleys. The majority of residents had been born in the local area or in neighbouring Glamorganshire, Monmouthshire or Breconshire parishes within a radius of some ten to fifteen miles, although the 1851 census shows a few incomers from Carmarthenshire and one from Wiltshire. Most of them lived on the scattered farms but some were enumerated in the small community that straddled the Rhymney river (and the parish and county boundaries) at Pontaberbargoed. The corn mill and textile factory were on the Glamorganshire side of the river as was the Old Mill Inn but the larger part of that community was on the east bank of the river in the parish of Bedwellty and county of Monmouthshire. The community had long been the focus of a lively Welsh culture with harpists and poets, and it is likely that nonconformists, both Baptists and Independents, met there in the 1820s and 1830s.

By the time of the 1861 census the area had began to change especially as Rhymney Railway was operating and its Bargoed Station was open for goods and passenger services. The population in the area that was to become Bargoed and Gilfach had increased by nearly 25% and, while the majority of people still originated in the three south east Wales counties (Glamorganshire, Monmouthshire and Breconshire) the process of inward migration already evident on a small scale in 1851 had gained momentum with incomers born in Carmarthenshire and Pembrokeshire, in the English counties of Somerset, Gloucestershire and Devon in the south west as well as Norfolk in the east. Not only had the population increased, but so had the housing stock and the numbers employed in the coal industry while the railway offered a new employment. In 1841 and 1851 there had only been 17 dwellings in the area that became Bargoed and Gilfach on the Glamorganshire side of the river, but that had increased to 28 by 1861 when there were also three in the process of construction and one that was uninhabited. The number earning a living in the coal industry had increased from 11 to 33, while 13 were railway employees and their dependants.

After centuries that had witnessed very little change in the local population (and housing stock), the rate of change continued to accelerate and the 1871 census shows that Bargoed and Gilfach were developing as two separate communities attracting migrants from rural areas in Wales and England as well as from older industrial communities in South Wales. There are no streets named on the 1871 census but 65 people are enumerated under the general address of Bargoed (most of those were in Pontaberbargoed) and 74 under Fos Las (probably the area in what was to become Bristol Terrace and Church Street). There was not much growth in the area that became Gilfach although several coal miners were enumerated at Gilfach Fargoed Fach including William Jones, born in Lisvane about 1807, and his sons whose birthplaces (Mynyddislwyn 1842 and Bedwellty 1848) suggest that the family had moved around the local area for work in coal mining. It is worthy of note that headmaster Mr Pullin and his family as well as a schoolmistress and nurse were enumerated at Pengam School while John Bowen, Lecturer to Gelligaer Charity, his family and a domestic servant, were at the nearby Vicarage. The First Edition O.S. map of 1878 shows not only Bargoed's new streets taking shape south of Pontaberbargoed near Rhymney Railway's Bargoed station to house, among others, rail workers and coal miners, but also the first nonconformist chapel, Calfaria.

At that time local people, whether born locally or incomers to the area, in common with their contemporaries across the country, were about to find that national legislation would intrude into their life and work over the coming decades in a way never experienced by their ancestors. The introduction of compulsory education and the extension of the franchise (votes) as well as legislation relating to public health and local government are just some examples of such laws.

The 1881, 1891 and 1901 censuses show the local population growth before Bargoed Colliery started to operate and the development of the emerging urban communities of Bargoed and Gilfach is shown on the extract from the Second Edition O.S. map of 1901 on page 162. Not only did the population increase in the last quarter of the nineteenth century, so did the housing stock, and the percentage of the population born in more distant counties of Wales and England was greater. The sinkers started work on Powell Duffryn Steam Coal Company's modern Bargoed Colliery in April 1897 and that anticipated the revolutionary growth that was to come as soon as the Colliery was fully operational in late 1903. Between then and the outbreak of World War I streets of terraced houses to house the rapidly increasing population linked the two communities of Bargoed and Gilfach while services were provided in what quickly became the largest urban area within the jurisdiction of the local council. In view of its recent rural background, the infrastructure was inadequate and, during the early decades of the twentieth century, local councillors faced exciting challenges searching for practical solutions in the hilly terrain. The 1911 census returns and electoral registers shed light on the local population in the era when large-scale migration (which continued to the late 1920s) into the area was a key feature and the effect of that is evident on the extract from the Third Edition O.S. map of 1922 on page 163

Some families came from distant parts while others did not travel far to find work and a home in Bargoed or Gilfach and the following examples serve to give a flavour of the people who moved into the area. Some of the people who moved into the rapidly expanding Bargoed and Gilfach communities were first time movers from rural South Wales or south west England while others were migrants who lived in other industrial communities after they had left the countryside. Others came from more distant parts of the UK as well as from other countries.

William Morgan, born in Gelligroes, Monmouthshire about 1826, was enumerated with his parents and siblings in Pontaberpengam in 1851. It is not clear when he got married or where he was when the 1861 and 1871 censuses were taken, but in 1881 he was a 55 year coal miner, head of a household comprising his wife and 25 year old Joseph, his unmarried son who was also a coal miner, at 22 Wingfield Road, Bargoed. The family was still in Bargoed ten years later when they were enumerated as two separate households in 11 Church Street. William and his wife together with a widowed male visitor (perhaps a relative) had three rooms while widowed Joseph and his 5 year old daughter Polly had two rooms. William had died by the time the 1901 census was taken but his widow, son Joseph and granddaughter Polly were enumerated in 11 Church Street again. According to the 1891 census, the family was Welsh speaking, but by 1901 they said they were able to speak both English and Welsh.

Two first time movers illustrate the fact that some men brought their skills with them while others adapted to work in an unfamiliar industry. On the one hand, Robert Henry Parton, enumerated as a live-in farm servant in Breconshire in 1891, was enumerated at 2 Bristol Terrace in 1901. A newly-married man, he had probably turned his back on farm work in favour of what he perceived as a more lucrative future as a coal-hewer. George Duggan, enumerated as head of the household at 23 Thomas Street in Gilfach, on the other hand, had brought his family from their native Hay, Breconshire, to pursue his skills as a stone mason in an area and at a time when they were at a premium. He was just one of many whose building skills were in demand in the rapidly developing communities of Bargoed and Gilfach.

Another incomer who found his skills in high demand in the rapidly growing community was Cardiganshire-born carpenter D. J. Thomas who, in 1908, made an amicable agreement to leave his building partner in Bargoed to establish his undertaking business and since then his name has been well-known and highly respected by generations of local people. He married a young lady from his native village and at first, they lived in McDonnell Road before, in 1914, 1 Wood Street, a dwelling in a more central place and better suited to his business, came on the market. When D. J. Thomas moved his family and his business there, a tank, a reminder of the contemporary European conflict, stood in front of the property on Trafalgar Square. As D. J. Thomas, undertaker and funeral director, did not have a hearse, he worked with P. Boobyer of 3 Wood Street, hearse proprietor, who garaged the hearse in Lower Park Road. As the years passed, the horse-drawn hearse was replaced by a motor hearse and after World War II, Davies Brothers, local furniture removers took over the hearse. D. J. Thomas' son, John, joined the business and pursued his vision to provide a Chapel of Rest. He realised that, in an era when more people died at home than in hospital, and most family homes in the local area were crowded with children and lodgers, the business could better serve the local community if it had a Chapel of Rest. Having purchased suitable premises, a former milk depot in Upper Wood Street, he converted it into a Chapel of Rest that, in spite of many sceptics, proved to be in much demand. The business was in the hands of two generations of the Thomas family for nearly seven and a half decades before it passed to Elvet Watson in September 1982, and he ran the business for nearly quarter of a century before it became part of Dignity Caring Funeral Services in 2006. By the 1980s, the Upper Wood Street Chapel of Rest was inadequate for its purpose, and so Elvet Watson purchased the Lesser Hall from the Methodist Church, and converted it into a Chapel of Rest that opened in 1993 and is still in use today.

The nature of the rapid urban development was noted in the introduction to a town directory published shortly before World War I: *Bargoed has very appropriately been designated the 'Metropolis of the Rhymney Valley'. But this is not its latest appellation, for it has just been titled 'The City on the Hill'. During the last decade there has been a wonderful metamorphosis in this district. From a quiet, rural, obscure village, Bargoed has sprung – as if by the movement of the magic wand – into an up-to-date, enterprising, progressive Town, whose doings often evoke the envy and admiration of less 'go-a-head' towns, not only in the Principality but beyond the border.* The same source continues: *Its elevated situation gives it a picturesque appearance and a bird's-eye view from a distance causes one to stand amazed at its magnitude and modernism. It commands a splendid view of the surrounding district...... Perhaps a collection of citizens of the world does not always serve to advance the interest and welfare of a town but the development and success of Bargoed, which has won for itself the distinguished title 'The Metropolis of the Rhymney Valley' is due in some degree to the Cosmopolitan character – which means the introduction of new ideas – of its population. Many of its business people, promoters of industry and professional men, though differing widely in religion, politics, and disposition, unite readily in a common cause and for the advancement of the town. The people are distinguished for their social entertainments, and there is never lack of countenance to any healthy form of amusement or recreation.* It was a thriving community and the source continues *Bargoed has been noted for its low percentage of paupers as compared with other places in the Parish of Gellygaer, the difference between the aggregate number of paupers in Bargoed to the number in the upper part of the Valley being enormous.*

When a decade or so later George Thompson recalled the cosmopolitan nature of the local community he noted some difficulties: *As industry developed, the need for labour grew: strangers streamed into the valley: Irishmen, many fleeing the oppressive Ironmasters of Dowlais and Merthyr; men of the Black country; tin-miners of Cornwall; Scotsmen; and the unfortunates seeking refuge from war-torn Europe. ... For years overcrowding was a problem. Families shared accommodation with relatives, and newcomers occupied cramped quarters with other homeless people in what were termed apartments. This influx of population frequently led to some community discord. Prejudice and cultural differences arose, but, with time, feelings of bigotry, even hatred, were overcome. Differing customs and accents became accepted, setting a pattern that gave the people an identity peculiar to the mining valleys.*

After decades when people had been attracted to move into Bargoed and Gilfach the pattern was reversed by the 1930s. The future of the coal industry looked less certain and the contemporary unemployment and depression encouraged some of the young and able-bodied people to leave the area. Some emigrated to start a new life in a new country while others moved to take employment in the new industries in places such as London and Coventry.

The Italian connection

The developing town of Bargoed, like so many other towns in the South Wales Coalfield, benefited from the influx of Italian families who opened up businesses to cater for low cost *luxury* items such as ice cream, sweets, chocolate and milky coffee as well as what some people regarded as *essentials* namely cigarettes and fish and chips. However, not all Italians were involved in the ice cream/cafe industry as some of them worked in the local coal industry.

By the 1880s Italian families started to appear in significant numbers in the old county of Glamorgan. Most of the first immigrants came from the Bardi area of Northern Italy, a mountainous region not far from Parma. By the middle of the nineteenth century that part of Italy was a fairly poor agricultural area with many small family farms operating at subsistence levels. The land was of poor quality and the equipment, such as it was, being very basic. Times were hard and so it was not surprising that many young men had to look for work elsewhere.

John Ricci, whose family still run a cafe in Bargoed today (2011), compares the story of his father leaving the Bardi area for South Wales with that of the countless men of similar age and ambition who left the small family farms of Cardiganshire in the same era. By the mid nineteenth century people found that their families' native land, whether it was Bardi or rural Cardiganshire, could no longer support the large families that were being reared and many of the younger people were attracted by the *money* of the coalfields where they could gain paid employment. At first a number of people, virtually all male, moved from Bardi to London but it was not long before the riches of the South Wales Coalfield became known to these immigrants: word got back to Bardi and a direct link was formed between Bardi and South Wales.

The Italian surnames of Assirati, Berni, Brachi, Conti, Lusardi, Rabiotti, Ricci and Rossi soon became quite familiar throughout South Wales as Italians arrived in numbers especially between 1891 and 1911. Not surprisingly, there were no people with Italian surnames enumerated in Bargoed and Gilfach in the 1901 census as the local urban communities did not develop until after Bargoed Colliery started working. However by the time of the next census in 1911 the picture had changed: Bargoed Colliery was working and the local communities were expanding rapidly.

In 1911 Luigi Massari, born in Italy about 1877, was enumerated with his wife and their four young children at 51 High Street where he was a shop keeper with Refreshment Room and ice cream manufactory. It is likely that the Massari family was the first Italian family to settle in the Bargoed area as his children were born there between 1904 and 1910. In 1911 his household was completed by four Italian-born male servants who like their employer were not able to speak English.

Zuizeppi Berni, who was born in Bardi about 1884, was enumerated as head of a household at 52 Hanbury Road in 1911. He described himself as a married man earning a living through his Refreshment Room and ice cream manufacturing. The thirteen young unmarried Italian males, aged from 14 to 23, enumerated at the same address were employed in his ice cream manufacturing business. Like their employer, they were born in Bardi and able to speak both English and Italian.

The Italian presence in the local area is confirmed in successive issues of Kelly's Trade Directory. Three Italian families were listed in Bargoed in the 1914 and 1920 editions: Berni Brothers, ice cream manufacturers of Hanbury Road and High Street, Fucito Brothers, confectioners of 4 Trafalgar Buildings and Luigi Massari with Refreshment Room at 51 High Street. By the time the 1926 edition was published the number of Italian businesses locally had increased and the following were listed: Berni Brothers of 52 Hanbury Road, 6 High Street and Trafalgar Square, Martha Berni, a fried fish dealer of 53 High Street, Fucito and Co. (fried fish) of 53 High Street, Giovani Conti, confectioner of 31 Hanbury Road, Massari and Sons with Refreshment Room at 51 High Street, shopkeepers Rissi brothers of 19 High Street and fish fryer Antonio Sidoli at 4 Trafalgar Buildings.

However the Italian families did not have a monopoly of the refreshment trade locally as the following non-Italian names were also listed in the 1914 Directory: John William O'Nions who had a fried fish shop at 45 Hanbury Road, William Parker with Refreshment Room at Hanbury Square, fried fish dealer Sidney Thomas of 1 Henry Street, fried fish dealer William Thomas of 36 Greenfield Street and 30 Hanbury Road and Frederick Wiltshire who had Refreshment Room at 46 Cardiff Road.

Ugo Zanasi, another Italian living in Bargoed, was listed in Kelly's 1926 Directory as a Physician and Surgeon. He had gained his qualification at the University of Bologna, which as it was probably established in 1088 is the oldest continually operating degree-granting university in Europe. As Bologna was in the mountains of northern Italy, many local immigrants from Bardi would have felt at home with Ugo Zanasi.

Walking south from the Railway Station through Bargoed's bustling town centre during shopping hours in the late 1960s one passed businesses run by nine Italian families. Assirati's *Cosy Corner Cafe*, and Pini's *Model* Fish and Chip shop were on opposite sides of Lower High Street near the Railway station. After that there was Rossi's cafe and another cafe run by the Assirati family. Lusardi's *The Conti* (comprising a fish and chip shop as well as a restaurant) was in Upper High Street while another branch of the same family ran Lusardi's *The Continental Cafe* opposite the Police Station in Hanbury Road and a little further on was *Hanbury Cafe*. Finally there was Mr Cresci's Trafalgar Fish and Chip Shop and Ricci Brothers' Cafe and ice cream parlour on Trafalgar Square. At the same time Gilfach had a cafe and confectionery shop run by the Opel family and a fish and chip shop run by a member of the Assirati family.

For decades the pattern of life and work of everyone in the local area, whether or not they worked in the coal industry, revolved around the colliery. The miners' days and hours of work (shifts) impacted on businesses and those, like the Italian cafes and fish and chip shops, that relied on capturing some of the leisure time of the miners and their families had to remain open for long hours. Gino Lusardi's father opened his Fish and Chip shop in High Street in the mid 1930s and Gino recalls that (including preparation and cleaning up times) his father worked from 8 a.m. until late (7 p.m. on Tuesday, 11 p.m. on Monday and Wednesday and to midnight on Friday and Saturday nights). The shop did not open on Thursday (early closing day for local shops) and on Sunday. As the years passed, Gino said, the hours of business reduced in the Lusardi shop as well as in numerous other local businesses for a number of reasons. In the 1950s and 1960s local people were increasingly likely to spend their leisure time at home watching their television or travelling by car to venues outside the local area. From the later 1960s onwards the Italian cafes faced competition from local public houses as they started to sell food as well as drink. Gino and his wife Rosa also recall that for a while the evening trade was sustained by the local Bingo halls but when they closed there was no point in staying open after 6 p.m.

Today the Ricci Brothers run a well established family business on Trafalgar Square that dates back to 1929. Originating in the Bardi area of Italy, the Ricci family arrived in Wales in 1905 and, after gaining experience in the ice cream trade in the Rhondda Valley, moved to Bargoed to start the cafe and ice cream business. There was a soda fountain in Ricci's cafe and for many years they offered sarsaparilla, cream soda, lemon and raspberry flavours for sale. John

Ricci recalls that orange was not added to the list until after the Second World War.

In the early years it was common to refer to the Italian cafes as Temperance Bars, as they did not offer alcoholic drinks for sale. Following the lead of their pastors and diaconate, the congregations of local nonconformist chapels opposed Sunday trading and made no secret of their disapproval of public houses and alcohol consumption which they blamed for many contemporary social ills. Thus they were faced with something of a dilemma regarding local Italian cafes: they welcomed them as alcohol-free refreshment rooms but disapproved of the fact that some of them were open on Sundays. Eventually all but the diehards accepted the Italian cafes as worthy alternatives to local public houses. John Ricci remembers that just after the end of the Second World War his father was able to produce a non-alcoholic drink that looked enough like beer, even down to the *head* on the top, to make it acceptable for celebrating a special occasion.

Two existing Italian cafes in Bargoed are run by families who did not come to the town as part of the first wave of immigrants in the early 1900s. On 23 January 1961 Jo (Guiseppi) Rossi and his bride of a few weeks opened a cafe at 51 High Street Bargoed. The premises had been occupied by the Massari family who are mentioned previously as probably being the first Italian family to come to Bargoed. Mrs Rossi had been living in Ebbw Vale with her parents (her maiden name was Antoniazzi) while Mr Rossi had been living with his family at Blackwood and his family still run the Square Cafe in that town. At Christmas time the display of high quality chocolates in their front window always attracted a lot of onlookers. Mrs Rossi recalls that the steak and kidney pies that were warmed by steam from the coffee machine were a particular favourite of her customers. After Mr Rossi's death and the demolition of their premises Mrs Rossi and her daughter opened a smaller cafe on the opposite side of the road, and just up the hill from their original premises. Both Mr and Mrs Rossi's family originated from the Bardi area. When Mr Rossi was alive they visited Bardi every year, but now visits are less frequent than before.

Just after the Second World War there was another influx of Italian workers into the area because the Italian economy was clearly suffering. In 1953 Pio Strinatti left the Bardi area for Cardiff. He had been running a successful poultry business in Italy but following a visit from his Uncle who was a partner in Astey's Cafe, Cardiff, he was persuaded to come to Wales. Pio married Renata Tedaldi who at the age of 14, had moved from Bedonia to Hirwaun with her mother and siblings. In 1968 Pio and Renata moved to Bargoed to take over the Continental Cafe (opposite the Police Station) and which had been run by the well known figure of Maurice Lusardi. The freehold of the Continental was owned by Mr Shibko who was reluctant to sell so Pio decided to purchase another premises which had been occupied by the Shapland family. The New Continental is now run by Pio's sons and is a popular local venue.

Emigration from Bargoed and Gilfach

From the mid nineteenth century to the late 1920s the general trend was inward migration, but there were also some examples of people who left the area. Some of these emigrants were descended from families that had lived locally for several generations but most were from families that had migrated (mainly within the country) several times. People moved from one area to another (whether in the same country or outside it) for a variety of reasons including a search of adventure or, as the local press suggested, a better future for themselves and their families than they were likely to experience in the local area as unemployment and depression grew in the inter-war era.

Some local people emigrated to U.S.A. In 1919 Levi Williams of The Shant (son-in-law of local musician Henry Smith), a popular miners' official who had been kept in U.K. by World War I, emigrated to join his family who had been in Scranton for some time. In 1923 David Prosser left his job in Wolfson's Clothiers to go to Michigan where he was joined soon after by his bride-to-be, school teacher Nellie Calvert of Gilfach. In July 1924, Mrs Sarah Rees and her three young children were entertained to a farewell tea by fellow-worshippers at Ainon Baptist Chapel, before they went to join husband and father who had been in America for some nine months.

Other local people chose to emigrate to places within the British Empire. After Alec Starling took his family from John Street to Canada in 1921, his son Gilbert corresponded from Canada with Elizabeth (Lily) Lake of Park Road before returning to Bargoed to marry her in St. Gwladys' Church in September 1926 and take her back to Canada with him. Albert Williams, his wife and two sons, left Plasnewydd Street in September 1926 to sail from London for a new life in Australia. While in Bargoed he had served on the rugby club's committee and proved himself a good cricketer. Following their respective marriages in 1926, two sons of the Jenkins family of Heolddu Uchaf left the area, one to work as an engineer for the Canadian Government and the other to farm in Australia. In 1927 local young ladies, Lily Spring and Lily Rogers, left the local area to join their husbands-to-be, abroad: Miss Spring joined D. Watkins in Australia and Miss Rogers joined Ernie Ariss in Canada.

Councillor A. S. Williams was probably accurate when, in August 1926, he spoke at a farewell to Reg Hibbs who was leaving for Ontario when he said that some of the best local men were leaving the area and taking their skills and services to serve other countries. He said Reg Hibbs was a good citizen, good craftsman and good workman, and he expressed the hope that the current industrial crisis would soon end and people like Reg Hibbs would be able to get well-paid work that would enable them to lead happy and comfortable lives in this country.

Sadly, sometimes the news that came back to Bargoed and Gilfach from local emigrants was not good. Only months after Levi Williams had left his 18-year old daughter Anna Mary suffered tubercular spinal meningitis and died. In April 1926 news reached the local area that David Griffiths, formerly of

Bargoed where, a fine baritone, he had sang with Bargoed Male Voice Party and Apollo Glee Singers, had died in hospital in Alberta, Canada, after suffering a fractured skull in a roof fall in the coal mine where he was employed. During 1927 two former residents died in Australia: in February Mrs Kinnersley of Gilfach heard of the death of her daughter-in-law and in October 20-year old Doris Arthur died after seven years in Australia.

Travel

Prior to World War II some local people may not have gone any further from home than they were able to walk for much of the year and for many local children the annual Sunday School outings to the seaside (usually Barry or Porthcawl) were something to look forward to. Other organisations also arranged trips and other treats for their members in the early part of the twentieth century and one such outing was that reported in *Merthyr Express* in June 1900, the tradesmen's annual trip to Weston, Ilfracombe, Lynmouth and Clovelly.

Judging by the number of advertisements that the various railway companies put in the local press in the first decade of the twentieth century, local people not only had a choice of destinations for both day trips and longer stays but also went on such journeys. The Railway Executive restricted travel but as soon as the railways were freed from government control in 1921 excursions flourished again. The popular destinations appear to include Newport Market and Shrewsbury Flower Show, as well as the bi-annual Scotland v Wales rugby international in Edinburgh. G.W.R. opened a new line to the new Fishguard Harbour in 1908 and offered day trips to Killarney.

Anecdotal evidence has it that pre World War I some local miners enjoyed holidays to seaside resorts such as Aberystwyth. Before 1914 and for a while after 1921 there was a summer rail service with through trains from Bargoed to Aberystwyth. Some local families took a holiday away from Bargoed and Gilfach to visit relatives, especially those who had remained in the rural community where their ancestors may have lived for several generations. It is likely that sometimes people accustomed to the amenities in Bargoed and Gilfach found it difficult to enjoy the rural isolation with its earth closets and no gas or electricity, especially if visiting a sick relative or attending a family funeral.

In the 1920s it was not unusual for the local press to report when some of the professional people of Bargoed and Gilfach were away on holiday. It was common for local clergy to take annual holidays, often lasting about four weeks, and for the local press to report on who filled the pulpit while the pastor was away. One such report was that of September 1924 noting that a Rhymney clergyman conducted the Sunday services in Hanbury Road Baptist chapel as pastor Rev. Emrys Jones was on holiday. The following holidays were among those reported in the local press in 1927: in July a relief stationmaster took over when local stationmaster Mr Boobyer was on holiday in Weymouth, and the following month Dr. and Mrs Turner visited Isle of Wight while another family from Hillside Park holidayed in Pembrokeshire. Sometimes former Bargoed and Gilfach residents returned to the area to spend time with friends and family as in the case of a bank employee who was transferred from Bargoed to Bangor and the numerous nurses and students who came home to visit their families. Holiday experiences were not always happy as shown by the sadness of Dr. Reidy and his family when his infant daughter died while the family was on holiday in North Wales. Probably one of the longest holidays with a distant destination enjoyed by a local resident prior to World War II started when, as announced in *Merthyr Express* June 1926, Miss Paul, assistant mistress at Bargoed Infants' school, set sail to California for a three month holiday.

Sometimes local people visited other areas for health reasons. It was not uncommon for working class families to spend some time in the Herefordshire countryside hop-picking, a matter that arose on more than one occasion when the question of absenteeism from school was being discussed. Most local people would not have been able to afford to follow the example of headmaster J. Sylvan Evans who, it was reported in the local press early in 1928, was about to leave for the south of England to aid his recuperation after an operation: they would have had content themselves with the fresh air on the local common.

Housing stock

For centuries, the local housing stock, as captured on the parish tithe map of the early Victorian era, was confined to farmsteads scattered across the area and Pontaberbargoed's labourers' and craftsmen's dwellings and public houses. Change started after the railway station was opened in 1858 but the First Edition O.S. map of 1878 shows that this had only limited impact on the housing stock.

The second edition O.S. map and the 1901 census enumerators' book combine to give a picture of the local population and housing stock at the start of the twentieth century. By 1901, the Pontaberbargoed community included Factory Road, Bridge Street, Old Mill Inn as well as Croft House, Gas House and Junction Hotel. Bargoed was emerging as a town and in 1901, occupants were enumerated in Bargoed's new streets of terraced houses (Bristol Terrace, Railway Terrace, High Street, Powell's Terrace, Hanbury Road, Elsie Street [later part of Greenfield Street], Cross Street, Capel Street, Greenfield Street, Heolddu Road, Wingfield Road [later part of Heolddu Road], Francis Street and Church Street), as well as in some scattered dwellings near the reservoir and old farmsteads. There was a growing community in Gilfach by 1901 as, in addition to the households in the farmsteads, people were enumerated in the new streets (Upper Park Place. Park Place, Commercial Street [including Gwerthonor Hotel], Maesygraig Street, Thomas Street, Llewellyn Street, Margaret Street and Gwerthonor Place), as well as Gwerthonor House and Brook Cottage and Pengam County School. Comparison between the Second Edition O.S. map of 1901 and the Third Edition O.S. map of 1922 (extracts of which appear on pages 162 and 163) indicates how the two communities had grown and merged.

This Ernest T. Bush photograph (from Reflective Images of Port Talbot) shows Gilfach's Maesygraig Street in the early twentieth century.

Most of the new residential development on the western side of the river Rhymney comprised rows of terraced housing, the *Valleyscape* described by John Hilling. Local geography dictated that streets such as Bargoed's Church Street and Heolddu Road were fairly steep and so it is not surprising that the town came to be known to some as the *City on the Hill*. Built of locally-quarried Pennant sandstone, the earliest houses in Bargoed and Gilfach, lacking front gardens, opened directly onto the pavement in the front, and the back gardens, with a detached building housing a water closet, gave access to a back lane. Inside, the typical early house comprised two rooms (parlour and kitchen/scullery) downstairs and a staircase leading to two or three bedrooms on the first floor. Such was the demand for houses that masons and carpenters featured prominently among the population enumerated locally in 1901.

Building Clubs, common in the growing communities in the South Wales Coalfield, helped augment the local housing stock. Members of these Clubs, many of whom were miners, made regular contributions and when the club had sufficient funds to build they did so and the house was allocated to the member successful in a club lottery. The process continued until all the members had been housed. In the short term they helped solve the housing problem and in the longer term they enabled working class men to become house-owners. It is difficult to find information about such Clubs in Bargoed and Gilfach but advertisements that appeared in *Western Mail* in the early 1890s shed some light on tenders for Gilfach Fargoed Fach Building Club houses.

As Bargoed developed as a service town as well as a railway and coal mining community, the area attracted middle class professionals, semi-professionals and business people and Bargoed and Gilfach became more well-to-do than some neighbouring communities. The housing stock reflected the varying social status of the residents. The better off among this middle class tended to live in Hillside Park, in large houses surrounded by fairly extensive gardens. Not only were there more and larger rooms than in the terraced houses in Bargoed and Gilfach, but these rooms were more likely to have decorations such as dado rails. Other middle class and professional people lived in streets like Park Crescent and Gwerthonor Road, in larger terraced or semi-detached houses, with bay windows as well as front gardens dividing the house from the pavement. These larger houses had three rooms (parlour, middle room and kitchen/scullery) downstairs and three larger bedrooms upstairs. It became increasingly common for local houses to have some form of ornamentation on the facades or roof, perhaps red or yellow brick around the doors and windows (the latter were often bay windows) or decoration on chimneystacks or roof ridges, although a few had more elaborate ornamentation.

There are a few houses in Bargoed and Gilfach dating from the early twentieth century that deserve special mention. Duffryn House (generally known locally as The Puzzle House) lies north of Bargoed and was built about 1908. Horace Davies, builder of such local properties as Bargoed Hall, Junction Hotel and The Emporium, built Oakland Hall, a large dwelling surrounded by extensive grounds. Many local people remember husband and wife, Alan and Eveline Withers, local solicitors living in Oakland Hall until the 1980s. It was demolished in April 1993, and before the end of the 1990s the site was developed for residential purposes.

Horace Davies built Bargoed Hall in 1907 for himself and much of the following information about it is taken from an article that appeared in *Western Mail* 16 May 1998. Local legend has it that he was known as *the silver king* because he always paid his employees in silver. However the widow of Dr. Trevor Lewis remembered a visit from an elderly lady who knew Bargoed Hall in her youth and she claimed it was because Horace Davies owned a silver Rolls-Royce which he kept in what they called the *motor* house. Bargoed Hall was a fine house with six bedrooms and, at that time, on the edge of a rapidly growing and prospering coal town. It is said that, one day in 1915, Dr. Thomas E. Richards knocked on the door and said he would like to buy it. Horace Davies agreed to sell it to him and build himself another fine house and that may have been Oakland Hall. Bargoed Hall became home to local doctors, first Dr. T. E. Richards, then his son, and after that, Dr. Trevor Lewis. On its flat roof Bargoed Hall had a summer house, accessed by its own staircase from within the house and surrounded by an ornate stone balustrade. This summer house has a pitched roof and its windows face in all directions to give fine views up and down the Rhymney Valley. Inside Bargoed Hall there is much stained glass including a leaded window depicting a knight's head in the drawing room and a rose patterned leaded window in the dining room while the stained glass in the main double doors pours colourful light into the hallway. The hall has a mosaic floor, panelled doors, a patterned cornice and attractively-worked architraving above the doors. There are lovely original fire-places: the fireplace in the lounge has carved mahogany pillars on either side and that in the dining-room is cast-iron in Adam-style. There is a glass veranda along the front and one side of the house and a large Edwardian conservatory on the other side. The gardens include a semi-circular lawn edged by flower borders, shrubs and mature trees and six high Victorian flower pots flank the steps up to the main entrance. There are two patios and a herb garden at the rear. This town property has its own driveway with cast-iron double gates, and there is parking space as well as the silver king's *motor house*, now a double garage with inspection pit.

There are two sizeable properties in Gilfach; Gwerthonor House and Springfield. In the 1890s H. P. Davies Phillips, a generous benefactor to local Anglicans, lived in Gwerthonor House. He allowed them to use a room in his home as a Sunday School and when that room proved too small for the growing numbers, he had an iron building, Gwerthonor Mission Room, put up on his land at the corner between Margaret Street and Gwerthonor Place. He left the house about 1896-1897 and, in 1901, 59 year old widow Ann Thomas headed a household of five in Gwerthonor House, comprising her two unmarried sons, 36 year old Lewis David, described as a gentleman and 29 year old William John, a physician and surgeon, a teenage daughter and a domestic servant. It is not clear how long the Thomas family lived there. By the 1920s, the Johnson family was there, as an oak altar rail (presented by Mr and Mrs Edward B. Johnson of Gwerthonor House in memory of a son and inscribed *To the glory of God and in memory of James Comport Johnson, born at Gwerthonor House, Gilfach, Sept 1921, died 14th August 1922: Lent 1926*) was dedicated at a service in St. Margaret's Church March 1926. Local Councillor, Moses Cadwgan Price, died at his home, Gwerthonor House, in June 1936. The Price family had moved to the area from Bedwellty parish about 1893-1895 and in 1901 they were enumerated at 8 Commercial Street, Gilfach. It is not clear when the Price family moved to Gwerthonor House, but it is likely that they remained there until the early 1970s when it passed to the present owners. The lease on Springfield, a large property near Lewis School Pengam and originally called Whitehall, started 31 October 1908, when it was jointly owned by Gelligaer Lectureship and Mrs A. Lewis. There does not seem to be an entry for the house in the 1911 census, although there is a property called Springfield (probably in Vere Street), and a 9 room property called Llys Aeron in which several servants were enumerated. Today Springfield is a small Residential Home.

The local council had not tackled the housing problem in the pre-World War I era and, especially as inward migration continued during the 1920s, there was a housing shortage in post World War I Bargoed and Gilfach. In September 1920 *Merthyr Express* carried a report on the charming and commodious architect-designed demonstration bungalow erected in Bargoed by local carpenter, builder and architect William Harris, who claimed it would solve some of the contemporary local housing problems. Situated in its own grounds with gardens at front and rear, it comprised a veranda leading to an inner hall that gave access to a large living room (15 feet square) with a bay added, three bedrooms (although one could serve as a sitting room), a scullery, bathroom and pantry. Built on stone foundations its walls and ceilings were panelled with fireproof material and the roof was fireproof. It was approved by the Ministry of Health as highly hygienic. At the time, G.U.D.C. was proposing to build about 900 houses in Bargoed at a cost of £1,000 - £1,200 per house, to be paid for by raising about £1million though housing bonds. William Harris claimed that fifty of his bungalows could be built quickly and sold to the council for £500 each. Not only would this provide an immediate part-solution to the area's contemporary housing problem at half the cost of the council's scheme but later G.U.D.C. would be able to sell these houses to the tenants (making repayments in instalments over a 15 to 20 year period).

Harris's design was not adopted when, in the later 1920s, Bargoed's residential area crept further up the mountainside as the area north and west of Moorland Road, McDonnell Road and Llancayo Street was developed for council housing while there was similar council housing development west of Gwerthonor Road in Gilfach. George Thompson noted that these council houses were *more modern than the terraced homes .... these had bathrooms and indoor toilets, innovations previously enjoyed only by the affluent.* There were lengthy debates in council meetings and committees on all matters relating to council housing. Councillor John Hill of Moorland Road died in 1923 and his obituary in the local press praised his moderate and sensible views and noted the respect he had earned for his constant fight to ensure tenants be charged reasonable rents for the new houses being erected in Bargoed.

It is clear that the problem of accommodation (particularly for unmarried male incomers) was one of the key problems in the growing communities in Bargoed and Gilfach in the first quarter of the twentieth century. Many miners' wives, already busy caring for their homes and families, took in lodgers, often work colleagues of their husbands or sons. The former woollen factory in north Bargoed was converted into a Lodging House and in June 1924 the local press reported on a fire that caused £8,000-£10,000 worth of damage when it completely destroyed *Factory Lodging House* and caused slight damage to the adjoining house, home of Benjamin Jarman, owner of the Lodging House. Lodger, Gilbert R. Williams told the press reporter that he was one of the first to see the blaze that started at the foot of the staircase in the *married quarters* from where it spread rapidly. Five Bargoed Police Constables arrived and then Bargoed Fire Brigade under Captain R. Williams, and, together with neighbours, they fought the fire and saved Benjamin Jarman's living quarters and furniture. The Lodging House usually accommodated 20-30 lodgers, but it is not clear how many were present at the time of the fire. Everyone present, including those who were in bed at the time, managed to escape in whatever clothes they were wearing at the time and no one was injured in the fire, although a dog, a cat and two kittens in the kitchen were burned to death.

In 1911 76 (70 males, including two boys, as well as five wives and one daughter) were enumerated in The Bargoed Metropole (Common Lodging

House) in Baldwin Street, Bargoed. It is not clear when the premises was built and opened. Anecdotal evidence has it that the building continued in use as a lodging house for several decades.

There was considerable economic and social distress in the country in the inter-war era but work opportunities locally meant that Bargoed and Gilfach still attracted many incomers in the 1920s. Some of these incomers came from older industrial communities especially in north Rhymney Valley and Cynon Valley. One such family was that of Shropshire-born Charles Owen who, with his wife, Emma, and their infant daughter, moved to live and work in Rhymney about 1902-1903. During the next two decades, Charles and Emma continued to live in Rhymney where they had a further ten children. With six sons and employment prospects looking grim in Rhymney, it is not surprising that the Owen family moved to Bargoed, where they lived, first in Baldwin Street, before moving to 10 Heolddu Drive. It is not clear when they moved house, and whether or not they were the first family to occupy the house on the new council housing estate.

The country generally faced a housing shortage in the post World War II era. Single-storeyed prefabricated houses, made in factories to be reassembled on site, were erected on what is now the Fairways housing development. Heolddu's *steel houses*, as they were generally known locally, were erected in the same era and are, with modernisation, still inhabited today.

By the 1960s there was very little space for further residential development in Bargoed and Gilfach. The only major development was that of the 1960s and 1970s when G.U.D.C. built the Gilfach Fargoed Estate, known locally as *The Site*, extending from west of Oakland Hall, Bargoed Grammar Technical School Playing Fields and Hillside Park to the edge of the moorland. Since then house-building has been generally confined to infilling (Marwyn Gardens and Fairways [where the post war prefabs had been]) and on sites formerly occupied by such properties as Oakland Hall, Union Jack Club in West Street and two schools (Higher Elementary in Park Crescent and Boys' School in Llancayo Street).

In the context of housing, several other developments in the second half of the twentieth century are worthy of note. Many local occupiers benefited from legislation allowing them to purchase the freehold of properties they had formerly held on leases (mainly from Pontypool estate) The relative prosperity of the 1960s and 1970s encouraged owner/occupiers (and sometimes landlords of tenanted properties also) to improve and modernise the houses. Sometimes this was simply converting a bedroom into a bathroom but it often involved changing the layout of the ground floor by knocking down a wall between the front and middle rooms and/or building a one or two-storied extension housing modern kitchen and bathroom.

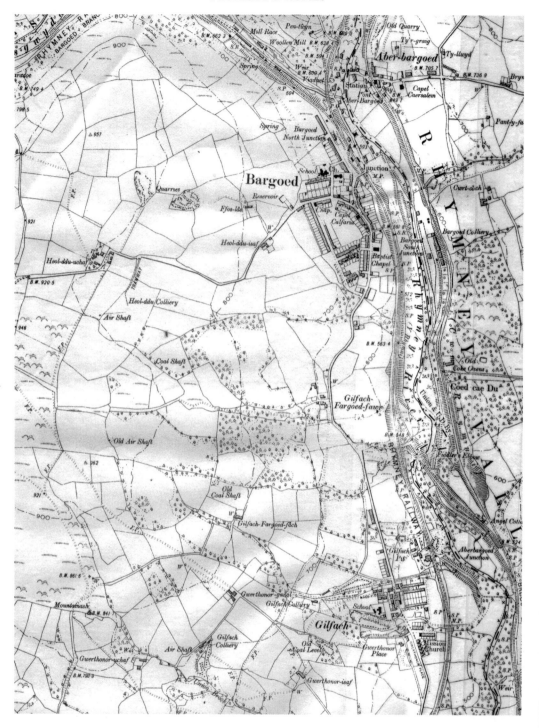

O.S. Map of Bargoed and Gilfach about 1900 (reduced from the 6 inch map).

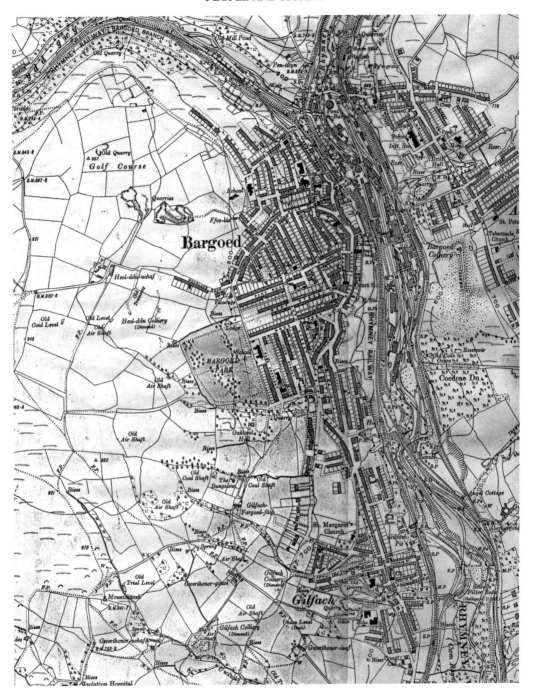

O.S. Map just over 20 years later (reduced from the 6 inch map).

CHAPTER 9
EVENTS 1900 ONWARDS

The beginning of the twentieth century

The Victorian era, with its revolutionary social and economic changes in the country in general, was drawing to a close, and the new century opened not only with the sinking of Bargoed Colliery but also with the South African War (1899-1902) in progress. Once Bargoed Colliery opened it was a magnet, drawing in thousands of people from other industrial communities in South Wales and elsewhere as well as from rural areas. The local area changed in the most revolutionary way as its rural environment gave way to a bustling urban community. Local newspapers shed considerable light on the new communities in Bargoed and Gilfach and their rapid growth with incomers from a wide variety of different backgrounds.

While the conflict in the southern hemisphere against the inhabitants of Transvaal and Orange Free State did not have the impact on the local area that other twentieth century conflicts had, it did not pass unnoticed. Some four months after the war started, John Davies of Groesfaen Farm had a *hearty send-off* from the crowds who accompanied him to Bargoed railway station to wish him and fellow members of Glamorgan Yeomanry success in the campaign, before a safe return. The headmaster of Bargoed Mixed School noted in the school log book that, on hearing the news of the British victory in 1902, they celebrated in the playground in April and with a holiday in June. Patriotic pride was on display in Bargoed again when, on Saturday 13 August 1904, Sergeant Edward Blayton was welcomed home by crowds at Bargoed Station after nearly five years in South Africa. He was carried shoulder-high and put on horseback. Then, he led the soldiers in uniform behind the Committee and Bargoed Brass Band, in a procession from the Station, via Hanbury Road, Greenfield Street (where his mother and step-father lived in Number 91) to the Pierhead before receiving a belated presentation of a watch inscribed *Presented to Private E. Blayton on his return from the Boer War, 1902*. (He had been promoted in the intervening period.) It seems that he settled in Bargoed later as his name appears in newspaper reports relating to local gymnastics as well as rugby.

People living in the new communities of Bargoed and Gilfach in the early twentieth century faced many difficulties especially as the infrastructure was inadequate for the rapidly developing urban communities. While water shortage was one key problem there were also occasions on which the area suffered from too much water especially because the drainage system was unable to cope with the water that flowed down from the mountain side during heavy rain storms. Although a letter in *Merthyr Express* in October 1900 drew attention to the inadequate drainage, and local inhabitants repeatedly appealed for improved drainage, the authorities did not act soon enough to save residents and business people from the difficulties arising from repeated flooding of roads and streets in the ensuing years. The owners of the Hanbury and McDonnell estates did little to deal with the surface water off their respective properties and the council did nothing to improve the drainage system. As a result, more than one hundred households and some business premises in Bargoed suffered when the 6 inch pipe failed to take the water pouring from the Heolddu mountainside after about an hour and a half of heavy rain on a Sunday evening in late October 1903. Not for the first time, the water flowed down Bargoed's main roads and streets, and, as the small traps near the houses were soon blocked, it had nowhere to go but flow through the houses. Homes in Greenfield Terrace, Elsie Road (later part of Greenfield Street), Francis Street, Bristol Terrace and Usk Street were among those badly affected as water, anything from 12 inches to 2 or 3 feet deep, flowed in through one door, through the ground floor before pouring out through the other door. Several business premises were also affected. At the same time, water pouring down Heolddu Road into High Street and around the Pierhead, was forceful enough to cut the road some 12 to 18 inches deep in several places, and deposit the road metalling from High Street on the road near the railway station.

Religious revival 1904-1905

The single-minded fervour of Evan Roberts and his associates, believing their church had lost its zeal and vision, was responsible for the religious revival in 1904-1905. In the course of their travels around Wales 25 year old Evan Roberts and his team of revivalists visited the local area. Years later local headmaster Walter Haydn Davies recalled how as a lad living in Bedlinog he had walked over the mountain to Capel Gwladys to hear Evan Roberts speak: *there were so many of us on Bargoed mountain that when the people in the front had sang the last verse, we in the back were still on the first!* In February 1905 *Merthyr Express* reported that *such was the enthusiasm to hear Mr Sydney Evans* (one of Evan Roberts' fellow revivalists) *that the crowd became so great it was impossible to move in Bethania Chapel, an overflowing will be held in the Calfaria Chapel*, and illustrated the impact of the revival by referring to the fact that Hanbury Road Baptist Chapel had 106 gains (97 by baptism and 9 had rejoined). The Vicar of the parish of Bargoed and Deri with Brithdir writing in the parish magazine, *Parish Messenger*, a century later, considered the medium and long-term impact of the Revival. He estimated that following the Revival there were about 3,500 worshippers in Bargoed (the total capacity of all the places of worship at the time). The impact continued into the second half of the twentieth century. In 1964 there were about 1,500 worshippers *and some of the more elderly still resonated with the stories of revival*. Social and economic changes locally and nationally may go some way to explain why there are substantially fewer regular Sunday worshippers a century after the Revival. However, successive issues of *Parish Messenger* testify to the depth of faith locally at the present time including opportunities for young people such as Heolddu C.U. (Christian Union) *a school lunchtime group for Christians and the curious.*

Tension and unrest 1910-1911

The beginning of the second decade of the twentieth century was one of rising tension and unrest in South Wales and beyond, and it became increasingly likely that police and/or army would be called upon to maintain law and order. Local miners, like those in Rhondda and Cynon Valleys, expressed concerns about minimum wage and interpretation of the 8 Hour Act, but, following the advice of their S.W.M.F. leaders, they made financial contributions to support striking colleagues while not taking strike action themselves. One of South Wales' most widely known events of that era, the Tonypandy Riots took place October 1910 and the Cambrian Colliery strike continued until the following August.

Local people, like those in the rest of the country, basked in a heatwave in the summer of 1911. After little rain during June and most of July the Rhymney Valley experienced freak weather conditions, a cyclone with shrieking wind that lifted an intense volume of dust high into the air followed by heavy rain and thunder in late July. At the same time, there was considerable patriotic fervour in the country in general with the Coronation of George V and Queen Mary in June 1911 and the Investiture of Edward, Prince of Wales (later King Edward VIII and Duke of Windsor) a few weeks later at Caernarvon Castle. Local schoolchildren celebrated the coronation during a week-long school holiday and, the following Tuesday, they made history when, on the invitation of the Managing Directors, they became the first local schoolchildren to see pictures of a Coronation in the town's Palace Cinema. At the same time, there were threats of war in the air as international events seemed to raise questions of patriotism and defence of the British Empire while Germany appeared to be deliberately provoking Britain and France by sending *Panther* to Agadir. On 21 July, in a speech at Mansion House, the Chancellor of Exchequer, David Lloyd George, made it clear he would not maintain peace at any price.

Summer 1911 saw strikes by the Seamen's Union and Merseyside Transport workers, continued bitterness among South Wales miners and the country's first ever rail strike. The local press had a gloomy view: *Merthyr Express* 19 August 1911 carried the headline *Seething discontent throughout the Country* and, the following week it compared contemporary anxieties, that a rail strike would bring famine and darkness, with the fears in the country at the time of the Spanish Armada. By mid August 1911, there was considerable uneasiness and tension locally especially as, prior to the opening of a new road link to Caerphilly in 1914, the communities of Bargoed and Gilfach were very dependent upon the railway. Local people were affected in a number of ways: housewives found that not only had milk deliveries ceased but also shops were running out of other fresh food commodities such as butter while workmen were stranded after work or unable to go to work. If the strike was prolonged, production at Bargoed Colliery would be affected and that would have a ripple effect on the income of all dependent upon the colliery.

On Friday 18 August, only four of the usual forty trains on the Rhymney Valley line ran, and there was considerable tension in the area around the railway stations all day. During the morning, about six hundred miners gathered around Aberbargoed Station (on Brecon-Merthyr line) as night shift workers tried to get home and day shift workers tried to get to work. When they realised why the train had not turned up, they moved en masse to Rhymney Railway station at Bargoed. There was vigilant picketing all day and when, the first passenger train arrived in charge of Company officials it was booed, but the railwaymen's union (Amalgamated Society of Railway Servants) was not willing for pickets to stop the train. During the evening, hundreds of miners and other sympathisers stood in gangs near the railway station but there was no trouble and the threatened looting of shops suspected of raising prices because of the strike did not occur. As no trains got through to Bargoed on the following day, *Pay Saturday* as it was called in *Bargoed Journal*, Powell Duffryn Steam Coal Company arranged for wages to be brought by road from Cardiff, but many miners had to walk some miles to collect their pay. News of settlement of the strike arrived in Bargoed on Sunday; it was approved by a mass meeting and greeted with great relief. The 4 p.m. train was the first to run through Bargoed.

The trouble in and around Bargoed and Gilfach on 23 –25 August 1911 when a number of shops were attacked by a stone-throwing crowd and the army was called in to assist police restore order is discussed in detail in Chapter 13 Retail. The first reference to Bargoed in the national press (*Daily Telegraph* 28 August 1911) was under the heading *Mob Rule in South Wales* and included the comment that *There are, however, signs that the forces of law and order have got the upper hand even in Bargoed.*

The disturbances in Bargoed and Gilfach were on small scale compared with those in some other parts of the country in 1910-1911. They were at a time when the country was going through a particularly difficult period: the *Agadir* crisis was still unresolved, waves of strikes and accompanying violence caused alarm, the army had been in the South Wales mining community for nearly a year, and there was bitterness at the failure of the Cambrian strike. The trouble in Bargoed and Gilfach was the product of the unusual and highly charged atmosphere prevailing during August 1911, exacerbated by the atypical weather of an unusually hot and dry summer.

Bargoed Labour Exchange

Prior to World War I the government set up a network of Labour Exchanges across the country and as they were linked by telephone they helped both employers seeking employees and workpeople seeking employment. The local Board of Trade Labour Exchange at 9 Upper High Street with resident manager H. W. Gardiner was formally opened 3 March 1911 by Sir T. Marchant Williams. By 1914 it had moved to Trafalgar Square and the Resident Manager was F. W. J. Angus of Hillside Park. Kelly's Directory of 1926 gives its address as 2 The Square (probably the same premises) when E. E. Lloyd was in charge.

World War I and its aftermath

Having enjoyed fine weather on August Bank Holiday, Monday 3 August 1914, most local people, along with those in the rest of the country, were surprised when war was declared the next day. Perhaps it should be noted that, at that time, the Bank Holiday was on the first and not the last Monday of August. While it is doubtful that the majority of them had any real understanding of the reasons for the war and the government's diplomatic policies, it is certain that they had no insight into the nature of the war that was about to bring traumatic change to the lives of so many people. For most people, with only the turn of the century South African War as a point of reference, war was remote with little or no impact on everyday life and work in communities like Bargoed and Gilfach. In spite of this, the majority of people supported Britain's entry into World War I. Many people, influenced by the Welsh nonconformist and pacifist tradition, had grown up with the idea that the army was a refuge for the destitute and desperate or for those who were unemployable in any other occupation. In spite of that and within a short time, some of them went to fight for a cause they barely understood, in places with names they often found unpronounceable. In November 1914, *Merthyr Express* reported that for three months D. M. Yorwerth worked ten hour days enrolling 1,315 recruits at Bargoed Labour Exchange, a process that involved him signing each recruit's papers in nine separate places. How relieved he must have been when that was reduced to seven signatures in November!

The large number of volunteers in the war's initial weeks and months suggested enthusiasm for the war: some may have been driven by economic necessity or patriotic feeling, while others were attracted by the chance of adventure beyond the confines of daily drudgery in a restricting society. Whatever their motives, most hoped and believed that the conflict may be over by Christmas. In the country in general there were some 16,500 conscientious objectors of whom about 1,000 were Welsh, including Morgan Jones, later to become the local M.P..

Many men who worked in the local coal industry remained in the area during the war, but some men from other walks of life left to serve their country either as volunteers at the beginning of the war or because they were conscripted later. School log books shed light on the way in which local schools were affected, and Gilfach School was not alone when the headmaster recorded that by December 1915 William Jones and Lewis Isaac were the school's only male teachers as the others had enrolled under Lord Derby's Scheme.

Wartime local newspapers, littered with reports of local service personnel reported wounded, missing and killed, give some insight into the anxious war years at home in Bargoed and Gilfach. The war was only a few weeks old when, 29 September 1914, 33 year old George Moyle became the first local man to fall in action. The issue of 17 February 1917 reported that Bargoed man Sergeant F. Gowing of Welsh Regiment was wounded while 40 year old Sergeant George Cornelius Knight of 25th Battalion Royal Fusiliers had died 4

January 1917 in Das es Salaam (Tanzania) to be mourned by his family at Wordsley, Gwerthonor Place. In September 1919 *Merthyr Express* reported on Bombadier Michael Weston of 33 Heolddu Road who was Bargoed's first military medallist in the war and on Pioneer James Harris who was serving in the desert. At the same time, there were reports on tribunals including that relating to Bargoed teacher Willie Jones.

Like the rest of the country, Bargoed and Gilfach took time to adjust to everyday life in peace time after the Armistice 11 November 1918. For some months the newspapers remained slim and some of the reports referred to men returning home safely and welcome home celebrations but these should be balanced with the sadness of the family and friends of those who did not return. The two sides were evident in the Sullivan household at 14 Wood Street: the welcome return of son Private James Sullivan in early 1919, did not allay the family's sorrow that his brother John had been killed in action in France in October 1918. The post-war community was ready to honour local heroes such as Sergeant J. C. Curtis of Bargoed whose bravery was acknowledged locally at an event in Lenox Club in May 1919. The citation for his award, Distinguished Conduct Medal (D.C.M.) appeared in Supplement to the London Gazette, 2 December 1919: *15216 Sjt. J. C. Curtis, 2nd Bn., S. W. Bord. (Bargoed) At Kruiseecke, on 29th September, 1918, for most conspicuous gallantry and determination. He led forward eight men to occupy a pill-box in advance of the line. The pill-box was found to be strongly held, and heavy machine-gun fire was opened. He led his men on, finally rushing the post and killing several of the enemy, the remainder running away. Still under heavy machine-gun fire he then went out and dressed three of his men who had been hit during the operation. He set a splendid example of courage and dash.* War service had disrupted the education of some local men as in the case of Captain Thomas Davies Evans, eldest child of headmaster J. Sylvan Evans, who had left his university studies in Aberystwyth for war service and returned afterwards to graduate B.A. in 1919.

There were numerous events and organisations centred on local ex-servicemen in the post World War I years. A Bargoed branch of Cardiff City Battalion Comrades, formed in 1919, held its first annual banquet at Hanbury Hotel in December. In the same month members of the National Federation of Discharged Soldiers met at Royal Hotel Assembly Rooms to hear speeches by various people including Mr T. Havard, Manager of Bargoed Labour Exchange.

Peace Day 19 July 1919

Although the Armistice was signed 11 November 1918, peace negotiations continued until the Treaty of Versailles was signed at the end of June. Britain's Peace Committee met in May 1919 and arranged that the country would celebrate Peace Day on Saturday 19 July 1919. Powell Duffryn Steam Coal Company made a grant of £450 for a children's tea in Rhymney Valley, and Peace celebrations were arranged. On Peace Sunday the various religious denominations of Bargoed and Gilfach united in procession to Bargoed Park.

The procession, led by the Salvation Army Band, and comprising the clergy and congregations of all local places of worship, made its way to Bargoed Park where they assembled before English and Welsh platforms. The English platform was presided over by Rev. Harri Edwards of Hanbury Road Baptist and the Welsh platform by County Councillor Rev. D. Leyshon Evans of Calfaria. Both platforms were supported by clergy and leading members of other local places of worship. The singing, accompanied by the Salvation Army Band, was conducted by men from the Primitive Methodist and Calfaria congregations. A memorial service for Bargoed men and boys who had lost their lives in the war was held in New Hall on a Sunday in mid September 1919. Neighbouring Aberbargoed provided Christmas entertainment for children who had lost their fathers in the war, and local people were disappointed that the same was not done on the Glamorganshire side of the river.

War Memorial

Over the decades Bargoed War Memorial has occupied three different sites in the town. First, it was in Trafalgar Square before it was moved to Bargoed Park, and, finally, to the position it currently occupies near St. Gwladys' Church in north Bargoed. Discussion about a local memorial to those who had not returned from the war started in Spring 1919 and a Memorial Committee was formed with Dr. McCrea as its first chairman. An Easter Monday Carnival and Sports in Bargoed Park was arranged to raise money for the Memorial Fund. G. W. Davies of The Emporium promised to contribute one hundred guineas (£105) if five others would give £100 each. Fund raising continued and *Merthyr Express* 23 August 1919 reported two such events: a Sunday evening concert by Apollo Glee Party and a memorial Eisteddfod in Bargoed Park on Monday.

By June Bargoed and Gilfach War Memorial Fund Committee was active and in discussion with G.U.D.C. regarding a memorial at Bargoed's Trafalgar Square. The idea of a Memorial Hall was discussed but rejected in June, and by July they were discussing a twenty foot high War Memorial at Trafalgar Square that would bear the names of those who gave their lives. Discussion continued about the nature of the War Memorial and whether or not it should occupy the whole or only part of Trafalgar Square. By early 1923, progress was such that they hoped the War Memorial at Bargoed's Trafalgar Square would be completed for an unveiling ceremony in February. Before the end of February, the War Memorial was erected and G.U.D.C. considering replacing an unsightly public convenience at the bottom of Trafalgar Square with underground lavatories. The names of local men who lost their lives in the Great War were inscribed on many War Memorials up and down the country but, in the early 1920s, Bargoed and Gilfach War Memorial Committee's decision to opt for a comprehensive inscription rather than the names of individuals met with the approval of the local press.

Bargoed's Trafalgar Square had been the scene of only two significant events before 1923: the first was the visit of a tank, part of the appeal for finance to continue the war to a successful end, and the second was the Peace

Celebration when C.C. Rev. D. Leyshon Evans had delivered an inspiring address. A crowd, estimated to be in excess of 10,000, congregated there on Thursday 31 May 1923 to witness the unveiling of a memorial recording their gratitude to those who had fallen in the fight for liberty and justice.

The Aberdeen grey granite War Memorial, the work of architect Idris Leyshon of Pengam, Surveyor to Bedwas and Machen U.D.C. and sculptors Messrs Clements and Sons of Gilfach, had cost £850. Its base was axe worked and the eighteen foot high column on a flight of forest stone steps was surmounted by the figure of a fully equipped British soldier with arms at the reverse. There was a wall of dressed stone with forest coping around the column and the rest of Trafalgar Square was tarmacadam. The unveiling ceremony was presided over by Ben Edmunds of Gilfach, then chairman of the Memorial Committee. The procession, headed by Salvation Army Band (conducted by Bandmaster H. Bosanko), comprising British Legion, D Company Mons Regiment, Bargoed Red Cross Contingent, Girl Guides, Church Lads' Brigade and Gelligaer Fire Brigade, made its way through the town's main streets before assembling at the War Memorial. Although Father O'Donovan, the Roman Catholic priest, was listed as being present at the ceremony he did not take part in the religious service.

Lieutenant J. O. Tyler unveiled the War Memorial and spoke both as a representative of the Pontypool Park Estate (the late John Capel Hanbury had formerly owned the land and had given the Square to Bargoed) and as an ex-servicemen. The first wreath was laid by 78 year old Mrs Trotman, who had lost two sons in the war. After that, wreaths were laid by British Legion, Red Cross Brigade, Dr. Richards, Officers D Company Mons Regiment, Lenox Conservative Club, Police of F Division, local press, local banks, New Club, R.A.O.B., East Glamorgan Golf Club, shops (Emporium and Bon Marche) and Housing Clubs. Then Councillor A. S. Williams, J.P., Chairman G.U.D.C. formally received the keys of the War Memorial on behalf of the Council and the proceedings concluded with the singing of the national anthem. The Council had agreed it should be open at certain times every day to enable families to place wreaths on the anniversary of the death of a relative.

Unfortunately, the event did not pass without criticism: at the G.U.D.C. meeting on the following Tuesday evening, Councillor W. Hammond of Tirphil complained that council members as a body and as individuals had not received invitations to the ceremony even though G.U.D.C. had been generous to the Memorial Committee. In response, Gus Jones of Bargoed informed that the Memorial Committee had not issued invitations but left it to anyone to attend as they wished while Chairman A. S. Williams said there was a misunderstanding as a fortnight earlier the secretary was ill and the letter mislaid.

It is perhaps a sad reflection on human nature in general that, only weeks later, the local press reported on anti-social behaviour at the War Memorial. The decision to inform the police and local press that flowers laid by relatives and friends on 28 July were stolen the following day was taken in the hope that it would lead to identifying those responsible. It was considered unlikely that children were the culprits as the War Memorial was surrounded by high railings but if it was, parents were reminded that it was their duty to punish them for this insult to the memory of those who had made the supreme sacrifice.

The local press carried reports on the annual Services of Remembrance. There was some measure of discord about the 1926 local Remembrance Day Service when, as nonconformist ministers had not received invitations, responsibility for the 1926 service fell on the vicar of St. Gwladys, Rev. T. O. Thomas, and Adjutant Whitter of the Salvation Army, who together conducted proceedings in a dignified and impressive manner. At least two local clergy, Father O'Donovan of St. Peter's and Rev. R. D. Griffiths of Gilfach Presbyterian, had served in the forces in World War I: the latter explained his absence in 1926 by pointing out that the time of the service clashed with his commitment to his Sunday School, an important institution in his eyes. In October 1927 *Merthyr Express* recalled the spate of letters concerning the absence of local nonconformist ministers at the 1926 service, and sought opinions prior to arrangements being finalised for the 1927 service. It concluded that, as local clergy and laity favoured a Remembrance Service of communal not sectional nature, the most popular and efficient solution would be for Rev. D. L. Jenkins, the senior minister in the locality, to arrange a preliminary meeting of local clergy to decide the form of service and select those best suited to take part. The following week *Merthyr Express* reported that, in consequence of its article, Rev. D. L. Jenkins had convened a meeting on Thursday when local clergymen agreed to prepare a representative communal ceremony. Several weeks later *Merthyr Express* reported on Remembrance Sunday, 6 November 1927, in Bargoed. The morning parade left the Workmen's Institute at 10.30 a.m. for St. Gwladys' Church where Rev. T. Thomas conducted a Special Service. In the afternoon, the members of the Parade, having assembled at the Emporium at 3 p.m., marched to the War Memorial at Trafalgar Square for a public service conducted by Rev. D. L. Jenkins assisted by other ministers and clergy. The Salvation Army Band, under Mr Bosanko, and Bargoed Town Band, under Mr W. Smith, accompanied the parade and Major J. R. N. Kirkwood was in command of the ex-servicemen.

The War Memorial was moved from Trafalgar Square to Bargoed Park in the 1950s where it remained until re-located in St. Gwaldys' Gardens and re-dedicated at a service on 5 May 2002. Since it has occupied this north Bargoed site plaques bearing the names of some local people who made the ultimate sacrifice in the Great War and later wars have been placed on the sides of the column of the War Memorial. A *Garden of Peace*, constructed on the site formerly occupied by Gilfach Presbyterian Chapel, opened St. David's Day 1996. The *Presbyterian* name stone, formerly above the doors of the original chapel, is incorporated in the wall and the plaque on the clock bears the inscription: *This garden is dedicated to the people of this community who have contributed to the Peace. May they be remembered for their efforts today and forever by the grateful residents of the village of Gilfach. Cysegrwyd yr ardd i bobl y gyuned hon a gyfrannodd tuag at heddwch. Cofir am eu hymdrechion heddiw ac am byth gan drigolion diolchgar pentref Gilfach.*

The inter-war years

The experiences of the first two decades of the twentieth century had helped the population of the new communities in Bargoed and Gilfach develop a sense of community and belonging. The people, predominantly incomers to the area, had come together through work and work-related organisations, places of worship and education as well as leisure activities (especially those associated with sport and music) and a vibrant and dynamic society had emerged thriving in tandem with the local coal industry. While the local communities were predominantly working class there was an influential middle class comprising ministers of religion, doctors, teachers, solicitors, accountants and business people and with their wives, they were well-known and highly respected for their contributions to the community especially in the places of worship and local societies. This community feeling was to prove important in helping the local community through the difficult inter-war years (1918-1939).

Perhaps, one of the most meaningful comments on how the local area changed in the first quarter of the twentieth century was the view of William Griffiths, who, although born in Breconshire in the mid 1870s, had been brought up in Church Street, Bargoed and educated at the local school under headmaster Thomas Myddfai Jones. He left the area for South Africa in the late 1890s and, in 1923, leaving his wife and five children in South Africa, he paid a six month long visit to the area where he had grown up. He told the *Merthyr Express* reporter that he noticed wonderful changes as Bargoed had grown from an insignificant little place to a busy bustling town, although he could not help remarking on the amount of gambling that was taking place locally.

The growing coal communities in Bargoed and Gilfach did not change as much as those in some other areas because of the war. Some young men left to join the forces but, demands for steam coal ensured there was work locally. Disputes between Coalowners and the miners' union had continued in the early years of the conflict as, with food prices rising and, it was believed, increased profits for the Coalowners, the Fed made regular bids for wage increases for miners. In 1916, in an attempt to ensure strikes would not endanger supply of coal to the British Navy, the Government had taken control of South Wales Coalfield (and of the other coalfields in the following year). Although the Royal Commission investigating future management and reorganisation of the coal industry reported in favour of nationalization in 1919, the Government handed the industry back to Coalowners' control in 1921 and the optimism of the immediate post war months faded. It no longer seemed *the land fit for heroes*: many miners felt let down especially as their unions, forced to negotiate district agreements within the Coalfield, faced South Wales Coalowners who, arguing that wages had increased too much under Government control since 1916, demanded miners accept lower wages or they would refuse to employ them. Not surprisingly, this ushered in renewed industrial unrest. During the 1921 lock-out, the Bargoed and Gilfach communities, in common with those in other parts of the Coalfield, supported local miners. Bargoed Canteen Committee, the treasurer of which was D. J. Evans manager of the local branch of N.P. Bank, provided 111,064 meals. After the three-months lock-out from April to June 1921 the miners returned to work on the Coalowners' terms.

Although production in the South Wales Coalfield increased by 1923 it did not reach the level of 1913, the year of peak production, and it was followed by years of steady decline with pit closures and fall in the number of working miners. Large companies like Powell Duffryn, expanding as they took over smaller coal companies, attributed the decline to the high cost of production and, in 1925, asked their miners to accept wage cuts as well as an extra hour on their working day. Another Royal Commission was set up to investigate the running of the industry and in 1926 reported that reorganisation would probably be followed by wage cuts for miners. The Miners' Union fought the Coalowners immediate wage cuts with the slogan *Not an hour on the day. Not a penny off the pay* and on 30 April 1926 British Coalfields came to a stop when miners who refused to accept local owners' terms were locked-out of work. Not surprisingly, in his 1926 May Day Speech at Bargoed's New Hall, Morgan Jones M.P. focussed on the coal crisis, urging miners to stand together in the big struggle facing them. T. D. Matthews, who presided over the meeting, expressed the feelings of many local people when he said that the country's 1¼ million miners, surviving on the bare necessities, depended on the support of 15½ million other British workers in their fight against the Coalowners' impossible demands. The TUC had promised to call all trade unionists out on strike if the miners were forced to accept the terms and the General Strike started on 3 May but nine days later the TUC called it off claiming the government wanted to negotiate a settlement. The miners felt angry and betrayed and continued alone until starvation drove them back to work defeated. When local miners went to collect their pay on Friday 7 May they found that 10 shillings had been deducted in respect of their tools. On the Saturday local men were among those who descended the various pits to bring out their tools so they could claim the amount deducted.

Local newspapers, consisting of fewer pages than normal during the months of strike, reported on the response in the Bargoed and Gilfach communities and by the second weekend in May 1926 it was clear that local people were united in their determination to ensure help for those in need, something that continued for the duration of the stoppage. The communities were little more than two decades old but the sense of purpose and unity was strong: business and professional people as well as local organisations of all sorts arranged activities to relieve both the suffering and tedium of those rendered idle by the industrial stoppage.

One of the first activities was on Sunday 9 May when Bargoed Salvation Army Band under conductor H. Bosanko entertained hundreds at Trafalgar

Square for about one hour after services at the various places of worship. By the middle of May, a variety of activities including concerts by local choirs, whist drives, dances and eisteddfodau was arranged to keep people active and interested as well as to raise money. From early May, proprietor Mr Withers made New Hall available free of charge for the local Canteen Committee's regular fund-raising boxing tournaments. It is not clear how much money these tournaments raised in total but as the local press reported that £23 12s 6d was raised at one event during October it was likely to have been a significant amount. Road races and sports were organised. On a Thursday in June, a crowd, estimated to be in excess of 2,000, forgot their problems for a while as they enjoyed fine weather and sports at Heolddu Ground. For some the highlight of the day came when they could indulge in a little betting on the Galloway race. By the Autumn the local Boot Fund was established and at least three fund-raising Dog Shows were held in the yard of Hanbury Arms.

Over the decades, local people have enjoyed their carnivals and those reported in *Merthyr Express* in June 1926 would have been no exception. Thousands lined the streets as Bargoed carnival procession make its way from St. Gwladys' Church Hall to Gwerthonor Hotel, through Gilfach's Thomas Street, Railway Terrace and Llewellyn Street and then to McDonnell Football Field where the judging took place. There were some imaginative costumes but none more so than the entry depicting a Coalowner leading a miner by a long chain attached to the miner's neck, a meaningful comment on the contemporary situation. It is not clear how much money this carnival raised, but a week later £11 17s was collected at that organised by Gilfach Workmen's Club. Then the procession started from the New Bridge and made its way via Park Place, Cardiff Road, Ruth Street to McDonnell Hotel and on through Heolddu Road, High Street and Hanbury Road.

Not only did local choirs perform fund-raising concerts within the Bargoed and Gilfach communities but some of them also travelled further afield. Bargoed Male Voice Choir under conductor W. Deri Bowen was appointed by the National Committee for Relief of Distress in London to make a fund-raising tour of various towns. It gave a concert in Bargoed's Workmen's Institute on a Monday evening in June before setting off on the tour the following day. The choir was accompanied by W. H. Thomas, Secretary of the Local Entertainment Committee. Later Bargoed Apollo Glee Party, under conductor Mr W. Williams and accompanied by County Councillor W. H. Hopkins, chair of Bargoed Canteen Committee, toured the Bournemouth area. There the choir performed in concerts associated with meetings where County Councillor Hopkins speaking on behalf of the striking miners, earned considerable praise in the Bournemouth press. By mid September they had raised £40 for Bargoed's Canteen Fund, £32 4s 6d for Cardiff Central Fund and £110 for Lady Slesser's Fund, as well as funding for boots and clothes.

It was reported in the local press that the Canteen Committee was up and operating from the start of the stoppage. Providing three meals a day for necessitous children, it was in receipt of substantial contributions from local tradesmen and professional people and organising fund raising events such as a road race. As the chairman County Councillor W. H. Hopkins spent some months with the fund raising choir in the Bournemouth area much of the work locally fell to vice chairman Fred Curry, secretary W. T. Lloyd and treasurer T. D. Matthews.

T. D. Evans B.A., auditor of the accounts of the Canteen Committee, presented his report on the accounts to a public meeting in May 1927. He noted that (taking into account a sum in the bank) the difference between income and expenditure was £68 13s 11d *due from the Treasurer*. After discussion on that sum it was decided to adjourn to enable the committee to investigate. The result of the investigation by the officers and auditor together with a sub-committee of six (Harold Bennett, William Redwood, Charles Roberts, Rodway Jones, Steve Walters and Ben Higman) was presented at the adjourned meeting on Saturday 20 August in the hall of Bargoed Workmen's Institute. The recommendation that £4 8s 1½d be deducted from the sum *due from Treasurer* was adopted. The Treasurer denied liability for the £64 5s 10d still to be accounted for and there was some conflict between him and the Secretary concerning the execution of their duties. It developed into a rowdy meeting that had to be adjourned as the business was not concluded before 7 pm when the hall was booked for a dance. The meeting resumed the following week with continued rowdyism and bad feeling. After much discussion it was resolved to consult solicitor T. W. E. Phillips of Tredegar regarding their course of action for recovery of the money. His report was presented at a meeting in November 1927 when the small attendance suggested that interest in the canteen inquiry had abated and there was none of the rowdy scenes that had characterised the previous meetings. In his letter of 17 October 1927, T. W. E. Phillips wrote that following his discussions with the deputation and his study of the auditor's report he thought *the committee would be ill advised to institute criminal proceedings* and that *as the auditor points out, the committee cannot be considered altogether free from blame*. No further action was taken.

Labour politician and trade unionist, Rt. Hon. J. R. Clynes, addressing a well attended Sunday meeting in Bargoed on mid November 1927, spoke of his pleasure at the increasing support for the Labour Party during the years of industrial strife and referred to Morgan Jones M.P. as one of the most promising young men in the Labour movement. He noted Labour's successes in local elections in the South Wales Coalfield and the miners' stand for their rights before expressing his hope that miners could move forward by appealing to their employers through reason rather than by suffering. When Moses C. Price, local Labour politician and chairman of the meeting, opened the meeting to questions the contemporary union conflict soon became evident and the meeting rapidly deteriorated into disorder as Bryn Roberts, Rhymney Valley Miners' Agent and Secretary, honed in on Clynes's reference to the Trade Union movement as the backbone of Socialism and accused the National Union of

General and Municipal Workers (of which Clynes was President) of poaching members from among the 10,000 plus miners in the Rhymney Valley district of S.W.M.F.. Chairman Price, trying to deflect the issue, claimed it was a matter for TUC but Roberts persisted and the large audience cheered and clapped in his support. Price tried to regain order and dismiss Roberts from the meeting but as Roberts shouted *Mr Clynes's speech was nothing but a hypocritical declaration, his union was a scab union*, the meeting was completely out of control. Clynes denied the allegations but Roberts was insistent. Eventually, Clynes said *In view of the impertinence of my friend who has described my speech as hypocritical, I decline to answer any questions from him*. Some semblance of order was restored and questions on other matter were taken before the meeting closed. Clynes and his union responded a few days later by stating that any charge of poaching was untrue and any complaint should be taken up through the TUC.

By the early 1930s life became increasingly difficult for many local people as not only was the local economy threatened as the coal industry faced an uncertain future but also the rise of Fascist regimes in Europe filled many with concern. Unemployment affected many families and youth unemployment was a matter of particular concern. Bargoed Juvenile Unemployment Centre opened in 1928 to train young people who were on the registers of the Labour Exchange but contemporary problems militated against its success. Further details about this Centre which eventually closed in 1937 appear in *Gelligaer* Volume XVII 2009. In 1931, when there were 9,461 persons registered as unemployed in Bargoed Labour Exchange, almost every court report in the local press included cases involving people stealing coal and/or men failing to make payments to deserted families.

There were numerous local efforts to help people in need in the 1930s. Rev. Leon Atkins of the Wesleyan Methodist Church tried to tackle the problem of unemployed youths in the local area. They were not eligible for unemployment benefit and many of them had considered pitching a tent on Bargoed Mountain, or going *on the tramp* to relieve pressure at home. He not only provided the lads with meals but was planning to provide sleeping accommodation in Wood Street's Lesser Hall while the Workers Fellowship, also based in the Wesleyan Hall, set up a youth football club, which would play on the McDonnell ground, where Bargoed AFC had played in previous years. The Children's Boot Fund was another local initiative. In 1932 committees of the unemployed organised fund-raising sports days for boys, girls and adults to pay for boots that would be distributed to the children of the means-tested deserving poor in time for the start of the new school year. Today children of some local councillors of that era still remember the supplies of boots in their home ready for their fathers to distribute to local children in need. With the contemporary depression and unemployment in mind, Bargoed Bowls Club organized a special singles bowls tournament limited to unemployed and retired members that resulted in a play-off between Ivor Davies of Church Street and Dai Davies of Park Crescent with

Ivor Davies winning the prize, a blazer donated by Harry Roberts. In another similar event George Hare defeated W. Pugh to win a pair of shoes.

The contemporary local press carried advertisements for items that the majority of local people could not afford. A collier's weekly wage was £2.9.6 and if he was on the dole he got £1.7.3. In 1933, H. Samuel of High Street Cardiff had a *Sensational New Offer* - a Gents Chromium Wristwatch with luminous figures and hands at just 8/6d. A loaf of bread cost 6d so a cheap watch cost 17 times more than a loaf. At about the same time a Merthyr cycle shop advertised a Raleigh Popular bicycle at a reduced price of £4.19.6 (about two weeks wages for a working miner).

Local people heard about international events, such as the spectacular and tragic accident to the airship R101 with no survivors, on the wireless set in home or through cinema newsreels. This event was marked by two minutes silence in memory of the victims prior to Bargoed RFC's game against Abertysswg on the McDonnell ground. Even the 1932 Summer Olympics in sunny L.A suffered as a result of the Depression. Few local people would have considered attending but, on a global scale, the cost of tickets and travel had deterred people from attending until big-name film stars offered to entertain the crowds as part of the attraction.

As the coal industry had a constant affect on the lives of local people it is not surprising that from time to time local people were credited with thoughts and inventions that could improve the lot of miners and their communities. In June 1923 *Merthyr Express* carried a detailed report on the Safety Sustaining Gear for mine cages invented and patented by E. R. Evans of Nythfa, Lower Wood Street that, it was claimed, would prevent disastrous damage in pit shafts and inclines as well as save lives. In 1927, following publication of his article *A Solution to the Coal Problem* Alfred Morgan M.E. of Devonia, Bargoed became a member of the Royal Economic Society. Alfred Morgan had studied in the L.E.A. Social Science and Economics class in Bargoed, one of the most successful such classes in the county year after year in the 1920s. Sometimes the coal industry created local panic as on one tea time in August 1933 when local residents rushed out of their homes fearing that an earthquake had hit the area. However, their fears were allayed when a Mining Engineer assured them it was underground 'shot firing' and therefore nothing for them to worry about.

The local newspapers of the period show that, in spite of the social and economic problems, Bargoed and Gilfach had an active social, sporting, cultural (including music) life, centred on places of worship, the Workmen's Institute and clubs and public houses. The cinema provided escapism and a glimpse of glamour while the wireless in the home not only kept increasing numbers of families up-to-date with the news and but also entertained them. Bargoed, especially because of The Emporium and the Cafe Ballroom, was a magnet that attracted shoppers and dancers from a wide area.

Spectacular fire at Bargoed Colliery's By-Product Plant 1926.

Probably, one of the largest and most spectacular fires fought by the Bargoed Section of G.U.D.C. Fire Brigade under Chief Officer T. H. Mather and Second Officer, P. J. Moody was at Bargoed Colliery's By-Product Plant in 1926. There had been a similarly spectacular fire at the Plant in 1920 but that had not caused extensive damage. The cause of 1926 fire, starting about 9 p.m. on a Thursday evening in early June and resulting in over £20,000 worth of damage, was unknown, although it may have started when naphthalene ignited. The stiff wind blew the flames northwards so that, within minutes, the distillery and other by-product plants were aflame. However, fears that it would spread to the gasometers and benzol plant were not realised. Thousands of people soon lined the hillsides to watch as flames soared high in the air for some hours and huge volumes of smoke formed a canopy over the area. The Police, including Inspector Herbert Evans of Bargoed and Sergeants Friend and Roper of Monmouthshire Constabulary, were in attendance on both sides of the valley, to keep the crowds back. They were forced to close all avenues of approach and hold up traffic around the north end of Bargoed Colliery. Occupants of Junction Hotel had to evacuate the premises and Bargoed Market (housed in what was originally the town's Skating Rink) seemed to be in danger. Anecdotal evidence has it that some Aberbargoed families removed themselves to the homes of relatives some distance away and it is possible that some Bargoed and Gilfach people did the same. Powell Duffryn Steam Coal Company officials arrived at the scene and superintended the operations. Bargoed Section G.U.D.C. Fire Brigade, Powell Duffryn Collieries Brigade and, on the Monmouthshire side of the river, Aberbargoed Fire Brigade, attended the fire, but, as they could do nothing to extinguish the flames, they concentrated on preventing its spread. Their hoses directed volumes of water into the middle of the flames with very little effect and the Tar Plant was absolutely burnt out before the flames died down. Eventually, the fire was brought under control about 11.30 p.m., and, soon after midnight, the final flames were extinguished, leaving only the charred remains of a splendid By-Products Plant, one of the world's finest of its kind. The local St. John Ambulance Corps was in attendance during the operation but, although the fire caused such damage to the Plant, they only had to deal with one injury, a facial injury sustained by a fireman.

Coronation of George VI in 1937

Extant school log books and the local press shed light on the ways in which Royal events, from Queen Victoria's birthday in 1900 onwards were celebrated locally. Bargoed and Gilfach schoolchildren enjoyed a week's holiday to celebrate the coronation of Edward VIII in June 1902, although the coronation, scheduled for 26 June, did not take place until 9 August because, after being diagnosed with appendicitis on 24 June, the King underwent life-saving surgery. They celebrated the coronation of George V and the investiture of his son as Prince of Wales in 1911 and, a year later, the Managers of the Gelligaer Schools granted a day's holiday to allow school staff and pupils the chance to see the

King and Queen when they visited South Wales to lay the foundation stone of the National Museum in Cardiff and to visit the colliery districts. The headmaster of the Higher Elementary School noted in the School Log Book that some of his pupils, particularly those from Fochriw, absented themselves the following day to go to see the King at Merthyr Tydfil or Dowlais.

During the 1920s and 1930s school children enjoyed a day's holiday to mark the weddings of three sons of George V (the future King George VI in 1923, Duke of Kent in 1934 and Duke of Gloucester in 1935) and George V's Silver Jubilee in 1935. Given the economic climate of the time, many local children enjoyed the tea that sometimes marked such celebrations. Local schools closed on the day of the funeral of George V in January 1936, and in November of the same year, there was an afternoon closure when Edward VIII passed through Aberbargoed at 3 p.m., on a visit to economically-depressed South Wales just weeks before his abdication.

However, all the earlier celebrations pale into insignificance when compared with the way in which the local community celebrated George VI's coronation in 1937. Bargoed and District Coronation Celebrations Committee, led by chairman A. L. Pritchard, vice chairman W. R. Baker (President Gelligaer NUT), treasurer H. Marson, and joint secretaries, W. Glyn Williams (of Lower Wood Street, Principal of Bargoed Juvenile Unemployment Centre) and W. Madley (of The Roath, Bargoed), and representing all organisations in the community, organised a four-day programme that ensured local people of all ages and interests could celebrate the 1937 Coronation in fine style. The residents played their part as flags and bunting – Union Jacks and Red Dragons – were displayed at most homes and *Duw Gadwo'r Brenin* hung at the entrance to most streets. A Special Souvenir Programme of Bargoed and District Coronation Celebrations, including photographs of the Royal Family, was on sale for 2d at various outlets including local newsagents and cinemas and the programme was printed in *Merthyr Express* 8 May 1937. The Chamber of Trade as a body as well as its individual members devoted energy and financial assistance to make the celebrations a success and *Merthyr Express* May 8 1937 aimed to dispel rumours that surplus funds from the local Coronation celebrations would subsidise Chamber of Trade purposes by emphasising that it had been publicly stated that all surplus funds would pass to local charities.

Due to the unavoidable absence of Albert Thomas, J.P., Miners' Agent, Dr. S. B. Turner presided over the official opening ceremony followed by a Community Singing Festival in New Hall on the evening of Sunday 9 May when Bargoed Salvation Army Band (conducted by Mr Bosanko) provided the music and P.D. Male Voice (conductor George A. James, Mus. Bac.) performed special items. On Monday and Tuesday, local school children, enjoying a week's holiday from school, were treated to free matinee performances at the local cinemas. Mrs Withers (wife of cinema owner Jackson Withers) and Mrs Cam (wife of the cinema manager) received presentations, tokens of thanks for these performances. On Monday they received boxes of chocolates from teachers, while, on Tuesday, pupils presented them with bouquets. That to Mrs Withers was presented by Eira M. Sallis, an 11 year old pupil of South Bargoed Girls' School (daughter of Mr and Mrs David Sallis of Park Crescent, a few weeks later, she headed the County Scholarship list for Gelligaer Urban District with 289/300) while Nancy Pickwick of Gilfach School presented the bouquet to Mrs Cam. After the cinema on Monday afternoon, school pupils assembled at Bargoed Girls', South Bargoed Boys' and Gilfach Boys' Schools, where teachers distributed Glamorgan County Council's commemorative Coronation Mugs decorated with Glamorgan Coat of Arms and portraits of the King and Queen, while the District Coronation Celebrations Committee ensured that all children not on a School Register also received mugs. On Tuesday afternoon, there were teas laid on in Bargoed and Gilfach Schools for all children over three. There were also organised teas for children in some localities, and one such event saw over eighty children from Heolddu Green, Heolddu Grove and Moorland Road sit down to tea before receiving 1d and a bag of sweets each.

On Monday evening, all local clergy with the exception of Rev. R. D. Edwards of Gilfach Presbyterian who had been called away to London, attended a United Service of Praise in Central Hall. The theme of the sermon by Rev. C. J. Griffith, vicar of St. Gwladys, was that the world needed people to change their outlook, motives, ambitions and spirit. Special Coronation Service leaflets were distributed to the congregation and the collection was donated to the Empire Cancer Campaign.

For an admission fee of half a crown, local residents, and those from other villages up and down the valley, had the chance to spend hours indulging their passion for dancing as the eight-strong Collegian Dance Band played in Cafe Ballroom from 9 p.m. on Tuesday. The spot prizes and novelty dances were directed by local men, G.L. Hirst, former rugby international, T. D. Evans, clerk to Gelligaer Governors, and J. S. Barrett, Manager of Bargoed Employment Exchange. Dancers did not have to worry about returning home as buses were arranged to convey them up and down the valley after the music stopped at 2 a.m.

Unemployed, old and blind residents were not forgotten. On Monday, at 5.15 p.m., Bargoed Labour Exchange presented all on the *live* register with coins: those over eighteen received half a crown while those under eighteen had a shilling. On Tuesday afternoon over 500 Old Age Pensioners and blind people enjoyed tea and musical entertainment at the Workmen's Hall, and half crowns were distributed to all OAPs.

It was expected that on Wednesday, Coronation Day, many people would listen to the Coronation Service from Westminster Abbey on their wireless sets at home. However, for the benefit of those unable to listen-in at home, the Committee arranged that, from 11 a.m., it would be relayed to those who went to Central Hall in Wood Street.

About 3 p.m., Bargoed's Grand Coronation Carnival Procession, headed by *Britannia* (Ivy Knibbs) and her attendants on a beautifully decorated lorry, left St. Gwladys' Church and proceeded via Hanbury Road, Gilfach Street, Park Place, Thomas Street, Railway Street and Llewellyn Street before returning along Park Place, Cardiff Road, Ruth Street and Upper Wood Street to arrive at Bargoed Park at about 4.30. The public had free admission to the Park where they could enjoy what the Committee described as an *Old Welsh Fair*. As well as witnessing the arrival of the carnival procession and watching the judging of the carnival competitions (for which cash prizes exceeded £25), they were entertained by Gilfach Page Boys Jazz Band display, schoolboys performing physical exercises, tug-of-war matches (an exhibition by a police team captained by Police Constable W. Knight and a juvenile competition won by Bargoed North Boys' School) and a comic football match in which *Borstal College* triumphed over *Old Dartmoorians* to win a cup presented by Police Inspector W. H. Williams. From 7.20 to 8 p.m., over 5,000 people listened to the relay (arranged by F. A. Cam, General Manager of New Hall) of the speeches of His Majesty King George VI and Empire representatives, before

continuing with their celebrations in Bargoed Park. Cambrian Glee Party performed some items and Bargoed Town Band (conductor W. H. Smith) provided music, there was dancing, a treasure hunt, pillow fights and a confetti battle. By about 10.30 p.m., those with energy for any more activity, progressed to the Mountain Gate, while others returned home, probably stopping to admire the town's floodlit buildings, such as Police Station, Workmen's Institute and Bargoed Secondary School. After a Royal Salute of 21 Maroon shells and a rocket display, Mrs Turner, wife of Dr. S. B. Turner, ignited a beacon, over thirty feet in height and erected by members of the British Legion overlooking the golf links. The *Merthyr Express* reporter estimated that nearly 10,000 people watched it burn and several thousand of them engaged in a confetti battle in the area lit by the blazing beacon. Spectators probably drifted home in the early hours of Thursday

This photograph, courtesy of Dr. David Williams, shows the 1937 coronation beacon.

morning but, it was reported, the beacon continued to burn for a week.

It is not clear if there were any Coronation babies born between midnight 11 May and midnight 12 May to receive the promised National Savings Certificate.

On a pleasant summer day about two months later, pupils from Bargoed, South Bargoed and Gilfach Schools, travelled (at the expense of the Local Coronation Committee) on the 8 a.m. train to Cardiff General Station, and then walked to Cardiff Arms Park, where the King and Queen were inspecting Juvenile Organisations.

World War II and its aftermath

Many of today's older residents remember life in Bargoed and Gilfach during World War II, a significant watershed in the history of the country in general. They recall family and friends who left the area to serve their country and especially those who made the ultimate sacrifice. As in World War I, the coal industry was important to the war effort and the number of men employed in the industry locally was swelled as Bevin Boys (young men conscripted to work in the coal industry) were drafted into the area. Women, who had not worked before the war were employed in munitions factories or other war-related work, while wives and mothers often had to struggle to provide for husband, children, other family members and lodgers at a time of rationing and shortages. Wartime families often enjoyed quality time together as well as plenty of exercise and fresh air while tending their allotment, the produce of which supplemented the family pantry. Mothers and older daughters were eager to enrol at local *Make-do-and-mend* classes in an attempt to make the best use of their existing wardrobe to clothe the family.

Life of the whole community was affected by the blackout and the air raids made life on the Home Front more dangerous than in previous wars. One of the most evocative images of life on the Home Front is that of children from Britain's larger urban and port communities being evacuated to less vulnerable areas like Bargoed and Gilfach. The following extracts from Gilfach School log book in 1940 and 1941 convey something of life in a local school during wartime. On 8 March 1940 the headteacher logged *School assembled to pay tribute and listen to A.B. Stanley Davies, a member of the crew of H.M.S. Exeter present at the battle of the River Plate, He was a past pupil of this school and was given a rousing welcome.* Before the end of that month an entry read *11 a.m. A.R.P. Test in sending children home in five minutes* and in May 1940 *School recalled on Wireless instruction owing to the International situation.* Evacuees arrived: in September 1940 the entry was *Sherness Junior Technical School – two classrooms given up to same,* in the following February the entry read *Evacuation. Admitted 26 Birmingham children. Merged into Glamorgan classes* while in June *admitted 10 Cardiff children* in the same way.

One highlight of the war years was in December 1941 when King George V and Queen Elizabeth visited Bargoed Settlement. The King signed the Settlement's Visitors' Book, and, it is said, that while he was in Bargoed he

This photograph (courtesy of Betty Williams) shows the King and Queen outside Bargoed Settlement.

heard the news of the sinking of *Prince of Wales* Battleship by the Japanese off Singapore. There was no school closure on that day but some schools sought permission to take their pupils to see the royals

The wartime privations did not cease with the peace and rationing continued into the 1950s. During the early years after World War II the post-war gloom was lifted by royal events and the 1951 Festival of Britain. Schoolchildren enjoyed a day's holiday for the wedding of Princess Elizabeth in November 1947 and a half holiday to mark the Silver Wedding of the King and Queen in April 1948. The headteacher of Bargoed Infants School recorded in the Log Book that, following the death of George VI in February 1952, they had been able to borrow a wireless and so, for the first time, local pupils and staff, teaching and non-teaching, assembled in the School Hall to listen to the Proclamation of Queen Elizabeth II from London and Cardiff before singing *God Save The Queen*. Just over a week later, they assembled again, to listen to the broadcast of the late King George VI's funeral service from Windsor Chapel and Westminster Hall, and observe two minutes' silence as a tribute to him. There was a certain measure of optimism at the time of the Coronation in June 1953 as people welcomed a new Elizabethan age. For many local schoolchildren, as well as the population in general, the coronation of Queen Elizabeth II was the first occasion when they saw television (perhaps at the one house in the street where there was a television) on that rather grey Coronation day in June 1953, although it was another decade or so before most families had a television in their own home. Local schools were closed on 9 July 1953 when Queen Elizabeth visited South Wales as part of a post-Coronation tour. Some local people still recall with pleasure their trip by train to the 1951 Festival of Britain.

The pattern of school holidays to celebrate royal events has continued during the reign of Elizabeth ll, including school closures to mark the birth of a Royal Prince in February 1960, the marriage of the Queen's sister, Princess Margaret, in May 1960 and of her daughter, Princess Anne, later Princess Royal, in November 1973, while some of the events, such as the marriage of Prince Charles and Lady Diana Spencer and that of their son, Prince William, as well as the wedding of Zara Phillips, also a grandchild of Queen Elizabeth ll, took place during regular school holidays.

Fire at New Hall

Many local people have vivid memories of what they were doing when they heard about one of the most memorable fires in Bargoed and Gilfach on 6 February 1958 at the New Hall Cinema and Nos. 1, 2, 3 and 4 High Street. The fire had started in the cinema some hours before it was discovered at 4.54 a.m. by a railway booking clerk, who immediately contacted the Fire Service. The cinema, a lofty building, partly of three and four floors, and constructed of brick and stone, had a slated roof supported by steel trusses. By the time the Fire Brigade arrived, the auditorium and roof were well alight and, a few minutes later, the roof and north and east walls sheared at the point where the original walls joined with the new construction built to increase its height, and the whole of the upper section collapsed on to the adjoining shop property (Nos. 1, 2, 3 and 4 High Street) making the work of the firefighters extremely hazardous. They had to call in reinforcements to deal with the fire and to prevent its spread to other commercial premises. The fire was eventually brought under control through the use of six pumping appliances and two turntable ladders. As the building was extensively damaged, it was impossible to ascertain the fire's cause. There were no serious casualties, but many local people mourned the loss of a popular social venue.

Third quarter of the twentieth century

Before World War II cinema and radio had increased local people's knowledge and understanding and in the 1950s and 1960s television and private family car helped to broaden their horizons further. The following two extracts describe the contrast between the difficulties of the inter-war era and the comparative prosperity of the local area in the post-war era.

Headmaster Walter Haydn Davies was acutely aware of how local society had changed from his youth in the early twentieth century to his retirement in 1967 as illustrated by his final entry in his school's log book:

In May 1953, I, Walter Haydn Davies MA, who was then Economics and Careers Master at the Boys' Grammar School, Barry, was appointed Headmaster of the Bargod Grammar School, which had then about three hundred pupils on roll, and I commenced duties in September of that year. It says much for the facilities afforded by the Glamorgan Education Authority, that I, who had been attending Evening Classes at the school in the early twenties (while employed in the Bedlinog Collieries) could acquire qualifications to enable me to become headmaster of this school.

I might state that there were many problems facing a headmaster in the post war years which had not existed previously. In the thirties, competition for teaching posts in schools of grammar school status, was keen and there were many applicants, but in the fifties, because of the dearth of qualified teachers, suitably qualified staff were difficult to retain. Such teaching posts had become plentiful and applicants could select their schools. Thus many staff changes became common, and after a short period of apprenticeship teachers moved elsewhere. The attitude of the majority of pupils and parents to the sacrifices involved in being afforded a prolonged education was also undergoing a change. Life had become easier, and social security had become the key-note, and in place of the years of endurance in the thirties, we had the never-had-it-so-good years of the fifties. Other social and cultural changes were having their effects. The radio and then television were to militate against home study, and the inherent cultural expression fostered by church and chapel were no longer so marked, and moral standards allied to social values were to be mainly generated from within the school community itself.

Elwyn Andrews, like Walter Haydn Davies, had grown up in a mining community. He was a schoolboy in 1926 and he could recall that shoes were distributed to miners' children during that strike and after he left school his father encouraged him to study in the library in the local Workmen's Institute. By the 1970s he was Miners' Union Secretary and is quoted in *Gruvarbetare i Wales*, a photographic and narrative interpretation on the eve of the closure of Bargoed Colliery:

When I came back to Bargoed after the War (World War II), *life was almost the same. There was no TV or Bingo and no one had a car. We used the Workmen's Institute in Bargoed to meet and talk. We had discussions and choirs and rugby teams, and I remember the Library in Bargoed Workmen's Institute. There was always a lot of people; if they didn't read, they played cards or talked to their friends but since the number of miners at Bargoed Colliery has decreased and people now have cars and TV there is not so much demand for the library. The windows are broken and books have been taken away. As soon as young people had money, they developed a taste for cinemas, dancing etc.. The manager of the Bargoed Colliery decided to try to save the Institute with Bingo twice a week. It worked for a while but then a big Bingo firm bought a cinema in Bargoed and started Bingo every night. It was the same in the Workmen's Institute in Aberbargoed.*

Of the 1972 strike Elwyn Andrews said:

I used to go to the Workmen's Institute where the strike committee met at 8.00 in the morning. People stood and waited to help with the pickets and they gave coal to the sick and needy.

One step down in the Institute, we had a small kitchen where the miners who came back from picket duty could get some tea and sandwiches. The men sat in the Institute and talked and waited for men, played billiards and held meetings. Nobody could afford to go to the pub for a pint. It was worse for bachelors. They had no wives to claim Social Security and they could claim nothing for themselves.

Bargoed and Gilfach after the closure of Bargoed Colliery

Sadly, after Bargoed Colliery closed in 1977 Bargoed and Gilfach declined rapidly and became broken-down and rather depressed places. Bargoed, formerly the premier shopping town in the area, declined as a shopping centre and closure of The Emporium in 1979 marked the end of an era. By then most local people in employment worked outside the area and many people did their shopping and spent their leisure time in places other than Bargoed and Gilfach.

It is unlikely that the local area can regain the life and vigour it had in the heyday of the local coal industry but the by-pass and town centre improvements, the result of some two decades of efforts by various individuals and groups, will undoubtedly contribute towards a better future.

Trafalgar Square. Showing Tip. Bargoed.

This photograph (courtesy of Reflective Images, Port Talbot) shows the War Memorial in Trafalgar Square and Bargoed Colliery Tip in the background.

CHAPTER 10
WORSHIP AND RELIGION

Introduction

Generations of people who lived west of the river Rhymney worshipped in their parish church, St. Catwg's Gelligaer (or in the Chapel of Ease, Capel y Brithdir) while their neighbours on the east side of the river worshipped in St. Sannan, the parish church of Bedwellty. As members of the Roman Catholic church they heard services in Latin, performed by their local priest. Most local people probably did not understood much about the changes in religion in England and Wales under Henry VIII and his children, but like most other people in Wales at the time they accepted them with indifference. They continued to attend the solid stone parish church to hear services by the same parish priest and most local people would have understood as little of the new English Bible and English language service as they had of the Roman Catholic Latin service. The translation of the Bible into Welsh in 1588 opened the way for greater understanding of the Scriptures.

Many local people would not have known much, and would probably have understood even less, about the complex religious, political, constitutional, social and economic conflicts of the seventeenth century but from time-to-time they were aware of the harsh realities of the Civil War era. From the seventeenth century onwards some people, failing to find spiritual satisfaction within the contemporary Established Church, were prepared to risk the penalties and seek their salvation with the emerging nonconformist sects, meeting in secret before they formed settled congregations and built their chapels. As the local population expanded, many new places of worship were erected in Bargoed and Gilfach during the last quarter of the nineteenth century and the first two decades of the twentieth century. Some of those are still places of worship but the most recent phase in the spiritual development of the locality has been characterised by closure and change of use of some places of worship erected about a century ago

Roman Catholic

For some 1000 years prior to Henry VIII's Protestant Reformation the Roman Catholic Church satisfied local spiritual needs and there may have been some pro-Catholic sympathisers locally in the following three centuries. Bargoed and Gilfach developed rapidly in the later nineteenth and early twentieth centuries and some of the incomers had their roots in Catholic communities in other parts of UK or further afield. Eager to practice their faith, it is likely that Catholics from Bargoed and Gilfach were among those worshipping in the corrugated iron shed in Brithdir (just a mile or so up the Rhymney Valley) that housed the first local Catholic church in 1903. In concert with the rapid growth of population, the increasing size of the Catholic congregation in Bargoed and Gilfach was such that they soon needed a place of worship within their own community.

There are probably not many Roman Catholics in the country who worship in a building that started life as a nonconformist place of worship, but Bargoed and Gilfach Catholics have done so since 1916 when local Congregationalists disposed of their Usk Road place of worship on moving to Trinity, Cardiff Road. The new Catholic church, dedicated to St. Peter (on the Graig) and consecrated by Most Rev. James Bilsbarrow, the first Archbishop of Cardiff, was intended to be a temporary place of worship for local Catholics. In both the early 1930s and early 1970s they tried to find a more accessible site but there was nothing appropriate available and so local Catholics remained in Usk Road.

Parishioners worshipped in its chapel-like environment for some years until, in 1933-1934 the parish priest Fr. Mahoney was instrumental in moving the altar centrepiece to a newly-extended sanctuary at the east end of the building and the sacristies to the Usk Road end of the building, and a pulpit, the gift of Dowlais parishioners, was installed. In the early 1970s, as the fabric of the church was in need of repair and internal changes were required to cater for the liturgical changes brought by Vatican ll, the building was renovated by enlarging the sanctuary with the altar moved forward to a more central position and new sacristies, and the facilities were enhanced, before it was rededicated by Archbishop John Murphy in April 1976. Further refurbishment followed in 2001.

The Usk Road church has never had an attached presbytery. The first presbytery, Penrhos, a large house in Hillside Park, was sold in the mid twentieth century and another Hillside Park property replaced it until the diocese purchased 46/48 Park Place as a presbytery and parish centre. When, in 1999, 46/48 Park Place needed renovation beyond that affordable by the parish, a smaller property, 25 Capel Street, became presbytery and parish centre, which in turn was disposed of in 2009.

The roll of incumbents of St. Peter's, listed in an article in *Gelligaer* XlV 2004, shows a considerable through-flow in consequence of the Church's policy of not allowing priests to be too settled in one place. While they have all made worthy contributions to parishioners and the community in general it would not be invidious to mention a few. Fr. O'Donovan (1920-1929) influenced the local council in much that it did at a crucial time in local development and he was highly respected by the wider community. Fr. Jim Boyle (1967-1981) was the instigator of the local Ecumenical Group of Clergy and initiated the concept of the Credit Union in Bargoed.

In common with other local places of worship, parish life flourished in the inter-war years: there was a thriving Sunday School while teenagers and adults enjoyed not only the spiritual life of the parish but its social activities as well.

From the mid 1930s to 1963 the strength of the parish was such that it could retain a curate to assist the parish priest. Over the decades St. Peter's has had the local area's most cosmopolitan congregation with parishioners from all parts of the UK and beyond. In *Gelliga*er XlV (2004), parishioner, Terry McCarthy, mentions the Italian immigrants of the early twentieth century, the Eastern Europeans of the post World War II years and more recently, some from the Far East, all of whom have enhanced the parish. In the final paragraph he writes *Like many upper Valley institutions St. Peter's is affected by the general decline in and aging of the population. However the spirit is still alive and it continues to provide its Catholic congregation with both its spiritual and social needs. ..... St. Peter's as a church and community has made a significant impact on the social landscape.* In 2008 as a consequence of a growing shortage of priests and declining congregations the Archdiocese decided that St. Peter's should share its Parish Priest with St. Thomas', Abercynon. Furthermore, 25 Capel Street, was considered to be in poorer condition than that in Abercynon, thus the Parish Priest moved out of Bargoed Parish and the house in Capel Street was sold. The decline also meant that on a Sunday there was only one Mass in St. Peter's and at major Feasts such as Christmas and Easter, services had to be shared; one year in Bargoed, the next year in Abercynon. Following the untimely death of Fr. Matus, the title of Parish Priest disappeared, replaced by a Priest-in-Charge, but at least they retained a regular Priest they could call their own.

Anglican

From the sixteenth century to the late nineteenth century most local Anglicans worshipped at Capel y Brithdir or in the parish church of St. Catwg.

St. Gwladys' Church was a chapel of ease to the parish church at Gelligaer, built and opened for worship in 1876 on a site given by the joint owners of the former Llancaiach estate. The parish history, *In the steps of St. Gwladys, A History of the Parish of Bargoed with Brithdir*, (1959) by Kathleen Lewis not only lists the subscribers who made the building possible but also provides considerable information on the subsequent history of the church to the mid twentieth century. When it was built, the new church occupied a central and prominent position in the growing community and was clearly visible from all directions. It was consecrated by the Lord Bishop of Llandaff on Tuesday of Easter Week 1876 and dedicated to St. Gwladys. In 1876, the chancel and sanctuary were of stone but the nave was a small temporary corrugated iron structure and that was replaced by a stone nave in 1893. Over the decades St. Gwladys' Church has been adorned by gifts testifying to the devotion and generosity of its members. While space does not permit all these to be listed, the stained glass east window given by shopkeeper D. S. Jones in memory of his wife in 1901 serves as one example.

The new parish of Bargoed with Deri and Brithdir was created in 1904 in response to the rapid growth of the local community following the sinking of Bargoed Colliery. The parish boundaries were redrawn in 1916 when Deri became part of the parish of Fochriw (a parish created in 1907) where it remained until the 1970s when the present parish of Bargoed and Deri with Brithdir was created.

This drawing of The Vicarage, Bargoed appeared in a pre World War I town directory. It was built in 1908 on land adjoining Bargoed Park. It no longer belongs to the church and today the incumbent lives in a smaller, more modern vicarage. In 1953 the church purchased a house in Moorland Road for the curate but that was sold in 1955 and a larger one in Hillside Park was purchased.

Bargoed Church Hall has occupied a site adjacent to the church since 1910. The plot was given by the owner and Fos Las Cottage, reportedly a one storeyed cottage with thatched roof and cobble stones outside, was demolished. Mrs Hughes, wife of Bishop of Llandaff laid the foundation stone in June 1910. Over the years it has been used by a wide range of different church groups including Mothers' Union, youth groups and operatic and sewing groups. It has also been used by outside bodies such as local schools and strike-time canteens. During World War II it became the local Food Control Office and was not returned for church use until April 1951. Most recently the Church Hall has been the temporary home of Bargoed Library.

St. Gwladys' parish magazine was first published in January 1906 but discontinued in wartime due to shortage of paper and difficulties of printing and publishing. It was reintroduced in January 1957 with the first issue of *Parish Messenger* and that has continued as a monthly publication to the present day.

The local press sheds considerable light on the spiritual and social life of St. Gwladys' Church especially prior to World War II. Rev. Thomas Richards, the first vicar, was well-known for writing beautiful hymns and early in January 1920 it was reported that some of these were sung at the Christmas services in the church. A few months later he left the parish and by July the parishioners were welcoming Rev. Trevor Owen Thomas as Bargoed's first vicar of the newly disestablished church.

St. Margaret's Church, Gilfach is part of the present day parish of Gelligaer. Our knowledge of the early history of the Anglican cause in Gilfach owes much to the work of Mr G. Trigg, an ardent church worker in early twentieth century Gilfach. His account of developments from the 1890s to the Bazaar held 23 and 24 October 1912 appeared in the bazaar programme and was reproduced in the local press at the time. As the expanding coal industry attracted more and more incomers, Gelligaer parish church and the new church in Bargoed, were unable to satisfy the spiritual needs of the rapidly growing industrial population in the area. At first, H. P. Davies Phillips allowed them to use a room in his home, Gwerthonor House, as a Sunday School. When that room proved too small for the growing numbers, he had a wooden building able to seat about one hundred people, put up on his land at the corner between Margaret Street and Gwerthonor Place, and the Bishop of Llandaff opened it in July 1894. It was known as Gwerthonor Mission Room and local laymen conducted morning and evening services there, and, before they left the district about 1896-1897, Mr Phillips played the organ while his wife conducted the choir. Men such as George Makepeace, Thomas Myddfai Jones (of Bargoed School) and James Coe (of Hanbury Road, died 1903) ensured the church flourished until 1906 when Mr H. James was appointed the first curate-in-charge. By then, as the Mission Room was inadequate for the still-growing community and they built a new iron church (known locally as the *tin* church) and Venerable Archdeacon Edmundes of Llandaff opened it in June 1906. The Mission Room was known as Gwerthonor as it was built on Gwerthonor land. The new Church, often known as Gilfach Church because it was on the land of Gilfach Fargoed, may have been called St. Margaret's after the old Church on Margaret Street.

The Anglican cause flourished in Gilfach due to the energy and enthusiasm of the curate-in-charge and his wife as well as the co-operation of church workers. By the time Mr G. Trigg was writing his history in 1912, St. Margaret's Church had a Surpliced Choir, a new organ, a Ladies' Guild; the Sunday School had grown to some 400 scholars, and the number of communicants had reached 150. In 1910, Mr James, having accepted the living of New Tredegar, left Gilfach and laymen carried on the work for five months before Rev. T. Llewellyn Evans served as Curate-in-charge until ill-health forced him to leave for the south of England.

Canon Thomas Jesse Jones, Rector of Gelligaer from 1890 to his death in 1930, was instrumental in ensuring that Gilfach Anglicans had the opportunity to worship in their community. He had supported Gwerthonor Mission Church and, in 1903, he launched an appeal for funds to build the *tin* church, St. Margaret's in Gilfach. Before his death in 1930, Canon Jones had prepared plans for a new church in Gilfach, the foundation stone of which was laid in May 1933. By 1933 Canon John Owen Williams (Rector of Gelligaer for about twenty years from 1931) had overseen the completion of this work with a new red brick church leaving the *tin* church to be used for the Sunday school and as a Church Hall. It was demolished in September 1988 since when the site has been developed for residential purposes. In *The History of St. Margaret's Church* in 1983, Reginald Lacey wrote that at one time the little wooden church was relocated and the three churches (the wooden church, the *tin* church and the present church) stood alongside each other.

Local nonconformists

Some people may have been influenced by, or worshipped with, local nonconformists, while others brought their nonconformist ideas with them from other areas of Wales and England. The nonconformist chapels that emerged in

Bargoed and Gilfach were more than just places of worship – they were centres of cultural activities in which people of all ages, but especially the young, were heavily involved. Some of the chapels had their origins in the last quarter of the nineteenth century but there was a real flurry of chapel building in the first decade of the twentieth century due to the rapid population growth and the 1904-1905 religious revival.

Baptist

Local people may have been among the Baptists from Gelligaer and neighbouring parishes who worshipped in secret in isolated farmhouses and mountain spots before Hengoed Baptist Chapel was erected in 1710. Later they may also have worshipped in Craig Fargoed, which opened as Arminian Baptist in 1750. By the 1830s some local Baptists were meeting in private houses in Pontaberbargoed, and Caersalem, a Welsh Baptist chapel, was built on the Bedwellty side of the river in 1839. It was rebuilt and extended in the following decades to accommodate the growing congregation that included worshippers from the expanding community on the Gelligaer side of the valley.

John Llewellyn (Inspector Rhymney Railway Company and a member of Caersalem) was instrumental in trying to meet the needs of English Baptists who wanted to worship in their own language in the expanding community. At first the English Baptists met in the homes of local Baptists such as Somerset-born John Knight (of Bargoed Gas Works) until in 1896 they decided to form a church and start a Sunday School in the Assembly Room of Plasnewydd Hotel. The church was officially constituted in November 1896 with the first administration of Baptism in December in an open air baptistery in front of the houses in Factory Road. It was accepted into the Monmouthshire Baptist Association at its Annual Meeting the following May. Immediately the members started a Building Fund and prepared to erect their own place of worship in Bargoed. Having agreed with the Hanbury Estate a 99 year lease of a site on Hanbury Road facing Capel Street (freehold of which was acquired 1924), they appointed trustees and plans were prepared for a substantial building with a Schoolroom in the basement. There is no photograph of the Schoolroom, opened April 1899, but an artist's impression was included in *60 years of Witness* a filmstrip made to mark the Diamond Jubilee of the local cause in 1956.

The first pastor of the church, Rev. Harri Edwards, inducted in April 1902, served the Bargoed congregation to 1921. He did much to enhance the spiritual and social life of his congregation with weekly prayer meetings as well as activities for the young. He also worked hard to guide and enrich the life of the community at large and, in common with other contemporary nonconformist clergy he was involved with local education as a member of both Gelligaer School Managers and the Board of Governors of the local secondary schools.

The Hanbury Road congregation grew because of the increased local population and the effects of the 1904-1905 religious revival and so they decided to build their chapel above the existing Schoolroom. While this work was being done they worshipped in a temporary wood building (that could seat 600) at the south end of Hanbury Road (on a site now awaiting redevelopment following the demolition of Bargoed Library). Sadly John Llewellyn died before the foundation stones of Hanbury Road Baptist Church were laid 2 April 1906, and so William Eynon M.E. laid one in his memory, while the other was laid by Rev. Harri Edwards on behalf of the various organisations in the church. The new place of worship opened 30 August 1906 with seating for 1000 people. Since then the building has been modified: gates and railings have been installed on the Hanbury Road frontage, the pulpit lowered, pipe organ installed (1933) and lighting and heating enhanced. At the time of writing the building is about to reopen as a place of worship and community facility following a major refurbishment: the Baptist congregation will worship in the basement while the ground floor and gallery will house the library and community hub.

While the recent refurbishment has been financed with the aid of outside bodies, the congregation's efforts were responsible for funding the original building. They secured loans both from members and from the Baptist Union Building Fund, and organised a variety of fund raising activities. By 1941 they had paid off the loans and celebrated with several days of preaching services and a children's service before H. J. Morgan, treasurer of 36 years, burned a pile of discharged notes, invoices, bonds, etc. in front of the assembled gathering at a social event. The Sunday School scholars were given commemorative book marks.

Over the years, Hanbury Road Baptist Church has received some well-known visitors including Sandy Macpherson (celebrated organist) in the early 1950s, and, in the mid twentieth century, several services were broadcast on the wireless (radio). Missionary Gladys Aylward has visited the church as Hanbury Road Baptist congregation, its Sunday School and Sisterhood have been in the forefront of supporting the missionary work of the Baptist Union and from time to time it has hosted exhibitions of missionary work such as that of November 1954.

The progress of Hanbury Road English Baptist Sunday School has been similar to that in other local places of worship. It started with thirty scholars and expanded to reach a peak of over four hundred scholars before it went into decline in the second half of the twentieth century. One of the highlights of the church calendar was the annual Sunday School Anniversary while the Nativity Plays were also popular. In 1952 Hanbury Road Baptist Sunday School was awarded the Shield for outstanding results in the Baptist Union of Wales and Monmouthshire Scripture Examination. The list of successful candidates is too long to reproduce but Margaret Pauline Luther deserves mention as, after gaining 96 marks in the examination, she won the Lower Senior Baptist Union Prize. By 1980, Hanbury Road Baptist Sunday School had declined to only seventy scholars and in his history of the cause 1896-1980, Alwyn Davies wrote *A decline in attendance has been noticeable since 1960, due mainly to the increase in the car influence and the television and an apathy with the parents for their children to attend* while the formerly annual Sunday School outings to the seaside (usually Barry Island) had lost their appeal as most children were taken on frequent seaside trips and they preferred the winter visits to pantomime in Cardiff's New Theatre.

Like most other local places of worship Hanbury Road Baptists had mid week activities for the young people. In 1904 Rev. Harri Edwards had been instrumental in the formation of a branch of the Young People's Society of Endeavour, a new evangelical movement, to help bridge the gap between Sunday School and the church. It not only helped young people gain knowledge, understanding and confidence but also prepared them for full adult membership and inspired some like Garnet Powell and Thomas J. Hamer to enter the ministry. At one time the local branch had Junior, Intermediate and Senior sections, all well-organised with officers and committee. Members attended weekly meetings and sent delegates to regional and national events, and they held an annual Christian Endeavour Sunday service in the church. The Band of Hope, aiming to encourage the young in total abstinence from alcohol, met weekly. Although the Hanbury Road Scout Troop started in 1927 with Wolf Cubs, Scouts and Senior Scouts, and the Rover Scouts (for those aged 17+) including a Deaf and Dumb Section, did not have much support from the diaconate and so moved to Trinity in Cardiff Road. The Girl Guides (with Brownies, Guides and Rangers), formed in 1930 were active until 1950. The Youth Fellowship formed in the 1970s was short-lived as it stopped in 1978 as it was purely recreational and members grew increasingly concerned about the damage caused to the fabric of the schoolroom. In September 1978 1st Bargoed Battalion of Boys' Brigade was formed and their weekly meetings included devotions and the members made a contribution to church life.

There were also mid-week activities for adult members of the Baptist congregation. Hanbury Road Sisterhood started in March 1927. The ladies held regular meetings and soon organised social activities: their outings started in 1929 and they held Christmas parties. The British Women's Temperance Association was initiated from Hanbury Road, and members visited and held services in local Lodging Houses at Factory Road, Baldwin Street and Gilfach. The Men's Own Movement was formed in 1952 and they held fortnightly meetings until the 1970s.

Over the years, numerous memorial gifts have enhanced the services and interior appearance of the building and those given prior to 1980 are listed in *The History of Hanbury Road English Baptist Church Bargoed 1896-1980* by Alwyn Davies (a longstanding member who served the church in various capacities). This is one of two histories of the church, the other being *History of Hanbury Road Baptist Church 1896-1941* by Rev. Harri Edwards, the first pastor.

Local Welsh Baptists held services in the home of Mark Old in the early twentieth century and the Foundation Ceremony of the new Welsh cause was in

May 1906 when 84 members were enrolled. They worshipped in Hanbury Road Baptist Schoolroom and then in Assembly Rooms in Hanbury Arms before Noddfa, their stone place of worship in Lower Park Road, opened in 1907. At first the Noddfa congregation was under the oversight of Rev. W. Jones of Treharris but Rev. George Bowen was appointed to take charge in 1908 when Noddfa's membership was 108. By 1937 they were experiencing difficulties with a decline in membership (partly because of the drop in the number of local Welsh speakers) and the associated financial strain. Their request to join the Hanbury Road congregation met with a favourable response when in March 1938, Fred Astin, Secretary of the Hanbury Road Church, wrote a formal invitation for Noddfa to unite with Hanbury Road. The merger of Noddfa and Hanbury Road Baptist congregations was a happy one. In July 1938, 23 members from Noddfa were received into membership at Hanbury Road with others following later, and in 1941 the diaconate of Hanbury Road was increased as two members who had transferred from Noddfa were co-opted.

Gilfach Baptists started to hold services in the Margaret Street home of Mrs Cross, but Ainon Baptist Chapel was built in Maesygraig Street in 1902 and remains open as a place of worship today.

Calvinistic Methodist (Presbyterian)

The local Calvinistic Methodist cause (also known as Presbyterian) dates from 1878 and their first chapel, in High Street, Bargoed, built the following year could seat about 150 worshippers. Rev. J. O. Evans, one of the first pastors of Bethania (who also served the congregation in the new Gilfach chapel for a few months from August 1894) was remembered by local Calvinistic Methodists with great affection for decades. Having cleared the debt on this building, the congregation embarked on building a larger chapel and the foundation stones of the new Bethania Chapel in Upper High Street were laid in August 1901.

Over the years the congregation was served by a number of clergy. Before the end of the first decade of the twentieth century, Rev. Daniel L. Jenkins started a lengthy pastorate at Bethania. By the 1920s, he and his family lived at Llwynteg, Hillside Park. He, his wife and their five sons were saddened when, in 1937, his daughter, a school teacher (at Radyr and later at Glanynant, Pengam) and an enthusiastic member of Bethana's Dramatic Society before her marriage to Charles Morris, died.

During three and a half decades spent in the teaching profession in Bargoed, from 1910 to his retirement in 1945, J. J. Davies became one of the best known members of Bethania's congregation. He was a deacon and, using skills developed in his professional life in Bargoed Higher Elementary (later Secondary) School, he worked with Bethania's children and young people. He was active in the work of Bethania's Sunday School and assisted the Young People's Society in a number of ways including presiding over their Eisteddfodau and helping with dramatic productions.

This pencil drawing by Ken Hamer (courtesy of Megan Hamer) shows the 1902 Bethania constructed on the site of the first chapel. The ground floor (or basement) was below the level of the road and comprised a spacious schoolroom to accommodate some 200 children and three classrooms fitted out with moveable back seats. The main chapel was well designed and finished with varnished pews of pitch pine with mahogany capping to seat 600, including 200 in a gallery running round three sides of the interior. The ceiling, panelled in the same wood as the pews, had six ventilations in the centre. The pulpit was panelled pitch pine with mahogany mouldings and handrail, while the windows were glazed with margin lights and amber centres (interior 30 feet by 49 feet, and height 20 feet) and artificial light came from incandescent burners. The walls were blue Pennant stone with York stone dressings.

This photograph (courtesy of Beryl Rowlands) is that shown on the front cover of Bethania's *Adroddiad am y Flwyddyn 1953*. The Report (Adroddiad) gives an insight into Bethania's strength and activities in Coronation Year and the list of preachers for the following sixteen months shows that they came from a wide area to preach in Bethania, probably travelling by train on the Saturday and then hosted by a family over the weekend.

This photograph (courtesy of Beryl Rowlands) was taken in the garden at the rear of Bethania on the occasion of a Sion a Sian in 1935. It shows the children in their costumes and, in the background, the outside steps leading to the rear entrance of Bethania

This photograph (courtesy of Beryl Rowlands) shows a group of members of Bethania Sisterhood on an outing to Penarth about 1950. Chapel life was not confined to the spiritual: it was an essential part of the social life of members of all ages

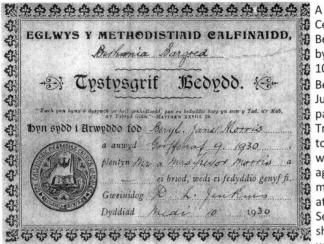

EGLWYS Y METHODISTIAID CALFINAIDD,

Bethania Bargoed

⁂ Tystysgrif Bedydd. ⁂

"*Ewch gan hyny a dysgwch yr holl genhedloedd, gan eu bedyddio hwy yn enw y Tad, a'r Mab, a'r Ysbryd Glân.*"—MATTHEW XXVIII. 19.

Hyn sydd i Arwyddo fod *Beryl Jane Morris*

a anwyd *Gorffenaf 9. 1930* ;

plentyn *Mr. a Mrs. Trevor Morris* a

_____ ei briod, wedi ei fedyddio genyf fi.

Gweinidog *D. L. Jenkins*

Dyddiad *Medi 10* 1930

A Christening Certificate, (courtesy of Beryl Rowlands), signed by Rev. Daniel L. Jenkins 10 September 1930. Beryl Jane was born 9 July 1930 and her parents, Mr and Mrs Trevor Morris, took her to Bethania where she was christened at the age of two months. She married Mel Rowlands at Bethania 22 September 1951 and she continued to worship in Bethania until it closed after which she, along with others from the congregation, went to worship in Calfaria (previously known as Bethel) in Greenfield Street. .

During three and a half decades spent in the teaching profession in Bargoed, from 1910 to his retirement in 1945, J. J. Davies became one of the best known members of Bethania's congregation. He was a deacon and, using skills developed in his professional life in Bargoed Higher Elementary (later Secondary) School, he worked with Bethania's children and young people. He was active in the work of Bethania's Sunday School and assisted the Young People's Society in a number of ways including presiding over their Eisteddfodau and helping with dramatic productions.

Music was an important part of the life of Bethania, and, over the decades, Bethania was served by a number of gifted musicians. For about ten years, J. Tudor Jones of Bristol Terrace served as organist in Bethania until he left Bargoed. On his return in October 1919, he became organist at Bethel. In the inter-war period, E. J. Owen, was, arguably, one of Bethania's most talented musicians and devout members. He was Bethania's organist when, holding a scholarship at the Tonic Solfa College, he won a College prize in 1923. The following year, he gained the Tonic Solfa College's diploma in voice training and music teaching, to become the only person in the Rhymney Valley with such a qualification. In November 1924, Bethania's Young People's Society celebrated the *Great Revival* of twenty years earlier with a lecture and revival hymns accompanied by E. J. Owen on the organ. His brother Richard, having started his ministerial career from Bethania, was a clergyman in Denbigh, and by 1926 E. J. Owen had started his theological studies in Lampeter, although he had to spend some time in Aberbargoed Hospital recovering after an operation. In the 1930s Tom Hoddinott was a member of Bethania and his young son, Alun, attended with him.

When Bethania ceased to be a place of worship its remaining congregation went to worship in the Greenfield Street chapel, Calfaria (originally known as Bethel). Later, Bethania was demolished and the site is now part of a public car park.

Programme - ONE PENNY

Workmen's Institute, Bargoed

Thursday, April 25th, 1940

Y FARGEN
T. JONES

: A :

CORLAN Y PENTREF
T. E. ARNOLD JAMES (Eudaf)

Presented by

Bethania Dramatic Society

Stage Manager : Mr. Gwilym Jones

Chairman - H. G. JOHN, Esq.
(Lloyds Bank)

Doors open 6-30   Commence 7 p.m.

Proceeds in aid of Church Funds.

PETER WILLIAMS

THE BARGOED
PRINTING WORKS
'Phone 46

This programme (courtesy of Beryl Rowlands) relates to production in Bargoed Workmen's Institute. Many of the performers were members of Bethania congregation and were well-known locally, including one who later taught in Bargoed Technical School and another who practiced medicine. It is interesting to note that the programme was printed by local printer, Peter Williams.

CHARACTERS

Y FARGEN

The Play Produced by Emlyn Williams.

Emrys Roberts, Trafaelwr	-	Trefor Morris
Mrs. Nell Roberts ei Wraig	-	Mrs. Trefor Morris
Selina, Morwyn yr uchod	-	Miss Beryl Williams
Edward Jones, Cymydog	-	George Lloyd Williams
Wmffra Hughes, Ffermwr	-	Brython Jenkins, B.Sc.

◇   ◇

CORLAN Y PENTREF

The Play Produced by Sam Davies.

Thomas Dafi, Teilwr	-	Fred Jones
Bet Dafi, Gwraig Thomas Dafi	-	Miss E. Bowen
Leisa Dafi, Merch Thomas a Bet	-	Miss Beryl Williams
Dafi Jones, Crydd	-	Sam Davies
Mari Jones, Gwraig Dafi Jones	-	Mrs. Gwilym Jones
Bili Jones, Mab Dafi a Mari Jones		J. B. Glyn Jones
Parch. Abel Owen, Pregethwr	-	George Lloyd Williams
Mrs. Gladys Owen, Gwraig y Pregethwr,		Mrs. E. A. Evans
Twm, Gwas y Pregethwr	-	Emlyn Williams
Marged, Morwyn y Pregethwr	-	Miss Bronwen Davies
John, y Gof		Iorwerth Matthews, B.Sc.
Cofrestrydd Priodasau		Gwilym Jones
Ifan William, Diacon	-	Brython Jenkins, B.Sc.
Clerc		Berwyn Jones
	Aelodau.	

SYNOPSIS OF SCENERY

Y FARGEN

One Act   -   Kitchen Scene

⊏×⊐

CORLAN Y PENTREF

ACT I
KITCHEN IN COUNTRY COTTAGE ; AFTERNOON

ACT II
ROOM IN REV. ABEL OWEN'S HOME

ACT III
Scene 1 : ON THE ROADSIDE.
Scene 2 : ROOM IN REV. ABEL OWEN'S HOME
Scene 3 : ON THE ROADSIDE

ACT IV
Scene 1 : REGISTRAR'S OFFICE
Scene 2 : ROADSIDE
Scene 3 : BEFORE HIS SUPERIOR

ACT V.
CHURCH MEETING

This Comedy is typical of Welsh Life 40 years ago.

BETHANIA C.M. WISH TO THANK ALL PATRONS.

This drawing by Ken Hamer (courtesy of Megan Hamer) shows the place of worship that was originally called Bethel, but was renamed Calfaria probably after the larger Calfaria closed and its remaining congregation went to worship in this chapel in Greenfield Street. This place of worship is still open today.

Welsh Congregational church 1874 present building 1962 at Greenfield Street.

The first service in connection with Bethel Presbyterian congregation was held at the West End Tea Rooms when the organist was Mrs Martha M. Kedward of Ruth Street (whose son was a well-known county councillor and school governor for many decades). It is not clear when Bethel in Greenfield Street was built. It flourished during the 1920s: the standard at the 1924 anniversary was (according to the report in *Merthyr Express*) that *of palmier days in the history of the church*, while in 1926, the same newspaper reported that many were turned away from the anniversary because there was no room. At the same time, the Sunday School scholars were successful in Scripture examinations, and the Band of Hope Choir, under musical director J. Tudor Jones, and the Young People's Society were active.

By 1893, architect William Harris and ironmonger Lewis Price, two recent incomers to Gilfach and members of Bethania, discussed the possibility of having a Calvinistic Methodist congregation nearer to their homes in Gilfach. They acquired hymn books and bible, and in 1893, opened a Sunday School in one of the houses then being built in Thomas Street. As each house was completed and let to tenants, the Sunday School with its seats (planks supported on piles of bricks) moved into the next house. The embryonic Gilfach congregation, having won the support of people of influence in the local community such as the headmaster of Lewis School, decided to build their own place of worship in Commercial Street. The foundation stones were laid in April 1894 and the chapel opened in June 1894. In August, it joined with Bethania under Rev. J. O. Evans and the first elders, Lewis Price, William Harris and Henry Rees, assumed office in October. The congregation was served by a number of clergy over the years, including Rev. Thomas Goshen Evans whose pastorate lasted from 1897 to 1902 after which he taught in local schools until his premature death in 1920.

The cause gained strength in Gilfach due, in part, to the increased local population, and especially because of the influence of an able and active intellectual pastor, Rev. John Williams, who ministered in Gilfach from June 1903 to his death in 1909. The decision to build a new chapel was taken in September 1904. William Harris, local architect and co-founder of the cause in Gilfach, designed the new chapel, connected to the old schoolroom by a porch, with galleries to accommodate 400 worshippers, vestries and a spacious lecture hall underneath. It was formally opened when, in June 1906, R. W. Jones, headmaster of Lewis School and a deacon of the chapel, unlocked the doors and the following Sunday, Rev. Dr. Cynddylan Jones of Cardiff preached to full congregations.

Aberystwyth-born Rev. R. D. Edwards had served abroad during World War I and was pastor in Gilfach during the 1920s. He was particularly interested in the younger generation of the 1920s and was proud to preside over a Young People's Guild with a good programme of activities. Local newspapers reported that, during the 1926 strike, he preached sermons appropriate to the times. In his leisure time he enjoyed golf and photography. His wife, considered by her contemporaries to be a very cultured lady, was closely associated with the Sunday School in Gilfach. G. W. Davies of The Emporium, his wife and daughter, Gladys, were loyal and hard-working members of the Gilfach congregation during the inter-war years.

In September 1926, the pastor, elders and congregation of Gilfach Presbyterian chapel decided to invite the Calvinistic Methodist Association of Wales to hold its 1927 Spring Quarterly Sassiwn in Gilfach. In April 1927 *Merthyr Express* carried detailed reports on this memorable event, the first time such a meeting had been held in Gilfach. Gilfach was one of the youngest Calvinistic Methodist Chapels to invite the Sassiwn and the presiding Moderator of the Calvinistic Methodist Church put the success of their invitation down to the energetic work of Rev. R. D. Edwards, chairman of the organising committee, and the support of the clergy and elders of Bethania and Bethel. The proceedings included a report on the church in Gilfach as well as inspiring preaching services in Bethania and Gilfach attended by crowded congregations. *Merthyr Express* reported that for several days the large numbers of sombrely attired ministers and delegates, hosted by local householders, gave the community a subdued appearance.

Gilfach's English Calvinistic Methodists (Presbyterians) worshipped in their chapel on Commercial Street for decades. After the congregation dwindled, the building stood unused for some years before it was demolished and a *Garden of Peace* now occupies the site.

Independent (Congregational)

It is likely that the history of the Independent cause (also known as Congregational) in the local area goes back to the 1830s when Rev. Edward Charles Jenkins (of Fleur-de-Lys) preached in Pontaberbargoed every Sunday afternoon. However, they did not develop their congregation and as Rev. Jenkins ceased his weekly visits and the Baptists built their place of worship, Caersalem, in 1839, the cause may have lapsed in Pontaberbargoed. Local adherents did not desert their faith as some joined congregations several miles away. By the 1870s, the local population was increasing and when some of the faithful decided to promote the cause in Pontaberbargoed once more the Uchdir congregation of New Tredegar proved to be very supportive. Mother and daughter, Mary Lewis (wife of Thomas Lewis publican of Old Mill Inn and

This drawing, courtesy of Dr. David Williams, shows the new Calfaria that was opened in 1874. Joseph Davies of Newport had the contract to build the new Chapel near the junction of High Street and Hanbury Road, a project that cost £1000. The foundation stone was laid by the wife of the Harpist Thomas Williams and her father loaned the money to pay for the chapel.

sister of Evan James) and Ann Thomas were among those who met in the Long Room of the Old Mill Inn. They used an old fashioned chair that converted into a table as a pulpit and, before long their numbers swelled. They were joined by Mary's husband, Thomas Lewis, son-in-law and daughter, Evan and Jane Davies of Bargoed, and two daughters of Ann Thomas, Miriam Thomas and Mrs Richard Rees. In 1871 their new Church was formally constituted and dedicated by Rev. David Jones of Cwmbwrla, Swansea and it soon started to attract more members. Mary Lewis, one of the original congregation, usually led the singing until Ben Powell was appointed as Precentor. During its first two years, the congregations depended upon local ministers and lay preachers and when they did not have a preacher, they held Prayer Meetings.

In the early 1870s the congregation considered building a chapel for themselves as not only was the local population growing but also the Old Mill Inn was for sale. Members were given collecting books to raise money for a new building. Rebecca Edwards went from door to door selling little articles in exchange for silver 3d pieces that she promised to give to the building fund. She died before the new Calfaria was opened, and her brother presented the 3d pieces totalling 23 shillings. The chapel, opened in 1874, was a small building with a gallery at one end and on two sides, but it served the purpose until the ever-increasing congregation outgrew its accommodation and facilities in the early twentieth century when a new building was built on the same site with a frontage extended by about 30 feet. The new chapel was an impressive building of native shoddy work in courses with Forest of Dean stone corners and traces round the windows. It had entrances on either side with spacious lobbies. Inside, it appeared compact with gallery all round, and a decorated ceiling. The gas lighting came from brass fittings round the walls, but there was no centre light. The front windows had six lead lights with tinted glass and the two vestry windows contained murrine glass. The galleries and seatings of pitch pine, could seat over 700 people. The floor was blocked pitch pine. The reopening services, in early July 1904, were spread over two days.

Over the decades, Calfaria was served by a number of loyal lay people and devout clergy including Rev. Daniel Leyshon Evans, as well as precentors who ensured the standard of hymn-singing, an important feature of their worship, improved. Over the years several members of Calfaria entered the Ministry. Three of them were descendants of founder Mary Lewis; her grandsons, brothers Edward and Gwilym Thomas, and great grandson David Prothero.

It is likely that local English Congregationalists had their first place of worship in Usk Road in 1903 but, during World War I, that building was sold and they started to worship in Trinity, a building that probably started life as a Welsh Methodist Church. The Trinity congregation dwindled and those remaining joined the congregation in Bethel (now known as Calfaria) and, since 1969, the former Trinity has been a Freemasons' Hall. There are probably few people remaining who remember Tabernacle, near Gwerthonor Road, as a place of worship. Although it was built about 1905 when Thomas Harris served as its pastor, there are few references to it in the local press. The building survives as an OAP Hall.

Methodist

Although John Wesley preached in Gelligaer on his journey from Breconshire to Cardiff in April 1744, and visited Llanbradach Fawr more than once in the later 1760s, there is no evidence of Methodist activities in the local area prior to the late nineteenth century when most local adherents were incomers. Before World War I, Bargoed had two separate English language congregations, Primitive Methodists and Wesleyan Methodists, as well as a Welsh Wesleyan Methodist congregation that worshipped in Trinity for a few years.

Bargoed's first English Wesleyan Methodist place of worship was a large building built before the turn of the century near Rhymney Railway's Bargoed station. Today, some older residents can recall hearing their parents and grandparents speak of worshipping there and the local press carried some reports on the services there. In 1900 the congregation, having bought an organ, marked the occasion with special Sunday services that included a musical programme by the chapel choir, with, on the Monday, a well-attended tea, followed by entertainment. The cause continued to flourish as shown by reports in *Merthyr Express* in 1904. The chapel was full for the annual services on the last Sunday in September, when, George Holifield conducted the splendid singing, accompanied by George Holifield, junior, and collections at each of the morning, afternoon and evening services were substantial, and again, they celebrated on the Monday when over two hundred people sat down for a tea. It is not clear why, in 1910, they built a new place of worship (later to be known as the Lesser Hall) in Wood Street. During the following two decades the Lesser Hall congregation was served by a number of clergy including Rev. John Roberts (whose sermons, always well-thought out and carefully prepared, captured the attention of his congregation), Rev. T. E. Deakin, Rev. E. Douglas Gibson and Rev. W. Soper Liddle. In late summer 1927, Rev. Handel Broadbent, arrived in Bargoed to take charge of his first church and set out to organise meetings where local young men could discuss topical social subjects. The Methodists organised a Wesley revival campaign in Bargoed late Autumn 1927 but sadly, on receiving a telegram that informed of his brother's fatal injuries at the Oldham mill in which he worked, Rev. Broadbent had to leave before the campaign was over. Early in 1928 he was successful in securing the support of local Miners' Agents for his planned series of lectures *Christ and Coal*.

Built on a site formerly occupied by tennis courts, the Methodist Central Hall, described in the local press as *The Cathedral of West Monmouthshire Methodism*, was a large building designed to accommodate over nine hundred people. Some of the construction costs came from donations but the largest part was from prominent Methodist, J. Arthur Rank. Rev. Joshua Holmes, Circuit Minister of Risca, presided over the stone-laying ceremony in August 1930, with the support of numerous local clergymen of various denominations and in the presence of a large congregation. The stone-laying was preceded by hymn-singing led by church precentor Dewi Bowen, prayers, and an address. Records show that 33 foundation stones were laid on behalf of various groups and individuals and the day concluded with an evening meeting. In the early 1930s it was hoped that the local Methodist congregations would amalgamate to worship together but, while some of the Primitive Methodist congregation joined the Wesleyans in the Central Hall, they continued as a separate cause.

From the 1930s to the 1960s, the Lesser Hall played an important role within the local community. Today, many remember the work of Rev. Leon Atkins in the Lesser Hall mentioned in chapter 9. From the 1930s and on through the 1950s, the Women's Sewing Circle was popular with housewives and mothers who sewed clothes and household items they could not afford to buy ready-made. At the same time, youth activities, including the annual pantomimes, were popular.

The Central Hall celebrated its Golden Jubilee in 1981 but, as membership dwindled and running costs soared, it proved impossible to maintain the premises and the Central Hall closed and was eventually demolished. The Lesser Hall, now owned by local undertakers, is still standing and is used as a Chapel of Rest. The congregation worshipped in the St. John Ambulance Hall

Over the years the Lesser Hall and the Central Hall were refurbished. The photograph overleaf, courtesy of Pat Davies, was taken on Saturday 12 September 1964, the occasion of the re-opening of the Methodist Central Hall after restoration and re-decoration.

Shown on the steps outside the front door of the Central Hall are (left to right) Councillor H. V. James, JP, Chairman G.U.D.C., and Mrs James, Rev. Dr. Maldwyn Edwards, Mrs Lloyd Edwards (aged 84, mother of Rev. Dr. Maldwyn Edwards) turning the key, Rev. Gresham Knapp and Mrs Knapp.

for a while before purchasing smaller premises where they now worship on the corner of Heol Fargoed and Park Drive.

The Primitive Methodist cause originated in 1809 and Bargoed Primitive Methodist congregation started to develop in the 1870s and the trustees signed an agreement in 1877 for the erection of their first local place of worship. The stone building, on land on the corner of Heolddu Road and Greenfield Street leased from Francis McDonnell of Usk, opened in 1878. Jonah Jones, one of the pioneers of the Bargoed Primitive Methodist congregation, remained an active member and local preacher to the early years of the twentieth century and he died in 1906. The Primitive Methodist cause flourished in Bargoed and, about 1897 they enlarged their Greenfield Street building. However, as that soon became inadequate for the rapidly expanding congregation, they sold it and built a new and imposing place of worship in South Street which was opened October 1903 by Sir Alfred Thomas MP. The fine new Gothic style place of worship, 66 feet long and 44 feet wide was the largest place of worship in Bargoed at the time. With a gallery at one end, it could seat nearly 700 and when side galleries were added it had the capacity to seat nearly 1000 people. For decades, when David Jones AC. directed the music at the anniversary services, it was common for the large chapel to be filled to capacity and repeat services held mid-week. Some of its congregation joined the Wesleyan

Methodists after the Central Hall was built and eventually the congregation dwindled. Its South Street building closed as a place of worship and was demolished in 1972, and the site is now occupied by a doctor's surgery.

The Welsh Wesleyan Methodists' first meeting may have been about 1904 in Hanbury Arms Assembly Rooms. From time to time they met in the Primitive Methodist Chapel, until, as their numbers increased, they built their own place of worship in Cardiff Road. Comprising a large vestry and classrooms on the ground floor, as well as the main room accommodating about 300, on the level of Cardiff Road, it was opened in November 1906. It is not clear how long this remained as a Welsh Methodist place of worship but after the Independents (Congregationalists) sold their Usk Road chapel they moved to this building. It is likely that Miss Bennett's St. Anne's school was held in the ground floor rooms. Although the Trinity congregation dwindled and those remaining joined others worshipping in Greenfield Street, the building remains as, in 1969, it became a Freemasons' Hall.

Holiness Mission

During the twentieth century, Bargoed-born Maynard Gordon James (1902-1988), played a significant role, nationally and internationally, in the Holiness Mission, a cause that had its roots in nineteenth century Methodist revivalism. Although Maynard James was born into a Baptist family his mother, Gwen, became involved in Bargoed's Holiness Mission and the young Maynard started to attend. He was baptised in 1920 and, when he was 21, he became a lay preacher in Cardiff. In 1927, he commenced study at Cliff College, the Methodist College, where he became known as *Holiness James*, and in 1930 he married Louisa Jackson of Bargoed. Through the following decades, he went on evangelical and revival campaigns in Britain and America. In 1934, he was one of the founders of the Cavalry Holiness Church and before the end of the 1940s he was working with their Beech Lawn Bible College in Cheshire.

Salvation Army

Bargoed Salvation Army Corps has played an important role in the local community since its formation in 1902. Today its citadel is in Greenfield Street. Although its first attempts to form a band proved unsuccessful, one was formed, conducted by Henry Bosanko, before the end of the first decade of the century. There are numerous press reports relating to the many and varied activities of this Band. Sometimes this was at united worship as when the Band headed the procession to Bargoed Park on Peace Sunday July 1919, while on other occasions it was more in the interests of entertainment as instanced by the Sunday evening performances on Trafalgar Square during the 1926 strike. There are references to numerous other examples of the Band's activities locally and further afield in *Gelligaer* Volume XVII (2009). The work of the Salvation Army extends far beyond that of the Band and over the decades the local Corps has been served by some admirable people. One such person was Commandant Boyce and, when he was leaving the area in 1920, the local press reported that he *had made a marked impression on the town*, remarking on his work as a Police Court Commissioner as well as the extent to which he won *general sympathy for and appreciation of* the Salvation Army.

United worship

In general the various congregations worshipped and socialised within their own premises, but there are some examples of occasions when they united, including the Peace celebrations in 1919 and the annual Procession of Witness (popularly known as Whitsun Marches). The local United Sunday School Committee formed a Sunday School Union in 1920 and, with representatives of most local Sunday Schools attending, it met regularly discussing among other things organisation of such annual events as the Whitsun Marches and the Sunday School outing. When, in 1963, artist L. S. Lowry captured the scene and mood of the Whitsun Marches in *Procession in South Wales, Whit Monday*, this aspect of life in Bargoed and similar communities in South Wales was all but dying out. However, it was an important highlight in the annual life of the Christian community for many years.

This photograph (courtesy of Pat Davies) shows some members of the Hanbury Road English Baptist Church on the 1959 Procession of Witness. The group is led by Alwyn Davies (who wrote a history of his church) and includes (from left to right) Garth Stephens, son of the minister, Colin Mapstone, Richard Williams of Greenfield Street, Geoff Harding, John Howells, David Bright, Roger Mapstone, Howard Jones (who later taught Maths in Pengam), Octavius Thomas (Ocky) of Heolddu Road, Rev. Emlyn Stephens and Percy Williams. To date the man in the trilby has not been identified.

CHAPTER 11
EDUCATION

Introduction

For centuries, the education of most local children in this sparsely-populated Welsh-speaking rural area was confined to what they learned within the home, workplace and their place of worship. However, some may have learned to read the Bible at one of the local Circulating Schools in the mid eighteenth century while others benefitted from the opportunities afforded by the Lewis Charity. Before the end of the nineteenth century, and especially in the twentieth century, local education provision expanded as successive governments broadened access to education and the demand for school places grew as the population of the local area increased dramatically. At first, local children benefitted from compulsory elementary education, and, as the twentieth century progressed, a growing minority could enjoy secondary education until, after World War II, it was available to all. Before World War II, few local young people experienced tertiary education, but, over the post-war decades, increasing numbers have studied in local or more distant further and higher education institutions. From at least the beginning of the twentieth century, local adults have had numerous opportunities to study vocational and non-vocational subjects in local societies and classes, until social and economic changes, including new initiatives (such as the opening of a Further Education College in Ystrad Mynach) contributed to a decline in locally-provided classes. Since the 1960s, Welsh–medium primary and secondary education has added a new dimension to local education provision.

Not everyone in post-1870 Bargoed and Gilfach area had a common view on education. There were some who argued in favour of wider educational opportunities, including access to post-elementary education for all, while others, fiercely proud of the local productive industry, opposed what they regarded as irrelevant extended academic education for working class children destined for manual labour. Some parents, seeing education as the means for intelligent offspring to climb the social and economic ladder from working to middle class, were prepared to make sacrifices for sons (and occasionally daughters) to attend secondary school, and, sometimes, college or university as well. However, especially in the pre-World War II era, children from working class backgrounds were less likely to benefit on equal terms with their more privileged peers, as social and economic factors, such as speech, dress and general demeanour, were likely to mitigate against academic progress. Other parents found it difficult to value anything beyond a basic elementary education, especially when the alternative was an additional wage to supplement the household budget.

The story of education in Bargoed and Gilfach from the mid nineteenth century to the present day includes continuing links with the Lewis Charity and local places of worship, as well as changes in line with the developing social and economic needs of a rapidly expanding population over the decades. Many thousands of children have been educated in local schools, some of which still serve as schools, by conscientious teachers who, especially prior to World War II, lived within the local community and played an important part in a wide range of community activities.

Lewis School -- School motto *Ni ddychwel doe* (Yesterday never returns)

The first major sign of change on the local education scene came when, 25 April 1848, the Trustees of the Lewis Charity School decided to move the school from its original site near Gelligaer Parish Church to a position nearer the emerging industrial communities. The school, founded in the eighteenth century, owed its existence to wealthy bachelor, Edward Lewis of Gilfach Fargoed.

Royal Commissioner R. R. W. Lingen visited Lewis Charity School in Gelligaer 26 March 1847 and his report in the Blue Books provides a snapshot of the school under George Bushell on the eve of the decision to move from Gelligaer. Although the premises were small, just one classroom measuring 22 feet by 16 feet and 8 feet high, accommodating 30-50 pupils aged 5-14, and the equipment limited to a blackboard and some locally-constructed wooden desks and benches, it compared favourably with many other contemporary schools.

On 28 May 1850 Dr. Ollivant, Bishop of Llandaff, laid the Foundation Stone of the new larger premises. The new building, comprising chapel, schoolmaster's house as well as classrooms, on a south-facing position near Pontaberpengam on land belonging to Tir-y-Bont farm, was an impressive structure with its Tower and Spire visible from a considerable distance. The first headmaster in the new buildings was Henry Cox (1853-54), and he was followed by James Tomlinson (1854-60), Rev. David Moseley (1860-67) and Alfred T. Pullin, B.A. (1867-74). Each of these headmasters and their families lived in the School House and their wives (in the case of Rev. David Moseley, his sister prior to his marriage), and some male and female monitors helped them teach the pupils. For two decades, they conducted a well-endowed Charity School that provided simple elementary education to pupils whose highest career goal was probably entering into an apprenticeship. The number of pupils on roll increased steadily: there were 90 on the registers in the late 1860s and that increased to about 200 by 1874.

The early 1870s witnessed considerable discussion within the school and across Gelligaer parish about education, and such debates were frequently coloured by religious issues. The petition, drawn up following a well-attended meeting in Nazareth Independent Chapel, Deri, late in 1871, was just one of a number of contemporary expressions of dissatisfaction with the Charity Trust. It showed concern that the Charity Trust did not serve the populous north of the parish well, and the composition of its governing body did not mirror the nonconformity of the majority of parishioners at that time. The Trustees and the Charity Commissioners considered local feeling and the changed situation and responded by preparing a new Scheme converting the elementary school into a grammar school for boys aged 11 – 16. The grammar school, financed by the enhanced School Endowment, would operate in the existing buildings under the management of a new Board of Governors, comprising ten elected and three co-opted members.

The new Board of Governors, with chairman George Thomas Clark, vice-chairman Charles Herbert James and clerk Frank T. James, met 8 September 1874 and resolved to continue the school as an elementary school with the existing staff for six months. It closed as an elementary school before re-opening 6 April 1875 as Lewis' Endowed School, locally known as the Grammar School, under new headmaster Rev. David Evans. It had 36 day scholars and 8 boarders (in Lower or Headmaster's House) and, as more applications were coming in, the Governing Body appointed Roger William Jones as second master, with boarders in Upper School House. The Governors negotiated with Brecon and Merthyr and Rhymney Railway Companies for cheap tickets for day scholars to travel up and down the valley, and, during 1876-1877, enhanced the accommodation for boarders at Lower House. By the end of the decade the number on roll was increasing steadily.

Rev. David Evans was the Grammar School's first headmaster, and, during his time in charge, from 1875 to his retirement to his native Merionethshire in 1887, he raised the school to a highly respected position: in reality, it offered post-primary rather than secondary education in the sense that it was a finishing academy on top of the normal elementary school. The curriculum was enhanced and boys could participate in sporting activities such as football and cricket. In successive reports to the Governing Body from 1880, the headmaster expressed his concerns that many day scholars did not gain any significant advantage from the school because of their unsatisfactory attendance and the brevity of their average length of stay in the school. One of the reasons for their short stay was probably the ready availability of local employment offering comparatively high wages.

Collier's son David J. Williams of Bargoed received his elementary education in Bargoed Board School under Thomas Myddfai Jones and, as was reported in *Merthyr Express* in November 1886, *when old enough he obtained a scholarship from the Lewis' Gelligaer Charity and entered the Endowed Grammar School at Pengam as a foundation scholar, where he was highly successful.* He gained Certificates of Cambridge Local Examinations in 1885 and by 1886, having passed its entry examination, he was studying in Llandovery College. Such was the pride of the local community in this Welsh collier's son that, it was reported in the newspaper, the leading residents of Bargoed were determined to assist him financially and he received the proceeds of a well-attended concert held at Plasnewydd Assembly Rooms. His studies

211

This photograph, courtesy of Greg Buick, was taken c1888 and shows headmaster R W Jones with about 30 pupils (possibly the 30 boys receiving aid from the Lewis Trust). Directly behind the headmaster is T W Lewis of Bontnewydd farm.

were successful and he went on to become headmaster of Bethesda County School.

R. W. Jones had proved a great asset to the school and deserved some credit for the reputation the school gained during those thirteen years. In addition he formulated ambitious plans for improvements and re-arrangements in the school, including a gymnasium and chemical laboratory as well as sub-dividing the Chapel into an Assembly Hall and three classrooms. He was appointed headmaster in 1887 and his plans were put to a Governors' Meeting in 1888. Many of them were implemented in the next few years, to make a more pleasant and efficient working environment for staff and pupils.

The Welsh Intermediate Education Act of 1889 ushered in a new stage in the development of the school. Under this legislation, each of the thirteen counties of Wales set up a Joint Education Committee empowered to levy a County Rate for Intermediate and Technical Education and to prepare a Scheme for such education specifying the Educational Endowments that ought to be used for that Scheme. Glamorgan Joint Education Committee's Scheme including the Lewis Endowment, provoked local reaction from the School Governing Body, Gelligaer School Board and groups of parishioners, such as those meeting in Bargoed 14 June 1892. Local opponents of the County Scheme, fearing the school would lose out and the Founder's Will would be set aside, expressed confidence in the fact that the school was already well-managed and supported. At the same time, they felt assured that, in coming decades, not only would increased coal royalties enhance the value of the Endowment, but also the local population would increase. Local people were not unanimous in their opposition to the County Scheme and there was a heated correspondence in the local press about the matter.

Glamorgan County Council voted in favour of the County Scheme at a meeting at Pontypridd Town Hall 13 April 1893. The School Governing Body and the locality appealed to the Charity Commissioners but failed to get the Lewis Endowment excluded from the County Scheme formally adopted by the County Council. In November 1895 the School Governors resolved it unwise to continue opposition to Glamorgan County Scheme and, on 13 May 1896, it was established and everything associated with Lewis School was transferred from the existing Governors to the Governing Body of Glamorgan.

The controversy relating to the Endowment and the County Scheme did not disrupt the life and work of the school and there was great intellectual activity, sound and thorough education, and firm discipline in the school in the early 1890s. The educational foresight of the headmaster was illustrated by the success of the manual training and woodwork lessons that put the school in the forefront of educational progress in the early 1890s. When the school was taken into the County Scheme in 1896 it had 57 boarders and 77 day-scholars. The high standard of education and achievement continued and was enhanced by the provision for instruction in mining and engineering as well as the weekly vocal music lessons.

A Central Welsh Board inspection in the late 1890s highlighted the inadequacies of the existing dilapidated accommodation, and so, by the turn of the century, the Governors and the County Governing Body, having found the cost of repair and alterations to be too high, decided to erect a new school. During the years of building the new school, designed by architect R. S. Griffiths and built by E. Turner and Sons, lessons continued in the Gymnasium, in Lower House and in a temporary corrugated-iron building. The Foundation Stone of the new school, was laid 16 September 1903 and most of the new buildings were ready for use by December 1904. When David Lloyd George, M.P., officially opened it in September 1905 he compared the school with the great English public schools and expressed his vision for similar schools to educate an elite across Wales.

In the first decade of the twentieth century, the school's mining and engineering education was enhanced with the appointment of a geology master, and geology, chemistry and physics helped bring the curriculum in closer touch with local industry. Pupil successes continued as illustrated by C. W. Judd of Bargoed. He gained the Certificate of Central Welsh Board with honours in July 1907, his scholarship at Aberystwyth was doubled in value due to his outstanding Chemistry paper, and he later became an eminent Industrial Chemist.

The school extended its extra-curricular activities. The Literary and Debating Society, although very popular, was short-lived because it was difficult for pupils living at a distance from the school to get home after it.

Welsh master, Mr Matthews, edited the boys' collection of local folklore and nursery rhymes, a publication that received favourable press notices. The first annual School Eisteddfod was held 28 February 1913 and a Boy Scout Troop was formed in the school in 1913. During the war years, 1914-18, some staff joined the forces but school work continued in spite of adverse conditions. Several Thrift groups saved for War Savings Certificates and a Cadet Corps started in the school, providing training in readiness for the war call-up. When the tank *Egbert* visited Bargoed in July 1918 (in conjunction with the Savings Campaign) Lewis School Cadet Corps in full uniform escorted it from Pengam Station to Trafalgar Square.

In 1919, R. W. Jones retired after 44 years service to the school. He had raised the school from a Grammar School of about 100 boys to a school second to none in Wales, and whose former pupils held important posts in Wales, Britain and abroad. Many former Ludovicans attributed their career successes to their training in the school, the foresight of R. W. Jones and the inspiration of his honourable and upright character. While not detracting from the excellent leadership of R. W. Jones and the hard work of his colleagues, it should be noted that the school was able to select the academic cream from a wide catchment area, an advantage it continued to enjoy until the 1960s.

The next headmaster, D. Vaughan Johnston, M.A., assumed control in 1919, and he remained in post until 1926 when he became Chief Inspector of Central Welsh Board. Perhaps his most important contribution to the development of the school's curriculum was in Science: he ensured older boys could study both chemistry and physics, while younger boys had a wider education in general elementary science, and in 1920, the Board of Education recognised the school's advanced course in science. Like his predecessors, D. Vaughan Johnston faced an increasing roll forcing changes in accommodation, so he had the Manual Training Room divided into two classrooms and a new Woodwork Room erected. During 1920, the school faced financial difficulties arising from the new County Scale of salaries for Secondary School Teachers. Glamorgan Education Committee was prepared to meet the extra cost for Glamorgan pupils but not for the Monmouthshire pupils in the school, while Monmouthshire was unwilling to contribute to a school outside their county and not under their management. There was considerable newspaper controversy and meetings of public, parents and staff, until an honourable settlement was agreed in June and the feared closure of the school evaporated.

D. Vaughan Johnston also had to oversee the school during the disruption caused when G.U.D.C.'s new road from Glan-y-nant to Gilfach was cut through the School playing field, separating the Headmaster's House from the rest of the school premises. G.U.D.C. sought to compensate the school for the disturbance and loss of land by erecting unclimbable railings on both sides of the road through the school grounds, with a hedge on the school side and a wall by the Headmaster's House, as well as improving sports facilities. They proposed to make changes to the football field and cricket pitch, and construct a new hard playground and a new fives court as well as a new tennis court by the Headmaster's House. By the time D. Vaughan Johnston left the school most of the work was complete, except for drainage of the new playing fields.

The next headmaster, Louis Stanley Knight, M.A., F.R.Hist.S., took up his duties 21 April 1926. He guided the school through the difficult years of economic depression, war and post-war reconstruction before retiring in 1950. Today many former Ludovicans have proud memories of the end of term in July 1950 when, after conducting his final assembly and receiving their presentations, L. Stanley Knight stood at the west door of the school and shook hands with each of his pupils before going to his study where he bade goodbye to every prefect.

The ensuing 50 years saw a number of significant changes, particularly in the character of the school. Headmaster, Neville Richards, B.Sc., J.P. (1950-66), was able to continue much as before, but the issue of the Monmouthshire pupils in a Glamorgan school was becoming an increasingly political matter, with County Councillor (later Alderman) Kedward, leading the clamour to change the status of Lewis School Pengam to that of a Grammar school whose pupils were derived entirely from the county of Glamorgan. His goal was achieved when A.T. (Fred) Evans, B.A. was headmaster (1966-69) when it was decreed that the Lewis Schools should take 40% of the pupils from a new Glamorgan-based catchment. It was during the headship of Glyn R. Rees, B.A., B.Sc., B.Comm. (1969-77) (appointed when, in 1968, A.T. Evans entered Parliament) that the implication of the loss of Monmouthshire pupils was felt. Local Government re-organisation, whereby the school came under the aegis of Mid Glamorgan County Council, followed soon after. Building on its predecessor's intentions, the new authority decided that grammar schools should be abolished in the county and plans for Lewis School to become a non selective, Boys Comprehensive School following a merger with Graddfa Boys Secondary Modern School in Ystrad Mynach were implemented.

Comprehensivisation rested uneasily on many of Lewis School's traditions, but adjustments were made and the Pengam site became the Upper School (the Lower School was in Ystrad Mynach) catering for boys of all abilities of 14 to 18 years of age. The catchment was considerably altered, though with the inclusion of Maesycwmmer in the new feeder area a geographical link with the former Monmouthshire returned. John S. Anthony, B.Sc. (1977-93) oversaw the transition to a more comprehensive ethos, guided the school through the requirements of the Education Reform Act, 1988 and was instrumental in the introduction of computers into both classroom and administrative systems. Christopher J. Howard, B.A., Ph.D. (1993 to present), has led the school through the educational morass of the late 1990s and first decade of the twenty first century. However, not all was bad. At the House of Commons St. David's Day Question Time in 1995, Ron Davies, M.P. for Caerphilly named Lewis School as one of two *slum schools* in the Rhymney Valley. A flurry of political activity led to plans for a new Lewis Boys' School, which was built. It opened in 2002, on the opposite side of the New Road to the buildings which, with successive enlargements and modifications, had existed since 1853. Sadly, these old buildings were subsequently demolished, despite their historical significance, but the name and many of the traditions continue, thus the spirit of Edward Lewis' covenant with the area and its young people is maintained.

Elementary education to 1938

Forster's Education Act (1870) created a national structure of locally-elected School Boards to implement compulsory elementary education, and the emerging communities of Bargoed and Gilfach were under the jurisdiction of Gelligaer School Board (set up 1871). When the 1902 Education Act replaced School Boards with Local Education Authorities, Glamorgan Local Education Authority administered the schools in Bargoed and Gilfach. To their credit, administrators and teachers, struggling with problems of overcrowding and understaffing in the North Bargoed, South Bargoed and Gilfach Schools, overcame difficulties to provide a commendable standard of education for local children until they attained the statutory school-leaving age and entered employment, prior to local reorganisation of education provision in 1938.

North Bargoed

An Anglican, Thomas Myddfai Jones and his wife, Jane, ran the first school in north Bargoed in two private houses in Factory Road. It aimed to provide a basic education for children from the community generally known as Bargoed or Pontaberbargoed, on both sides of the river Rhymney. Mr and Mrs Jones had long associations with education in north Bargoed as they continued in charge when the school moved to new purpose-built premises in Church Street. Thomas Myddfai Jones remained in charge of the Mixed (and after 1906 Boys') Department until his retirement March 1913, only to resume control when his successor, David Davies left for war service 1916-1918. Jane Jones was an able Mistress, as witnessed by successive H.M. Inspectors' reports noting the good instruction given to the pupils and the order maintained in the school, in face of difficulties such as overcrowding and understaffing.

The Pontaberbargoed community expanded with new streets constructed near Bargoed Railway Station on the Gelligaer side of the river. The facilities soon became inadequate to accommodate the growing number of children, and so, the Board of Education agreed that Gelligaer and Bedwellty School Boards should find a suitable site for a new school. After some months of discussion and correspondence, Gelligaer and Bedwellty School Boards, at separate meetings in May 1873, passed a resolution approving agreement that the two School Boards combine to build and manage a new purpose-built school to serve the community on both sides of the river Rhymney. Each of the two Boards should provide four School Managers and the costs would be in proportion to the number of pupils from each Board's area every half year. At the outset, there were 111 pupils, 46 of whom were from Bedwellty and 65 from Gelligaer. Although the new school designed by architect John Williams, was jointly provided by Bedwellty and Gelligaer School Boards, it was deemed provided by Gelligaer because it was to be built within that Board's area, and so Frank James, Gelligaer School Board Clerk, conducted the correspondence, and provided plans, specifications and costings to the Board of Education. By the time they came to build the school at the bottom of Church Street, not only was the local community, especially on the Gelligaer side of the valley, growing, as fifty new houses had been completed and others were in the process of construction, but also Lewis School Pengam was about to close as an elementary school. Frank James, arguing in favour of accommodation for 270 pupils, far more than the Board of Education thought necessary, wrote *collieries are rapidly developing in the locality and the number of houses within reach of this school is increasing every day.* Having supplied estimated, not actual, costs amounting to £2,280, Frank James incurred the disapproval of Board officials when he requested a further £265 in September 1874. The Board pointed out his error and, on the reverse of his letter denying error on his part, a Board official described him as an *offhand gentleman who evidently thinks himself the biggest man in Glamorganshire* and he should be sharply admonished. Frank James replied accepting that, as he had not noticed the words relating to tender costs, he had used the Architect's estimated figures. A Board official noted on the reverse of the letter that Frank James will read things carefully in future, and the additional £265 was granted. The new school opened with two rooms each for Infants' and Mixed Departments, and a residence for the Master.

Successive Reports of His/Her Majesty's Inspectors of Schools in the decades to the 1930s, highlighted problems of overcrowding in consequence of population growth in the emerging community in this rapidly expanding part of the South Wales Coalfield. Over the decades, the problem of overcrowding in local schools was addressed in a variety of ways: sometimes the existing facilities were enhanced or extended or some classes were housed in temporary rented accommodation nearby, and new schools in south Bargoed and in Gilfach were erected. By the early 1890s, the premises were inadequate for the growing school population and, in January 1892, Frank James, submitted an application for an extension to the Mixed Department. In spite of the fact that some children had moved to the new Gilfach Mixed and Infants' Schools that opened in May 1898, further extensions and improvements were necessary before the end of the century to relieve the overcrowding in the Mixed Department especially as further residential developments on the Gelligaer side of the river took the average attendance to over 300, (Bedwellty increase to 51.6 and Gelligaer to 249). Bedwellty School Board believed that Gelligaer Board's contribution should be higher while Frank James predicted an imminent increase in population in Bedwellty. The 1873 Agreement between the two School Boards had not included any provision to settle such a case and, when asked, the Board of Education were unwilling to give advice.

In the early twentieth century, the school faced overcrowding problems on a far greater scale than in previous decades, as the earlier population growth was nothing compared with the huge local population explosion that followed the sinking of Bargoed Colliery. The incomers were predominantly young adults eager to carve out a better life for themselves and their families. Many of them were newly-married or arrived with young families, so the demand for elementary school places soon became a matter of urgency to be addressed by Gelligaer School Board and its successor, Glamorgan Local Education Authority.

The first response to this dramatic increase in the school population was to prepare plans for a new Infants' School, with eight classrooms and a Hall, adjacent to the existing school so freeing the existing Infants' Rooms for the Mixed Department. In the meantime, some Mixed Department classes occupied temporary accommodation in local chapels until the former Infants' premises became available to them when the new Infants' School opened April 1903. Pupils enjoyed a holiday and a tea to mark the opening of Bargoed Infants' School in April 1903 and the Infants moved into the new premises on 1 May 1903 when the headmistress recorded in the School log book *very proud the children seemed to be in their new buildings*. The school's new superior premises were not problem-free. During the winter 1903-04 it soon became clear that the heating was not satisfactory and the headmistress recorded temperatures, sometimes below 40° F (4°C) in the log book, before some improvements were implemented. The use of temporary premises to cope with the problem of overcrowding in the school continued until Bargoed South Infants' School opened in 1913.

Even though Standard I boys and girls remained in the new Infants' School, where there was excess accommodation as about fifty infants from Bedwellty parish had left to attend the new Aberbargoed School that opened in June 1902, there was considerable overcrowding in the Mixed Department and, it was suggested that Standard II girls should also be housed in the new Infants' School. In addition to the problems of overcrowding, the Mixed Department still faced difficulties as the furniture in the former Infants' rooms was unsuitable for them. In 1903, it was decided to split the Mixed Department into two single-sex departments, with the girls housed in the existing premises and the boys in new premises to be constructed on a new site nearby. The first site chosen for the new building was rejected as being so steep that levelling would have been too expensive and so they opted for a site about 200-300 yards higher up the valley side where the land was more level. At the same time, and in an attempt to provide a long-term solution to the problem, they identified a site for the proposed South Bargoed Schools.

The plans for the new Llancayo Street Boys' School, comprising seven classrooms, a central hall, teachers' room and store room, were approved August 1904 and pupils celebrated its opening with a tea on Monday 29 January 1906 and, on 2 February 1906, headmaster, Thomas Myddfai Jones, noted in the school log book: *The Boys of the Mixed School were drafted to the New School on Tuesday morning – the girls remaining in the old Mixed and Infants School.*

The lads as is expected are highly delighted with the change but it is with great difficulty that they have been kept within bounds – the large and even playground is to them an especial delight.

The problem of overcrowding in the Boys' and Girls' Schools, coupled with large classes consequent upon an unfavourable pupil:teacher ratio, continued, eased in part by the construction of additional classrooms in the Boys' School 1910-11 and the use of temporary classrooms in Usk Road Chapel in 1914. In 1924, Glamorgan's Chief Education Officer, refused to designate the central hall in the Boys' School as a classroom so, the following year, the two classrooms at the north end of the school were converted into three classrooms, and a handicraft centre, including a woodwork room, was built in 1928.

The new Bargoed Girls' School opened in the former Mixed School, under headmistress Selina Jane Viner, who remained in post for three decades until her retirement in October 1936. The premises underwent considerable alterations and extensions during 1908-1909, to provide facilities for the girls to have lessons in cookery and other domestic subjects before they reached the statutory school-leaving age. Before the end of 1906, facilities in Bargoed Girls' School's received recognition of suitability to accommodate 54 girls in a cookery demonstration lesson and 18 in a practical lesson. While the premises were being altered, some classes were held in the school's central hall while others were in hired premises such as the nearby Church Hall, and efforts were made to ensure that the girl's cookery lessons continued. In 1908, HMI Miss Sillitoe observed a satisfactory cookery lesson but she was concerned that it was given in the Teachers' Room of the Infants' Department, a room that was not only not recognised for the purpose, but was also not fit for purpose. The room was only 9 ½ feet high, its ventilation was defective and lighting was poor. While it had a gas stove, it did not have a cooking range or grate, and there was no sink. The girls had to carry hot water, boiled on an open grate at the bottom of the staircase leading to the room, upstairs for cooking and scullery work, and they had to carry slops and refuse downstairs. As a result of her report, the grant for cookery instruction was refused, until the L.E.A. explained the circumstances, pointing out that as it was a temporary arrangement using part of the school premises, it had not been thought necessary to make a formal application for approval. By the following year, the school had new commodious cookery facilities, and girls from other schools, including Gilfach, attended for instruction. By 1911, the school was equipped so that, in addition to cookery, laundry work could be taught, and before World War I, homemaking and housewifery were also taught in the school.

The problem of overcrowding in the north Bargoed schools disappeared as the number on roll fell in the 1930s, and there was spare capacity in the schools when they were prepared for the local reorganisation of education in 1938. The Infants' School remained open but the single-sex north Bargoed Schools closed as elementary schools on 31 March 1938. Boys and girls aged 7 - 11 were transferred from the Boys' School in Llancayo Street and the Girls' School near

St. Gwladys' Church to Bargoed South Junior Boys' and Girls' Schools in Park Crescent and the staff was deployed in the new Bargoed Senior Schools or in other local elementary schools. On 31 March 1938 David Davies, B.A. (headmaster since 1913), made his last entry in Bargoed Boys' School log book before he took charge of South Bargoed Boys' Junior School 1 April 1938, filling the vacancy created by the death, in October 1937, of 53- year old Joshua Christmas Williams, the previous headmaster: *Keys of School handed to Mr W. L. Richards, B.A., Head Teacher of the new Senior School, and every good wish for a successful professional career at the building in which I have acted as Head Teacher for the past 25 years.*

South Bargoed

It was decided in 1903 to meet the needs of the rapidly growing Bargoed community and address the problems of overcrowding and understaffing in the existing schools by building schools in south Bargoed. The initial plan had been for Glamorgan County Council to purchase a Henry Street site, but, within two decades, three schools, designed and built under the supervision of the County Architect, D. Pugh Jones, occupied a long, narrow site, approved March 1910, on the east side of Park Crescent.

The plans for the first of these schools, South Bargoed Infants', were approved July 1911, and the following year, work started on the construction of a single-entrance detached block at the south end of the plot. With four classrooms to accommodate 200 children, a Medical Inspection Room, a small hall and a basement shelter it was completed by 1 March 1913 and opened under headmistress, Miss Kate E. Jones.

A few weeks before the Infants' School opened, plans were submitted for the Junior Mixed School on the north side of the Infants' School. The plans included 6 classrooms, arranged for cross ventilation and opening off an 8 foot wide corridor, together with two cloakrooms, teachers' room and store room, and were approved in August 1913. The building was not completed until April 1918 when it opened, as Junior Mixed School for 292 pupils, with Miss Ceridwen Roberts as headmistress. It became a Girls' School when the boys were drafted to the new Boys' School 9 January 1923.

Sanction for South Bargoed Boys' School, at the north end of the site, was granted in May 1914 with plans approved in March 1915. The application was renewed in April 1919 but in August it was decided to hire existing buildings to compensate for any shortfall in local school provision rather than proceed with building a new school. The loan to cover the cost was in place by late 1920 and in May 1921, the L.E.A.'s opinion that it was *imperatively necessary to proceed with the erection of the proposed new building for boys*, prompted H.M.I. Mr Evans to investigate local provision for elementary education. He noted the congestion in the existing Bargoed and Gilfach schools as well as the sizeable housing schemes that would bring further incomers to the area and, in July 1921, the scheme had consent to proceed. During 1922 the contractors, Messrs

Williams and Davies, of Pencoed and Caerphilly, constructed a substantial modern building providing for 300 boys with part of the Park Crescent site available for a school clinic. *Merthyr Express* 13 January 1923 carried a report on the formal opening of the school before a meagre attendance, including some local notables and very few parents. Lewis Edwards, J.P. of Bedlinog presided and Daniel Davies of Bedlinog, one of the oldest members of the School Managers, performed the opening ceremony. The two main themes running through the speeches related to the important role of parents in the education of their children. While Glamorgan L.E.A. was in the forefront of education and aimed to meet the needs of the community, it seemed that many parents lacked enthusiasm and failed to give careful attention to their children's education. At the same time, it was clear that some Welsh-speaking parents failed to provide a Welsh-speaking home environment for their children and Gelligaer Managers had not placed the Welsh language high on their agenda. School work started the next day under the school's first headmaster, Lampeter-born Joshua Christmas Williams. The opening of this school in 1923 meant that, at last, Bargoed and Gilfach had adequate elementary school provision. The 1925 inspection report showed the school was building a worthy tradition of attainment and conduct.

By the time Bargoed South Boys' School opened, Gelligaer School Managers had fixed the boundaries of the catchment areas of local schools. The dividing line between the North and South Bargoed Schools ran behind Park Road and through Capel Street, and children from Lower Capel Street and Cross Street were to attend the north Bargoed schools. However, after modifications, all children in Cross Street and Capel Street were added to the South Bargoed catchment area. Children living south of East View Terrace and Capel Hotel, as well as those in Alfred Street and Hillside Park belonged to the catchment area of the Gilfach Schools. It was not long before a deputation on behalf of some parents in Alfred Street and Hillside Park asked Gelligaer Managers to move them to the South Bargoed Schools' catchment area as it was closer to their homes than the Gilfach Schools. Discussion continued for some time with objectors claiming that they only wanted to include them because they were rich, and two of the children had previously attended a private school that had closed. Before the end of 1923, Gelligaer Managers and Glamorgan L.E.A. agreed that, subject to confirmation by the Board of Education, Hillside Park and Alfred Street should be part of the catchment area of the South Bargoed Schools, but those parents who wanted to keep their children in the Gilfach Schools were allowed to do so.

On local reorganisation of education 1 April 1938, the older pupils in South Bargoed Boys' and Girls' Schools transferred to the new Senior Schools in north Bargoed, and their places were taken by the transfer in of the younger pupils from the north Bargoed schools. Initially, South Bargoed Boys' and Girls' Schools did not have room for all their classes and so Standard I boys and girls were accommodated in South Bargoed Infants' School, thus increasing the roll in the Infants' School.

Gilfach

Gilfach started to develop as a coal mining community in the second half of the nineteenth century and, by 1895, *Merthyr Express* was carrying reports about Gilfach Ratepayers' requests for a school and the possibility of establishing a temporary school in the emerging community. Gilfach Mixed and Infants School was formally opened by Rector of Gelligaer on 16 May 1898, in front of an audience comprising Board members and Gilfach villagers. Schoolwork started the following day with a staff of eight under Thomas Cornelius Jones, Head of the Mixed Department, and Mary Ann Morgan, Assistant in charge of the Infants Class. Thomas Cornelius Jones remained in post until his retirement in September 1938, proud of over thirty years overseeing changes in staff and buildings. At the outset, Gilfach School, designed to accommodate 90 boys and girls and 65 infants, went some way towards alleviating the overcrowding problems in Bargoed. However, it soon faced the same problems of overcrowding as did Bargoed, and similar solutions were employed, namely using local chapel vestries as classrooms before new purpose-built accommodation was erected.

The problem of overcrowding was highlighted in the HMI Report published at the beginning of 1902 and recommendations included a new school for the infants so that the Mixed Department could use the existing premises. Temporary adjustments were made to cope with the growing number of pupils on roll. In February 1903, Messrs Lattery & Co. of Cardiff had the contract for the extension and alterations to the existing building, and when building work started in April, the noise and general disruption made it difficult for the school to operate properly. They failed to rent alternative accommodation in local chapel vestries during May and June 1903, but, by the end of June some classes were accommodated in Ainon Baptist chapel. When the school reopened after the summer break on 31 August, the main room of the Mixed Department and two Infant classrooms were finished and in use, but the new desks and partition did not arrive until late October, when carpenters returned to the school to install them.

The population in the local area continued to grow rapidly and there were further problems of overcrowding by 1906. Writing in the school log book the headmaster recorded that there were insufficient desks for the pupils and the school's budget was stretched to provide reading and exercise books for the increasing roll. By October 1907, Standard I was housed in the schoolroom of the Presbyterian Chapel, where, as they did not have any desks until January 1908, instruction was limited to oral lessons for several months. Although the problem of overcrowding was eased a little when Gilfach Infants' School, opened January 1909, so allowing the Mixed Department to occupy the premises previously used by the Infants and, in 1910, when some of the older pupils transferred to the new Bargoed Higher Elementary School, but they continued to use temporary premises until Gilfach Girls' and Boys' Departments opened in 1913. The 1910 Inspection report highlighted deficiencies in the ventilation in the classrooms used by the Mixed Department, especially those on the south side of the building, and recommended hoppered opening in the lower parts of the windows. They also noted that dry rot was causing problems in some of the rooms and had led to total abandonment of the Master's Room.

During 1912, the school operated under difficulties including noise and disruption caused by the builders and continued overcrowding, but the Inspection Report noted that there were no signs of any fall in the standards of education provided through the supervision and guidance of the headmaster and the work of the strong staff of teachers. The building work was completed by the Spring of 1913, and the Mixed Department ceased to exist on 7 April 1913 when the new Boys' and Girls' Departments opened. The catchment area of the Gilfach schools extended northwards to help alleviate overcrowding in the Bargoed schools only to contract following the opening of Bargoed South Boys' School, when Thomas Cornelius Jones wrote in the school's log book 9 January 1923: *All boys north of the Capel Hotel who attended this School are being transferred for Bargoed South Boys' today. As the district consists of good houses, the type of boy is among the best in the neighbourhood and among the 59 boys transferred from the various classes are some of the brightest children on our books.*

Only months before his retirement, Thomas Cornelius Jones recorded in the school log book that, at about 10.45 am on 23 January 1928, several prestigious visitors arrived unexpectedly at Gilfach Boys' School. Mr A. Price HMI and Lord Eustace Percy (President of the Board of Education) were accompanied by Lady Eustace Percy, Mr Percy Watkins (Permanent Secretary of Welsh Department Board of Education), Alderman William Jenkins (Chairman of Glamorgan Education Committee) and another gentleman. After spending some time with Thomas Cornelius Jones, discussing the problems of the neighbourhood they heard reading in Standard IIa, before pupils, with teacher Walter Jones, B.A., conducting and Miss Doris B. Davies accompanying them on the piano, performed four Welsh folk songs. After that, the visitors left to attend the opening ceremony at Caerphilly Miners' Welfare School.

By the 1930s the number of pupils on roll decreased and it soon proved unnecessary to use the central halls as classrooms. The numbers on roll dropped further when 11+ pupils transferred to the new Senior Schools that opened in north Bargoed 1 April 1938.

Life and work in local elementary schools before 1938

Up to the middle of the twentieth century these elementary schools aimed to teach the basics in arithmetic, reading and writing, and to broaden the pupils' knowledge and understanding of their environment through object lessons in subjects such as geography, history and science. In the early decades after

Forster's Education Act, there were few qualified teachers in the local elementary schools but, as the years went by, an increasing number were able to train at institutions such as Cardiff Day College. In his final entry in the log book of Gilfach Boys' School, Thomas Cornelius Jones noted how, over three decades, he had seen teaching colleagues of varying degrees of competence come and go. When he started at Gilfach in 1898, he worked with apprenticed teachers and pupil teachers, but, by the time he retired in 1928, most of the classes were taught by certificated teachers. The effect of this is evident in the local attempts to implement the Dalton Plan, a scheme designed to cater for the needs, interests and abilities of individual pupils while encouraging them to work independently and become responsible. The elementary schools also tried to cater for the physical health of the pupils. At first this was confined to routine drill exercises done without the aid of any equipment. Later the pupils did a wider variety of activities sometimes accompanied by music, at first played on the school piano, and later, from gramophone records or the wireless. School log books record that Bargoed Higher Elementary School purchased a piano in 1911 but South Bargoed Infants' School did not have a piano until 1930. After World War I, they played team games: Bargoed Boys' School earned an enviable reputation in soccer in the 1920s before they turned to concentrate on rugby in the 1930s which, after 1934, they played on land at Heolddu rented by the L.E.A..

Children who did not attend school regularly were unlikely to achieve the levels of literacy and numeracy that should follow the introduction of compulsory elementary education. Local Attendance Officers (such as Rees Saunders) paid regular visits to the schools but did not make much impact on the somewhat irregular attendance at school that limited the educational progress of many pupils in local elementary schools from the later nineteenth century to the middle of the twentieth century. Gilfach schools, serving a far more extensive catchment area than any of the Bargoed schools, faced the biggest problems associated with absenteeism. There was a wide range of reasons for absence from school during these decades. Some absences were unavoidable, as in the case of illnesses and inclement weather, especially heavy rain that made it impossible for little children to negotiate the resulting muddy roads approaching the schools, or icy conditions and heavy snowfalls. However, many were coincident with local events or arising from home circumstances, while others were, according to the head teachers, attributable to neglect by the mothers.

From time to time, both pupils and teachers suffered illness that forced their absence from school. It is likely that some of these illnesses were spread in the over-crowded, inadequately heated and ill-ventilated school premises, while their effects were greater among the more malnourished pupils. Another indication of local poverty, namely lack of boots and suitable overcoats, accounted for absences especially during extremely bad weather, while embarrassment about the nature of underclothing often accounted for absences coinciding with medical inspection.

Pupils were frequently absent from school to attend local functions, especially Singing Festivals and treats, such as teas or outings, in or organised by their place of worship. Other local events, such as sports, carnivals and eisteddfodau, also led to absences from school. Occasional visits by circuses and menageries attracted the children's interest and, if they could afford it, they attended performances where they saw the acrobats' daring feats, clowns' antics as well as displays by exotic animals they were unaccustomed to see. New local facilities also attracted children's attention as witnessed by the absences generated by the opening of Bargoed's new Palace Theatre in 1910. Mabon Mondays (a miners' holiday on the first Monday of each month) and closures on Labour Day were frequently followed by absences during the week.

Sometimes, the absences from school were for more practical reasons in the home: to fetch water for the household, to pick coal and sticks on the tips, a common practice during times of strike in the coal industry, or just to run to the shops for the mother. In the early decades of the twentieth century, it was not unusual for busy mothers to keep daughters at home. This was particularly prevalent on Friday afternoons, when they would be expected to help with household tasks or care for younger siblings as well as frail and ailing family members, all duties that supplemented and reinforced what they learned in their homecraft lessons in school. At the same time, boys missed Friday afternoon classes if they could earn money by *carrying out* for local shopkeepers. Children often missed days or half days of lessons for the seasonal pursuits of wimberry and blackberry picking on the local hillsides: not only did this give them plenty of fresh air and time out with their families but it also helped provide the family with healthy additions to a sometimes extremely meagre diet. Local School Managers discussed the more lengthy absences caused by hop-picking outings to Herefordshire on numerous occasions in the 1920s. Some argued that working class parents should not be prosecuted for taking their children out of school to enjoy a working holiday in a healthy environment, while others believed it wasted local educational resources and that the air on the local Common was just as beneficial.

As Gelligaer School Board, as well as local teachers, realised the importance of regular attendance at school if pupils were to make satisfactory progress in their studies, they introduced School Board Prizes for attendance at school and awarded half-day holidays to schools with a satisfactory attendance record. Thomas Myddfai Jones recorded an attendance prize-giving at Bargoed in the log book September 1903:

Mr Llewellyn, a member of the Gelligaer School Board, attended school this afternoon to distribute the prizes given by the School Board for regular attendance. The number of attendance to qualify for a First Prize was 437. Two only were intitled to a First Prize, namely Maggie A. Morgan and Willie Ridge. Fifty six boys and thirty six girls received a Second Prize.

This practice continued after Glamorgan L.E.A. assumed administrative control as witnessed by reports in local newspapers. In 1926, County Councillor and School Manager, W. H. Hopkins attended Bargoed Girls' School to present attendance awards in early February and similar presentations were made at the South Bargoed Infants' Girls' and Boys' Schools on St. David's Day and at the Gilfach Schools in late April.

Apart from the regular Christmas, Easter and Summer Holidays, and the shorter mid-term breaks, local schoolchildren enjoyed a number of other holidays during the year. St. David's Day was routinely celebrated in the schools with Welsh dramas, songs, dances or lectures during the morning and a half holiday in the afternoon. Other half holidays were granted as rewards for satisfactory attendance records, and early closures were often arranged when there were special events such as a visiting circus or menagerie, or a tea in one of the places of worship. Often holidays were granted to allow school pupils to join in national celebrations, such as Queen Victoria's birthday and the Relief of Mafeking in 1900 and royal events such as coronations and weddings, and there were several days *Victory Holidays* at the conclusion of both World War I and World War II. In addition, schools sometimes closed for local events such as Royal visits to South Wales, the funeral of a local notable and for Bargoed Shopping Week in October 1937.

Other school closures occurred for a variety of reasons. For decades, many of the elementary schools regularly closed on election days as the premises were used as polling stations. Sometimes the schools closed when the Labour Examinations were held, while on other occasions the closure was to allow a local place of worship use of its facilities to accommodate a special event. From time to time, school holidays were extended when repair and decoration work overran the estimated time, and on other occasions, the Medical Officer of Health enforced closure for weeks, or even months, in order to control the spread of disease, as in the case of measles in Bargoed Mixed School in 1897.

Private education

It is likely that some of the new middle class professionals who moved into the growing communities of Bargoed and Gilfach sought private education for their children. Sometimes they achieved this by sending their children to boarding school while, in other instances, children travelled by train to Cardiff schools where they were enrolled as day pupils. St. Anne's School was a private school in Bargoed and Gilfach. It is not clear when the school opened, but *Merthyr Express* 2 August 1919 reported on the scholars of St. Anne's School celebrating Peace Day. In the early 1920s the Principal was Miss C. A. Bennett and classes were held in the schoolroom of Trinity Chapel in Cardiff Road. *Merthyr Express* 4 August 1924, while announcing that the next term at St. Anne's School would start on 18 September, referred to successes of some of its pupils in music examinations and in the entrance examinations to Lewis School Pengam and Howells' School Llandaff. While most families in pre-World War II Bargoed and Gilfach would not have considered sending their sons and daughters to a private school, it was not uncommon for them to pay for their child to have music (mainly piano) lessons from one of the numerous local people who offered lessons in their homes.

Post-elementary education to 1938

Glamorgan L.E.A., believing that education was the key to progress, was determined to extend its provision of post-elementary education to satisfy the rapidly growing population in communities like those in Bargoed and Gilfach, through opening Higher Elementary (later re-designated Secondary) and Senior Schools, while, since the later nineteenth century, the Lewis Schools offered single-sex grammar school education for boys at Pengam and girls first at Pontlottyn and later at Hengoed.

The Education Acts of 1870 and 1902 had concerned themselves with elementary education only, but the 1918 Education Act raised the question of education for 11+ pupils. Glamorgan L.E.A.'s first response, submitted to the Board of Education in 1920, included Middle or Free Secondary Schools for scholars aged 11+ to 16 who did not gain entry to the Secondary (including Intermediate or County) or Junior Technical Schools. This proposal was abandoned, partly because of its cost and partly because there was no compulsion for young people to attend. When the 1926 Hadow Report recommended some form of post-primary education for all children aged 11-15, Glamorgan L.E.A. prepared plans for non-selective Senior Schools for all 11+ scholars who did not go to a Secondary or Junior Technical School. The headteachers of these Senior Schools (with rooms equipped for Woodwork, Domestic Science, Arts and Crafts and Practical Science, as well as classrooms and a gymnasium, and, if possible, playing fields) should operate them like Secondary Schools, with the teachers, of whom at least 50% would be graduates, assuming responsibility for a subject in which he/she had specialist knowledge. However, they would be different from the other 11+ schools in that they would be free of the demands of external examinations and of prescriptive guidance from both Board of Education and Glamorgan L.E.A. and so able to experiment and develop in response to the needs of their pupils.

Local reorganisation of schools in 1938

By the mid 1930s, the elementary school population had fallen from its peak, and there was spare capacity in boys' and girls' schools in Bargoed and Gilfach. Provision for the education of Infants continued in all three centres, north and south Bargoed and Gilfach, but, in 1938, that for children aged 7 – 14 was reorganised. During 1937-1938, the north Bargoed single-sex elementary schools were subject to disruption as contractors moved in to work on the alterations necessary to adapt the school premises for the new non-selective Senior Schools. The Girls' School had a commodious new wing while in the Boys' School the 1925 conversion of two classrooms into three was reversed and the classroom constructed in 1911 was absorbed into a further extension including a store room, art and craft room, science laboratory, headmaster's

This photograph of the outside of Bargoed Higher Elementary School was taken from the north (Wood Street) side of the building. Mr Thomas, school caretaker during the school's first decade, is leaning on the railings. He had to deal with a number of problems associated with the new buildings in 1910 including two explosions in the boiler furnace in the early months.

room and indoor staff toilet and cloakroom (part of which was partitioned off to form a kit room). The new single-sex non-selective Senior Schools for pupils aged 11 – 14 opened in 1938. They closed at the end of 1947 to reopen in January 1948 as single-sex Secondary Modern Schools.

Bargoed Higher Elementary School, *Tua'r Goleuni* (Towards the Light)

As the early twentieth century Liberal Government opposed Higher Grade Schools by refusing to sanction funding them from Government grants to L.E.A.s for elementary education, Glamorgan L.E.A. planned 39 Higher Elementary Schools. Higher Elementary Schools, attracting a higher rate of grant than ordinary elementary schools, aimed to provide a three-year course for some of the more able older pupils in the elementary schools who were not able to attend County (Intermediate) Schools like those at Pengam and Hengoed. Although it was intended that these schools would be staffed by teachers as well qualified as those in the County Schools, the curriculum would be less extensive and there was no *leaving certificate*.

Bargoed Higher Elementary School, opened in February 1910 by Sir T. Marchant Williams, Stipendiary for Merthyr Division, was one of six such schools that Glamorgan L.E.A. opened, before the outbreak of World War I, in areas where there was both a significant increase in the local population and insufficient secondary school provision. Designed by County Architect, D. Pugh Jones, and built by T. F. Howells of Cardiff, it was a fine example of a modern school at that time. Designed to accommodate over two hundred boys and girls, the premises, erected on the west side of Park Crescent at a cost of £7,819, comprised an assembly hall, six classrooms, a science laboratory (to

This photograph shows a class of boys and girls in the science laboratory of Bargoed Higher Elementary School with science master J. J. Davies in the background

accommodate 24 pupils), facilities for handicraft and housewifery, and a dining room, with a spacious playground outside.

Its first headteacher, James Sylvan Evans, B.A., laid the foundations of a great tradition. The curriculum of practical subjects and useful arts aimed to prepare boys and girls for their future life, satisfying the demands of the education-conscious parents of the time. The first pupils would have felt proud of their school caps with badges – a mark of distinction – and in awe of their dignified headmaster and his staff in their academic gowns. Most of the

This photograph shows J. Sylvan Evans, first headmaster of Bargoed Higher Elementary School, working in his office in the school

This photograph shows the staff of Bargoed Higher Elementary School in 1910.
Stand left to right: E. W. Rees, Evan T. Davies, J. J. Davies (headmaster 1931-1945) and W. H. Evans
Seated Left to right: Miss A. M. Evans, Miss M. S. Lloyd, J. Sylvan Evans (headmaster 1910-1930), Miss E. V. Salmon and Miss A. C. Brooks.

following information on this school is based on *The Story of Bargod Grammar Technical School 1910-1960*, compiled in the school in 1964 by which time the name of the school had changed several times.

In 1910, the school had a team of School Managers, comprising local ministers of religion and Councillors. The first meeting of its Managers was 22 November 1910. Rev. Daniel Leyshon Evans of Calfaria and Rev. Harri Edwards of Hanbury Road Baptist, were the first elected chairman and vice-chairman, with the former serving until his death in 1919. In the early twentieth century it was not unusual for Ministers of religion, spiritual mentors and guides for many working class people, to assume public office to further the cause of social progress. The Managers had a variety of weighty educational issues to deal with but they also had to make decisions that appeared to have little to do with education as in the case of 18 March 1912 when they decided to fix springs on the school gate to prevent sheep straying into the school yard.

From the first, the school was eager to develop and display its talents. The first school concert was held 23 March 1911, and a piano was purchased from Dale Forty and Company at a cost of 36 guineas (£37.80). Concerts continued to be held, including one in which a war memorial, carved and erected by Mr Thomas, the school caretaker, was unveiled in the school hall.

The first headmaster was also Organising Secretary of pioneering technological and further education evening classes held in the school. There were over twenty technical classes with nearly 400 students on roll and he visited the classes nightly to stimulate and encourage the students. The classes were especially popular among young men who had passed the Labour examination and who had started work, usually to make a necessary contribution to the family budget, but wanted to extend their knowledge and broaden their culture.

This photograph shows the school's first workshop facilities, a handicraft room, lit by gas brackets suspended from the ceiling and with *Manual Room* carved in stone over the doorway, in which pupils were taught by one trained teacher. Later, following merger with Bargoed Mining and Technical Institute, pupils and teachers enjoyed enhanced facilities in the West Street premises.

During the second decade of the twentieth century, Higher Elementary Schools, frowned upon by both County and Elementary Schools, were increasingly criticised by educationalists for their narrow curriculum. Thus, early in 1920, Glamorgan LEA, prepared to turn them into Secondary Schools, and, in September 1920 the headmaster received their letter instructing him to conduct the school as a Secondary School. The staff of the school remained the same but the syllabus was extended to provide a 4 or 5 year education for the pupils. In July 1923, the first pupils of the school sat Central Welsh Board

When Bargoed Higher Elementary School opened housewifery was an important subject for girls, training them for domestic service before marriage and a home of their own. This photograph shows a class of girls and their teacher, Miss A. M. Evans, in a cookery lesson.

examinations. The school's reputation grew during the 1920s, and, before the end of the decade, the school had outgrown its limited accommodation. In 1930, G.U.D.C. made part of Bargoed Park available for extensions to the school and they were opened in 1931.

When Bargoed Higher Elementary School became a Secondary School, a Board of Governors replaced the School Managers. The first meeting of this governing body, 21 December 1920, was to prepare for the change in January 1921. Rev. Harri Edwards was elected chairman of the Board of Governors but he left the district before the end of 1921 and he was succeeded by a succession of chairmen over the next decade.

On the retirement of the school's first headmaster in 1930, J. J. Davies, B.A., B.Sc., a member of staff since 1910, became headmaster. His headship (1931-45) spanned difficult years of economic depression in the 1930s and the duration of World War II. During the 1930s, he was able to enhance the school's facilities by ensuring there were well-equipped laboratories, a gymnasium and playing fields, a Dining Hall and a suitable room for teaching Art. As Organising Teacher for the evening classes in Bargoed Mining and Technical Institute in the academic year 1931-1932, J. J. Davies was able to secure the use of some of the new facilities for Bargoed Secondary School while the Secondary School was being enlarged.

The school inspection in May 1935 highlighted the fact that the school had no playing fields of its own. Pupil's physical activities were limited to dancing lessons in the hall and netball on the sloping yard, although the headmaster, as one of the Trustees of the Miners' Welfare Fund, had secured the school use of the Miners' Welfare Ground, about ¼ mile from the school. It was clear that, given a change of headmaster in the future, this privilege would not necessarily continue, and that the school, with 188 boys and 160 girls on roll, needed its own playing field. The L.E.A. was already taking positive steps to provide the school with a suitable level playing field, but, given the local geography, this was not an easy matter. After trial boreholes showed there was sufficient depth of soil above the rock, they agreed to purchase a freehold plot (a little over 8 acres, 20,025 square yards) at the rear of Hillside Park from Arthur Moss. After spending £30 on legal costs and an estimated £6,300 for preparation, including levelling and draining the land, the playing fields opened in the Summer Term 1938.

The Board of Education approved plans and specifications for the erection of a Dining Hall of 1,620 square feet with entrance lobbies, kitchen, vegetable and crockery stores, larder, laundry, W.C. and heating chamber (totalling 857 square feet) on 5 December 1935. When it opened in 1939 it was a boon, especially for those pupils who lived some distance from the school.

J. J. Davies fostered choral music in the school and, as a loyal member of Bethania's congregation, he was proud of the enthusiastic hymn-singing in the morning assembly. The first annual Speech Day was held in Central Hall on Thursday 29 March 1934 with guest speaker, Morgan Jones, M.P., then

Parliamentary Secretary to the Board of Education. School Eisteddfodau during the 1930s were public and held in Bargoed's Workmen's Institute.

Prior to World War II, teaching posts were scarce and teaching staff tended to remain in post for a long time, sometimes for their entire teaching career. Bargoed Secondary School was fortunate to be served by many competent teachers. However, during the war years, J. J. Davies had to contend with numerous staff changes and the difficulties of finding replacement teachers, something that became increasingly difficult as members of staff (and many ex-pupils) were called up to serve their country. Staff and pupils had to adjust to the war in other ways also: the difficulties of travelling during the blackout necessitated a change in the school day so school started at 9 a.m. and often finished by 2.30 or 3 p.m., and while they were in school lessons were liable to interruption by the air raid sirens.

After forty years in the teaching profession, J. J. Davies retired in January 1945 and left the local area to enjoy retirement in his birthplace, Llangrannog, Cardiganshire. The next headteacher, E. John Saunders, M.A., served from 1945 until ill-health prompted his retirement in 1953. Mr Saunders took over the school during a period of bad weather when few pupils were able to attend school. Soon after he became headmaster, the school had another change of name, becoming Bargod Grammar School. It was Grammar consequent upon R. A. Butler's Education Act of 1944 and the spelling *Bargod* was adopted in preference to Bargoed as approved by the Board of Celtic Studies and Grammar. The examination system also changed when Welsh Joint Education Committee's General Certificate of Education Ordinary, Advanced and Scholarship levels replaced Central Welsh Board's School Certificate and Higher School Certificate.

By the 1920s, the school's Old Students were active and the Old Students' Association organised reunions and games against school teams before the school closed for the Christmas and Easter holidays each year. After World War II, the Old Student's Association held a meeting to organise a memorial fund in memory and honour of former pupils of the school who had given their lives during the conflict. In November 1947, a memorial plaque and a two-manual pedal organ were dedicated during a service at the school, and during the academic year 1947-1948 they initiated two Old Student's Association Memorial Prizes. These prizes (£10 towards the cost of books and instruments required in their studies) would be presented as rewards for academic and cultural achievements of two pupils of Form IV and V who expected to continue full-time education. Also in the late 1940s the former pupils held their Athletic Club in the school gymnasium when members enjoyed activities such as badminton, basketball and table tennis. They opened a weekly Social Club in the Buffet Room of Bargoed Workmen's Institute on Friday 13 October 1950 and they advertised their Christmas Reunion in Café Ballroom in the first issue of *Yr Eryr* (the school magazine).

Walter Haydn Davies became headmaster in September 1953 and he remained in post until his retirement in 1967. He had started his working life in Bedlinog Collieries. As headmaster he wrote in the school magazine about experiences in Bedlinog Reading Room and debates in the Committee Room that inspired him to study. While still working, he had regularly walked over the mountain to attend evening classes in Bargoed Secondary School in the 1920s and he attended Higher Education Summer Schools. He was able to turn his back on the dangers of working in the coal industry when he acquired the necessary qualifications to enter the teaching profession. His early experiences remained with him as shown in his Reports delivered at successive Speech Days.

As a teacher and as headmaster, W. Haydn Davies was acutely aware of the social and economic changes in the decades since his youth. He knew that a pupil's development depended on innate ability, the competence and commitment of the teachers and encouragement from parents. He recognised that, while in the 1950s and 60s the material and moral well-being of homes was reflected in the pupils' cleanliness, dress and good behaviour, some parents and children did not necessarily view education as the important key to future success as he had done in the 1920s. He realised that radio and television in the home was likely to limit the time spent in home study and that the decline in church and chapel attendance impacted on contemporary culture. In successive Speech Days, he endeavoured to encourage parents to ensure they did everything possible to provide a proper atmosphere for study in the home as education was a privilege that had been won by efforts of earlier people and in the 1950s and 60s they should show their appreciation by diligent study.

W. Haydn Davies and his staff knew the pupils and understood their home backgrounds. He knew that some parents made sacrifices to keep their children in school and so he was determined to ensure that, in spite of difficulties in retaining competent staff for lengthy periods at that time, the pupils were given every educational opportunity in school. He appreciated that, while Glamorgan LEA's selection policy creamed off the most academically-gifted pupils to the neighbouring single-sex Lewis Schools, this school could never match their academic reputations and earn the same regard among parents. However, he was proud of the balance of academic and social activities and the nurturing of citizenship and fellowship in the school. A School Film made in the early 1950s and reports in *Yr Eryr* illustrated the school's range of cultural and social activities. There was a happy relationship between staff and pupils, with staff actively involved in extra-curricular activities, including drama, concerts, Urdd, eisteddfodau, Christmas parties as well as visits to places of interest at home and abroad.

School life underwent some changes while W. Haydn Davies was headmaster. He introduced Current Affairs into the Sixth Form timetable and that included accepting an invitation from County Councillor Hancock to visit County Hall to hear the County Council in session. His first school concert, in

October 1953, to raise funds to enable the school to purchase a tape recorder, culminated in a showing of the School Film. A Parent Association, formed during the school year 1953-54, displayed an enthusiastic interest in the school: it aimed to raise money to buy a sound recorder and it presented two cups to be awarded to the best readers in morning assembly. During the 1953-1954 school year, he oversaw the introduction of distinctive ties, caps and badges, designed by the Sixth Form for the Sixth Form.

When the question of a Pavilion on the school playing field was discussed in staff meetings in the early 1950s, it was decided that the proceeds from the next Annual School Play should be used to purchase a suitable building. The play, *Noah*, by Andre Obey (translated from French by Arthur Wilmurt), produced by Mrs E. P. Walters and performed 8, 9, and 10 February 1955, raised £100, and that was used to purchase an ex-R.A.F. pavilion advertised for sale in *Western Mail* during Spring 1956. It was opened Wednesday 10 April 1957 by Alderman Llewellyn Haycock, J.P., Chairman of Glamorgan Education Committee. Although it was a utilitarian veranda, it provided shelter in wet weather and a place where any pupil suffering a sports' injury could be treated.

After 1959, the West Street building was transformed to provide superior facilities in two spacious, well-equipped workshops, one for woodwork and one for metalwork, and a commodious and comfortable drawing office for engineering drawing. In the new woodwork room, older pupils were able to start a course of cabinet making that had not been possible in the inadequate former workshop in Park Crescent. The new metalwork room was about the same size as the woodwork room as two rooms were made into one for it. It had up-to-date machinery and equipment installed and new workbenches. The drawing office needed new drawing tables.

Up to 1958 school Speech Days had been in the Church Hall or Workmen's Institute but that of 1959 was the first to take place in the Central Hall. In 1959, the school underwent another change of name when it merged with Bargoed Mining and Technical Institute, in West Street, to become Bargod Grammar Technical School. That merger meant that the school's workshop facilities were enhanced, and with its excellent science facilities, the headmaster was confident that the school was well-placed to prepare pupils for careers in the changing post-war economic climate in South Wales and beyond. The merger meant not just a new name for the school, but it also increased it from a 2-form to a 3-form entry. As the increased numbers worked up the school it would eventually increase the size of the Sixth Form and probably increase the size of the Science classes in the Sixth Form to make further use of the excellent science facilities.

The school celebrated its Golden Jubilee in 1960 by installing two stained glass windows in the main School Hall, a physical reminder of this landmark in the history of local education, and by establishing a Jubilee Fund. £350 was invested in 5% Defence Bonds and the first Golden Jubilee Award was presented to ex-pupil, surgeon Dr. Brychan Morris at Speech Day, Wednesday 16 November 1962.

The anticipated increase in the school population prompted the headmaster to stress the need for increased accommodation. In his Report at Speech Day November 1962 he noted that two additional classrooms (one for music and one for arts and crafts), as well as a Sixth Form Library to replace the small, unsuitable Library, and improved cloakroom accommodation were essential. On his retirement in 1967, W. Haydn Davies was succeeded by Keri Edwards, M.A. (later J. P. and, after his retirement his literature research earned him a doctorate), Deputy Principal of Bargoed Mining and Technical Institute before becoming Head of English in Bargod Grammar-Technical School. During a headship, which lasted to 1984, he guided the school through its merger with Bargoed's two single-sex Secondary Modern Schools to become Heolddu Comprehensive School in September 1973.

Over the decades pupils enjoyed a variety of cultural activities and one of the annual highlights was the St. David's Day inter-house School Eisteddfod that became so popular with parents and the public that the School Hall could not accommodate them and so it was moved to the Central Hall. Pupils enjoyed successes in Urdd Eisteddfodau, with their greatest achievement being the five firsts and one second prize at Pontardulais National Urdd Eisteddfod. The school was actively involved in the National Eisteddfod in Caerphilly in 1950. The school earned a reputation for excellence in dance and drama with performances in the school and in the Workmen's Hall and Church Hall when pupils and teachers performed with scenery and costumes made by schools pupils under the guidance of the craft teachers.

Bargoed Mining and Technical Institute

Bargoed's Mining Training Centre was one of five Centres for Senior Stage Work planned for the Glamorgan section of the Coalfield. A suitable freehold plot in West Street was identified as early as 1926 but Bargoed Mining and Technical Institute did not open until 12 June 1930. For sale at a cost of £400, the 3,212 square yard site would be easily accessible to students, being only 3-4 minutes from a bus route and 8-9 minutes from the railway station. However, the cost of levelling the uneven ground would be considerable and further expansion was limited as the site bordered West Street, a narrow street on the north side, cottage property on the east, and a back lane behind the Wood Street houses on the south. In 1926, the Board of Education recommended that the L.E.A. should also purchase an undeveloped plot with a 70 foot street frontage on the west, between the original plot and Bargoed Park, and, either build the Institute on it or keep it for future expansion of the Institute. By January 1927, it was clear that was not feasible as a trading concern had already acquired it, and so negotiations continued for the original designated site.

During the later 1920s, there was considerable correspondence between the Board of Education and the L.E.A. regarding costs. As the travelling teachers would become fixed, their travelling expenses would be saved when the Institute opened and it was estimated that running costs such as caretaking, lighting and heating of the new premises would cost about £300 a year. The

£7,186 16s 11d final cost of the building (including boundary walls, outbuildings and playground, installation of heating, lighting, furniture and equipment, including laboratory fittings, and salary of clerk of works) was met by a Miners' Welfare Fund grant of £5,500 towards the costs of constructing and equipping the new Institute topped up by a loan secured by the L.E.A..

In 1930 the Mining Institute opened to provide technical education in the Rhymney Valley through day and evening classes. The stone and brick building, with a slate roof, and solid woodblock and tile floors laid on concrete, comprised five teaching areas (two classrooms, a drawing room, a physics laboratory and a chemistry laboratory) as well as dark and prep rooms, a small store area, staff room, cloak room and lavatories and a cleaners' store. It was important that the dark room, for the examination of colliery firemen candidates, should be very well ventilated, as, when in use, irrespirable gas could pollute the air. It needed a separate exit so that the examinee did not walk back into the prep room, temporarily darkened to allow waiting candidates to grow accustomed to darkness.

The Junior Technical School opened September 1931 and in May 1932, the Secondary School Governors accepted responsibility for management of the Junior Technical School and the Evening Classes. The pre-World War II aims of the Junior Technical School are shown in the following extract from the 1938-39 prospectus: *The aim and object of the Junior Technical Day School is to provide continued education and practical preliminary training for boys who intend to enter one of the industries of the district. It is not intended to teach a boy a particular trade, but rather to develop his faculties so that by the time he is ready to commence work, he possesses not only a general knowledge of the principles which underlie the particular trade he wishes to follow, but also such intelligence, reasoning power, and adaptability as will help him to understand and take an interest in his work. It is intended that the education received should be a preparation for the whole of life. It should educate for labour and for leisure.*

At that time, the school accommodated 75 boys from the catchment area, 25 of whom were admitted annually based on performance in a competitive examination in English and arithmetic. At the same time, there was a wide range of Evening Classes on offer including technical introductions for the building, engineering, metallurgy and mining industries, certificate courses on Mechanical and Electrical Engineering, courses for those who wish to qualify as teachers of Handicraft and for those seeking to matriculate, as well as courses for serving miners. Females were attracted by the Domestic and Household course that included needlework (art and plain), dressmaking, quilting, handwork (including leatherwork) and cookery and the Shorthand-Typist Course taught in Hengoed Girls' County School. From the early 1930s, the Mining and Technical Institute used the nearby Secondary School's handicraft facilities and later it used its gymnasium, playing fields and art room, and, the pupils had their midday meal in the new Dining Hall.

Before World War II, most of the Institute's work involved evening classes together with two groups of part-time day students on courses in Engineering and Mining. During World War II, it assisted in training men directed into the mining industry (Bevin Boys). Its work increased in the post-war era when, in 1946, part-time day courses in Engineering and Mining were re-introduced on a large-scale, and, in 1947, it introduced a new system of training mine entrants. By 1950, the Institute catered for about 70 day school pupils, many evening class students studying a variety of subjects, at least five day-release classes and four groups of full-time mine trainees who, during a twelve-week course, spent alternate periods of two weeks at the Institute and the Colliery Training Centre. When H.M.I. Mr G. Grattan inspected the Institute in November 1954, the existing accommodation was inadequate for the number of students and range of courses, and so workshops, classrooms and gymnasium in other premises, including Bargoed Colliery, Bargoed Educational Settlement and Gilfach Y.M.C.A., solved some of the accommodation problems but created administrative difficulties. By that time the L.E.A. had decided to erect a new College of Further Education at Ystrad Mynach and, after nearly three decades, Bargoed Mining and Technical Institute ceased to exist as an independent entity in 1959. It lost most of its adult classes to the newly-completed modern and well-equipped College of Further Education in Ystrad Mynach, and the Technical School was combined with Bargod Grammar School to form Bargod Grammar Technical School.

Under successive principals (who also acted as headmasters of the Junior Technical School), D. T. Jarman, B.Sc. (1931-49), Oswald Thomas, M.Sc., A.R.I.C. (1950-53), and G. C. Sumption, M.Sc. (1953-59) and their staffs, Bargoed Mining and Technical Institute made a valuable contribution to industry and culture. Adult students studied vocational and non-vocational subjects, preparing themselves for important managerial posts in collieries and engineering works. The annual printed transactions of Bargoed Mining Society ensured information about modern mining techniques and machinery was disseminated to distant parts of the world. Over the years, nearly two thousand boys studied in the day school. Although they did not have the academic ability of contemporary Grammar School pupils, many of them eventually achieved Higher National Certificate of Engineering, at least ten pupils won scholarships for full-time study at Treforest College of Advanced Technology, while some boys who wanted to enter the professions applied successfully for transfer to a Grammar School. Critics of Bargoed Mining and Technical Institute pointed to its limited curriculum and the fact that the comparatively small number of day pupils precluded extra-curricular activities such as sports, drama and eisteddfodau.

Post World War II Tripartite system of secondary education

In the post-World War II era Glamorgan County Council implemented the 1944 Education Act and all Bargoed Secondary Schools were governed by one Governing Body, comprising 12 members, ten Representative Governors (five representing and nominated by the Glamorgan Education Authority and five representing and nominated by the Caerphilly and Gelligaer Divisional Executive) and two Co-optative Governors nominated by the Governors. At least two of the Governors (one of the five representing and nominated by the Caerphilly and Gelligaer Divisional Executive and one of the Co-optative Governors) had to be female. The Governing Body met twice a term and its clerk was the Divisional Executive Officer. The Governing Body had a comprehensive constitution that laid down in detail the regulations relating to the terms of office of a Governor. A Governor held office for a 3 year term. Teachers in the school being governed were not eligible to be members of that Governing Body. The headteacher of the school attended every Governors' Meeting but was not a member of the Governing Body. The Governors' duties were laid down in the Fourteen Articles of Government. The Governors did not appoint the headteacher but they appointed the teaching and non-teaching staff. The aim of the Governing Body was to ensure that pupils, staff, parents and the Education Authority worked together to offer the best possible education the school could give. By the mid twentieth century, local councillors were likely to be elected chairman and vice-chairman of the Governing Bodies and the Bargoed Secondary Schools were served by some experienced men including W. H. Lee and W. J. Kedward, O.B.E., J.P..

When the post-World War II selective tripartite system of secondary education was implemented in January 1948, the two single-sex Senior Schools became single-sex Secondary County Schools and pupils who did not gain places in the local grammar or technical schools were educated there until the introduction of comprehensive education in 1973. In the early 1950s H. M. I. of Schools who reported on these two schools noted that the area had a high (approximately 40%) Grammar School intake: the most successful cohort in the 11+ examinations earned places in Pengam (boys) or Hengoed (girls) Grammar Schools, while other successful pupils were offered places in Bargod Grammar School (formerly known as Bargoed Secondary School and later to become known as Bargod Grammar Technical School) or Bargoed Mining and Technical Institute (boys only). Some of the pupils who attended the County Secondary schools transferred to a Grammar school following a Casual Vacancy examination and there were instances of pupils transferring from a Grammar School to a County Secondary.

Bargoed Girls' County Secondary School occupied premises built in three stages: the oldest part at the back dated from the late nineteenth century, the middle part from 1907 while the commodious new wing was constructed in 1938 for the new non-selective Senior Girls' School. When the school was inspected in June 1951 there were a number of limitations that made for difficulties in providing an entirely effective education for the 199 girls on roll. As the two adequately-sized Housecraft rooms on the ground floor, one with bedroom, sitting room, bathroom and lavatory attached, had not been updated they did not meet the needs of the 1950s. The main teaching rooms around the

Assembly Hall (that also served as gymnasium and dining room) included a spacious Science laboratory that was suitably furnished in most respects, but, as it lacked black-out facilities it could not be used to show filmstrips. The school was ill-equipped for physical education: outdoor activities were limited as the school only had two small playground areas, each about 30 feet square, and it did not have a playing field. The Assembly Hall was used for physical education but there was no adequate storage space for equipment and, as it was between the two pupil cloakrooms, on wet days the floor was dirty and unsuitable for the full range of activities. Dining facilities were inadequate: a sliding partition between two rooms had been removed to make a long room for the teaching of Arts and Crafts, and that served as a dining room with any overflow directed into the Assembly Hall. In spite of these difficulties at the time of the Inspection (June 1951) the school, under the control of an experienced headmistress full of vitality and initiative with a conscientious, hardworking and appropriately qualified staff comprising eleven full-time female teachers and a part-time male teacher (for instrumental music), was successful.

Prior to World War II, many of the girls who left school on reaching the statutory school leaving age went into domestic service. However, that was a far less popular career choice in the post-war era, when changing social and economic conditions coupled with the advice and information offered by the Youth Employment Officer, meant that girls were more likely to opt for light factory work, or jobs as shop assistants, clerks and waitresses.

Over the years, the local County Secondary Schools faced numerous challenges but perhaps none was so traumatic as the sudden increase to the numbers on roll following the fire that closed Pontlottyn Secondary School after which the Girls' County Secondary took over the three classrooms vacated by the Welsh classes in the neighbouring Infants' School.

Bargoed Boys' County Secondary School, in Llancayo Street, opened in January 1948 in premises built in 1906 as an all-age Boys' School. After additions and conversions in 1911, 1925 and 1928, it was adapted to house the non-selective Senior Boys' School. In January 1948 Bargoed Boys' County Secondary School opened with a catchment area including the local Boys' Junior Schools and those to the north including Brithdir, Deri, Pantywaun, Tirphil, Pontlottyn, Fochriw and Butetown. At the time of the inspection (May 1954) the school was under the control of Walter Jones, a graduate headmaster who was appointed in January 1953, Senior Master George Elwyn Blyton, and ten other full time assistants as well as a part-time teacher for instrumental music.

As the school did not have a gymnasium, physical education was generally taught in the Hall. However, this was not satisfactory as its floor was uneven and slippery with loose blocks, and there was inadequate space for the boys to change. The school's playing field was a ten-minute walk from the school and it had no changing facilities.

Like the Girls' School, this school had a good relationship with the Youth Employment Bureau, whose Officer arranged visits and talks that enhanced the boys' understanding of the world of work that they expected to occupy for some five decades after leaving school. The inspectors who visited the school in May 1954 reported that recent leavers had entered coal mines, engineering works (including some apprenticed to Electrical Engineering and Allied Trades), railway, navy and the Distributive Trades.

Primary education from 1938 to the present day

The two South Bargoed single-sex junior schools continued from 1938 until September 1974 when they closed, only to emerge as two mixed schools housed in north Bargoed: St. Gwladys' Junior School in the former Girls' County Secondary School in Church Street and Y Graig Junior School in the former Boys County Secondary premises in Llancayo Street. Since then Y Graig Junior School has closed. Its pupils were transferred to the new Park Junior school housed in the Park Crescent premises originally built for Bargoed South Girls' and Boys' Schools and the Llancayo Street premises have been demolished and the site developed for residential purposes. At the present time, St. Gwladys' Primary School, the result of the merger of the Infants' and Junior Schools near St. Gwladys' Church, occupies the north Bargoed premises near St. Gwladys' Church while Park Primary School, formed by merging the South Bargoed Infants' and Y Graig Junior Schools, is housed in the former Boys' and Girls' Junior Schools (premises that were for some time used first by Heolddu Comprehensive School and then by Ysgol Gyfun Cwm Rhymni) in Park Crescent. Bargoed South Infants' School has been demolished and the site offers additional playground space for Park Primary School.

As indicated previously, in 1938 there were three schools in Gilfach, one infants school adjoining the Bowling Green, a boys junior school just off Commercial Street and a girls junior school next to the infants school in Vere Street. During the 1960s changes occurred generated by declining rolls, whereby the boys were transferred to the Vere Street site, thus Gilfach Junior School became a mixed school. The former boys school was taken over by the nascent Welsh Primary school, as indicated below. At a later date the Junior and Infants sections were merged to form a Primary School all on the Vere Street site, where it still exists.

The development of the large Gilfach Fargoed housing estate by the local authority in the 1960s gave rise to demand for a new infants' school easily accessible from the housing estate. This was provided in Park View, where it remained until the declining birth rate rendered it uneconomic, thus its potential pupils were 'bussed' to Gilfach Primary School, to which they would have been sent at 7 years in any case.

Welsh medium education

Welsh language and culture played an important role in the emerging local communities as witnessed in the information supplied in the 1891 and 1901 censuses and in the number of places of worship that conducted their activities in the Welsh language. Those who had grown up in other parts of Wales retained their Welshness, while the school children were made aware of their Welsh heritage especially as St. David's Day was celebrated annually by activities in the school in the morning and a half holiday in the afternoon.

By the 1960s when the Welsh language and culture was under threat across the country, efforts were made, locally and elsewhere, to secure Welsh medium education to help ensure the survival of the language. At first, a Saturday morning class was held in Hanbury Road Baptist Chapel Vestry but perhaps the real starting point of Welsh-medium education in Bargoed and Gilfach came in October 1963 when a Welsh class, taught by Mrs Eirlys Thomas, was inaugurated in a classroom in Bargoed Infants' School. There were only nine pupils on the first day but over the following months and years the numbers grew, more teachers and additional classroom space proved necessary. They outgrew the facilities available in Bargoed Infants' School and, by July 1968, a move to Gilfach was under consideration. That move was not effected until January 1970, when the three classrooms they had occupied in Bargoed Infants' School, were handed over to the Girls' County Secondary School to help them cope with their increased roll following a fire that closed Pontlottyn Secondary School. The Welsh School in Gilfach flourished, and is still providing primary education through the medium of Welsh in the building built for Gilfach's first primary school in 1896 and which later became the Boys' Junior School.

In the 1960s, 70s and early 80s, those pupils who wanted to continue their Welsh-medium education at secondary level had to travel to Rhydfelin before Ysgol Cyfun Cwm Rhymni was opened to serve a wide catchment area in north east Mid Glamorgan and west Gwent. At first it used disused school premises in Aberbargoed before, in 1983, the Park Crescent and West Street buildings formerly occupied by Heolddu Comprehensive School, were also used. In 2002 they moved to purpose-built PFI (Private Finance Initiative) accommodation in Warne Street, Fleur-de-Lys.

It should be noted that, while only a minority of local schoolchildren are currently educated through the medium of Welsh, the Welsh National Curriculum is ensuring that, in common with those in other parts of Wales, local children acquire at least some knowledge and understanding of the language, culture and history of Wales.

Comprehensive education from September 1973 to present day

Comprehensive education was under discussion for some years before it became a reality in the local area as witnessed in *Yr Eryr* volume 15 1965. Heolddu Comprehensive School was a mixed school with a catchment area extending from Gilfach in the south to Butetown in the north, on the west (Glamorgan) side of the river Rhymney, as well as the communities of Deri and Fochriw. In its first year, it was a multi-site school housed in the former County Secondary and Grammar-Technical buildings as well as part of the new accommodation being constructed on Mountain Road. By its second year the school no longer used the former County Secondary premises as more of the new building was ready for occupation while the two youngest year groups were housed in the former Grammar-Technical school buildings and the shortfall in accommodation was made up with the vacated premises on the east side of Park Crescent (as South Bargoed Junior Schools had moved into the former County Secondary premises). It became a single-site school on the purpose-built Heolddu site in 1983. Both before and after it became a single-site school any shortfall in accommodation was met with temporary terrapin classrooms on the already rather small schoolyards. After Keri Edwards retired in the summer of 1984 he was replaced as headmaster by D. Michael Howarth, B.Sc. who in turn was followed by Michael P. Doyle, B.A. on whose retirement in 2006 Philip Jones, BA (Hons), MA (Ed), NPQH became the headmaster.

As outlined above, Lewis School became a single-sex comprehensive school in September 1973 by combining the Grammar School in Gilfach (Pengam) with Graddfa Boys' Secondary Modern School in Ystrad Mynach to form a split-site comprehensive school that faced problems of long-distance commuting between its two sites. In 2002 the school moved into purpose-built PFI accommodation and reverted to its former name of Lewis School Pengam. Lewis Girls' School had moved from Hengoed to Ystrad Mynach in the 1960s and remains there to the present.

Adult Education

Over the decades, there has been a wide range of opportunities for education and learning for adults in Bargoed and Gilfach. As well as evening classes in Bargoed Higher Elementary (later Secondary, Grammar and Grammar Technical) School, and Bargoed Mining and Technical Institute, courses and debates were held in Bargoed Workmen's Institute (built in 1913) and Bargoed Settlement (opened in 1933) in the early and mid twentieth century. Further details about Bargoed Workmen's Institute and Bargoed Settlement appear elsewhere in this volume while *Bargoed Settlement 1933-1998* by Nesta Williams provides a more in-depth study of that institution. Over recent decades, provision for adult education has changed to meet society's needs and classes, offered by a variety of providers, are held in several local venues. Today it is increasingly likely that local people will also attend adult courses in more distant venues to study a range of subjects including the Welsh language.

Library facilities

The library facilities in the Workmen's Institute and Settlement that played an important role in the past are discussed elsewhere in this volume as are the library in Hanbury Road (1972-2009) and the present refurbishment of Hanbury Road Baptist Chapel.

CHAPTER 12
SOCIAL LIFE

Introduction

Over the years, local people have spent their leisure time in a wide variety of different ways and music and sport have figured large. In the later nineteenth century sporting activities became increasingly popular both with participants and spectators while in the early twentieth century, literary and musical groups attracted much interest. For decades the social life of many, especially young people, centred on the mid week activities in local places of worship of all denominations. Some clubs and societies flourished for years and still exist today while others have floundered for a variety of reasons including the attractions of both home-based entertainment such as television and that offered in more sophisticated venues outside the local area.

As Bargoed and Gilfach grew rapidly in the early decades of the twentieth century so the range of entertainment facilities expanded. The pre-World War I years saw new hotels and public houses as well as clubs, playhouses, cafes (those run by Italian incomers were popular as they were alcohol-free) and dance halls and, for some years the roller-skating rink near Bargoed railway station had its resident band.

Hotels and public houses in Bargoed and Gilfach

The pre-industrial community, as well as travellers, were served by several inns and public houses at Pontaberbargoed. The only one on the Glamorgan side of the river was the Old Mill Inn while nearby Smiths Arms, Greyhound (demolished in the late 1960s), Quarry Arms and Travellers Rest as well as Duffryn Hotel (built about 1910 at the top of the hill and later used as Council Offices before being converted for residential purposes) were on the Monmouthshire side of the river. Another public house was marked on the parish tithe map: it was west of the area that became Bargoed and Gilfach on land belonging to Capel Hanbury Leigh Esq. where Gwerthonor borders the Common. It may have been there for a long time, presumably serving travellers over the Common. Both the identity of the occupier, William Perrott, and the date when it ceased to operate as a public house are unclear.

The name of Old Mill Inn in Pontaberbargoed refers to the corn mill and it may have originated in the eighteenth century or earlier. The story of the mill and the inn in the 1860s and early 1870s was linked to the family of Evan James, composer of Wales' National Anthem, as his brother-in-law, Thomas Lewis was the publican, while his nephew, Daniel Lewis was the last miller at the nearby mill. The early history of the Congregational cause in the local area was linked to the inn's Long Room and to the Lewis family. The property was up for sale in the 1870s and Slaters Directory of 1880 lists David Jones as the innkeeper. It is not clear how long he was there as Breconshire-born Thomas

Williams appears as innkeeper in both 1881 census and Kelly's Directory of 1884 but he died before the 1891 census when his widow Martha was Innkeeper and she was listed in Kelly's Directory of 1895. Joseph Davies was listed as an Ale House Keeper in Glamorgan Constabulary's Licensing List of 1897 and in October 1900 *Western Mail* reported that his application to move the Old Mill's licence from the original premises to that on the other side of the road (the site of the present Old Mill Hotel) was granted and that is probably when the name changed from Inn to Hotel. He was enumerated as Hotel Proprietor at Old Mill Inn in 1901 but Kelly's Directory of the same year described the establishment as Old Mill Hotel. It is not clear how long the Davies family was associated with this establishment but the Walters family was there by May 1902 when Eddy Walters of The Old Mill was named as Secretary of the Cricket Club in the local press. Mrs Margaret Walters was listed as landlady of Old Mill Inn in Kelly's Directory of 1906 and she may have been succeeded by Benjamin Augustus (Gus) Jones (an expert Dog Judge and formerly a butcher in New Tredegar) as the Innkeeper in Kelly's Directory 1920. It is likely that the Jones family link with the Old Mill ended soon afterwards as Kelly's Directories of 1923 and 1926 listed John Walters at the Old Mill Hotel, Bridge Street. The Old Mill Hotel continued to serve the community under a succession of landlords and landladies through the twentieth century. In the early twenty first century it was renamed The Gold Mine but closed after trading for a short time, before reopening in 2010 with its former name.

The majority of the locality's new inns and public houses were large buildings to serve the needs of both local residents and visitors in the rapidly expanding communities. Local newspapers shed light on the property auctions, inquests, meetings of local societies and organisations and celebratory events of all sorts that were held in them.

Not surprisingly, a hotel was built near Bargoed railway station for the convenience of rail travellers visiting the area. These included mining experts and engineers who commuted between Britain's coalfields as well as commercial travellers eager to promote their products and exploit the potential market in the rapidly growing and prospering communities of Bargoed and Gilfach. At first it was a small establishment called Railway Inn but that was demolished and replaced by more spacious premises. It was listed as Junction Inn in Slaters Directory 1880 with William Matthews as the innkeeper but he was no longer there when it was called Junction Hotel in the 1881 census. Kelly's Directory of 1884 listed Evan Lewis as the Hotel Keeper but Somerset-born Alfred Henry Stowell was enumerated as the Hotel Keeper in the 1891 census and he was listed in Kelly's 1895 and Glamorgan Constabulary 1897 Licensing List but the Wells family was enumerated at there in 1901. Local newspapers indicate that the Junction Hotel was the preferred venue when auctioneers Messrs. Phillips and Jones had local property to sell in the early twentieth century and numerous local inquests were held there. The premises underwent alterations in 1905 and the entry in Kelly's Directory of 1906 not only named Benjamin Newton as the proprietor and listed its telephone number (21) but also illustrated the services offered and the clientele it wanted to attract. It *had Special XXX ale on draught brewed by Rhymney Valley Brewery Co. and wines, spirits etc of best quality as well as good accommodation for commercials, cyclists and parties and good stabling.* It is not clear who took over when Benjamin Newton died in the autumn of 1909 but William Henry Mills, a rugby player from Llwynypia, was landlord after World War I and he was listed as such in Kelly's Directory of 1920. He died in 1922 and probate records show that he was a fairly wealthy man with an estate valued at over £3,500. Kelly's Directory of 1923 named Mrs Mary Mills, his widow, as the landlady. This hotel did not continue to prosper in the second half of the twentieth century because fewer visitors arrived by train or sought accommodation locally. It ceased to trade and eventually the premises were demolished.

It is not clear whether Breconshire-born William Prothero, *Butcher and Beer Seller*, enumerated at Plasnewydd Public House in 1881 and listed in Kelly's Directory of 1884 was its first landlord. His wife was Miriam Thomas (granddaughter of Thomas Lewis of Old Mill), and they had two sons, David (born in Cardiff about 1878 and who went on to become teacher and pastor in Bedfordshire) and William H. born locally in 1880. The following decades saw a succession of different landlords at Plasnewydd: Kelly's Directory of 1895 listed James Rees, while William Morgan appeared in Glamorgan Constabulary Licensing List of 1897 and Kelly's Directory of 1901 named Joseph B. Thomas. There are not many specific references to the local area in *Merthyr Express* prior to 1900 but there are several references to fortnightly music and literary entertainment at Plasnewydd Assembly Rooms, an early indication of such cultural interests in the area. According to reports in the local press, this establishment attracted a great deal of business in the early twentieth century: it was an ideal venue for a wedding reception (for those who could afford it) and in the years prior to the outbreak of World War I the monthly meetings of the local Chamber of Trade were held there. Ernest E. George, a former Pontypridd rugby player who had won Welsh caps in the mid 1890s, had a somewhat longer tenure than his predecessors at Plasnewydd Hotel as he arrived there no later than June 1904 and he was still there in 1920. Kelly's Directory of 1923 listed Edmund Jones and referred to the position as Upper High Street. Since then Plasnewydd Hotel has had a number of landlords and remains in business today.

It is likely that Gwerthonor Hotel was the one referred to in notices in *Western Mail* in 1894 and 1895 concerning construction and licensing of a hotel in Gilfach. George P. Thomas was listed as its hotel keeper in the 1897 Glamorgan Constabulary Licensing List and in 1901 Welsh-speaking Sarah Watkins was enumerated there as hotel manager. *Merthyr Express* carried a report on a fire in the premises in December 1906. In the early twentieth century auctions and inquests were frequently held on the premises and, prior to World

War I, it was the meeting place for local organisations including Gilfach Cricket Club and Gilfach Chamber of Trade. A large part of the premises was demolished in the 1990s but what remains still operates as licensed premises today.

An application to build a hotel was rejected in 1910, but permission was granted later on a different site and the large and prestigious Royal Hotel was erected in a prime position on the town's main street. According to Kelly's Directory, Mrs Blodwen Williams was its hotel keeper in 1920 and David Thomas Jones in 1923. For decades its Assembly Rooms were frequently used for a variety of purposes and a post-match Glamorgan County Police Rugby team supper in April 1923 is just one example. However, it was closed and demolished in 1960s, and a supermarket with a wide pavement separating it from the thoroughfare was built.

Three local establishments bear names associated with landowners. Both Hanbury Arms and Capel Hotel bear names associated with the landowning family of Pontypool while the McDonnell Hotel is a reminder of Francis

This photograph from Gelligaer Historical Society's collection shows Bargoed's Hanbury Arms. It is not clear when and why the photograph was taken and the identities of the men in the foreground have not been established.

McDonnell also of Pontypool. In May 1903 *Merthyr Express* carried a report on a new hotel, Hanbury Arms. The entry in Kelly's Directory describes it as a *Commercial Hotel and Posting House* with a good billiards table and reports in the local press confirm that it had a billiards team playing in 1904. In its early years it was the meeting place for many local organisations including R.A.O.B., and local cycling and soccer clubs and meetings and inquests were frequently held there. In the post World War I era ex-serviceman Charles Rowley was the hotel keeper and his name is listed in Kelly's Directory of 1920. Notable among later landlords was W. H. (Bert) Burgess. The application for a license for Capel Hotel was made June 1913. During the inter-war years its landlords included Jenkin Morgan, Trevor Price and Philip White. Both Hanbury Arms and Capel Hotel are in business today. McDonnell Hotel, known locally as *The Mac*, dates from 1907 and is still in business today.

What remains of the various large licensed premises serve as a reminder of the rapid growth of Bargoed and Gilfach in the quarter of a century prior to the outbreak of World War I. There was no further development until the Barley Corn opened in the 1970s to serve those living on the new Gilfach Fargoed housing site but it has closed as a public house and the building has been converted for residential accommodation. The Park Hotel and restaurant opened in 1980 in premises that had formerly been residential and is still in business today.

Clubs in Bargoed and Gilfach

During the twentieth century Bargoed and Gilfach had a number of clubs including Bargoed Labour Club on the corner of Wood Street and Henry Street, Bargoed Social in Church Place, Gilfach Workmen's Club, Gwerthonor Social Club in Commercial Street and West Street's Club Lenox. They each had a lively programme of activities including sport, musical entertainment and outings and those of the Union Jack Club serve as an illustration.

Bargoed branch of the British Legion (Royal British Legion since its 1971 golden jubilee) has been active for about nine decades. Its Union Jack Club probably opened in Spring 1923 as a report in *Merthyr Express* 10 March 1923 noted that the new British Legion building near Bargoed Park was near completion. Activities in the *Shot and Shell*, as it was affectionately known by many local people, in the 1920s are documented in the local press and include reference to a well-attended Saturday evening talk against Prohibition followed by a musical evening in Spring 1924, the 1926 case of two brothers remanded in custody for a week after a court appearance for breaking and entering the premises, stealing a quantity of whisky and assaulting a local policeman, its fourth anniversary celebratory supper and concert in 1927 and, later in that year, another concert when William Teague received an inscribed oak clock for five years' service as Secretary. In the post World War II era the Chard family played an important role in the history of the Club. Thomas and Caroline Chard were steward and stewardess for two years prior to Thomas' sudden death in 1964, after which their son Basil served as steward until 1966. Another son

The original building was corrugated as shown in this photograph (courtesy of Marlene Shaw) that shows George Harrison and Ronald Chard on either side of a man so far unidentified with the building in the background. Thomas Chard (junior) was one of the men who worked with builder Mr S. C. Sheen to rebuild the outside by rebricking it, and he made and painted the Union Jack and British Legion signs for the Club.

Thomas (junior) and his wife Myra, a popular singer and entertainer in the Club, were steward and stewardess in the early 1970s until following an accident Thomas was unable to continue. Son Basil, with his wife Anne, were steward and stewardess in the early 1980s.

The Union Jack Club had an active and varied programme in the second half of the twentieth century. It earned a reputation in the local area for its entertainment and some members recall joining long queues in West Street to gain access to the popular Christmas and New Year functions in the 1970s. It had skittles and darts teams, with one of the darts teams entirely composed of sons of Thomas and Caroline Chard. Many local men have fond memories of playing league football as members of the Club's football team. Like many other local clubs, the Union Jack Club organised annual outings to the seaside each summer for members and their families. Stan and Freda Bodman were steward and stewardess for some time. Brian Jeremiah and his wife were the last steward and stewardess before the Union Jack Club closed and after that Brian Jeremiah ran it as a private Club called BJ's for a short time before it was sold, the building demolished and the site developed for residential purposes.

In 1947 a group of ex-R.A.F. personnel met in Hanbury Arms and formed Bargoed Branch of the Royal Air Forces Association. Their first club was sited in premises they acquired in 1953 in Bristol Terrace and when they wanted to move to larger premises they purchased the farmstead of Gilfach Fargoed Fawr in 1968 and the club has remained there ever since.

This photograph (courtesy of Terry McCarthy) was taken about 1980 and shows the exterior of the Gilfach Fargoed Fawr, the oldest building in the Bargoed and Gilfach area.

This scraperboard by Jeffrey Carter shows Bargoed Workmen's Institute as viewed from the south west. It appeared in *Yr Eryr* Volume 13 1963

Bargoed Workmen's Institute

The local area developed rapidly as a mining community and there would have been a degree of pride and optimism when the six foundation stones on the front of Bargoed Workmen's Institute were laid. The 'Stute, as it was often called, was built in 1913 and funded by donations and the miners' weekly penny contributions. Local people celebrated when the debt was cleared. On 13 July 1925 headmaster, David Davies, B.A., recorded in Bargoed Boys 'School Log

Book: *The Schools were closed for the whole day (Monday) because of the Celebration Tea and Sports organised by the Workmen's Institute Committee to celebrate the clearing of the debt on their Institute. All the children in the town were given tea etc free.* The foundation stone on the extension built on the north side of the original building, was laid by Albert Thomas Esq., J.P. on behalf of the Trustees in December 1939. In its heyday it provided recreational and cultural facilities that complimented those available in other local places of worship and education. Some men enjoyed its sporting activities such as billiards while others were more interested in discussing politics, trade unionism, economics and social sciences, reading in the library or debating in an ante room. Union and political meetings that often concluded with singing *The Red Flag* as well as social events such as dances were held in the large hall. Prior to World War II, Workmen's Institutes, regarded as the miner's universities, contributed to every aspect of miner's cultural and social life. By the 1960s the heyday of the Institute was over: the decline in its importance in cultural and social life is illustrated by the number of books borrowed from their libraries, which, in the case of Bargoed was 33,021 books issued in 1931 but only 2,661 in 1961. As the coal industry declined so did the Institute and after Bargoed Workmen's Institute closed it was used for a variety of purposes including some time as a temporary doctor's surgery, a sewing factory employing some local women and a gymnasium/fitness centre.

Playhouses and cinemas

The speed with which places of entertainment were opened reflected the area's rapid growth in the decade and a half prior to the outbreak of World War I. Travelling cinemas set up under Rhymney Railway Viaduct were popular in the early twentieth century and when permanent venues were opened, they were well patronised by local people, especially in the decades from the 1920s to the 1960s when the cinema provided a couple of hours of glamorous escapism from a daily life often dominated by hardship. The early films were silent with sub-titles and accompanied by live music, but by the 1930s the talkies had arrived. To mid twentieth century cinema-goers, the stars of the light-hearted romances and westerns became as familiar as family and friends, while *Pathe News* kept them up-to-date with news and events outside the local community and, during World War II, the films were also preceded by short Ministry of Information films of instruction and guidance. By the 1960s, the attractions of the cinema in the country in general faded, especially as most families sought entertainment and news updates from the television set in their home. Since then, further advances in technology have made it possible for people to watch films, on affordable video and DVD players with high quality picture and sound, in the comfort of their own home and at a time to suit themselves.

In 1907 the New Hall Playhouse opened on the east side of Lower High Street as a venue for live performances and with its ballroom and cafe, the premises remained popular for over five decades. The headmaster of Bargoed Boys' School noted in the School Log Book that one of the reasons for poor attendance immediately prior to Christmas 1907 was the fact that children were admitted for 3d. to *Wreck of the Argosy* in New Hall. *Merthyr Express* reported that Miss Madge Belmont, a popular music hall and variety artiste, was among those who appeared at New Hall in June 1919. Her autographed photographs were sold and profits of the variety evening went to local men who had returned from war service. Within a few months of the end of World War I, Jackson Withers, owner of New Hall, made it clear that he wanted to erect an up-to-date modern theatre and, during the 1920s, the Playhouse was converted to New Hall Cinema (generally referred to locally as Cafe Cinema or Hall Cinema). Its management, having prided itself on keeping up to date with the latest and most advanced developments in the science of sound reproduction long before the days of the talking film apparatus, did not spare any expense when they installed the most up-to-date equipment in January 1937 to enhance patrons' enjoyment. Local schoolchildren enjoyed cinema visits on the occasions of the 1937 and 1953 coronations: entries in school log books show that, in 1937, Mr A. Withers, owner of New Hall Cinema, provided school children with a free programme celebrating the coronation of George VI, and in June 1953, they enjoyed the film *A Queen is crowned*. It was not only school children who enjoyed films in New Hall Cinema as many local people remember the long queues that formed up and down Lower High Street as patrons waited eagerly to gain admission to the stalls or circle.

The attached New Hall Cafe could seat over 200 diners who were served by waitresses in Art Deco style uniforms. It was a dining place of distinction as shown by the fact that it was the chosen lunch venue for the guests at the third annual Horticultural Show in 1920. The lower part of the building housed the popular Cafe Ballroom. In the 1940s and 1950s young children attended dancing lessons in Cafe Ballroom, before as young teenagers, going to the Church Hall on Friday evenings where, for 3d., they could dance for about three hours to gramophone records. As they grew older they joined people from the town, surrounding villages and further afield, dancing on New Hall Ballroom's sprung dance floor, jiving, jitterbugging, waltzing or quickstepping in styles peculiar to this venue, to the music of local bands. One of the best-known and most popular of these bands was that of Aneurin Thomas (1906-2011). Countless local couples, many of whom have celebrated Golden Weddings in recent years, recall that their romance blossomed on the dance floor at the Cafe Ballroom, often when the young man was home on leave from National Service.

In the inter-war period New Hall hosted numerous prestigious social events, many of which were annual functions and reported in some detail in *Merthyr Express*. One of these was the annual Jewish Ball and Whist Drive, the first of which was probably held in 1918. That of 1926 was described as successful with people from Swansea, London, Leeds, Manchester, Porthcawl, Cardiff, Merthyr and Rhondda making it one of the main social functions in Bargoed. During the later 1920s Gerald and Cyril Barnett and Nathan Joseph were among the organisers of the event. Some of the events were fairly small, as in the case

These two drawings appeared in a pre World War I town directory and they show The New Hall and The Palace, two places of entertainment facing each other on opposite sides of Lower High Street.

of the fourth annual Bargoed Branch Railway Clerk's Association Dinner attended by over sixty people in December 1924 while there were over four hundred people at Bargoed Bon Marche annual whist drive and dance in aid of Cardiff's King Edward VII Hospital in February 1926. Sometimes the event was a group celebration as in the instance of the reunion of Bargoed's mining students in May 1920, while on other occasions, it was to celebrate an individual as in the case of a presentation to William Evans of Lower Wood Street on completing 25 years service to Refuge Assurance Company in May 1926.

Year after year, May Day was celebrated in New Hall. In 1920 Miners' Agent, Walter Lewis, J.P. expressed his disappointment with the meagre attendance as well as his concern that people's indifference was jeopardising the work of the Labour Movement. The main issue in the speeches that followed was S.W.M.F. resolution relating to nationalisation. No doubt he was more cheered to preside over the large attendance in 1924 when Captain Griffiths spoke on Labour and Noah Ablett addressed the meeting on the mining industry. Morgan Jones made a May Day Speech at New Hall in 1926 and, during the following months, there were numerous boxing tournaments in aid of the local Canteen Fund at the same venue, including one in October attended by four members of the National Sporting Club and Mr and Mrs Frank Moody of Pontypridd. Perhaps the boxing highlight of the year was in the autumn, when, having brought the film of the Dempsey-Tunney fight by car on Sunday, it was on screen at 11 a.m. on the Monday, making Bargoed's New Hall Cinema one of the first cinemas in the country to screen it.

Many people recall with sadness the winter day in 1958 when fire destroyed the premises, but they still have happy memories of their time in Cafe Ballroom, especially if they met their marriage partners there. The site was redeveloped and occupied by F. W. Woolworth's until its closure in January 2009. Since then this property, boasting the largest retail floor space in Bargoed and close to the railway station and the pedestrian link to the bus station (opened June 2011), was purchased by Caerphilly County Borough Council and early in 2011 it was leased to the national retail store, Original Factory Shop, with hopes that it would help breathe new life into north Bargoed shopping area.

Following demolition of a row of cottages on the west side of Lower High Street in 1909, Palace Cinema was built and owner William Haggar opened the new cinema on 10 November 1910 with free entertainment for all who attended at 2 o'clock. The Managing Directors offered the pupils of Bargoed Boys' School free admittance on a Tuesday afternoon in June 1911 to see pictures of the Coronation. The Palace Cinema was not used solely for entertainment purposes as, early in 1913, the headmaster of Bargoed Boys' School recorded in his school's Log Book that the pupils of Standards IV, V and VI attended there to hear Dr. Morris's lecture on T.B. It was taken over by Jackson Withers Group in 1926 and the tradition for using it for educational purposes continued as, in January 1938, school log books show that local schools closed for an afternoon to allow teachers to see a film on Physical Exercises for school children at Palace Cinema.

The Electric Theatre opened on Trafalgar Square in 1914. Later known as Hanbury Cinema, it too eventually became part of the Jackson Withers Group. At first, it had an unremarkable façade and a shed-like auditorium, but later the façade was improved with a more practical foyer and entrance, pleasant windows onto Trafalgar Square and advertising posters above the canopy and stills in glass display cabinets. Local people recall that although Hanbury was smaller than Palace Cinema its superior facilities including a bigger screen meant that they were more likely to patronise it. The heyday of cinema-going in the country in general was over by the mid 1960s when Palace closed as a cinema and bingo was played there seven days a week. Hanbury Cinema continued to show films until 1973, when the then owner and operator, Circle Cinemas, transferred bingo to Hanbury and Palace reopened to enjoy a short life as Cameo Cinema. In 1994 and 1995, although *Screen International* carried advertisements offering Cameo Cinema for lease, it did not reopen as a cinema. The premises were demolished and a modern three-storey office block now occupies the site. After Hanbury Bingo Club closed, the building remained empty. Plans by Brian Bull (who had cinemas in Cardiff and Barry) to reopen it as a cinema in 1990 came to nought and today the building stands empty.

In recent years, local families have enjoyed films such as *Happy Feet*, *Polar Express* and *Ratatouille* at The Big Screen, a free open-air cinema event held several times a year in Hanbury Road Car Park. In April 2011 the classic children's fairytale, *Gulliver's Travels* starring Jack Black, Amanda Peet, Emily Blunt and James Corden was shown in Emporium Car Park.

Sport in Bargoed and Gilfach

Sporting activities became increasingly popular in the expanding local communities of late nineteenth and early twentieth century Bargoed and Gilfach. Some of those early sporting organizations still exist while others have not retained their appeal. The continuous history of rugby in the local community can be traced from 1883 when Bargoed and Gilfach were small communities, through the decades when the pool of potential players expanded as the local population grew, to its centenary and on to the present day when, although the game and its organization have changed, it is still a vital part of the local sporting scene. For decades the club had its headquarters in whichever local hotel had a landlord who favoured the sport until they established their club in premises at the south end of Hanbury Road car park before moving to the present Gilfach Street club. Similarly, golf has a considerable history in the local area from the formation of a club in 1910, generally known as East Glamorgan Golf Club in its early days, to the present day. However, other sporting activities and clubs have been more ephemeral. Prize-fights were popular entertainment in the nineteenth century and it is likely that some Bargoed and Gilfach residents were among a large gathering on Bedwellty Common at daybreak on a Monday in May 1886 to witness (and lay bets on the outcome) two *bruisers* from further north in the Rhymney Valley take part in a contest that ended in a draw. From the early twentieth century onwards many local groups organized competitive sports involving activities that did not require much, if any, special equipment or facilities apart from a fairly flat piece of ground. Usually these were on Saturdays or other days off work, and they were often designed to raise money for some cause, such as support of miners' families during periods of strike.

It is likely that the history of cricket in the local area dates from 1900. In June 1900 *Merthyr Express* reported on a movement to organize a cricket team in Bargoed and during the following three months it played some games. A cricket club was formed and young Eddy Walters of Old Mill Inn was elected as its Secretary at a meeting in Hanbury Café at the start of the 1902 season. The team was defeated in several games but not disgraced and it was evident that there was sufficient talent for them to be successful if they practiced more often. By February 1903 Bargoed Cricket Club had joined the new Rhymney Valley Cricket League and in May of the year they opened the season with a dance before starting to play on the new pitch laid at Heolddu. In spite of their rather unmanly name Bargoed Lillies was an active men's sports club in the decade or so prior to World War I: it seems that the men played rugby in the winter and cricket in the summer.

One of the early references to soccer in the local area was a report in *Merthyr Express* in August 1903 when a large and enthusiastic group of men met at Hanbury Arms and decided to form a local club, with its headquarters at Hanbury Arms. It would apply to join the Cardiff District League and ask Mr Edwards of Gilfach Fargoed Fawr for a playing plot. Soccer continued to be played after World War I as the local press reported how Bargoed AFC was adversely affected by the industrial crisis in the early 1920s: the 1922-1923 season was the poorest in the history of the club as not only did its playing record leave much to be desired but in June 1923 it was suspended from the Welsh FA for not fulfilling fixtures. It ceased to function and its players joined Bargoed branch British Legion football team to play in the Second Division of the Welsh League. Local soccer lapsed in the mid century but was revived in 1960 when the new Bargoed Football Club played its first game under the auspices of Bargoed and District YMCA (a body whose remarkable contribution to local sport merits detailed appraisal). Bargoed Football Club celebrated its fiftieth anniversary with a match against a team comprising representatives from South Wales Amateur League at Bargoed Park on Saturday 28 August 2010 for the Dean Shorey Memorial Shield.

As the local population expanded so did the range of sporting activities as well as the facilities, and that was reflected in the substantial coverage in the local press especially in the inter-war years. It is clear from the pages of the local press that while unemployment and hardship dominated life in the 1920s and 1930s for many local people, sport, both for participants or spectators, gave them something to be cheerful about. During the inter-war years, many South Wales mining communities benefitted from improved sports facilities as some 300 schemes were supported and part funded by the Miners' Welfare Fund. Playgrounds were opened for children, many of whom had formerly played on slag heaps where several fatal accidents had occurred. Parks, playgrounds and recreation grounds built between 1932 and 1938, often through grants giving work to the unemployed, made paddling and swimming pools, football and cricket pitches, tennis courts and bowling greens available to all. In the medium term these public leisure amenities helped improve the physical health of the population.

The detailed reports that appeared in *Merthyr Express* include references to some local star players, still recalled as sporting legends, as well as other facets of the contemporary competitive spirit in soccer, rugby, cricket, hockey, bowls and tennis. They also highlight some of the difficulties facing organizers and players. Then as now, soccer and rugby games were called off because of the weather: what was described as boisterous and inclement weather meant that the soccer match against top-of-the-League Tredomen and the rugby match against Mountain Ash were among the games called off early in 1931. The local terrain presented problems and *Spectator* reporting in *Merthyr Express* included scathing comments about the Welfare Ground *on the slopes of Bargoed Mountain* with changing rooms about a 10 minute walk away, in his report on a game when Bargoed lost to visitors Ynysddu 9-8 early in the 1929-1930 season. Teams regularly had problems getting a side together as matches started before players could leave work. In view of contemporary unemployment problems, a player could ask to finish early, but was hardly likely to make a fuss if this was refused. Jobs were few and far between and with the best will in the world, no man was going to risk his job to play a match. Early in 1931 the local rugby team missed out on a game when opponents Merthyr were unable to field a team. In December 1931, Bargoed was unable to fulfill a soccer fixture against Caerau as the local colliery bosses would not let the men leave work early. Having got a side together, they did not always encounter a situation like that facing Bargoed Thursdays when, in September 1924, they were about to board the charabanc taking them to an away fixture when Bargoed Fire Brigade commandeered the vehicle to go to a barn fire in Gelligaer and the footballers had to wait for its return before they could set off.

Bargoed and Gilfach were soccer communities in the inter-war era. The following paragraphs focus on the years between 1929 and 1933 when there was a bewildering plethora of local teams including Bargoed Town AFC (usually referred to in the local press simply as Bargoed), Bargoed Harlequins, Bargoed Athletic, Bargoed Ivy, Bargoed Wheatsheaf, Bargoed Robins and Bargoed Thursdays. Gilfach AFC also played regularly and one of their goal-scoring players was Jack Norman. They did not all play every week nor did the local press report on all of them on a regular basis. Some played in leagues while others played on a more ad hoc basis.

In September 1929 efforts were made to resuscitate the old Merthyr area Thursday Association Football League, which included teams like Bargoed Thursdays. Often referred to as *shoppies*, such teams played on Thursdays, half-day closing, and so workers in shops and small businesses had the chance to play. The Thursdays League was soon up and running but concern was raised on the sporting pages about funding for their matches. In early February Bargoed Thursdays were trounced 5-1 by Pontlottyn and dropped towards the lower end of the league table. They continued to play from time to time during the following seasons and enjoyed a fairly successful 1932-1933 season reaching the semi-final of the Thursday League. In that match the referee's decisions *repeatedly aroused the ire of the spectators*. This was hardly surprising as he had failed to see a hand-ball! After a quick goal, the hand-ball was recognised following protests from the Thursday players and consultation with the linesman resulted in a goal kick. The referee also failed to notice that a linesman was frantically trying to draw his attention to the fact that time was up. It turned out that the referee's watch had stopped! Bargoed were declared the winners. The crowd invaded the pitch and attacked the referee. The police were called to restore order.

In the late 1920s and early 1930s press reporters frequently commented on the *sparkling* play of Bufton in Bargoed AFC games and opponents soon realised he should be closely marked. In the 1929-1930 season he led Bargoed to a victory over visitors Tredomen, an *undoubtedly superior team* as well as Treharris Corries before, in mid March 1930, defeating Troedyrhiw, a team that turned up 36 minutes after the appointed kick-off time. However they ended the 1929-1930 season in sixth place in a league of eight. With some new players to start the 1930-1931 season, Bargoed AFC was victorious over Troedyrhiw in an exciting and high scoring game, with Bufton *sparkling* (as usual) while scoring the fourth goal in a match that ended 5-3. They followed up in good form the next week, with a new player, Islwyn Jones, the youngest player on the field, justifying his selection by *smart footwork and heading ability*, and beat Abertysswg by 4 goals to 3. However, by May 1932 Bufton had taken his *sparkling* talents over the mountain and was playing for Trelewis.

Year after year local clubs played against other local teams on a home and away basis at Christmastime. In 1929 Bargoed AFC played against Bedlinog on Christmas Day with a return match on Boxing Day and the following year they defeated Gilfach twice over the Christmas period. In 1931 train-loads of passengers (people who had left the local area to seek employment in south east England) had travelled from Paddington to Cardiff and on up the valleys for a few days with their families. If any of them were supporters of Bargoed Harlequins they were disappointed with the result of the Christmas game against Rhymney.

Members of local sporting clubs of all sorts valued those people who served the club whether in a playing or administrative capacity. In particular they marked their passing with respect as witnessed by a local press report on Valentine's Day 1931. Before Bargoed's match against top-of-the-league Tredomen kicked-off, the crowd stood in silence in memory of Henry Hill, a club official, and the Bargoed players wore black armbands as they held Tredomen to a draw.

In early September 1932 a new club, formed from Gilfach and Bargoed Harlequins, was to be called Bargoed and Gilfach United AFC although, almost from its inception, the sports reporters renamed the club Gilfach/Bargoed United and continued to do so in subsequent reports and tables. In the trials match T. Evans and E. Payne scored two goals each and Bob Baggott, G. Gummer and M. Lewis were described as *showing promise*. The new side kicked off the season spectacularly, defeating Abertridwr Stars 5-0. In the first round of the Welsh League Challenge Cup, a local derby between the new side and Aberbargoed, Baggott opened the scoring but Percy Williams scored the *best goal of the match* and the game ended in a two all draw. Gilfach/Bargoed were soon into the upper half of the Eastern Division and was described as *doing well* in *Merthyr Express*. Having secured Frank Harris to replace goalkeeper Sid James (who had transferred to Aberaman), the side defeated Llanbradach in early February and was in 6th position in the Eastern Section, with 8 teams below them, a status which they maintained the following week before dropping to eighth position then returning to sixth place. They carried on their winning ways beating Treorchy Juniors 3-0 with T. Jones, O. Jones and Billy Binks singled out for good play. At the end of the 1932-1933 season Gilfach/Bargoed finished a commendable 5th in the Welsh National League, Division 2 and *satisfaction was expressed that the working of a strenuous season had shown a small profit* and Bob Baggot's captaincy skills were praised at the A.G.M..

In the 1920s and 1930s the *Merthyr Express* banner headline was *Soccer, Rugger and General Sports Notes* but it is not clear whether the hearty, hairy-armed valley men who played with the oval ball referred to it as *rugger*. The fears of the ubiquitous *Merthyr Express* reporter *Spectator* who managed to cover many of the Bargoed games was concerned that rugby (also referred to as *The Handling Code*) would be subsumed by soccer proved unfounded especially as rugby was played in local schools including Bargoed Secondary and Lewis School Pengam by the early 1930s. As both rugby and football were often referred to as *football* in the press, it not always clear which game was being described without counting the number of players listed on each team. *Spectator* and fellow reporters wrote about the club's facilities, crowd behaviour and sportsmanship as well as about the game and, as they did not always give the final score, it is necessary to read the whole article, experiencing the excitement and suspense, to discover which team had won.

Rev. William Hopkins, one of several local clergy in the inter-war era to have been actively involved in local sport, was curate in St. Gwladys' Church. He was a member of Bargoed Golf Club and a billiards enthusiast and he played an important part on the field for Bargoed RFC until, at the end of August 1933, he left Bargoed to take up an appointment as Curate-in-Charge of Ynyscynon.

There was a strong link between Bargoed RFC and the local police in the inter-war years and when Police Inspector Herbert Evans was at Bargoed Police Station Bargoed folk were never quite sure if he recruited rugby players for the police station or policemen for the rugby team. In the later 1920s and early 1930s numerous young policemen who served in the local station played not only for Bargoed RFC but also for the county constabulary team. Police Constables Cliff Williams (Bargoed's 1929-1930 captain who sadly died just after the season finished), Percy Payne, Wilfred Rosser, W. A. Davies, Sandham and Tommy Rees all played for the local team. In Sandham's first game for Bargoed in Autumn 1931 he played alongside fellow officer Percy Payne against Mountain Ash in the Glamorgan League but he left in mid December to join Cardiff Athletic. Time and again the reports show that Tommy Rees played a crucial role in helping Bargoed to victory. When Bargoed lost 3-0 to Talywain in the 1932-1933 season they were without him as he was playing in the Welsh Trials. Rees later transferred to Newport (where he was the heaviest player to play for them) and went on to win eight Welsh caps 1935-1937. Cliff Williams (captain 1929-1930 season) and Percy Payne justified their selection by helping to trounce Aber Valley 21-0 and by October 1929 there were four 'Bobbies' and the local curate, Rev. William Hopkins, in the squad as well as a number of miners. When Bargoed beat Abercynon *Spectator* commented *No better play has been seen this season on the Bargoed ground* and *sporting feelings prevailed*. Captain Cliff Williams suffered a broken nose in a *friendly* game played in atrocious conditions at the start of 1930. When Cardiff Currans visited later in January 1930, many of Bargoed's usually faithful supporters and players, even the redoubtable Percy Payne,

It has not been possible to identify all the people in this photograph that was taken outside Bargoed Hall in the late 1920s. The captain (seated left of the uniformed police officer) is Billy Sims while Tommy Wardrupp is to his left. Two of the players standing have been identified: Jim Taysome is second from the left and third from the left is Glyn Williams.

decamped to Edinburgh to support Wales in the International against Scotland. Bargoed's team included the Rev. William Hopkins at inside half and, with a 14-0 victory it seemed that the home team had God on their side, if not the full force of the law. When Bargoed beat Machen 6-0 *Spectator* mentions that Rev. Hopkins initiated forward movements on several occasions. In March visitors Mountain Ash fielded five policemen while the home team had three *Bobbies* and a curate.

In May 1930 Bargoed RFC played Aberaman in their last home game of the 1929-1930 season. It was no surprise that it had the best gate for some time and was described as *the keenest game of the season on Bargoed's ground* as the winner was to play Treorchy in the final of the Glamorgan League Cup. Heavy rain made conditions difficult but the final score of 12-3 put the home team through to the final. That final did not take place until early the next season (when Joe Williams was captain) when Bargoed lost 3-0 to Treorchy despite the fast feet of J. Taysome on the left wing and the efforts of Payne, Hanney and Alcock. Sadly in June 1930 Cliff Williams died at his home in Llangenech, near Llanelli, following a brief illness. At his funeral 82 police officers were in attendance and some of the Bargoed RFC players were pall bearers. On 20 December 1930 the club held a presentation evening (for the presentation of Glamorgan League Cup runner-up medals) at Capel Hotel and, before a large gathering, a posthumous award was made to the late Cliff Williams.

The link between Jim Taysome and Bargoed RFC started in the mid 1920s and continued in various capacities for many decades. His successful playing career (including a season as vice-captain) was undoubtedly enhanced by his summer races in the later 1920s and early 1930s. Summer after summer the local press carried reports of his successes as illustrated by the following from 1927: in June he won his heat in Cambrian Dash in Pontypridd before finishing equal third in the final, in July he won his heat in the open 100 yards event at Tonypandy Sports and in August he was one of three Bargoed athletes who won their heats in the Welsh Powderhall Sprint (over 130 yards) at Pontypridd but lost in the semi-final and, in the same meeting, he won his heat in the 300 yards event but was disqualified. This all helped to ensure that the rugby team would not only be strong but also fast in the new season.

Bargoed RFC, looking forward to the 1931-1932 season with all the advantages of strength, speed and experience, was optimistic about forthcoming fixtures under the captaincy of Ivor Jones. They played some hard-fought matches and players such as Taysome, Payne and Wardrupp earned plaudits in the local press. Bargoed's 1931-1932 season, was summed up in *Merthyr Express* as being *creditable* and Naughton Davies, presiding over the end of season meeting, announced that it had been a successful season for Bargoed RFC despite the *inclement weather and decline in gates*, the latter a reflection of the contemporary economic climate.

Tom Wardrupp was appointed captain for the 1932-1933 season and during that season, as in previous seasons, his play was frequently praised in the local press. Alongside policemen Prosser and Tommy Rees he was described as *prominent* in a game when Bargoed was defeated by Kenfig Hill in October and he scored in a 22-0 victory in a friendly against Ystrad Mynach on the last Saturday of 1932. The early months of 1933 were not good ones as his club lost to Tredegar in the Glamorgan League before several games were called off as wintry weather rendered the ground unfit. By mid-March the weather and Bargoed's fortunes had improved when they drew away to Tredegar. Before the end of the season the club played their first game (against Penygraig in the Glamorgan League) on their new ground, estimated cost of which was £1,200.

No account of local rugby can ignore the question of *union v league*. In the early 1920s Billy Jones, Bargoed's centre three quarter, was a local sporting hero. Playing for Glamorgan County he scored the winning try against Monmouthshire at Tredegar and dropped a goal against France at Toulouse to score the only points in that game. However, soon after he left the Rhymney Valley to go to Rochdale Northern Union Club for £400. The money on offer to those who *went north* was an important factor in the inter-war years of unemployment and depression. Later *Merthyr Express* reported on discussion about a new league to promote *The Oval Code* and one of its founders was W. J. Ellis, former secretary of Bargoed RFC. However it was in connection with Rugby League and not Rugby Union and never came to fruition.

In the 1930s, the various costs of playing meant that golf was perceived as the domain of those in professional, well-paid secure jobs and so precluded the majority of local people who were out of work or whose wages could not run to *luxuries*. The local golf club had a thriving membership including men and women proficient at the game but the local press carried few reports of golf successes by Bargoed and Gilfach people. The report on the AGM in November 1930 included the election of officers and the presentations of the Bon Marche Bowl to Miss D. M. Williams, the Simscott Shield to D. J. Amwell Jones and the Barnett cup to E. W. Rees and A. Marsden. The following year, Dr. A Richards of Bargoed won a medal in a singles competition organised by Newport Golf Club. Bargoed's vicar, Rev. C. J. Griffiths, had been a sports master in Nottingham prior to his ordination and his success in a Cardiff and Newport Golf Association event in 1932 was reported in the local press. In 1933 Stanley Jones B.A. scored a hole-in-one on Bargoed's 7th hole, a distance of 98 yards (only the second time this feat had been performed on the course).

There were a number of local cricket teams playing during the summers of the inter-war years. Although the fixture lists of the major local cricket clubs such as Bargoed Welfare and Bargoed Bethel promised much the results were generally disappointing. In the mid 1920s St. Gwladys' Church Cricket team was very successful. It included much talent but none so great as the curate and captain Rev. Dalis Davies M.A. On one occasion he won a cricket bat for his bowling against Treharris where the scoreboard showed that he took nine wickets for no runs. With talent like that, small wonder the local press commented on the team's run of wins. At the beginning of the 1930s one of the most active local cricket sides was Bethel Cricket Club and their star player was D. Wyatt Day, Bargoed's 'Demon Bowler', with a record breaking 7 wickets for 6 runs in a game in which his team lost to Argoed. By mid June 1930 he had a record of 50 wickets for the very low average of two runs each but unfortunately, his team mates had problems scoring runs, a pattern that continued for the rest of the season and into the following one. Bethel's move to Gilfach Albions football ground in mid-season 1931, and a wicket of *new green coconut matting* improved their performance when they met Deri, and R. John in the middle-order scored 19 not out. D. Wyatt Day showed his skill at the crease in the match against Tredegar Wesleyans with 33 runs, helping Bargoed to victory on that occasion. It is not clear if Bethel Cricket Club continued to operate but by 1932, D. Wyatt Day was taking wickets and scoring runs for Bargoed Harlequins. Early in 1933 Bargoed and District Cricket League was set up with F. C. Sheen of Ruth Street as Secretary. It was reported at a meeting a few weeks later that among others, St. Gwladys' Church, Bargoed Harlequins, and Bargoed Thursdays had joined the League. Bargoed Thursdays soon made their mark in the League and Bargoed Church also got off to a good start with L. Bettany (captain) and F. Renton listed among the run-makers.

It is not clear when Bargoed Hockey Club started but it was active in the inter-war era. It had some good fixtures including matches against St. Fagans, Cardiff Y.M.C.A. and Treorchy and its players included the Jenkins brothers of Heolddu Uchaf. Unlike the local soccer and rugby clubs of the time, the Hockey Club had both men's and women's teams and Misses Susie Davies and Muriel Bowen were its star female players. The club played its home games at Pencaedrain Ground and when that was not available at Heolddu. As the years passed and hockey was taught to girls in the local secondary schools, the sport became more associated with female players and the local club played regular fixtures in the later twentieth century.

Local people have long excelled in bowls and two of the best local bowlers in the early 1930s were Percy Holloway and Amwell Jones. They won a Rhymney Valley Pairs competition in 1931 and early in 1932 they were presented with gold medals having won prizes in the Rhymney Valley Bowling League. Percy Holloway was a County player, one of four Bargoed players to be selected to play for Glamorganshire against Monmouthshire early in the 1930 season and in July he was called on to play for his county against Herefordshire. Further county honours followed as early June 1931 he was selected to play for Glamorganshire against Monmouthshire and Devon. In 1933 he was selected to play against Carmarthenshire while both he and Amwell Jones were selected to play for Glamorganshire against Monmouthshire. In the same year Percy Holloway was also selected to play at the Welsh International trial. Teacher D. J. Amwell Jones was an all-round sportsman, excelling in golf and bowls and, in his younger days, he had played for Bargoed RFC. His successes in bowls were numerous as illustrated by the following successes in the 1931 season: he was part of the winning Rhymney Valley League team against the Eastern Valley League and he won a bowls competition especially for club secretaries. Thomas Morris was one of the leading players in Gilfach Bowls Club in the late 1920s and early 1930s. In August 1932 he defeated W. Roberts, to win a pair of woods, while the Dr. Turner Cup and medal went to W. Roberts and a clock to G. I. Woods. Bargoed and Gilfach Bowls Clubs played against each other frequently. In the first round of the Miners' Welfare singles competition in 1933 E. Thornley of Bargoed beat Tom Morris of Gilfach 21-14.

When, in March 1932, the Welsh National Women's Bowls Association was formed to develop the game for women in Wales, there were only 7 clubs in Wales compared to 40 in England. There is no evidence in the local press of any women bowlers in Bargoed and Gilfach at that time but not too far away, in 1933 Mrs I. Williams, Mayoress of Merthyr, rolled the first wood at a match between an International English Ladies team and Thomastown Park Ladies team, a successful team that won the Welsh Women's Bowls Association rose-bowl trophy that year. Over the years the picture changed and by the last quarter of the twentieth century, local women were bowling with some of the best in the country.

By the beginning of the 1930s tennis was popular and affordable and local people could avail themselves of courts in public parks or join one of the several clubs in the Rhymney Valley. Bargoed Tennis Club did not enjoy a good season in 1930, losing to Nelson at home and away in May. When *Merthyr Express* published Rhymney Valley League tables in June it was in bottom place, having lost all of their eight matches and with no points. The Club retained this lowly position through July and into August but end of season victories over New Tredegar and Gilfach gave them hope for 1931. Bargoed Tennis club started the 1931 season, with a match in which Mr. O. N. Taylor and Miss Bongard defeated Mr. A West and Mrs Taylor at the Bungalow Courts. Neither the Men nor the Ladies teams enjoyed success in the Rhymney Valley League and by early June both teams were in bottom-but-one position. However, some younger club members had some individual success: Miss Violet Fenn and Miss Phyllis Barnett, Ladies doubles winners at the Nelson Open Tennis Tournament, were the only undefeated couple in Rhymney Valley Ladies League and Miss Phyllis Barnett won the Ladies Junior Lawn Tennis Championship. While Bargoed Tennis Club may not have had a fine playing record its members enjoyed its social functions such as the dance held in September 1931.

Sport, a welcome relief from contemporary economic problems in the inter-war period, played its part in raising money to help alleviate some of the problems especially with money-raising activities during the 1926 strike. In the inter-war period local hospitals were highly dependent on fund raising activities of all sorts and, in addition to their league commitments, local teams competed in a variety of sports for Hospital Cups. During the 1929-1930 Aberbargoed Hospital Cup tournament Bargoed Town defeated Llanbradach while Bargoed Athletic beat Fleur de Lys, and in the final a crowd of 6,000 watched Bargoed Town defeat New Tredegar. However, the following season Bargoed was knocked out of the competition by Cefn Forest. Local bowlers also competed for a Rhymney Valley Hospitals Cup In August 1932 W. H Evans was victorious in a singles competition and won a cheque as well as Rhymney Valley Hospitals Silver Cup for Bowls. In 1933 Percy Holloway and Amwell Jones won the final of the Pairs Rhymney Hospital tournament and the cup was presented to Amwell Jones following a *repast at the Park Pavillion* only a week after Aneurin Bevan MP, speaking at Rhymney Carnival, expressed his sorrow that hospitals had to be funded in that way.

Prior to World War II the local area replicated the national and international picture with most sports being regarded as male preserves. However in the Bargoed and Gilfach area reports in the local press show that some local women were competent tennis players and the hockey club had a ladies team, while anecdotal evidence has it that some local women played soccer in the inter-war period. However, employment or domestic duties meant that few local females had the time for sport in the inter-war era and even if they did they were effectively excluded from those sports based in the local pubs and clubs, grim spit-and-sawdust places where swearing and bawdiness was common.

Nevertheless, some women did have something to offer to sport. The local press reported that Bargoed RFC's ladies section played an important part in the success of the club with activities such as the mid April 1930 dance in the Workmen's Institute and their regular fund-raising whist drives became a tradition continuing to the 1960s. Menna Hughes (nee While) recalls how, when her older brother was playing on the wing for Bargoed RFC, her mother and other ladies *decided to meet in a 'quiet' room at the Hanbury Hotel on a Tuesday night following the Selection Committee Members' meeting on the Monday. Their aim was to be able to provide the team with a proper sit-down meal after a game.* They raised funds through a weekly raffle and the Committee granted them some financial support. What Mrs Burgess of Hanbury Arms could not supply in the way of chairs, tables covered with white table cloths, crockery, cutlery and condiments were supplied by the ladies and they served *slices of boiled ham and chips, pickled onions and pickled cabbage, bread and butter, followed by a selection of cakes and a nice cup of tea!* Menna recalls that *200 home-made iced cup cakes left my mother's kitchen that first Saturday morning and were soon joined by plates of Welsh cakes and slices of fruit cake, cooked and brought by the other ladies.*

This section, with its focus on football, rugby, cricket, hockey, bowls, tennis, and golf in the late 1920s and early 1930s has merely scratched the surface of the story of sport in Bargoed and Gilfach. There are other eras to study and other sports, notably boxing, to consider. Over the years there have been teams in the clubs and pubs of Bargoed and Gilfach participating in activities as diverse as quoits, skittles, table-tennis, bagatelle and air-rifle shooting, and today there is a wide range of indoor and outdoor activities on offer in venues such as Heolddu Leisure Centre that have not been touched on. Despite both the fine indoor facilities locally and further afield for participants and the wide range of high quality sport available on satellite TV for spectators, local people still play the outdoor sports in all weathers and turn out to support live events and cheer on their teams because nothing beats the smell of the *Wintergreen* as the players run on to the pitch and the satisfaction of basking in the reflected glory of a home win and saying after the match *I know 'cos I was there.*

Music

Music, both religious and secular, has enhanced the lives of generations of local people: it was part of their worship in church and chapel and it played an important role in their limited leisure time within the home and elsewhere. In the early nineteenth century, local people gathered at the Old Mill in Pontaberbargoed to enjoy the week long annual Pastai-y-bont (Bridge Pie), the origins of which are lost in the mists of time, with feasting on Welsh mutton and apple pie, and singing and dancing accompanied by local harpists. Bargoed and Gilfach were centres of culture and musical excellence in the later decades of the nineteenth century and first half of the twentieth century. There were numerous choirs, including those associated with places of worship, in Bargoed and Gilfach, rehearsing regularly and performing in concerts locally and further afield, as well as people who performed as soloists in concerts and eisteddfodau, and others who excelled in musical composition or direction. Such was the reputation of local musicians that some of them were in demand as well-known and well-respected adjudicators across the region. The number of musical and dramatic organisations and performances in the local area has declined in recent decades, partly because television was able to bring world-class performances into the home, and partly as venues in Cardiff and elsewhere proved more attractive that those locally. However, the local music tradition has not been lost as, in the early twenty first century, some fine performers excel locally as well as further afield.

Harpist William Morgan ap Siencyn (1867-1937) was born in Cwmsyfiog and once lived with his parents at *Greyhound Inn* (on Aberbargoed Hill). He took to music at an early age, and noted Welsh harpist, Taliesin Jones, taught him to play the harp. His harp-playing skills earned him success and world-wide praise in the later nineteenth century: he won first prizes at National Eisteddfodau at Merthyr in 1881, and Swansea, Rhyl and Pontypridd in successive years 1891-1893, and, in 1893, he won the World Harpist Championship at Chicago World Fair. He played the harp before royalty and his teaching was such that his pupils included about twenty National Eisteddfod winners. In 1900 his World Championship was recognised locally when, at a social evening in Plasnewydd Hotel, the chairman of the local male voice party presented him with an inscribed gold pendant. He also received local recognition for his sporting prowess: a talented centre three-quarter, he was a pioneer of rugby in the area and he excelled in boxing and billiards and was a good shot. It is not clear how long he remained in the Bargoed area as he died at *Farmers Arms*, Maesteg, aged 69. His contribution to music was recognised at his funeral as two harp-shaped floral tributes were placed on his coffin. He was buried in Llangynwyd.

Henry Smith (1859-1924) was a gifted musician who earned a living and met his premature death in the mining industry. He was born about 1859, into a working class family in the mountain top hamlet of Pantywaun. As, at the age of 10, he started what was to be a 55-year career in the coal industry, it is unlikely that he received much formal education. He was an ardent Welsh man, influenced by poetry, music and religion and, in his youth, he grew to love the Welsh language and the poetry, music, institutions and traditions of Wales. On one occasion, he won a prize for a few verses of poetry. Known affectionately as *Smith Bach*, Henry Smith was a dapper, debonair and cheerful man with an optimistic and humorous outlook on life. He was a choir conductor of long experience and wide repute who, over some thirty five years, led a number of mixed and male voice choral groups (in both Rhymney and Merthyr valleys) to victory in competition. He also conducted children's choirs in churches where he served as choirmaster and he helped raise hundreds of pounds for churches and charities through performances of oratorios and other religious works. Although he competed three times at the National Eisteddfod he never won top honours there but earned the highest commendation. After he moved to the Bargoed area, Henry Smith was actively involved in the musical life of the community and that included conducting the award-winning Mixed Choir (alternatively known as Bargoed Music Lovers). His family faced sadness when, early in 1920, they heard of the death of his 18-year granddaughter in Scranton, U.S.A.. The family experienced unhappiness again when, July 1924, in the course of his work as a repairer at Britannia Colliery, 65-year old Henry Smith was crushed by a stone weighing about one ton and died instantaneously. At the inquest into his death, at Junction Hotel, Bargoed, the coroner returned a verdict of accidental death. His death was a sad loss to the community and especially to his family, left to cherish a fine oil painting as well as the medals, metronomes, chairs and batons, won over his illustrious musical career.

Thomas Gabriel FTSC (1869-1938) was one of a number of gifted musicians who lived and worked in Bargoed in the first half of the twentieth century. It is not clear when he gained his qualification as Fellow, Tonic Sol-Fa College. Tom, as he was generally known, was a Monmouthshire boy, born into a working class family in Argoed about 1870 and probably educated in the local school before commencing work as a collier in the Sirhowy Valley but he was described as a music teacher when he was enumerated in 11 Bristol Terrace in 1901. He was an unassuming yet competent all-round musician, active and highly esteemed in the Bargoed area as well as further afield for many years, His association with Aberbargoed's Caersalem Baptist Church as choirmaster, organist and deacon lasted for about four decades. As a music teacher, he was an authority on tonic sol-fa and served as music teacher in Lewis School Pengam for over a decade until 1927 when the school authorities decided that the subject was important enough to warrant a full time Master. His judgement as an adjudicator at eisteddfodau was always valued and respected. He was a highly respected conductor who had conducted many performances of classical oratorios in the local area in support of religious and charitable organisations. During his time as Musical Director of Bargoed and District Choral Union, their performances raised funds for causes such as Cardiff Royal Infirmary and St. John's Ambulance Brigade. It is perhaps as a composer that he was most widely known. In 1919 Swansea music publisher David John Snell, purchased a series of Tom Gabriel's compositions for £160, but Snell blamed the contemporary economic downturn when he offered a lower price for further compositions in 1926. The correspondence between the two was rather acrimonious before they agreed on £60, probably as Tom Gabriel was keen for Snell to publish all his work. Soon afterwards, they settled on 12 guineas for compositions of Tom Gabriel's father John (1844-1913). Tom Gabriel's anthem *A'r Lan'r Iorddenen Ddofn*, was one of the best-known pieces of its kind ever written by a Welsh composer: often the test piece at eisteddfodau, it was sung at National Eisteddfodau and by Welsh people across the world during the composer's lifetime. It was sang at his funeral service in Caersalem in 1938, the attendance at which reflected the esteem in which he was held by musicians, public bodies and the general public. In 1936 Sir Walford Davies, Master of the King's

Musick, paid tribute to Tom Gabriel: *It is most heartening to know that, through many difficult years, the Bargoed and District Choral Union, under its faithful conductor, Mr. T. Gabriel, has been able to carry on so finely. The work done by this choir – and others like it – cannot be too highly valued. It annually presents in its own district, for the delight of those who have ears to hear, the great choral classics which otherwise would seldom be enjoyed outside the larger towns; and by its many successes the Bargoed Choral Union is enabled to give generous support to various charitable causes. It is with warm appreciation that I recall this Union as one of the many choirs that helped to make memorable the Welsh week at Wembley in 1924.*

David Jones AC (Advanced Conductor in Tonic Sol-fa) (1877-1949) was a modest and unpretentious but accomplished poet-musician who became known as *Bargoed's colliery hymnologist.* He lived in John Street and, for about quarter of a century, he earned a living as a collier before becoming a postman. His love of music was evident early in his life and he soon learned to play the violin, cornet, cello as well as the organ. Having composed his first verse during the miners' strike of 1898, he set it to music and won a prize. He followed that with a long series of successes in musical competition. His service to music in Bargoed's South Street Primitive Methodist Chapel started before 1900 and continued until his death in 1949. In the decades when he directed the music at the anniversary services, it was common for the large chapel to be full to capacity, with repeat services held mid-week. He was a choral conductor of long experience whose work also included scores of rehearsals and United Festivals in South Wales and Monmouthshire. He wrote hundreds of hymns and tunes and published his own works, issuing *Cambrian Series* of original hymns and tunes including anthems and choruses. As they were written in tonic sol-fa and staff notation, they proved popular in musical festivals, Sunday School anniversaries, choral contests and marches, in Britain and beyond. His anthems *The army of God* and *Blessed are they* together with *Victory*, a sacred chorus, have been deposited in National Library of Wales, while other works are in Winding House CCBC Museums and Heritage Service Collection. The enduring quality of his music is evident as several organists still play his music in local places of worship today.

Two eminent twentieth century musicians, Sidney Northcote and Alun Hoddinott, had links with the local area in their youths. Sidney Northcote (1898-1968), was probably the first child of Alfred Northcote and his wife, Margaret, née Llewellyn. As his father was an accomplished pianist and his mother's ancestors were well-known harpists and violinists, it is not surprising that young Sidney was talented and interested in music. When he was nine years old, Sidney conducted a male voice party, and he was pianist to Bargoed Male Voice Party. A talented boy soprano, he was awarded first place in the 1908 National Eisteddfod at Llangollen. In 1909, he gained a scholarship to Lewis School Pengam, where, during his three years of study, Tom Price, FTSC, visiting music Master at the school from 1896 to 1915, influenced him.

The family lived in Cross Street, Bargoed, and his father worked as a miner in Gilfach Pit. However, his father's health deteriorated and, so that he could afford to pay for Sidney's four-year course at Royal College of Music, London, he found employment as a guard on London's Piccadilly Tube, so breaking the family link with the local area. As a musician, writer, editor, composer, arranger, adjudicator and administrator, Sidney Northcote earned a reputation not only in Britain but also worldwide, as illustrated by just two of his achievements. In 1959, largely due to his lobbying and fund-raising, Trinidad had a fine venue for musical performances when Queen's Hall opened in Port-of-Spain. (It is worthy of note that, although Central Hall fulfilled the function for some six decades, Bargoed, the place where Sidney grew up has never had the fine concert hall that the local press, both before and after 1900, claimed it needed although, in 1904, there were discussions about building such a hall near Hanbury Arms.) Closer to home, and of more significance to musicians in Bargoed and Gilfach, he was co-editor of *The National Songs of Wales* (*Canaeuon Cenedlaethol Cymru*) published by Boosey and Hawkes, a publication that included some 43 of his own arrangements. Welsh composer and academic Alun Hoddinott (1929-2008) was born in Bargoed 11 August 1929, son of Thomas Ivor Hoddinott and his wife Gertrude (née Jones). *Merthyr Express* reported that his father, a teacher in South Bargoed Boys' School, arranged the programme for the school's St. David's Day celebrations in 1926. As a child, Alun learned to play the violin under the tuition of Morfydd Meyrick at Bargoed Settlement and he may have been part of the excellent youth orchestra she formed there. Educated at Gilfach Fargoed Boys School when J. H. Garnet was headmaster, Alun performed a recitation and a violin item at a school concert in 1937 when, according to the report in *Merthyr Express*, the audience was so large that many parents failed to get into the school hall. The family moved from the area on his father's appointment as headmaster of Penllegaer School after which a talented and enthusiastic music teacher in Gowerton Boys' Grammar School nurtured Alun's natural flair for composing music. His long and distinguished career earned him an enviable reputation and his name lives on in BBC Hoddinott Hall (Neuadd Hoddinott y BBC), the specially built 350-seat concert hall, new home of BBC National Orchestra of Wales in Wales Millennium Centre, Cardiff that opened in 2009.

The Annual Chair Eisteddfod organised by Bargoed and District Workmen's Libraries and Institute started at the end of the first decade of the twentieth century and continued after World War I and it was just one of many such eisteddfodau organised by various local groups over the decades. In 1920, *Merthyr Express* carried detailed reports that shed light on the eleventh Eisteddfod when the Eisteddfod Committee, chaired by Mr W. R. Maddocks and including a number of local notables, worked hard to organise the event held at New Hall on Thursday 16 September 1920. The Eisteddfod, conducted by Rev. Llew Morris (Ogwy) of Pengam, attracted large attendances and, while competition was keen throughout, the choral competitions attracted especial attention. About six weeks before the Eisteddfod, the Committee had adopted its Music sub-committee's suggestion to establish a choir, and John Owen of Deri was unanimously elected conductor of the new Bargoed United Choir that went on to share the honours in the chief choral competition with Caeharris. The Male Voice Choir Competition attracted keen interest and competition and, having heard two fine performances of the test piece, Dr. Parry's *The Pilgrims*, the adjudicator awarded first place to Ebbw Vale. T. R. W. Lewis' Bargoed Choir (with soloist Jenkin Llewellyn excelling) was beaten into second place to win £10, one of Dr. Richards' special prizes.

Many people, in Wales and beyond, associate Wales with the choral music tradition that developed in the mid nineteenth century especially as young, often unmarried, working men in industrial communities sought recreation and company after work. Although, unlike some other male voice choirs in South Wales, those in Bargoed and Gilfach did not go on to achieve worldwide fame, they were in frequent demand to perform at concerts within Bargoed and Gilfach and the surrounding area.

Bargoed's Apollo Glee Singers came together during World War I. With conductor T. R. W. Lewis and accompanist Lily, eldest daughter of Tom Gabriel, the Singers aimed to bring cheer to thousands of wounded sailors and soldiers by performing concerts in hospitals and distributing cigarettes to wounded servicemen and continued both during and after the war. They claimed to be the finest combination of male voices in Wales and continued after T. R. W. Lewis left the Party. During the 1926 strike, accompanied by County Councillor W. Hopkins, conductor Mr W. Williams took them on a tour of the Bournemouth area. There, they performed in concerts associated with meetings where County Councillor Hopkins, speaking on behalf of the striking miners, earned considerable praise in the Bournemouth local press. By mid September they had raised £40 for Bargoed's Canteen Fund, £32 4s 6d for Cardiff Central Fund and £110 for Lady Slesser's Fund, as well as funding for boots and clothes.

T. R. W. Lewis was a talented musician who, over the years, was not only a composer but also the successful conductor of several choirs in Bargoed and neighbouring communities. After he left Apollo Glee Singers he became conductor of Bargoed Male Voice Choir (Choral Society) in October 1919. That choir opened its competitive career with a fine triumph at Llanbradach in July 1920. Over the years, it went on to win hundreds of pounds at Eisteddfodau, including winning three prizes, value £80, in one day.

There were a number of male choirs in the local area in the inter-war years but it is not clear how long each of them was in existence. Cambrian Gleemen had probably been in existence for some time when, in March 1924, it celebrated its association with Gwerthonor Hotel with a social. Presentations followed an excellent supper: Mr Thomas (of Gwerthonor Hotel) received a walking stick, his wife, a silver-mounted salad bowl, and the conductor, David Jones, was presented with a purse of money for his faithful service. In his speech of thanks, Mr Thomas referred to Cambrian Gleemen's great work for charitable and philanthropic institutions in Bargoed and Gilfach and throughout South Wales. May 1923 saw the formation of Handel's Concert Party. With J. Handel Jones as conductor and musical director, this small party of eleven was soon performing publicly. In June 1923, their concert was broadcast from Cardiff Broadcasting Station, and in September 1923, they performed in the Banqueting Hall at Caerphilly Castle with Cliff Jones of Deri as the baritone soloist. In 1924 John Owen of Deri was appointed conductor of Bargoed Gleeman's Party. Bargoed Orpheus Male Glee Party, with conductor Gabriel Jenkins and Organising Secretary Octavius Thomas, was performing charity concerts in Bargoed and the surrounding area in the later 1930s. In June, 1937 Ross Powell, the Party's principal baritone soloist, was awarded a first class certificate at Cheltenham Music Festival, the third largest such festival in the British Empire. At about the same time Bargoed and District Philharmonic Society, under conductor Edward Jenkins, was enjoying success in choral competitions at places as far apart as Cilfynydd, Brecon and Abergavenny

Powell Duffryn Steam Coal Company Male Voice Choir practised in Bargoed. They travelled to London to perform in a St. David's Day concert, patronised by Duke of Kent, in 1937 to raise funds for Aberdare and Rhymney Cottage Hospitals, both areas having suffered especially because of the depression in the coal trade. Before going to the concert in Queen's Hall, the choir laid a wreath at the Cenotaph. In Queen's Hall they performed before an audience of some 1,500, including Captain Harry Crookshank, (Secretary for Mines 1935-1939), and all the directorate of the Powell Duffryn Steam Coal Company.

The local section of the Choir for Welsh week at the 1924 Wembley Exhibition started rehearsals under the direction of Tom Gabriel in late July 1924 to prepare for the performance at Wembley during Welsh Week at the end of August. Tom Gabriel's daughter Lily was the pianist for rehearsals and her husband, John Prosser, worked with a strong committee to organise the venture. The choir had started with some 120 volunteers and, by the time Sir Walford Davies accepted the invitation to attend a rehearsal the week before the concert, it had increased to about 150. Welsh Week started on 25 August and reached a grand finale with a festival concert in Wembley Stadium on 30 August when more than thirty choirs united in singing from the Welsh Festival Book specially prepared by Sir Walford Davies. The choristers were not the only local people to visit the Wembley Exhibition, as there were numerous organised visits from the Bargoed and Gilfach area. Morgan Phillips of 20 Francis Street organised a train excursion for Monday 25 August and arranged that Morgan Jones M.P. and Earl de la Warre would meet their special train when it arrived in Paddington and take them on a tour of Houses of Parliament, Westminster Abbey and St. Paul's Cathedral.

Brass bands were popular in communities like Bargoed and Gilfach and the local press made regular reports on the activities of Bargoed Salvation Army Band both locally and on their tours to more distant places. Reports in *Merthyr*

Express suggest that Bargoed Town Band did not have a continuous history. There was a Bargoed Brass Band as early as 1887 as *Merthyr Express* carried a report noting that it was given permission to practice in the school rooms. In 1920 Bargoed Town Band, with Secretary Rees Davies of Gilfach, held a meeting on 23 June at Royal Hotel Assembly Rooms to form a Committee for the Band for a Flag Day for St. Dunstans Institute for the Blind on 10-11 September. It seems that the Band went out of existence as in September 1926, in the middle of the strike, the local press reported that Bargoed Town Band was formed with twenty-four members under conductor Mr W. Smith. Their headquarters was in Royal Hotel Assembly Rooms and Gwilym Jenkins was chairman and Mr J. Carter its Secretary.

It is not clear when Bargoed and District Operatic Society (sometimes called Amateur Operatic Society, and sometimes Amateur Dramatic Society) was formed, but reports in *Merthyr Express* indicate that it was active during the mid 1920s. When Bargoed and District Operatic Society started rehearsals in August 1923 the conductor was W. Deri Bowen (baritone) and the accompanist was Miss Doris Kedward Williams. In March 1926, the local press reported in detail on its performance of *Pirates of Penzance* at Hanbury Cinema, an operetta not staged in Bargoed since a 1912 performance in New Hall with conductor Caradog Davies and accompanist J. S. Chambers. The producer in 1926 was Mr W. H. Williams and the accompanist, Doris Kedward Williams. The excellent chorus was conducted by John Owen of Deri, the orchestra was conducted by Mrs Bush and the secretary was David Jones. In previous years, the Society's performances had included *Ben Hur*, *Highwayman's Love* and *Dogs of Devon*. The *Merthyr Express* reporter praised the Society for its hard work and fine performance but was scathing about Bargoed which saw itself as the *Metropolis of the Rhymney Valley* yet its people did not give much support to local Societies and did little to encourage the works of the foremost musicians.

The male population of Bargoed and Gilfach in the inter-war period did not have a monopoly of music as there were some fine female musicians associated with the area including accompanists Doris Kedward Williams and Lily Prosser (née Gabriel). Although not a local person, Marie Novello (1884-1928) who owed her professional name to adoption by Clara, mother of Ivor Novello visited her birth mother, Annie Bedlington Williams (née Kirkhouse) and sister, Mrs David Davies (formerly Lily Kirkhouse Williams and wife of the schoolmaster) in Bargoed. Bargoed Blue Danube Ladies Glee Party was directed by Madame D. Rawlings and early in 1937, it gave concerts at Cardiff Prison and at Talygarn Miners' Convalescent Home. Madame Ada Esther Davies (wife of John Davies, grocer in South Street) was a well-known singer in the area and, together with her husband, an active member of Bargoed Amateur Dramatic Society. There are further details of the musical career of Morfydd Meyrick (later Williams) in *Gelligaer* Volume XVII (2009). She grew up in Cemetery House at Gwaelodybrithdir and much of her early music training came from Bethania, her family's place of worship, and Kathleen Newman of

Capel Street, her teacher. After World War II she was one of only two female members of the re-formed 31-strong BBC Welsh Orchestra under conductor Mansel Thomas and she remained as a member of that orchestra under Rae Jenkins, when it starting touring Wales and appearing on television.

The idea of establishing a Youth Choir in the area was mooted by Evan Lewis in his address at Bargoed and District Philharmonic Society's concert early 1948. Its aims and objectives from the outset were as set out in the 1956 constitution:-

- *The promotion of good music among young people.*
- *To form a link between school age and the age at which members might normally be expected to join adult choirs.*
- *To form a nucleus to which adult choirs can look, and from which they can draw new members as time advances.*

Evan Lewis and an advisory committee organised the venture. A disappointing nine young people aged 15 to 20 turned up at the first meeting in the Lesser Hall in Wood Street on Friday 17 September 1948 but the following

This photograph (courtesy of Pat Davies), shows the choir that, on 11 May 1957, beat off nine other choirs to win First Prize at Glamorgan Youth Eisteddfod at Porthcawl. Seated in the front centre are Mervyn Burtch (accompanist) and Iorwerth Thomas (conductor) and the choristers include Mary Bowen, Enid Jones, Dinah Evans and Margaret Richards in the back row with Ena Hopkins, Dorothy Cook, Sheila McCarthy and Margaret Morgan standing in front of them, while Wendy Evans, Pat Davies and Sally Carter are among those seated.

week there were forty there, and Bargoed and District Youth Choir came into being under conductor Iorwerth Thomas, with accompanist Mrs J. T. Hughes and her deputy Ivor Thomas. The choir, at first mixed but later girls only and with junior (aged 10-13) and senior (up to age 25) sections, rehearsed every Friday evening in Hanbury Road Baptist chapel schoolroom. One of the highlights of the early years was taking part in the opening concert of the 1949 National Eisteddfod (in Caerphilly). They held annual concerts in the Central Hall and, as time passed, these became celebrity concerts as they shared a stage with artistes such as Stuart Burrows, Margaret Price, and Treorchy and Pendyrus Male Voice Choirs. The choir also competed in Eisteddfodau and performed concerts outside the local area, nearly always in support of charity. The choir had a varied repertoire including major works such as *Messiah* and *The Creation* and attracted choristers from all over Rhymney Valley between its creation in 1948 and disbandment in 1961 when the conductor's professional career took him to a school headship in Trelewis.

It is clear from reports in the local press that the tradition of male voice choral singing developed as the communities of Bargoed and Gilfach grew. It had lapsed during World War II but revived in 1961. Lewis Price of Moorland Road met with fellow enthusiasts at the Court Room in Bargoed on 2 September

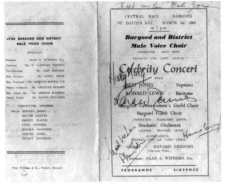

1961 and they decided to contact all local men who had formerly been associated with male voice singing. A list of 140 men was drawn up and a further meeting held at Central Cafe on 18 October when it was agreed to contact even more choristers and to hold a meeting in Royal Hotel on 29 October. That meeting, sponsored by the local branch of the Rotary Club with a £10 donation to start choir funds, saw many men volunteer to pay a year's contributions in advance. A committee was elected and it was decided to approach Alun John, a BBC music studio manager from Pontycwmmer in the Garw Valley, to take the baton. He agreed to accept the

This autographed programme of Bargoed and District Male Voice Choir's Celebrity Concert (courtesy of Pat Davies) refers to other contemporary choirs that shared a stage on St. David's Day 1962, the Choir's first annual celebrity concert

post of conductor and the Choir commenced with twice-weekly practices at the Lesser Hall before they performed their first annual celebrity concert on St. David's Day 1962. Since those early days the Choir has been fortunate in having Musical Directors and accompanists of outstanding ability and has excelled over the years, winning eisteddfodau and other competitions, especially under the baton of Clifton Horrell. The Choir, under Mr Horrell, was one of the first to introduce male voice arrangement of popular music into their repertoire, something that is now commonplace. Bargoed MVC has travelled extensively, touring the U.S.A., Germany, Austria, Belgium, France, Poland, the Czech Republic and Ireland, as well as performing concerts throughout the UK. There have also been many television appearances, the highlight of which was appearing on the highly popular *This Is Your Life* with the unsuspecting Ruth Madoc. This was followed up by an appearance on *Home on Sunday*. Under the musical direction of Lionel Hughes, the Choir built up an extensive repertoire of traditional male operative arias, modern light music and many songs in their original languages, thus catering for and pleasing varied tastes. The Choir held its Fiftieth Anniversary Concert at Lewis School Pengam on 1 July 2011 and returned to Ireland in September 2011 where Lionel Hughes conducted his final concert after 28 years service as Musical Director. He is succeeded by his former assistant, the gifted musician Jonathan Polson.

The contemporary music scene is different from that of earlier decades but none the less just as talented. Many local people are involved in choral music: Bargoed Male Voice Choir continues to flourish while a number of people travel outside the local area to sing with other choirs. In recent decades, three former pupils of Heolddu Comprehensive School have made names for themselves in the music world: in 1992 Amanda Normansell was still in school when she impersonated Patsy Cline to win ITV's *Stars in Their Eye*, Samantha Link discovered her musical theatre voice when cast in a school production of *Joseph and the Amazing Technicolour Dreamcoat* while James Fox's professional music career took a new direction after he participated in BBC's *Fame Academy* in 2003 since when he has represented UK in 2004 Eurovision Song Contest and in 2010 received complimentary reviews for his part in the revival of the musical *Chess*. Perhaps Samantha's daughter Scarlett is also heading for a career in entertainment as, at just ten days old she played Nessa's baby Neil in BBC's comedy series *Gavin and Stacey*. The last decade has seen Bethan Watson, a young harpist, make a name for herself. In recent years Bargoed's four-piece band *4th Street Traffic* made their mark on the Welsh music scene, performing live shows across the UK and their busy 2010 schedule included a prestigious support slot with their Welsh rock idols, the Stereophonics, in concert in Cardiff's City Stadium 4 July 2010 as well as a performance for the Wales rugby team after their game against New Zealand in November.

Societies and Organisations (other than sport and music)

Over the decades, a number of clubs and societies with different interests have flourished in Bargoed and Gilfach. Some of them attracted working class members while others were more likely to appeal to the middle class professionals in the community.

For decades Bargoed prided itself on the excellence of its Literary and Debating Society, one of the first societies to appear within the growing community. It is not clear exactly when and where it first met, but it activities were reported regularly in *Merthyr Express* from 1900 onwards. In those early years of the twentieth century, members met in Hanbury Cafe and debated some

274

weighty contemporary issues: in March 1900 members listened to papers on both sides of the argument before declaring *Denominationalism was an advantage to Christianity* while in December of that year their verdict was against *Conscription*. *Lit and Deb* was not all about serious matters as the local press also reported on their arrangements to celebrate events such as St. David's Day and New Year with supper followed by musical entertainment.

For centuries, local people had been largely self-sufficient and, in the late nineteenth and early decades of the twentieth century, many local families (especially incomers who earned a living in the emerging industrial community) depended on the produce of their allotment for a healthy and varied diet for the family. They grew vegetables and herbs for the kitchen table as well as soft fruits, like gooseberries, currants and raspberries, and kept a clutch of hens to supply the family with eggs. In addition, they took pride in selecting their finest produce (vegetables and flowers) for the numerous local horticultural and floricultural shows. In 1895 the local council prepared to let thirty allotments (20-25 perches each) on a designated four acre site at a rate of 7d per perch per annum free of rates and taxes, according to these rules, as defined by the Local Government Board: *He shall keep the allotment free from weeds, and well manured, and otherwise maintain it in a proper state of cultivation. He shall not plant any trees or shrubs so as to be injurious to any adjacent allotment. He shall keep every hedge that shall form part of the allotment properly cut and trimmed, and he shall not cause any nuisance or annoyance to the tenant of any other allotment.* In October, the plan of the site, drawn by Mr E. W. Lewis of Hengoed, was on public display at D. S. Jones' grocery shop in the main street, and notices inviting applications for the allotments were displayed, not only in the shop but also in numerous other public places locally, and those interested could pick up application forms in D. S. Jones' shop.

In the early decades of the twentieth century several organisations held competitions for the produce of gardens and allotments. R.A.O.B.'s annual Flower Shows at McDonnell Hotel were reported regularly in the local press in the 1920s but the grandest local events were Bargoed Horticultural and Floricultural Shows, organised by Bargoed and Gilfach Allotment Holders Association at Bargoed Park. The reports in the local press show that the show weekend was special: local public houses were granted extended opening hours on the Friday and Saturday and, at least on some occasions, the event was rounded off with a concert. *Merthyr Express* carried a detailed report on the successful third Annual Show in 1920 when there were about 1,200 entries in the vegetable classes and ideal weather encouraged thousands to attend. At the commencement of the show, the platform party included Councillor G. F. Forsdike (Lord Mayor of Cardiff), Prince of Jalahwar (India) and Right Hon. Sybil Viscountess Rhondda, as well as local people, Dr. T. E. Richards, J.P. and Mrs Richards, Rev. Trevor C. Thomas (vicar of Bargoed), Mrs Ebsworth, Councillor Gus Jones and Mr T. D. Matthews. Dr. Richards started the formal proceedings by introducing the Lord Mayor who, in his speech formally declaring the show open, noted that, while it was unusual for a civic leader like him to be invited to open a show in another town, he had been pleased to accept the invitation as it was important for neighbouring towns to be on good terms. He congratulated the Committee, especially the energy and enterprise of F. C. Brooks, general secretary and organiser, and praised the fine show of flowers, fruit and vegetables produced by amateurs. He recalled the recent Royal Horticultural Show in Cardiff and told of his hopes for a Royal Horticultural Society for Wales that, like the National Eisteddfod, would visit all parts of Wales. After Dr. Richards and Councillor Gus Jones had thanked the Lord Mayor, the party left for lunch in the New Hall Cafe before visiting Bargoed Hall, home of Dr. and Mrs Richards, where they viewed Mrs Richards' fine collection of rare antique china. The judges, including local people, such as Dr. and Mrs Richards and schoolmasters David Davies and Sylvan Evans, agreed that this was the best such show they had attended in 1920. Mr J. Tambling, vice-chairman of the Committee and Bargoed Park Keeper won prizes for plant in foliage, flowers including begonias, dahlias and carnations, vegetables including beans beetroot, parsnips, turnips and potatoes as well as herbs. The day included a carnival, fancy dress football match, a Band contest and a special feature, a magnificent balloon ascent and parachute descent by Miss Spencer of London. Not all of the shows were as successful as that of 1920. In 1923, although there were record entries, the attendance was disappointing partly as the weather was poor and perhaps because of competing attractions of the Band Contests and Big Eisteddfod in Bargoed and the extended opening hours in local public houses on the Friday and Saturday. The contemporary financial problems meant that the 1926 Horticultural Show was disappointing and so the Horticultural Society Committee organised a Sunday concert in December to try to compensate but attendance at the concert was also disappointing.

Cultivating an allotment became increasingly less fashionable during post World War II decades as families began to rely on purchasing their food from supermarkets. At the same time, local shows declined and the remaining devotees were more likely to compete at larger regional shows or the Royal Welsh Show. However, recent years have seen a reversal of that trend, as people become more aware of *food miles* and the value of fresh produce grown without the help of too much chemical fertiliser. Thus, it is not surprising that local people are currently taking a new interest in horticulture and, if they cannot get an allotment, they grow vegetables and herbs in pots in their small gardens In more recent decades Bargoed Gardening Club has been active and since the early 1990s has organised an annual show raising over £10,500 for charity.

In the decades prior to World War II some local people, interested in the new technology of the era, helped establish local photographic and wireless societies. It is likely that Bargoed and District Photographic Society started meeting in 1908 and lapsed during World War I before re-forming in 1922. It had a large and keen membership by the time it organised its first Annual Exhibition in Spring 1923. That exhibition attracted over seven hundred people on the first day and its success was attributed to the efforts of Stanley J. Hood of Bargoed, Exhibition Secretary, and Society Secretary, D. S. Blatchford of Gilfach. The Society continued to make excellent progress with interesting and instructive lectures weekly in the 1920s and 1930s. Later, perhaps about 1942, it became known as Bargoed Camera Club. Today it is one of seven clubs in South Wales Photography League and meets weekly in Bargoed Settlement, encouraging beginners and more experienced photographers to enjoy learning about photography in all its formats. Messrs Jones Bros of Cardiff Road played an important role in the success and popularity of Bargoed and District Amateur Wireless Society. The Society came into being a few weeks prior to the opening of Cardiff Radio Station in February 1923 and attracted large attendances to its weekly meetings in The Settlement. One of its first activities was a Wireless Concert under the auspices of Calfaria's YPG when Councillor A. S. Williams presided and Messrs Jones Bros fixed up the apparatus free of charge. In the 1920s the government decided that the wireless, new technology capable of delivering entertainment and information, was to be financed, not by advertising, but, by a compulsory radio licence (from November 1922 to February 1971). During those decades the wireless, powered by electricity or accumulator batteries, played an important part in the life of local people as more and more households were equipped with a wireless set. Many local residents have fond memories of listening to programmes such as *Dick Barton Special Agent*, *Take It From Here* while an extant prospectus of local Evening Classes in 1938-1939 shows that V. A. Williams, B.A., was the tutor for a weekly Wireless Listening and Discussion Group.

There were several local societies devoted to birds and animals. Bargoed and District Pigeon Flying Club organised annual shows and that at Junction Hotel in 1937 attracted over one hundred entries. Benjamin Augustus (Gus) Jones, a butcher in New Tredegar before he became landlord of Old Mill Hotel, was an expert Dog Judge and exhibitor as well as being Chairman of Welsh Canine Club. The revival, during 1924, of Bargoed and District Canine Society, a society that was formerly very successful in the district, can be traced in issues of *Merthyr Express*. The Society organised several dog shows in the yard of Hanbury Arms and Frank Morris was one of the local members to have success in Cardiff Championship Dog Show. In early July, the Society had 74 entries at its Members' Sanction Show at Hanbury Arms. Before the end of October 1924, Bargoed and District Canine Society was advertising its first Annual Open Show (under Kennel Club Rules) at Bargoed Workmen's Institute with admission from the time of opening at 10 am to 3 pm being 1/6d, or just 1 shilling from 3 p.m. to closure at 5.45. There were cheap tickets from all G.W.R. stations within a 60 mile radius. The 470 entries to the show exceeded expectations and the detailed report in the local press included names of judges and prizewinners.

New clubs and societies emerged, reflecting a new range of interests, as local people in Bargoed and Gilfach readjusted to life in the post World War II era. Freemasons and Rotarians started to meet locally. Two new societies, Bargoed and District Art Society and Gelligaer Historical Society, started in Bargoed Settlement and, while they are both still active and attracting members from Bargoed and Gilfach, neither of them hold their regular meetings in Bargoed and Gilfach.

In the early decades of the twentieth century local men like solicitor L. Arnold Williams, policeman J. H. Folland and auctioneer I. B. Barnett, had belonged to the Freemasons' Lodge in Rhymney, to which they had probably travelled by train. However since 1946 freemasons have met locally and in 1969 the former Trinity chapel in Cardiff Road became a Freemasons' Hall. Bargoed Rotary Club started in 1955 and their website shows numerous examples of the ways in which they have worked to improve the lives of people within the local community, including fixing bird boxes to the wall of St. Gwladys' School and supporting the annual *Youth Speaks* competition.

Bargoed and District Art Society has a proud history recorded in its Society Cuttings Books. In the immediate post World War II era, about ten people enrolled annually at evening art classes in Bargoed Settlement where, taught by Bargoed Grammar School's Art Master, the students worked in oils, on still life and landscape subjects, and they had exhibited some of their work. Bargoed and District Art Society was founded in Bargoed Settlement in 1960, and owes a great deal to its early members including Alban Thomas, Stuart Florence and Ruby Lewis. In its early years it met in Bargoed Settlement, then in Bethany Chapel Schoolroom Ystrad Mynach, before moving to its present home, Llancaiach Fawr. Its membership, artists and those interested in art, drawn from a wide area, meets regularly and holds annual exhibitions displaying members' work in a range of media. At first, these were held in Bargoed Settlement before they moved to larger premises in Ystrad Mynach Church Hall, but recent exhibitions, including that of 2010 celebrating fifty years of amateur art in the area, have been held at Llancaiach Fawr. Within the Society, the supreme award is the Withers Cup, which was won in 2010, the Society's Golden Jubilee year by Eleanor Whiteman.

Gelligaer Historical Society was formally inaugurated at a meeting held at Gelligaer Urban District Council Offices in Hengoed on 22 November 1961; its officers and committee were appointed and the provisional programme for the first session was outlined. The research team responsible for Gelligaer Urban District Council's Golden Jubilee publication, *The Gelligaer Story*, formed the nucleus of the new society, but membership was open to all interested in the history and heritage of the area. Reflecting the contemporary revival of interest in research and interpretation of local history and heritage, it started with a programme of lectures, discussions and visits, and produced its first journal, *Gelligaer*, in July 1962. Gelligaer Historical Society regularly met in Bargoed Settlement until, in the late 1970s, it moved to the purpose-built Bargoed Library constructed in the early 1970s, before moving to Llancaiach Fawr in 2007 in anticipation of the demolition of that Library building. The founder members would be proud that Gelligaer Historical Society retains not only the interest and enthusiasm that inspired them in the early 1960s but also has a popular programme of lectures and a thriving research interest. They would be amazed at both the dramatic changes that have taken place in the former Gelligaer Urban District and the technological developments that have wrought a revolution in research and publication methods in the intervening decades.

Local newspapers and photographs in family albums shed light on Scout and Guide groups both before and after World War II. Former Scouts and Guides recall with fondness and gratitude the role such activities played in their social life as young people as well as the way in which they helped them through adulthood. In the 1950s some Gilfach girls went to Brownies and Guides attached to the Presbyterian Church and they remember, first Mrs Jenkins (wife of the minister) and then Mrs Alloway (whose husband was an award-winning fireman) as Captains. Judy Ellis was in Gilfach Brownies from its first meeting and she joined Guides in 1955, the year after it started, and later became a founder member of 1st Gilfach Land Rangers.

This photograph, courtesy of Judy Ellis, shows a happy bunch of uniformed Gilfach Guides washing up in the kitchen of the hall underneath the Presbyterian Church after one of their tea-parties in the 1950s. Pictured are: back left to right:: Mrs Jones? who helped with Brownies, Unknown, Greta Walters, Sheila Owen, Gillian Lewis, and front left to right::Judith Davies, Wendy Mayo, Gillian Brookes.

In the late 1940s and early 1950s the annual pantomimes and shows performed in Lesser Hall provided much entertainment for adults and children, both performers and spectators. Sheila Little (formerly McCarthy) recalls *that for months beforehand, the large cast of players rehearsed their lines, songs,*

This photograph (courtesy of Sheila Little) shows the cast of The Minstrel Show in which the rendering of the Al Jolson style solo *Mammy* brought the audience to their feet at every performance. Included among those pictured are (adults) Tom Jones, Reg McCarthy, Mrs Perrins and Haydn Williams and (children) Graham Cross, Pat Davies, Enid Jones, Marion Jones, Sheila McCarthy, Gaynor Morris, Gaynor Perrins, Linda West, Sylvia Williams, Graham Harris, Glyn Ricketts, Barbara Smith, Doreen Pritchard, Lily Carpenter, Shirley Williams, Margaret Rogers and Glenys Pritchard.

tap and ballet dances,while mothers stitched up miles of satin, net and sequins .... and fathers built and painted stage sets. Scripts were written by Reg McCarthy with Tom Jones who, together, also comprised the comic duo each year.

Social life since the 1970s

For decades the social life of many local people centred on their family, school and place of worship as well as the activities (especially sport and music) already mentioned in this chapter. In addition, Bargoed Park with its open-air swimming pool was popular and attracted people of all ages from the local community and further afield, while the fresh air and open spaces on the local Common was all that some people wanted in their spare time.

In the post World War II era Bargoed Grammar Technical School offered its pupils an active social life complimenting their more formal education. Both before and after reorganisation of secondary education in 1973, the local secondary schools had a range of extra-curricular activities, especially in music and sport, that enhanced the social life of participants. However a variety of factors including comprehensive reorganisation itself, early school closures during the drought of 1976, more pupils taking weekend jobs and a work to rule by a teacher's union, meant that many who were pupils during the last three decades or so, do not look back on school as an important part of their social life.

The McCarthy siblings received their primary and secondary education locally in that era and, apart from extra-curricular music activities, they recall few other ways in which school enhanced their social lives. Far more important were local Scouts and Guides and YMCA. Jenny played netball in YMCA and Robert and Chris played football. Later Jenny, having been introduced to hockey in school, played for Bargoed Ladies Hockey Club while Robert enjoyed Bargoed Badminton Club. Both Robert and Chris went to Bargoed Model Railway Club, then held in Bargoed Workmen's Institute. As they grew older they found little to attract them to spend leisure time in Bargoed and Gilfach and so went further afield, to Ystrad Mynach or Cardiff.

By the 1970s many people, with more disposable income than earlier generations as well as motor cars to take them out of the area, were more likely to spend their leisure time in what they perceived as more desirable venues in Cardiff or further afield. By going to cinemas, theatres and sports venues as well as shopping centres outside the local area, they were helping to close down the leisure opportunities in Bargoed and Gilfach itself. However, the picture is not altogether dismal as witnessed by the number of people using the facilities at Heolddu Leisure Centre and other local sports grounds, and the many Bargoed and Gilfach residents who are involved in a whole range of choral, craft and cultural activities both within Bargoed and Gilfach and neighbouring communities today.

Bargoed Male Voice Choir (photograph Courtesy of Barrie Jones)

CHAPTER 13
RETAIL

Introduction

After centuries of self-sufficiency the local area changed in the later nineteenth, and especially in the twentieth century. Not only were local farmers unable to grow enough food to feed the rapidly expanding population but also the range of goods required began to expand. In the early twentieth century the new communities of Bargoed and Gilfach both developed as shopping centres but of very different kinds: while Bargoed, with its large stores, served a wide hinterland, Gilfach's village-like shops were generally patronised by local residents to satisfy their day-to-day needs.

Lewis Lewis and his son Edward Lewis

Lewis Lewis established the first retail business in the area in the late 1820s and his was the first goods consignment for Bargoed on the new Rhymney Railway line in 1858. Successive census returns show that at first the business was run from premises on the Bedwellty side of the valley but by the last quarter of the nineteenth century it had moved to Croft House (close to the Old Mill Hotel) on the Glamorgan side of the river. Lewis Lewis died in 1888 and his son Edward (shown in this cartoon that appeared in *Merthyr Express* February 1911 and depicted Edward Lewis Postmaster and *General Looker-After of Bargoed*) expanded the business when, in 1890, he opened the  first Post Office in the district on the Glamorganshire side of the river. He continued trading until his retirement in 1914 brought an end to the 86 year history of the business.

Bargoed: "The Premier Shopping Centre of the Rhymney Valley" (a snapshot of the town in the decades before the Second World War)

In December 1913 *Merthyr Express* described Bargoed as *the Premier Shopping Centre of the Rhymney Valley* and, as many of today's older generations will recall, it retained its right to that graphic description until well into the third quarter of the twentieth century. However, Trade Directories show that its emergence as a centre of trade came relatively late in the history of the Rhymney Valley. In Slater's Directory of 1859, Bargoed was not considered significant enough to warrant an entry in its own right: it appears under the heading *Risca*, and is described as *a village and station on the Rhymney and Cardiff line, partly in the parish of Bedwellty and partly in Gellygare...the only trade carried on in this village is a small woollen manufactory. Population in 1851, 315.* Most of those people (including the traders) were resident on the Bedwellty side of the river. The tradespeople listed in the publication included three boot and shoemakers, three retailers of beer, a blacksmith, a butcher, a carpenter and joiner, an enterprising shopkeeper Edward Jenkins, (who was both a grocer and a draper), a maltster, a saddler, two surgeons, and a woollen manufacturer. There was also one Public House listed, the Smith's Arms. A station master, John Duckett worked for the Rhymney Railway, which ran a goods and passenger service. Even in Kelly's Directory of 1885, a quarter of a century later, whereas Brithdir and Ysgwyddgwyn (later known as Deri) were listed as valley communities of note, Bargoed was not, and the "most populous part of the parish" was Pontlottyn with a population of 6,587.

All this changed with Powell Duffryn Steam Coal Company's sinking of Bargoed Pit. Within a decade of opening, it resulted in, as a Medical Officer of Health remarked in his report, a *phenomenal immigration of the large industrial population*. By 1912, the population of Bargoed had increased to 13,014. Ten years later, almost 2,500 men were employed at its colliery alone.

The implications for trade were immense. The first decade of the twentieth century saw this little village transformed into a commercial centre and its new status was reflected in national Trade Directories. By 1907, in Cope's South Wales and Monmouthshire Directory, Bargoed had 'made it'! It had achieved an entry in its own right, its name in bold, thus:

Bargoed
Including Gilfach, Brithdir, Deri, Pengam, Hengoed & Gelligaer.

The types of tradespeople in Bargoed at that time were indicative of the way in which the town had become industrialized. There were, for example, Courts the Coal merchants, Powell Duffryn Steam Coal Colliery Company Ltd., Williams the hauliers, three ironmongers, and three quarry owners. There were also ten Builders and Contractors, illustrating the demand for new houses and businesses. The wealth generated was reflected by the fact that, not only were there plenty of essential stores in Bargoed and Gilfach - no less than seventeen grocers and seven fruiterers, seventeen boot and shoe makers, and ten tailors and clothiers - but other shops which were proof of a thriving local economy. There were two accountants, six hairdressers, two artificial teeth manufacturers, four watchmakers and jewellers, four milliners and dressmakers, a sewing machine shop, Refreshment rooms, two ice-cream makers a photographer (Mr. Horace Dale Riden – a name which might resonate with many valley people even today!), a musical instrument dealer, three tobacconists, a wallpaper dealer and Bargoed and District Window Cleaning and Carpet Beating Company of Cardiff Road. By 1916, the local press described the town as *the metropolis of the Rhymney Valley*. Nevertheless, an ominous sign that poverty was never too far away, was the presence of Shibko's, the pawnbrokers, in Hanbury Road.

The town also had its own printer, responsible for a local newspaper. *New Tredegar, Bargoed and Caerphilly Journal* had been established in 1904. This entertaining newspaper paints a wonderful picture of a bustling Bargoed. In an article of 1904, a visitor gave his impression of the town. He remarked that Bargoed was still *a young and immature community*, but that there were "*ever-increasing signs of development.*" He went on to comment that *it is with pleasure that one sees... the enterprising tradesman, the commercial traveller, the 'man-about-town'... the up-to-date shops, bank buildings and municipal improvements... Walking up the main street, one sees most of the shops ... possessing imposing frontages and signs that would do credit to many a large city.*

This optimism is also reflected in the foundation and success of Chambers of Trade both in Bargoed and Gilfach and reports in *New Tredegar, Bargoed and Caerphilly Journal* shed light on their early history. Established in 1902, Bargoed Chamber of Trade was confident enough to celebrate in style a year later by inviting the local MP, Sir Alfred Thomas to speak at its *annual banquet*, held at the Plasnewydd Hotel. On that occasion, Councillor Lewis, the President, reminded his fellow members of their *important social and financial responsibilities.* Gilfach Chamber of Trade was set up in November, 1905, and its first meeting, held at the Gwerthonor Hotel, was reported in the local press. The Chairman, Mr. C. E. Forrestier Walker, J.P. of Pengam, commented that *some might laugh at the idea of such a small place as Gilfach having a Chamber of Trade. But ...there would very likely be a great increase in the place in the near future.* His committee pledged to carry out whatever was *useful and beneficial to the district.*

These Chambers of Trade were, in fact, extremely influential and became instrumental in lobbying the local council to make improvements in the town in such basic areas as street lighting, roads and transport. Their members were thus key figures in the development of the town. Many had started out from humble roots, possibly as shop assistants themselves. Most had grown wealthy as Bargoed Colliery brought in more workers and money. Some still lived above their shops but others moved *over the fields* – the phrase which signified the 'wealthy' area of Hillside Park. All were involved in several civic organizations. At the turn of the century, Bargoed was represented by two members on the local council and, often, one of these would also be a member of the Chamber of Trade. Aspects of the life and work of D. S. (Davy) Jones and Gus Jones, two personalities who epitomize these early entrepreneurs, are described below.

D.S. (Davy) Jones was the first ever President of Bargoed Chamber of Trade. He had arrived in the town in the 1870s, taking over the management of a small grocery store at 15, High Street in 1874. Today, the sign 'Davy's Shop' can still be seen, engraved in stone, above that address. In 1910, towards the end of his life, he was awarded the honour of being elected permanent President of the Bargoed and District Grocers' Association. In announcing this, a 'sketch' was written about him in the trade magazine, *Grocer*. Describing him as *the father of the grocery traders of the town*, the article went on to say that *it has often been said of him that he figured second only to the great Powell Duffryn Coal Company in the development of the district. He has played a considerable part in the devotion of time to public service, having served on the County Council and the District Council and on the latter authority he has filled the*

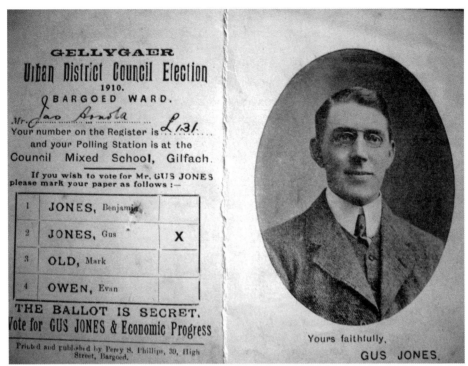

Gus Jones' 1910 G.U.D.C. election poster. courtesy of Michael N. Jones, Director of Gus Jones Jewellers, and grandson of Gus Jones.

position of Chairman which carried with it the duties of magistrate for the period of office. His last candidature was with the Board of Guardians. It may be added that last year Mr. Jones was one of the judges at the Grocers' Exhibition in London. Mr. Jones, but for his innate modesty, would be a star among public men. According to *New Tredegar, Bargoed and Caerphilly Journal* he was regarded by some as *the financier* of the town and, in 1906, credited him as being the chief force in persuading Lloyd's Bank to start a branch in Bargoed. He certainly amassed a personal fortune but tales of his generosity to local people in times of need were legendary. In 1912 *Merthyr Express* recalled how *in the great strike of 1898, when numbers of business establishments had to close temporarily, Mr. D.S. Jones's goodness of heart played a right good part in allowing his own pocket to suffer to help numbers of families through to the end.*

Gus Jones was another leading figure in the town, and was present at the first ever meeting of the Bargoed Chamber of Trade. He had been brought up in Pontypool. His father was a tobacconist, who later became interested in photography. Young Gus, though, entered the trade of his grandfather – watchmaking. He started work as a shop assistant in Abertillery and, by 1903 had saved enough money to open his own shop at 65, Hanbury Road, Bargoed. Like other traders, he took up politics, becoming an Independent member on the local council. He served twice as Chairman of the Council (in 1916 and 1927), as well as being Mayor of Bargoed and a Justice of the Peace. In 1915 *Bargoed Journal* claimed that it would be *difficult to now name a public man in the valley, who is held in higher regard by his colleagues than Mr Jones.* He did all he could to encourage visitors to the town, was an organizer of Bargoed and District Flower Show, President of the May Day Show as well as being instrumental in many important decisions at this crucial time in the development of the town. Today, Gus Jones' shop in Bargoed still stands, at its original address.

This photograph, courtesy of Myra Jones of Deri, shows Bargoed's Emporium at the Pier Head before the clock was put in place. Several generations of residents and visitors grew to know the clock as a familiar and much-loved landmark and were saddened when, in April 1970, it had to be removed for safety reasons.

During those early years of the twentieth century, shops opened which were to become household names in the valley town, and beyond, for many years. In 1911 a Bargoed Trade Journal described 'The Emporium' as *the largest and most flourishing business in the Rhymney Valley.* From relatively humble beginnings as *Bargoed's cheapest shop*, formerly Burns and Evans, it reopened in March 1906 at 33 and 34, High Street, Bargoed, with Mr. G. W. Davies as its proprietor. As Bargoed prospered, so the Emporium expanded: the size of the premises increasing significantly four times between 1906 and 1911. Its frontage in 1906 was 40 feet but by 1911 this had become 150 feet. It was in one of the most prominent positions in the town, the Pierhead Buildings being a natural meeting place for local people. Construction of the magnificent Emporium clock tower started in 1909, and, after taking some three years to build, it was to remain one of Bargoed's most famous landmarks until 1970. It was an eight-day striking turret clock. The dials were 7 feet 4 inches overall, with the words 'The Emporium' in copper letters engraved across the clock face. It was reported in *Bargoed Journal* in 1911 that *The business is devoted to the sale of drapery, clothing, millinery and furnishing of every description.* In March 1911 *New Tredegar, Bargoed and Caerphilly Journal* reported that the large staff employed on its premises is an indication of the immense business transacted. Much later, in 1936, the *Merthyr Express* commented that *the name Emporium is synonymous with quality and shopping.*

By 1910, Bargoed was attracting shoppers from all over the valley and so large stores from Cardiff, and beyond, found it profitable to open outlets in the town. One of the most successful was Roath Furnishers, which opened in 1908. *All goods are made at its factories in Cardiff, and therefore it is little wonder they are able to sell at 'razor-edged' prices. The Bargoed branch in High Street is one of the most flourishing.* In 1913 *Merthyr Express* reported that it sold, *beds, chairs, tables, linoleum, carpets, washstands, coal scuttles, fire-irons, lamps, rugs, mirrors.* The store was to remain in the town for over 50 years.

Another example of a chain store which came to Bargoed was the 'Maypole' which opened in April, 1911 and was famous for its dairy goods. Lipton's was also established in the town in this period.

Chamber of Trade members were constantly attempting to find enterprising ways of bringing more people into the town. They were insistent about the need to forge a better link between the town and Aberbargoed. In 1903, they proposed the erection of a viaduct between the two places but this created outrage in some quarters because of the impact on ratepayers. Nevertheless, similar projects were suggested almost annually. In 1910, Mr Lewis Watkins addressed the Chamber, proposing either a light footbridge from the Skating Rink in Bargoed (opposite the train station) to School Street in Aberbargoed, or a light traffic bridge. By early January 1911 *New Tredegar, Bargoed and Caerphilly Journal* reported that these ideas led Gelligaer Council members to brand the plan *a wildcat scheme* and to suggest *severing its connection with*

This advertisement sheds light on the special opening prices at Bargoed's Maypole.

the Chamber. In a lesser scheme, in 1909, Mr. Jackson Withers (of the Hall Cinema) made £25 available for the Chamber of Trade to advertise Bargoed as a business centre throughout the Valley and Gus Jones' idea was to use this to advertise the town on the hoardings of 24 Valley Railway Stations. At various other times, they subsidized cheap railway tickets to attract shoppers in. Their members were also prominent in setting up committees to organise popular, crowd-pulling events – a May Day Show and Parade, Bargoed Flower Show and the local Eisteddfod. In 1905, the Eastern Glamorgan Agricultural Society Show was held in Bargoed so, according to *New Tredegar, Bargoed and Caerphilly Journal, marking an epoch in the history of the town and district.*

However, there were problems in the town, just as in any burgeoning town at the turn of the century. One source of grievance was the fact that the Post Office had not moved with commerce: it was still in Edward Lewis' premises near the Old Mill (dating from the days when that area was at the heart of the community). The *Journal* voiced its objections frequently – as in the following comment in May 1912 *When we want a penny stamp on a Thursday afternoon or a postal order, or to send a telegram, we have to walk from the centre of town, and even from Gilfach, down to the head post office, by the Old Mill – imagine the people of any other town having a general post office on the outskirts of town.*

Another worry was the lack of what we now think of as basic facilities, such as a good water supply, lighting and refuse collection. In the summer months, there was often a shortage of water. In the autumn and winter, many shops were affected by flooding as there was too much rain! Even when the rain had stopped the roads were impassable. In 1905 *New Tredegar, Bargoed and Caerphilly Journal* reported that several Bargoed tradesmen complained to the council that their business suffered on account of the heaps of mud that were lying about the streets... *Between the entrance to Bristol Terrace and the Workmen's Club the road was covered with mud 10 inches thick.* It was decided to appoint a Committee of the whole council to deal with the matter (April 1905). But still the same newspaper reported in 1912, *Hanbury Road and other main streets are in a scandalous state.* It seemed little was done to remedy the situation in this busy town. In 1913, Councillor Gus Jones bemoaned the fact that the main road was in serious need of repair because of the heavy traffic in the town - an average of one vehicle a minute passing along the road from Bargoed Station to Pengam Bridge!

Lighting the town was difficult and expensive. There were no street lights in Bargoed in the evenings, even though most shops were open until at least 9 o'clock. On winter days, even lighting premises inside was hard. By 1906, Bargoed had gas lighting but the Chamber of Trade was campaigning to replace this with electric throughout Bargoed and Gilfach, even though some on the council declared this to be a *luxury* the area could ill afford. In August 1904 *Bargoed Journal* reported that the Chamber criticized the *irregularities of supply* with gas, noting that *there are at least two shops in Bargoed with large frontages, that have had to resort to candles more than once, which looks very bad indeed!* In March 1906 it reported that postmaster Edward Lewis complained that *he had used as many as 30 candles to light the Post Office at Bargoed.*

Furthermore, the rapid growth of the town meant that there were basic problems in sanitation. An angry letter to *New Tredegar, Bargoed and Caerphilly Journal* in 1905 described how there were, *defective and leaky refuse carts, uncovered, being drawn through the busy and thickly populated thoroughfares, scattering the contents on its journey...equally dangerous is the storms of road dust driven into every shop, settling on provisions which are exposed for sale...*

Collection of refuse seemed to be a sore point. In 1908, there were complaints to the Council about the smells from heaps of refuse in some streets, caused by the fact that some fishmongers were in the habit of throwing their fish on to the refuse instead of burning it, giving rise to the *Bargoed Journal* headline – *Fishy, Niffy Bargoed! Rotten Fish on the Streets.*

Moreover the town's prosperity was soon to be threatened. Bargoed traders inevitably depended on the coal community which they served. The pre-war years were difficult ones, as hard times hit the coal industry throughout the Valleys. This resulted in several incidents during that period, which were to test relationships between shopkeepers and traders within the town.

1911 was a year of industrial unrest throughout South Wales. In August, a rail strike resulted in food shortages. This led some shopkeepers to put up prices. It was believed that some were profiteering and, with feelings running high, attacks were made against their shops. *Bargoed Journal*'s front page railed: *One of the worst features of the strike was the rising of food commodities to famine prices and all in a moment. We cannot find words too strong in reprehending this action on the part of tradesmen in the valley. One can regard it as criminal on the part of the shopkeepers to seek to make a good profit on the backs of poor peopl*e. This happened in several towns and the anger of townspeople erupted in an *epidemic* of rioting which broke out in places such as Ebbw Vale, Cwm, Rhymney and Bargoed.

There was a sizeable Jewish community in Bargoed at the time and when the shops of some of them were targeted, the incidents took on unpleasant anti-semitic undertones. It was claimed that *the valley from Bargoed to Rhymney appears to be a seething state of discontent and full of racial hatred.* Additional police were drafted in and soldiers were stationed at Tredegar, Ebbw Vale, Rhymney and New Tredegar.

The Bargoed Riot took place in the early evening of Thursday 24 August 1911 and was reported in the local press. Because it was half-day closing, there were no shop lights and the streets of the town were in darkness. A crowd of almost a thousand men, women and children gathered around the Pierhead. A contingency of 40 police (30 of them having being drafted in especially because of the unrest) encircled the protestors. At first, there was good humoured banter between police and crowd but, at about 8.30 p.m., the smashing of glass could be heard, as a stone went through Mr. J. D. Jarman's shop-window in Upper High Street. It was the signal for more stone throwing and a portion of the crowd made their way up Hanbury Road. The newspapers made the most of the dramatic events which followed. The *Merthyr Express* headline was *Bayonets at Bargoed!.*

The crowd's next target was the jewellery shop owned by Mr. Isaac Barnett. One of the crowd urged the others on, calling *Come on, boys! At 'em!*. A shower of stones hit the shop and Mr. Barnett stood in the doorway, armed with a revolver, yelling – *Stand aside, I am going to shoot!*. Fortunately, he was dissuaded from this course of action by Inspector Canton and the crowd moved further up Hanbury Road. At this stage, volleys of stones were being hurled from the back of Hanbury Road over the roofs of business premises to smash windows on the opposite side of the street. Mr. Rubenstein's furniture shop was damaged as were the premises of Mr. Protheroe (furnisher); Mr. James (tobacconist): Messrs Masters (clothiers): Mr. J. A J. Wilcox (fruiterer): Mrs. Newcombe (confectioner) and Messrs Hipp Ltd (clothiers).

Upper High Street (courtesy of Reflective images of Port Talbot)

Eventually however, the police managed to surround the crowd and, marching down Cross Street, charged with batons drawn – the crowd had only one means of escape –Capel Street – they rushed there pursued by the police who, according to the local press, used their truncheons *right lustily*. In the meantime a message had been dispatched to the troops stationed in Rhymney. In less than 15 minutes, a special train had been run through to Bargoed with troops from the Worcestershire Regiment. But the crowds had disappeared, many in the direction of Gilfach, others towards West Street or Heolddu Road. By midnight everything was quiet. A lesson had been learned about the fragility of relationships within the town in times of stress. For the most part, however, community bonds were strong. Within a year, the same traders and townspeople, who had in 1911, faced each other in a 'stand-off', were united in a fight against poverty.

In 1912, the South Wales coalfield was beset by a series of bitter strikes. *Merthyr Express* reported on a meeting at Bargoed in March of that year, to express concern that *the gaunt figure of starvation would be staring many families in the face* and to form the Bargoed and Gilfach Relief Committee to alleviate *the distress of the poor*. Many of the leading members were local minister and businessmen, such as G. W. Davies (of the Emporium) and Gus

290

Jones, who proposed *discovering and dealing with the urgently necessitous cases*. The *Bargoed Journal* of April 4th published a list of those who had donated in cash or kind up to the end of March. All the butchers gave meat and bones for soup, while all Churches and Chapels made notable cash donations, as did numerous trades people and organizations, such as:

Businessman / Organisation	£.	s	d.
Mr. Jackson Withers	3	0	0
Roath Furnishing Company	2	2	0
Home and Colonial Co.	2	2	0
Hipps Ltd	0	10	6
Liptons Ltd.	1	1	0 (value in goods)
Masters and Co.	0	10	6
Mr. Wolfson	0	5	0
Hodges and Co,	0	10	6
Co-operative Society	80 loaves of bread as long as strike continues		
Mr. W. B. Lloyd	84 loaves of bread as long as strike continues		
Mr. L. Thomas, milk vendor	Gallon of milk weekly as long as strike		
Mr. J. D. Jarman	24 loaves of bread.		
Mr .A. S. Williams, coal merchants	Half a sheep		
Mr. Boobyer, fruiterer	Potatoes, carrots, parsnips, onions.		
Mr. I. B. Barnett	Pair of boots.		
Messrs Williams and Co. Royal Stores	56lbs of rice.		
Mr. Aaron, grocer	800 buns and 12 loaves of bread		

The trading community suffered another dramatic major blow in 1912, when a serious fire started in the Bon Marche, Hanbury Road and spread to destroy several shops. Fire was a constant danger because so many of the shops in the town were crowded with combustible goods and had wooden shop fitments. The episode, described in *Merthyr Express* 4 May 1912, also illustrates the primitive nature of the Bargoed Fire Brigade at the time. Towards midnight, one night in May 1912, fire broke out in *one of Bargoed's high-class establishments*, the Bon Marche. People who were leaving the 'Picture Palace' noticed flames. Bugler D. Jones was notified, and in time honoured tradition, gave the fire call to rouse each of the Brigade members. To do this, he was *frantically rushing from street to street*, blowing his bugle outside each fireman's house (as there was no telephone link!) By the time the Brigade arrived, *the fire had a tremendous hold upon the highly inflammable contents of the premises* and had spread to several others. A very strong easterly wind was blowing on to the rear of the building and forced the flames out on to the main street......large balls of fire were also carried away by the wind over the houses into Greenfield Street, Cross Street and Capel Street. By this time a crowd of helpers had arrived – *there was great excitement and women rushed wildly to and fro*. The Brigade connected their hose to the hydrant near the Hanbury Baptist Chapel but the water pressure was not strong enough to be effective. Mr. T. W. Evans, mechanic at the Powell Duffryn Colliery ran a hose from the Pit Head, under the metals of the Rhymney Railway, to the buildings in Hanbury Road but there was still not enough pressure. Meanwhile, other firemen were trying to assemble their sectional ladders to reach the top of the buildings. The ladders were not long enough and buckled under the weight of the firefighters – one fireman, Alf Nile, falling several feet when a section of ladder snapped. Longer ladders had to be borrowed from the New Hall Theatre. Finally, by 12.30a.m., with considerable help from tradesmen and townspeople alike, the fire was under control.

The damage done was extensive. The 'Bon Marche' was *completely gutted* and the *Denture Institute* at 8 Hanbury Road (only opened in December 1911 and *beautifully equipped premises*) was totally *burnt out*. Mr. Parfitt's shop (a tobacconist and hairdresser) was also practically destroyed. Other shops damaged were the Home and Colonial, Messrs Hodges and Sons, the Butter Cream Shop and Palmer Bros. Boot Shop. On the other side of the road, tailors and hatters Scriveners and Sons was badly damaged as were Olivers shoe shop, Masters and Co. and Mr. Marston the butchers.

Both Bargoed Journal and Merthyr Express decried the damage done to the main thoroughfare of Bargoed. The Journal particularly criticized the antiquated and ludicrous method of calling out members of the Fire Brigade. The papers, voicing the feelings of many in the town, demanded that the Council invest more money in updating the Fire Brigade with modern appliances, sufficient length of hose and adequate pressure of water in the mains to throw a strong volume of water on the blaze. They also demanded that the Fire Brigade be on the telephone with electric bells placed in all firemen's houses.

However, little was done and, in May 1914, another serious fire broke out, this time in High Street, in the large block of buildings known as Bank Chambers. The shop and ware house of the Pontypridd Furnishing Company were destroyed, as were the offices of Mr. Ebsworth the solicitor and others. Lloyd's Bank was saved by its strong rooms, though the premises *suffered severely. Merthyr Express* lamented the way in which the *brigade is being handicapped for appliances...they had to borrow ladders from builders in the district to enable them to carry the hose to the upper windows.......The ancient method of calling out the Brigade by means of the Bugle is again to be condemned.* It seemed lessons had not been learned.

Working conditions for shop assistants in Bargoed, as across the whole of Britain were often hard and hours were long. The campaign for a 60 hour week for shop workers eventually resulted in the Liberal Government passing the 1911 Shop Hours Act but, like other contemporary government legislation, the details of the measure had to be negotiated locally. Gelligaer Council could not get a local agreement amongst all traders. In August 1912 the local press reported that some traders did not want to shorten their evening hours, claiming that they would suffer financially by such a step, because *the main part of their business is transacted after the hours of 7 o'clock in the evening of every day of the week.* One manager, who had worked in other Welsh valley towns, stated that hours in Bargoed were in excess of any other place he had ever known and were *a disgrace*. Eventually a consensus was achieved across trades and, 8 June 1912 *Merthyr Express* reported the working week was as follows:

Day	Shops open until
Monday:	8 p.m.
Tuesday:	7 p.m.
Wednesday:	7 p.m.
Thursday:	1 p.m.
Friday:	9 p.m.
Saturday:	11 p.m.

Yet, by 1913, a small minority of shopkeepers would still not accept the principle of half-day closing on Thursdays, so Bargoed Branch of the National Shop Assistants' Union organized a protest meeting in December of that year. A torchlight procession of shop workers from Bargoed and other towns in the Rhymney Valley marched to the Skating and Boxing Pavilion in Bargoed, where they held a demonstration against those tradesmen who opposed the closing order of Gelligaer Council. There were some traders who attended the meeting and who spoke out for the workers – one being Mr. Jarman. Rev. W. F. Phillips also gave his support, claiming that workers had the same right to leisure time as employers. The march might well have had an impact, for, shortly afterwards, half-day closing on Thursday was introduced in the town.

Regular checks were kept on conditions for workers. Contemporary newspapers contained accounts of prosecutions made against Bargoed traders for continuing to break the regulations on hours. Thus in 1912, for example, a local butcher was fined for employing young children to deliver baskets of meat after 9 p.m.. Another shopkeeper in 1912 kept a young 15 year old boy for seven and a half hours without a break for food. The health of workers was not only affected by these long hours but also by the conditions within some of the buildings. In November 1911 *Merthyr Express*, quoting F. Meyrick, calculated that in 1910 about 50% of deaths among shop assistants were due to consumption, the result of the *foul atmosphere of the shops*.

However, it took many years to reduce working hours significantly. Even in the 1930s and 40s, many shops remained open until 8 p.m. on Friday evenings and 9 p.m. on Saturdays – some even later. Roger Jones, whose father, T. G. Jones kept a newsagency in Bargoed for many years, recalls the late working days of the 1930s. Much of the week was quiet, so as a very young lad he was allowed to play in the shop. But Fridays and Saturdays were incredibly busy – the time when people came to pay for their papers. Next door to them was a butcher's shop. In the days when there were no fridges, meat had to be bought daily. On a Friday and Saturday night (after payday), some would go to the pub, then at closing time go and collect their meat from the butcher on their way home. As they would call into the newsagents as well T. G. Jones stayed open until 10.30 or 11 p.m. at night and he would be up at 4 a.m. the next morning to get the morning papers from the station.

Also of concern to many was the *living–in* system. The rooms above shop-level which were used for the accommodation of staff can still be seen in Bargoed town centre today. At a time when hours were so long and transport both expensive and irregular, it was convenient for many traders to provide living accommodation for their staff. This obviously varied and was very good for some, who were treated as part of the family. A larger store, like the 'Emporium,' had to provide more dormitory-type accommodation for their staff.

Judy Ellis (formerly of Gilfach) remembers what a friend told her about being a live-in apprentice shop girl at the 'Emporium' in the 1920s and early 30s. There was *a 'matron' in charge of the residential floor, which was on the second floor (Upper High Street side). The entrance was half way along the building...and there was a women's end (up the hill I think) and a men's end, guarded by the 'matron'. Staff had Sunday and a half day on Thursday as holidays and had strict curfew every night, but especially on Saturdays when they would go to the local dances at the Miner's Institutes up and down the valleys.* Chris Jones recalls that in her days at Powell Duffryn Offices in the 1940s, she met some girls who had left the 'Emporium,' seeking more freedom. They had earned 5 shillings a week there but their wages had to be spent in the store itself. Living-in also meant that many were disenfranchised and *Merthyr Express*, quoting F. Meyrick, noted that less than 5% of male shop workers had the right to vote in 1912 (of course women workers could not vote anyway!).

The promise of prosperity which had seemed so real at the turn of the century, proved illusory for Bargoed traders. After a period of industrial tension, World War 1 broke out, bringing other problems with it such as shortages of food and other goods and difficulties of recruitment, as male shop assistants enlisted to fight for their country. The post-war years saw more trouble in the South Wales' coal-field, with particularly bitter strikes in 1921 and the General strike of 1926. More hardship followed in the late 1920's and early thirties as the 'Great Depression' took its toll on the town. The Chamber of Trade ceased to meet.

Yet new businesses did open during that period and shops did change hands. T. G. Jones moved to Bargoed from Mountain Ash to take over the newsagents in Hanbury Road in 1924. The premises had been converted from a house originally, the 'front room' being utilized as the shop, the family living above. His son Roger remembers growing up there in the 1920s. Bargoed then was extremely diverse – its earlier prosperity had attracted new settlers, not just from other parts of Wales, and Roger played alongside the children of first generation immigrants from England, Italy and China. There were large Catholic and Jewish communities as well as Anglican and Welsh Nonconformist. Transport was very different too. Few cars or vans could be seen about the town. No post van - the postman pushed a red painted handcart to take the mailbags from the Hanbury to the station, to be sent on trains up and down the valleys (in 1936, the last post was collected at 8.45 p.m.!) Every milkman and coal man had horse-drawn carts, and, at the bottoms of the streets which fed into Hanbury Road and High Street, were pitched stones, so that horse traffic could get a grip. Butchers' boys cycled out to the outlying villages first to take weekly orders from customers, then to deliver them at the end of the week. Hotels in the town – the Royal, the Hanbury, the Plasnewydd, the Capel, grew up to provide accommodation for the many commercial travellers who frequented the town, providing goods for the shops. The 'reps' would arrive by train, then hire horse and trap from local farmers to take their business to the surrounding villages. The horses would be stabled in the hotels and for years, the Hanbury carried the sign *Good Stabling*. One of the Hanbury's rooms also bore the window inscription *commercial room* – a lounge for the commercial travellers to get together in the evenings. When cars became more affordable, the reps stayed in hotels in larger towns like Pontypridd and spent less time in Bargoed.

In the 1920s, most shoppers visited the town on Friday and Saturday evenings – after pay day. For families who lived in the surrounding villages, it was a weekly event – one for which you 'dressed up' and (in the days before the 'Blue Fleet' buses run by Lewis and James of Newbridge started) took the train! Myra Jones from Deri remembers going there almost every Saturday evening with her sister and parents. A typical evening's shopping would start with a call to get their fruit and vegetables from Ruthers or Onions. Then they would pop into Lipton's, where her mother would buy a couple of slices of luncheon meat as a treat for their Sunday breakfast. It seemed to a child that there were always exciting things to see – crowds of people thronging the streets, the indoor market near the station and Longstaff's 'Penny Bazaar,' displaying tables of trinkets and everywhere, goods hanging outside shops enticing shoppers in. At Parfitt's, Myra's father Will would often stop to look at the multitude of different sized and coloured leather pieces which were hanging outside. Her father would choose one which he would later use to 'tap' (repair) his shoes at home on his cobbler's last.

Christmas was the special time. Shops did not start to dress their windows for Christmas until December and then even the grocery stores made a great effort. At Pegler's, the window contained massive mounds of sultanas, raisins and currants. In those days, most families made several cakes and puddings. They then took them to be baked in the large ovens of one of the local bakers, such as Charlie Raynes of Greenfield Street. Myra's favourite Christmas display was that of 'The Realm', a confectionery shop. In their window, every year, there would be three giant Christmas stockings. Each seemed about 5 feet tall and was full of toys and sweets. Myra's parents bought tickets for the shop's raffle on Christmas Eve, hoping that they would win one of the stockings – but they never did!

When she was older, Myra was a pupil at Bargoed Grammar School. She walked through town every day on her way to catch the train home to Deri. On Monday she and her friends would love looking in the window of Riden the

Photographer, where the wedding photographs from the weekend would be on display. A very enterprising photographer, Mr. Riden took photographs of most families in the valleys, attended the important occasions in the Bargoed calendar and at Whitsun would place his camera in the grounds of the Police Station – a brilliant vantage point from which to capture the Whitsun 'turn-out,' as the churches and chapels marched through the town.

Nearby was a Chinese Laundry, 'Sou Yicks,' the window of which was covered with a huge white sheet. It was always busy, as there was a huge demand for starched white collars amongst the business community. Across the road, passers-by could smell the leather from Hiles the Saddlers. Mr. Hiles (another of the very early town traders) was a properly apprenticed saddler from Newport, who originally made saddles and harnesses for the horses of the local collieries. When those days passed, the shop provided leather satchels for generations of schoolchildren. Further down the main street (at 33 Hanbury Road) was Shibko's the pawnbrokers, with a window full of gold–rings, bracelets, pendants and watches of all kinds.

Phil and Eira Mantle remember shopping in the Maypole as young children with their parents in the 1930s. The shop was always immaculately clean. All the assistants wore white overalls and hats. The walls were white and the glass counters shone. The tiles on the floor were beautiful. In the 'Maypole', as in other grocery stores, butter would be kept in a big block or 'tub'. The assistants would weigh out the amount the customer wanted, then, using wooden paddles, would pat it back and forth until it was the right shape, then pack it up expertly.

Bacon and cold meats were put on to slicing machines to be cut. The customer was asked what thickness they wanted on a scale of one to five (most customers knew their 'number'). Dried fruit such as raisins and sultanas were kept in sacks and the assistants would make up the amount required in packets in the room behind the main shop room.

Yet, for many, the Emporium was the favourite place to shop. At the time of its heyday in the 1940s, the 'shop under the clock' had a reputation for being one of the finest department stores in South Wales, selling quality goods. Judy Ellis remembers the store in the 1940s: *The ladies' department was on the first floor. My overwhelming impression was of light – it had huge windows on both sides and cheval mirrors which caught and angled the light....Counters and mirror frames were of mahogany and gleamed rich reddish brown. The cabinets had glass fronts and 3 sided drawers so that customers could see what was being displayed.* What almost everyone remembers about the Emporium was the cylinder/railway system of paying! Judy goes on to describe this in detail: *The thing which fascinated me was the system for sending cash to the cashier. The Emporium had a vacuum system, rather like that used in modern Sainsbury's. The woman at the counter – and they were all women, not girls – took the payment, twisted it so that the money was held securely, opened the trap in the pipe behind the counter and put the cylinder in. As soon as the trap was closed there was a whoosh and it was transported (on an overhead railway system) to the cash desk. A few minutes later it returned, with any change and the receipt. It seemed like magic!.*

Bargoed's shopping streets, Hanbury Road and High Street, in the 1920s (courtesy of Myra Jones of Deri)

In 1936, the Chamber of Trade was reconvened. Its members organized *Bargoed's First Shopping Week* in an attempt to encourage more shoppers to the town, with bargains galore and entertainment for the whole family. The local M.P. Morgan Jones (formerly a Bargoed councillor for 11 years) opened proceedings on Monday 2 November. In his speech, he appealed to the people of the Rhymney Valley that although Bargoed had *fallen on days of adversity,* they, the shoppers, could help by spending in the town. *Try and get rid of that snobbish thought that by going to Cardiff you get better things for your money......I hope this shopping week will be the turning point in the industrial history of the town.* A procession, including the Glamorgan Constabulary, Gelligaer Fire Brigade and the Ambulance Division, marched from the New Bridge, Pengam, to the Savoy Assembly Rooms, where the opening ceremony took place, headed by the Bargoed Town Band.

The chief attraction on the Tuesday was the roasting of an ox. This was held near the centre of the town with a crowd of nearly six thousand people, who had, paid their pennies to see the ox roasting and there was a ready sale for the slices and joints when the ox was cut up. The week of events finished with a torchlight procession to Bargoed's Trafalgar Square, where there was community singing. The streets were crowded and the lights were extinguished when the procession marched through the town. The square was floodlit for the community singing, attended by hundreds of people, in a downpour of rain. The week proved such a success, that others followed in those few years before the outbreak of World War Two.

It had been hoped that the week would really signal a revival in the trade of the town. Alderman Tom Evans, speaking after the 1936 shopping week, said that he *believed the coal industry would again prosper...and Bargoed would enjoy to the full its prosperity.* In November 1936 *Merthyr Express* echoed those sentiments in words which might have some resonance today - *Bargoed still has a great future, if the spirit which gave her such a splendid start still survives.*

Griffith William Davies (1879-1937) and The Emporium

The story of the Emporium reflects the fortunes of the local coal industry and of Bargoed, the premier shopping centre of the Rhymney Valley.

In 1937 *Merthyr Express* carried detailed reports on the death and funeral of G. W. Davies, owner of Bargoed's chief retail outlet, the Emporium. Born about 1879 at Bryngwyn Farm near Lampeter, Cardiganshire, G. W. Davies was adopted by an aunt after becoming orphaned by the age of four. On leaving Arthen School in Cardigan, he went to Llandeilo where he worked as an improver for £10 a year (saving £5 out of his first year's wages to lend to an older brother to open a grocery business in Tonypandy). His next employment was in charge of the men's department at the store of Messrs Powell and Jones in Abertillery. About 1905-06 G. W. Davies walked from Abertillery to Bargoed to establish his business. At first, he purchased premises adjacent to

Calfaria Chapel. His business increased and, through his boundless activity and enterprise, he went on to build the Emporium establishing what was considered by many of his contemporaries, to be the largest one-man business in Wales. For decades, the imposing Emporium building in Bargoed town centre was a striking monument to his ability and perseverance.

Although he was one of the largest tradesmen and major ratepayers in the Rhymney Valley, G. W. Davies did not play a prominent part in public life, preferring to devote himself to his extensive business. However, he was placed on the Commission of Peace and his fellow magistrates gave him a warm welcome when he took his place on the Bench at Bargoed late in 1920. Over the ensuing seventeen years, he won the confidence and respect of magistrates and all others who had business in the court.

G. W. Davies was a member and generous benefactor of the Presbyterian Church in Gilfach, where he served as Treasurer for over twenty years prior to his death. His considerable generosity was not confined to his own place of worship as there are numerous references to his financial support of other churches as well as worthy and needy institutions and people in the local area. One such beneficiary was Lewis School. In the later 1920s, he gave a bardic chair to the school and when its assembly hall was converted into the chapel he paid for panelling in front of the platform and staining the organ case to match. He also subscribed to the school sports prize fund and provided decorations for numerous school events. Small wonder the headmaster of Lewis School, wrote the following words in the school magazine in Spring 1937: *For all these things we of Lewis' School unite with numberless others to hold him in grateful remembrance.*

He and his wife, Mary Ann, had two children, a son David Howard who became a physician and surgeon, and a daughter Gladys. It is not clear where he lived in his early days in Bargoed but, by the time of his death he had a family home at Pentre, Abergavenny, as well as quarters on the top floor of the Emporium building. Employees in the Emporium from the 1940s onwards have vivid memories of admiring these beautiful rooms with mirrors above the marble fireplaces and windows, with leaded glass in the top half offering enviable views of Bargoed town.

Although G. W. Davies had been in poor health for some time prior to his death at the Emporium 28 February 1937, he had visited warehouses in Plymouth, London and Manchester in preparation for the store's 31st birthday sale to be held during the first week of March 1937. He was busy in the Emporium on the Saturday evening and, because of the snowstorm on Saturday night, he had not gone to his Abergavenny home as usual. He died when he went from his Emporium home above the shop to his office below to get a key for a member of staff. His funeral was held at Gilfach Presbyterian Chapel on the following Wednesday. His coffin was carried by members of his Emporium staff, while numerous other staff, as well as representatives of the local clergy, magistracy and council, and a large number of townspeople, paid their respects to one of the leading citizens of the Rhymney Valley. Business was suspended in the town when, following the service, the mile-long cortege headed by a posse of Glamorgan Police under Bargoed's Inspector W. H. Williams, and including scores of cars, proceeded to Gelligaer Churchyard for interment.

The Emporium survived the death of G. W. Davies in 1937 and retained its position as the area's premier store into the second half of the twentieth century. When Macowards, the second owners of the Emporium premises, sold the property it was purchased by the local council who then sold it to Mr Joseph, an optician in the town.

Joan Thompson is just one of a number of former employees who recall with enthusiasm and pleasure her decades of loyal service in a store they had almost as much affection for as they had for their family. When she started working in the store in 1942 the country was at war and she was a 14 year old inexperienced school-leaver. She started work on the wool counter when knitting wool from firms like Patons and Sirdar was in short supply but there was plenty of demand for the hanks of wool. (Today many older people recall how when they got the hanks of wool home it had to be wound into balls before they started knitting.) At that time the farthing [¼d] was still in use and she remembers that when the bill came to 1/11¾ most customers actually paid 2 shillings as they did not ask for the farthing change. Joan had spent two years working on the wool counter when a girl working in the cash office was called up for war service, and so Joan applied for that position and was able to extend her experience with two years in the cash office before she left paid employment when she got married. Over a decade later, when her daughter was settled in school, she returned to work in the Emporium, working seven years part-time followed by three years full-time for the then owners, Macowards. In 1967 Mr John Jenkins, Mr Fred Jones and Mr Tony Williams (all formerly of another fine Bargoed store, George, Rees and Jones) took over The Emporium. Fred Jones did not stay long but Mr Jenkins and Mr Williams were her bosses for the next 22 years and Mr Williams' wife Edna was in charge of the office work. Apart from the management, Joan was the last member of staff, leaving only when the store closed in 1989.

During the war years, the staff was predominantly female, with just a few male employees who were too old to be called up for war work, and the stock in the various departments was severely limited by wartime restrictions and the basement was emptied of stock so it could be used to store sandbags. Certain items like *Dinky* curlers and hairclips as well as talcum powder and cosmetics were put under the counter for senior staff to sell to favoured customers while the limited supply of silk stockings and silk petticoats was rarely available to anyone except the wives of managers of other prestigious stores such as Roath Furnishers.

After the war, the male staff returned to the shop and the various sections, including the toy, china and hardware departments in the basement, reopened. Business was soon booming in the post-war era. The store had its own

Provident and Premium agents and there were two Club Offices, one on the ground floor and one on the floor above, dealing with the agents who covered Bargoed and the surrounding villages such as Deri and Ystrad Mynach as well as more distant towns like Merthyr Tydfil and Tredegar. From time to time, the Emporium had late night openings when the staff enjoyed a half hour break before working late to serve the customers who came in on the buses.

For decades the Emporium had a full range of staff covering all aspects of its business. It employed its own tailor and tailoress as well as its own carpenter with a workshop. The buyers in the various departments played an important part in the success of the business. Miss Rees (who had been brought up in the shop as her mother was the Housekeeper in the days when many of the staff lived on the premises) and Mrs Pugh were both successful buyers, the former in the fashion department and the latter in drapery, as they knew how to select items that would appeal to their customers. When Macowards replaced the store's buyers with their area buyers, Bargoed store had the same stock as that in their Newport, Cardiff and Swansea stores but, while it may have sold in those stores it did not sell well in Bargoed.

Mr Ford, the manager, was a dignified figure who regularly walked through the store observing what was going on in all the departments. He never disciplined any of the staff directly but instructed his private secretary to speak to any member of staff who needed correction. Whenever necessary he was chauffeured by one of the two van drivers employed at the store as he was not able to drive. Mr Price, formerly a window dresser and under manager at the Emporium, replaced Mr Ford as manager, and oversaw the store as it started to decline partly because of Macowards buying policy and partly as pit closures in the villages further north in the Rhymney Valley meant that local spending power declined. The Emporium was forced to close first its basement (and that retail space was taken over by the Maypole grocery shop) and then its shoe department on Lower High Street. The Emporium carpet department was accommodated in the Upper High Street premises that Woolworths occupied before moving to new premises in Lower High Street. When Bargoed Colliery ceased operation the days of the once-splendid Emporium were numbered and when landlord Mr Joseph (an optician in the town who had purchased the premises from the local council who in turn bought it from Macowards) increased the rent Mr Jenkins was forced to close the store in 1989.

Shops in Gilfach

Gilfach's shopping centre was very different from that of Bargoed. While Bargoed, with its large shops, served not only the town but also its hinterland, Gilfach's shopping facilities catered for the needs of its own residents. It had a range of shops as shown by its entry (as one of several communities listed under the heading of Gelligaer) in Kelly's Directory of 1926 that listed over forty retail outlets in Gilfach. Local housewives of that era, shopping daily as their homes generally lacked facilities to keep food fresh, had a choice of shops in Commercial Street and Park Place. In addition to New Tredegar & District

Cooperative Society Ltd. store on Commercial Street, Gilfach had five grocers, two butchers, two greengrocers as well as one dairy, five confectioners and four fried fish dealers (to supply the occasional luxury of a fish supper). In addition there were nine people simply listed as shopkeepers who presumably stocked a range of frequently purchased items. At the same time, Gilfach's shopping facilities included two drapers as well as Wolfson's clothiers and a supplier of hosiery, while there were three businesses dealing with repair or sale of footwear and two hairdressers (presumably men's barber shops). Gilfach also had two newsagencies and a stationery shop which housed a sub-post office, a drug store, as well as a cabinet maker and an upholsterer, and two hardware outlets. While there was no bank or other commercial offices or professional services in Gilfach, the village had both a local estate agent and a Friendly Society agent.

Arguably one of the best known Gilfach traders of that era was butcher Ben Edmunds. Not only did he run a successful business from the late 1890s, but he also played a significant role in public life. He served as chairman of Bargoed Male Voice Choir and, as chairman of the War Memorial Committee, he presided over the unveiling ceremony in 1923 An item in the local news column of *Merthyr Express* in November 1923 described him as *a most useful citizen, and is associated with the religious, social and educational life* of the area.

This advertisement for Ben Edmunds' business is taken from a pre-World War I local Directory.

Today

The present state of the local shopping centres owes much to a combination of various factors including changes in the coal industry and widespread private car ownership combined with the attractions of more distant shopping centres. It remains to be seen what the next phase in the retail history of Bargoed and Gilfach holds as the area prepares for the 56,000 square foot store Morrisons, on the recently constructed plateau overlooking the new by-pass.

CHAPTER 14
HEALTH AND WELFARE

Introduction

Today, local people visit one of several surgeries or chemist shops when they feel ill, but those who lived and worked in the pre-industrial community relied on a variety of remedies handed down through the generations to alleviate pain, cure sickness, soothe and heal sprains and strains, or deal with difficulties in sleeping. There was no known local collection of remedies like that of the Physicians of Myddfai, but generation after generation of wives and mothers depended on their understanding of local products such as herbs and honey, coupled with whatever national and continental medical knowledge filtered through to this part of the Rhymney Valley, to cure ailments ranging from common coughs and cold to the more serious and to alleviate the pain of those who suffered accidents. News of their successes and failures, mingled with a belief in magic and spirits surviving from medieval times, became part of local folklore, passed on through the generations, as medical knowledge (sometimes interpreted as magical healing) ranked alongside gossip and story-telling in the verbal world of the small pre-industrial community.

This extract from Rev. Gwilym Thomas' personal memories provides an insight into the nature of medical care in the last quarter of the nineteenth century: *We were a healthy group with good appetites. I remember that my brother Dan was ill. Mother sent for the doctor who lived three miles away. He was popular but a little unreliable because he often got drunk. He turned up to see Daniel a week later. When he arrived we were all round the table having food. The doctor asked mother which one was ill. She pointed at Dan who was eating bread and cheese. The doctor could not restrain himself from laughing, he told my mother not to be concerned with him as he seemed to have recovered.*

There was no organisation or supervision for local health matters until, in the second half of the nineteenth century, locally elected bodies began to address issues of public health and civic amenities. At the same time the formerly sparsely populated rural area was starting to change as it attracted workers seeking jobs in the area. That rapid growth inevitably created problems, including those of public health which the local councils found difficult to remedy quickly as shown in the earlier discussion of the provision of local services.

A revolution in health and care

There has been a revolution in health and care in the decades since Bargoed Colliery was sunk and the communities of Bargoed and Gilfach emerged. Medical knowledge and expertise has advanced considerably over the decades. The reforms of the pre-World War I Liberal government made health and care part of the business of government by introducing legislation to improve the lot of vulnerable groups in society; children, the old, sick and unemployed. Collectively such reforms had an impact on health and care and paved the way for the Labour government's post-World War II revolutionary changes, especially the establishment of the publicly-funded National Health Service in 1948.

The log books of Bargoed Infants' School shed some light on the ways in which the reforms were implemented locally. In February 1910 the headteacher recorded not only the visit of Mr Saunders, Attendance Officer, but also that of Dr. Evans, School Medical Officer, who spent several sessions conducting a medical inspection. It is not clear which age group he inspected or whether or not the *great many children* noted to be *away from school owing to sickness (Bronchitis etc)* were examined. Regular references to medical and dental inspections as well as visits by the *nit nurse* continued to be recorded. Before the end of the 1920s and continuing through the next decade, the nurse, often Nurse Brazell, paid a regular visit to conduct a cleanliness survey in the school. In the early 1930s these were complimented by entries such as that of October 1932: *Dr Roberts inspected the children for the purpose of discovering malnutrition cases*, a reflection of the contemporary economic situation. No doubt may former Bargoed and Gilfach pupils of all ages have vivid memories of lining up for inspection by the *nit nurse* or school dentist. Some of today's older generation may recall the embarrassment when examination by the school doctor (as well as changing for sports activities) revealed the poor state of their under garments while younger former pupils can recount stories showing the care administered by the school nurse in schools like Heolddu Comprehensive.

Sources also point to improving care for others in the community. Kelly's Directory of 1926 listed a number of local midwives including Miss Elizabeth Dorsett C.M.B. of 64 John Street, Mrs Sarah Jane Evans C.M.B. of 24 Henry Street, Miss Elizabeth Greenaway C.M.B. of 1 North Street, Mrs Leah Thomas of 16 West Street and Mrs May Lane of St. Mary Street Gilfach as well as a nurse Mrs Lily Adelaide Stannard of Gilfach. In April 1926 *Merthyr Express* carried a report on the opening of a new Infant Welfare Centre converted from the former Fire Station in Hanbury Road. Local Councillor Miss Hettie Jones, having worked hard to ensure the Council's support for a facility she believed to be of great importance to the community, performed the opening ceremony that was also attended by Dr. J. Gilmore Cox (the local Council's lady doctor), Nurse Skey, who was to take charge of the Centre, and nurses Lewis and Rees.

Government help for the other end of the age spectrum included old age pensions for those over 70 (7/6 a week for married couples and 5 shillings for individuals). Prior to World War II the age profile of the local area was such that the number qualifying for such pensions was limited and sometimes merited mention in local newspaper reports, for instance Mr and Mrs Thomas Brown of Aeron Place who celebrated their Golden Wedding in February 1923 when Mrs Brown collected a pension on the day of their Golden Wedding. In

1948 the qualifying age was reduced to 60 for women and 65 for men, but increased life expectancy coupled with financial considerations mean that in the early twenty first century the qualifying ages for the state pension are under review.

For the unemployed, the Liberal government established Labour Exchanges in 1909 to help the unemployed find work. The National Insurance Act of 1911 introduced a system whereby those in work made weekly contributions to insure their right to medical treatment and sick pay when illness prevented them from working, as well as unemployment pay during periods when they were without work.

Local newspapers and school log books are among the sources that shed light on the way in which local communities rallied at times of crisis including during strikes in the coal industry. Today many local people associate *soup kitchens* with the 1926 strike but they are not always aware that the community rallied to support striking miners' families at other times. In March 1912 the headteacher of Gilfach School logged: *The feeding of necessitous children commenced today at the Presbyterian Vestry* and *Today Breakfast and Dinner are given the children. Much of my time is occupied on writing out Tickets for children and investigating needy cases* followed by *My time nearly wholly occupied with the feeding of Children.* Again in 1921 he wrote *As the feeding of necessitous children has been in force since last Monday April 25th and feeding of children commenced on Wednesday 25th my time has been altogether taken up with the work.*

There has never been a hospital within the communities of Bargoed and Gilfach, although that constructed in Aberbargoed was considered to serve the communities on both sides of the river. Although it was suggested in 1900 that a parish Isolation Hospital should be built in Bargoed because of its central position, it was eventually built near Gelligaer village. In recent decades local people have been served by a comprehensive range of hospital facilities over a wide area extending from Abergavenny and Merthyr Tydfil in the north to Newport and Cardiff in the south, with occasional recourse to specialist hospitals further afield. At the time of writing (2011), local hospitals including the cottage hospital in Aberbargoed (opened in 1909) and that in Caerphilly known locally as *The Miners* (opened in 1923), are about to be replaced by the new Ysbyty Ystrad Fawr. Today's hospital care for both in-patients and outpatients is a far cry from that experienced by pre-NHS generations. The following examples reported in *Merthyr Express* in 1927 refer to some hospital stays by local people. In June 1927 William Harris returned home to Ruth Street after a successful operation and a seven week stay in Cardiff Royal Infirmary. David, the young son of J. J. Davies (senior master and later headmaster of Bargoed Secondary School) and Mrs Davies was in a Cardiff nursing home during a serious illness in 1927. During the autumn William Langley of Park Crescent, senior deacon at Trinity English Congregational Chapel, was treated in Cardiff Royal Infirmary. J. Sylvan Evans had an operation before spending several weeks in a Cardiff nursing home to return home before the end of the year and then spend some time convalescing in the south of England early in 1928.

Before the 1950s it was common for local people to travel by train to hospitals other than that in Aberbargoed. This is illustrated by the 1937 reports in *Merthyr Express* relating to Rev. W. R. Lewis, pastor of Hanbury Road Baptist, who suffered a heart attack on the train while accompanying his wife on her way to receive treatment in the Infirmary in Cardiff. In recent decades it became increasingly common for people to travel by road, in the family car or, especially in the case of more elderly patients nowadays, in a taxi. While this is often more convenient it is not without its problems including congested roads at certain times of day and the difficulties of parking on hospital premises. *New CLURV* is a worthy local voluntary group that aims to relieve patients, especially cancer patients, of some of the stress associated with travel to and from hospital visits for consultation and treatment by providing door-to-door transport.

Common diseases (especially among children)

In the late nineteenth and early twentieth century many children in the streets of Bargoed and Gilfach were at best grubby, with scabby knees and runny noses, and particularly susceptible to a range of diseases because of malnutrition and poor housing. For decades, many children and adults lived in crowded conditions that contributed to the spread of infectious diseases. At the same time, countless wives and mothers, weighed down by endless household drudgery and family responsibilities, struggled to put enough food on the table to feed their hard-working menfolk and growing children. It is not surprising that in such conditions and with very restricted access to the medical expertise of the times, a variety of illnesses frequently cast a cloud over families in pre World War II Bargoed and Gilfach. George Thompson, writing some seven decades later, recalled that in the 1920s, *pavements were continually bespattered with spittle and phlegm, offensive matter wrenched from the victims of those diseases* (smallpox and tuberculosis), *and also with the virulent discharges from the gas-rotted lungs of returned soldiers, or spat out by colliers suffering dreaded occupational diseases. .... Most children lacked the basic principles of hygiene. Few were taught to use a toothbrush and most neglected to wash their hands after a visit to the toilet. Many were victims of lice and impetigo ....* boys wiped their noses *on the sleeves of their jackets or jerseys* girls wore *a handkerchief or a piece of linen pinned to their dresses.* Extant log books of local schools shed some light on the illnesses that affected the schoolchildren in that era, sometimes of epidemic proportions that caused the Medical Officer of Health to order school closure in an attempt to limit the spread of the disease

Coughs and colds, as well as influenza and bronchitis, were common causes for absences from school. They spread quickly in the crowded homes and schools. Some local people suffered in the 1918 pandemic. There was a severe influenza epidemic locally in 1921 but that of January-February 1927 was more extensive numerically. There are numerous references in school log books to cases of scabies, sores and itch that like the highly contagious ringworm (a fungal infection of the skin causing inflamed circular patches on the skin) passed by skin contact or on towels and bedding and spread easily in crowded homes and schools, and it is likely that some local children suffered from rickets.

There are numerous references in the log books to epidemics of chickenpox, diphtheria and enteric fever (typhoid) with the latter more likely to be prevalent in the warmer seasons in the rapidly growing communities of early twentieth century Bargoed and Gilfach. In June 1901 the headteacher recorded in Bargoed Infants' School log book that there were three cases of diphtheria among the pupils and one child died. In 1902 and 1903, the Medical Officer of Health, reporting at a meeting of the local council, noted cases of enteric fever in Bargoed. In August 1902 when most of Bargoed's six cases of enteric fever were in Greenfield Terrace, he explained that cases of diphtheria and fever were becoming common in that particular part of the growing community because of the old insanitary tip traps, and so recommended the council should order their immediate removal. A month later, he reported on fresh cases of enteric fever in Bargoed and enteric fever was prevalent again in Bargoed by May 1903.

To the mid twentieth century, infections such as measles, mumps, and whooping cough swept through Bargoed and Gilfach like wildfire from time to time as shown in school log books. There were major epidemics of measles in 1897, 1905 and 1914, and of whooping cough in 1894. Sometimes such epidemics forced the Medical Officer of Health to close the school for a period to try to limit the spread of the disease, as in the case of the measles epidemic in 1907. In recent decades, cases of measles, a common virus until the 1960s when a vaccine was developed, have been rare but, as some parents refused it when it was incorporated in the MMR (measles-mumps-rubella) jab, cases of measles nationally have increased in recent years.

Some people who suffered scarlet fever, an airborne infection, were sent to isolation hospitals, but, if these were overfull, sufferers stayed in their bedrooms, isolated from other children. It was not until the discovery of bacteria and, later the invention of antibiotics like penicillin that an effective treatment was found.

From time to time, cases of smallpox occurred in the area. In May 1903, *Merthyr Express* reported the case of William Allen, who had been mixing with people in Bargoed for about ten days when he was found to be suffering from smallpox and taken from the town to Penybank Isolation Hospital. In October 1924, Councillor Gus Jones urged that local councils cooperate to establish a much-needed smallpox hospital in the valley. Local Sanitary and Health officials were trying to limit the spread of the smallpox epidemic in Bargoed in June 1927 and they urged everyone in the densely populated area to do all they could to prevent further contagion. Six cases from Bargoed, all young people, had been taken to Gelligaer Isolation Hospital. In November 1927, Thomas Cornelius Jones, headteacher of Gilfach Boys' School wrote in the school log book: *There is an outbreak of Smallpox in this neighbourhood and several school children are suffering from same such as Boys Stuckey and Lane of St Mary Street. Also boys from these homes are excluded.*

Tuberculosis (usually referred to as TB, or sometimes consumption or white death) had spread quickly and fatally in the nineteenth and early twentieth century. At the start of the second decade of the twentieth century, King Edward VII Welsh National Memorial Association was set up to tackle the disease. The local area was at the forefront of this campaign as local bodies organised meetings to support the anti-consumption campaign. Early in 1913, the Association's exhibition was in Bargoed Skating Rink for a week and, in the log book of Bargoed Boys' School, headmaster Thomas Myddfai Jones noted that the Education Committee had arranged for Standards IV, V and VI (children aged 10 – 13) to visit the exhibition and to attend a lecture given by Dr. Morris at the town's Palace Theatre. He also recorded other occasions when this on-going nation-wide campaign against TB was waged in his school, including instances when Owen Williams B.A. (in May 1924) and Miss Edith Rowlands (in January 1930) lectured the boys on TB. The incidence of TB cases in the country generally began to drop after the development of treatment that eliminated resistance. However, health experts have identified a recent rise in the number of drug-resistant cases in the country and, globally, TB is an enormous resurgent phenomenon.

The general improvement in public health and living conditions coupled with the impact of the NHS combined to explain a fall in the incidence of many formerly common childhood diseases in the second half of the twentieth century. As post World War II children not only had a better diet and generally lived in homes with superior facilities to those of earlier decades, but were also protected by vaccination and immunisation, it seemed as if some of the diseases were all but eradicated. However, in the last decade or so, the health picture nationally is less positive: the number of cases of diseases such as measles and TB has increased and a new problem namely childhood obesity, a consequence of the contemporary lifestyle, looms large.

Coal industry related diseases, injuries and fatalities

The dominance of the coal industry in Bargoed and Gilfach inevitably meant that many men carried the blue scar marking where coal dust had entered a break in the skin, and coal industry related diseases, such as silicosis and pneumoconiosis, and injuries were common for decades. The decline of the coal industry in the last quarter of the twentieth century had adverse economic effects on the community, but it brought an end to such injuries, although many local families continue to live with health issues that are the legacy of the local coal industry. While major mining disasters of South Wales and beyond have received much attention from historians and others, it is also important to remember the large number of injuries and fatalities in smaller and less publicised incidents. There was no major incident resulting in significant numbers of injuries or fatalities in Bargoed and Gilfach collieries but, local people were touched by incidents in nearby collieries as well as those further afield.

One of the major incidents that affected people in Bargoed and Gilfach was that at Darran House Coal Pit, little more than a mile north of Bargoed and linked underground to Gilfach Colliery (an important element in the rescue bid) on 29 October 1909. Bargoed headmaster Thomas Myddfai Jones wrote in his school's log book *A serious disaster took place this morning in the Darran House Coal Pit and a number of men lost their lives through an explosion. Many of the boys of the upper standards absented themselves from school this afternoon in order to visit the scene of the disaster. I suppose that it is the usual thing when these unfortunate events occur for people to crowd to the top of the pit.* The Manager of Darran House Pit, W. T. Bowen, who lived in Bargoed, was one of the victims of the explosion and Gomer Griffiths of Gilfach Street and David Lewis, under manager of Gilfach Colliery died in the attempt to rescue the trapped miners. The Bargoed and Gilfach community shared the sadness and, the following week, Thomas Myddfai Jones noted that *some of the boys stayed away some afternoons to witness the funerals of the poor fellows who lost their lives as a result of the terrible explosion.*

The local community was affected by the disaster in No 1 and 2 Pits, Marine Colliery, Cwm, in 1927. Powell Duffryn Steam Coal Colliery Company agents, Major J. R. N. Kirkwood (who later received St. John Ambulance Certificate of Honour for the work he did there) and Harry Thomas attended there as well as Albert Thomas J.P., Bargoed Miners' Agent whose kind actions in comforting the bereaved were deeply appreciated. Rhymney Valley St. John Ambulance men made themselves useful and a number of Bargoed doctors offered their services. Bargoed Women's Branch of St. John Ambulance Brigade under Superintendent Mrs Turner were thanked for their offer of help but were not needed in view of the excellent response from the more local brigades. A contingent of Rhymney Valley Salvation Army members also went to help.

For decades, the local press was littered with reports on injuries and fatalities in the local coal industry, and the inquests that followed the latter, and the following examples serve to convey a flavour of the trauma to families and the community. The fatalities during the sinking of Bargoed Colliery included 47 year old Thomas Reed, who early in 1900, left widow, Ann, and seven children to live the nightmare that countless local families dreaded. The inquest into his death was held at George Inn, Brithdir before foreman John Evans (Ioan ab Dewi). William B. Lloyd (sinking contractor) and William Jones gave evidence concerning the apparent solidity of the part of the earth that fell and explained the position of the timber and other precautions taken, while the manager, D. R. Morgan, fully explained the plan. Mr Robinson, Inspector of Mines, and Mr Pigott (sinking contractor) were also present and a verdict of accidental death was recorded. There were injuries of all sorts in the local coal industry and they did not always happen underground as witnessed by a report in *Merthyr Express* May 1903. Mechanic Mr Lewis was supervising some work at the colliery saw mills when he got his hand jammed near the revolving saw, and the top of one of his fingers was cut off. In 1905, *Merthyr Express* reported on a fatality at Groesfaen Pit (in the Darran Valley, about a mile north of Bargoed) when the victim was sinker, William John Jenkins of Bargoed. A few months later, in September 1905, the same paper reported that Gwilym Jones of Francis Street was in a critical condition in Cardiff Infirmary following an injury at Bargoed Colliery. In May 1909 there was a report that a Pengam coal trimmer was killed at Gilfach colliery. It was not uncommon for inquests to be held in one of the local hotels as illustrated by the following two inquests of 1910. In early July, the inquest into the death of Bargoed rider, 24 year old William John Jones, who was caught by a roof fall, was held at Plasnewydd Hotel. Some months later, the inquest into the death of George Trigg (junior), a 25 year old married man of 6 Llewellyn Street, was held in Gwerthonor Hotel. This was not the first time that he had suffered an injury at work, as he had been injured in May 1910 when he was working at Groesfaen Colliery.

In July 1919, 28-year old David Morgan of North Road died from injuries suffered in South Pit and Thomas Casey, a 52-year old sawyer, was fatally injured on top of the House Coal Pit. Before the end of 1919, Mrs Cullum of Llancayo Street and five children faced a future without husband and father following a roof fall at South Pit. Coroner, J. B. Walford, returned a verdict of accidental death at the inquest at Aberbargoed Police Station, when Mr McVicars, represented Powell Duffryn Steam Coal Company, Mr McBride, the Home Office, and Albert Thomas, the Miners' Federation. The night foreman, T. J. Yorath, gave evidence saying that he was satisfied that the five hundred yards (including the spot where the incident took place) under his examination was efficiently timbered, while the deceased's workmate, Frederick Capel, confirmed that the necessary precautions had been taken and the roof was regularly sounded prior to the incident. Sadly, a stone broke off and, together with debris weighing about half a ton, it fell, pinning 46 year old Thomas Cullum by the legs. He was released almost immediately and the ambulance men administered first aid of excellent quality before Dr. McCrea arrived to examine him at the pithead. Thomas Cullum, paralysed as his spine was fractured high up near the shoulder blade, was taken to hospital where he died two days later.

In May 1920, Stanley Arthur was taken to Rhymney Hospital after being injured in a fall at Gilfach Pit. April 1923 saw a double funeral in the local area when a family said goodbye to elderly grandfather, William Campbell, and his unmarried 21-year old grandson, William Jones of Upper Plasnewydd Street. The young man, a rider at Bargoed Colliery, was fatally injured when he was buried by ten tons of debris in South Pit. Later in 1923, there was a double fatality when 24-year old Frederick Ayres of Aberbargoed and 17-year old Herbert William Helps of Llancayo Street met their deaths in South Pit in

October. In November 1923, *Merthyr Express* reported on another inquest at Aberbargoed with an accidental death verdict. Timberman John James of Park Place, Gilfach, died in Aberbargoed Hospital shortly after a sudden roof fall of about three tons at Bargoed Colliery knocked him down the staging on which he was working. He left a widow and five children. In July 1924, local musician Henry Smith, a repairer at Britannia Colliery (a Powell Duffryn Steam Coal Company colliery, sunk 1910-1913 about a mile south of Gilfach on the Monmouthshire side of the valley) was crushed by a stone weighing about one ton and died instantaneously and the coroner returned a verdict of accidental death at the inquest at Junction Hotel, Bargoed.

In 1926, during the course of his work as a repairer at Groesfaen Colliery, 48-year old David Jones of Bristol Terrace lost his life when a roof mass gave way while he was putting up a post. He was mourned by a widow and eleven children (seven of whom were under 14 years of age) and by Caersalem Choral Society of which he, a keen music lover, was a member. Tom Gabriel conducted the singing at his funeral and he was buried in Graig Cemetery near his Rhymney Bridge birthplace. During the same month, William Hall of Baldwin Street was taken to hospital with serious injuries and assistant timberman William Roberts of Church Street was injured. Early in 1927, 17-year old Sidney McCarthy was working with his 48-year old father Thomas, when he saw his father killed by a roof fall in Bargoed House Coal Pit. The events of that morning were recounted at the inquest before coroner R. J. Rhys. Thomas and Sidney had already filled two trams when Thomas sounded the top as usual. The sound of the fall that followed brought a collier nearby rushing to them only to see Thomas's hand protruding from under a stone measuring about 4 feet long and 8 inches wide. In February 1928, there was a memorial service in John Street's Christian Spiritualist Church for 16 year old Reginald Seymour Hicks of Moorland Road, victim of an accident in Bargoed Colliery and son of two ardent church workers.

The catalogue of misery and hardship could go on. The names of those who were badly injured or killed in the small incidents underground as well as at the pithead are not carved on monuments but that does not lessen the sadness of their relatives and friends and the impact on the community at large.

Housing and Pithead Baths

One of the reasons for the general improvement in the nation's health since about 1960 is that living conditions are far superior to those of earlier generations. The local council's new housing developments in Bargoed and Gilfach included indoor flush lavatories and bathrooms while landlords and/or owner-occupiers installed them in many of the terraced properties. Before the mid twentieth century many people bathed in a tin bath in front of the fire or used a bowl of water on the kitchen table, washing the top half first and then the bottom half of the body and the only time they could bath in private was after other members of the household had gone to bed, a situation almost unimaginable to many today when people take hot running water and facilities for daily showers for granted and often forget that earlier generations generally had to be content with washing their hands and faces regularly and bathing infrequently.

For decades, hundreds of local wives and mothers had the back-breaking task of preparing baths for menfolk who arrived home from work dirty and often wet after a shift in the coal mine. There were pithead baths in German collieries in the early twentieth century but none in Wales before World War I and the Pithead Baths Movement had a long, hard struggle, lobbying at national and grassroots level to convince government and mine owners, as well as miners and their families, of the need for pithead baths. It was reported in *The Times* (31 May 1919) that Elizabeth Andrews (of Rhondda) spoke for miners' wives in general when she told the Sankey Commission of the benefits that would accrue from pit-head baths and better houses. Until there were pit-head baths, miners would continue to carry the dirt and dust of the mines to their homes and their wives would have to dry the pit clothes in overcrowded kitchens and strain themselves lifting heavy bowls of hot water. Locally, the campaign for pithead baths included a well-attended miners' meeting presided over by Walter Lewis, J.P. at Bargoed's New Hall on a Sunday evening in November 1923. Miners were shown pictures of pithead baths in operation and Dr. E. Colston Williams and Edgar Chappell (Cardiff) delivered lectures emphasising the importance of having pithead baths at every colliery so that the homes of miners would be cleaner and healthier. The meeting also paid tribute to Robert Smilie (miners' leader) who had advocated a law for compulsory pithead baths and made an appeal to miners that, when balloted, they vote for pithead baths.

The Miners' Welfare Fund, established in 1926, was administered by the Miners' Welfare Committee (renamed Miners' Welfare Commission in 1939) and its income came from a levy of 1d on every ton of coal mined. Between 1921 and 1952 the Miners' Welfare Commission spent about £30,000,000 on many pithead projects that improved the lives of millions of men, women and children. It regarded pithead baths as important and so, from 1926, an additional levy of 1 shilling was raised on every £1 of royalties specifically to provide funding for a national pithead baths-building programme. In 1929 the Miners' Welfare Committee established its own architects' department to find the most cost-effective way of constructing, equipping and operating pithead baths and it soon developed a house-style based on modern methods and using glass and reinforced concrete to create modern functional buildings with robust fittings and fixtures. Miners generally were unenthusiastic about the pithead baths but once their womenfolk knew what was available, the men could not expect to find a bath prepared at home. The introduction of colliery pithead baths, heralding an architectural revolution through their modernist designs, changed the face of mining communities for ever: the health of workers and their families improved, the perception of the communities changed. Bargoed Colliery had Pithead Baths for the officials in the late 1940s and, in 1949 they were adapted so that the Duchess of Kent could use them on her visit. Facilities for the majority of the miners came later.

Child injuries and deaths in the home and the street

Local newspapers of the pre-World War II decades carried many reports on child deaths in the home and the following examples are just some of a number involving open fires or water boiled in kettles and pans in local homes. A five year old girl from West Street suffered burns in July 1905. A 3½ year old boy from Moorland Road suffered burns and died the same day in Aberbargoed Hospital about a week before Christmas 1919. The coroner, R. J. Rhys, returned a death by misadventure verdict after hearing evidence suggesting that, while the father, was at his pigeon cot in the back garden, the child's clothes had caught fire after he put a bit of paper through the fireguard. In January 1923, an inquest held at Junction Hotel heard that Dr. Turner attended a 12 month old boy scalded by the contents of a hot teapot, but he died two days later. A 4 year old South Street boy died as a result of scalds in March 1924. In July 1924, a delicate 3 year old girl from Commercial Street clambered down from the sofa where her grandmother had put her and fell over a bucket of hot water on the hearth, fitted and died of her injuries the next day. In November 1924, a Llancayo Street boy, aged one year eleven months, died following scalds when his mother boiled the copper to do the family laundry. A Bridge Street boy was just twelve months old when he died in Aberbargoed Hospital in March 1926 as a result of burns received earlier in the day.

Prior to the mid twentieth century children were often ill-trained as far as road safety was concerned and there were numerous incidents involving children on the local roads as shown by the following incidents from the early twentieth century The road was crowded with children on their way home from school when, one Thursday afternoon in October 1902, a five year old girl was knocked down by the horse attached to the cart of fruiter on the bridge some fifty yards from her Margaret Street home. The inquest, held at Gwerthonor Hotel, heard that she had made a sudden dash towards the other side of the road immediately in front of the horse and a verdict of accidental death was returned. In October 1910 a Bargoed child was run over by a cart from Heolddu stone quarry and killed.

Over the decades, better education and increased wealth combined to make homes safer and healthier: not only did families have access to clean, running hot and cold water together with gas or electrical cooking, washing cleaning and heating facilities, but they also grew more safety conscious, and the number of accidents concerning children and boiling water and open fires was reduced. Homes were cleaner and healthier as electrically-powered domestic equipment including washing machines and vacuum cleaners made domestic work easier and more effective. Similarly, greater awareness of safety coupled with speed limits and pedestrian crossings on the roads help improve safety outside the home. Sadly, while the number of serious accidents (including fatalities) in local homes and on local roads may have reduced they have not been removed.

Workplace accidents (other than the coal industry)

Coal industry related diseases and injuries were not the only work-related health issues in the local area as people in other walks of life, especially the service industries, were also vulnerable, until, in recent decades, heightened awareness alongside a plethora of health and safety regulations has helped reduce the number of accidents and illnesses in the workplace. One such case was that reported in *Merthyr Express* in October 1919 concerning Ted Broad, a hump-backed Liverpudlian aged about 40 who lodged in Alfred Street. He suffered fatal injuries during the course of his employment as a haulier for Bargoed Cooperative Society. While he was attaching his horse, the fully loaded bread van overbalanced and tipped up, hurling him over the cart to hit the road. He was taken, unconscious, to Aberbargoed Hospital where it was discovered he had a fractured skull and he died later the same day. Over the years local railway employees have suffered accidents, including fatalities, as illustrated by the following two examples relating to railway porters at Bargoed Station. Late 1909 19 year old William Ewart Griffiths of Gilfach Street died in Cardiff Infirmary after being hit by a train during the course of his work as a porter in the employ of the Rhymney Railway Company. He was taking a bundle of newspapers from one platform to another when the noise of the wind and the rain together with that of the outgoing train meant that he did not hear the incoming train that struck him. In 1921 some sheep got on the roof of Bargoed Station and when porter Alf Wallace went up to try to bring them down both he and the sheep crashed through the glass roof onto the platform. He suffered severe injuries and was taken to Rhymney Cottage Hospital where he died without regaining consciousness.

Health and lifestyle

Prior to the second half of the twentieth century, many local people worked long hours in difficult and dangerous conditions while they lived in crowded homes with inadequate facilities and frequently had too little to eat. Their enforced lifestyle increased the likelihood of sickness and/or accidents that often resulted in poverty (as they were unable to work) as well as premature death. In recent decades, increased knowledge and understanding of the way in which the human body works and the creation of the NHS as well as a general improvement in living standards in this country, means that more and more people in the country in general live longer and healthier lives and statistics on life expectancy improve year on year. However, today's relative affluence and the associated collective lifestyle raises concerns about the future health of individuals and of the financially-stricken NHS as people not only eat too much but opt for the wrong type of food, over-indulge in alcohol and take insufficient exercise. This lifestyle may be compounded by smoking and drug abuse as well as the soul-destroying consequences of unemployment (often long-term). The Westminster and Welsh Governments have a role to play in this but individuals have the final say in their lifestyle.

In the past, except in conditions of extreme weather, especially rain, children had plenty of exercise and fresh air as they went out to play, especially so as not to be under the feet of busy mothers who were responsible for a multitude of household tasks as well as frequently having to care for sick or elderly relatives. Today, children tend to spend more time indoors; partly because of the attractions of television and computer-based activities and also the perception that society outside the home has become more dangerous than it was several generations ago. At the same time while the quantity of food eaten by children is rarely insufficient, its quality has deteriorated. Formerly for most families the only food that was not home-cooked was the bread from the local bakery and the occasional meal of fish and chips. Most fruit and vegetables were grown on the allotment and many families also kept poultry to supply them with eggs as well as a pig for slaughter in the autumn. In recent decades, however, more and more people are eating processed junk food readily available in supermarkets and take-away restaurants. By today, in the second decade of the twenty first century, obesity has become a serious health problem: it puts a strain on a financially-stricken NHS and is the leading cause of preventable and premature death.

Smoking

Attitudes towards smoking have changed over the years. Many men, and some women, smoked cigarettes, cigars or a pipe, and for decades it was regarded by many as a fashionable pursuit while others claimed that it helped them clear their chest. Medical knowledge and understanding proving smoking to be a danger to health and a significant cause of preventable and premature deaths coupled with recent legislation banning smoking in public buildings has contributed to a decline in the number of adult smokers in the country in general.

There are numerous references in local newspapers in the first half of the twentieth century to presentations of smoking equipment to worthy members of organisations as illustrated by the following two examples. Suitably inscribed cigarette cases were presented by Bargoed Hockey Club to Harry Jenkins, the eldest son of the family at Heolddu Uchaf and one of their star players and members, to mark his leaving Bargoed to take up employment as an engineer under the Canadian government and to Dr. S. B. Turner by Bargoed branch St. John Ambulance Brigade's.

The popularity of smoking among the male population in the decades before the Second World War is illustrated by the fact that, from time to time, *Merthyr Express* carried reports on smoking concerts in numerous local venues and for a variety of reasons. In October 1903 the newspaper reported on Bargoed Rifle Club's successful smoking concert in Hanbury Arms Assembly Rooms and the same issue carried a report on a more healthy activity, a walking concert, promoted by auctioneer Mr Williams, covering sixteen miles from Hanbury Arms south to Llanbradach and back. Local groups and societies, such as the Comrades of the Great War (May 1919) and the R.A.O.B. (in Capel Hotel in

1923), organised smoking concerts. Sometimes smoking concerts were held for the benefit of local deserving people. Ted Harris of Britannia (who had not been able to work since he was discharged from the forces) benefitted from a smoking concert in Capel Hotel in early March 1920, while William Price of Bargoed (who had been ill for over two years) was the recipient of the proceeds of that held in Royal Hotel in November 1923. In late May 1924, the local R.A.O.B. held a smoking concert in Capel Hotel when the proceeds went to one of their members who had been unemployed for several years. The New Year's Eve smoking concert at Lenox Constitutional Club, as 1923 turned to 1924, and, some four months later, a smoking concert to mark the third anniversary of the National Workmen's Club Institute, are just two examples of smoking concerts that were held for celebratory purposes.

Ambulance

Ambulance provision has been discussed as one of the local services within the chapter on economic activity.

St. John Ambulance Brigade

Over the decades countless local young people and adults devoted many leisure hours to Bargoed branch of St. John Ambulance Brigade. While the efforts and achievements of students who earned certificates for their first aid skills are praiseworthy, no account of the Brigade's activities locally can ignore the sterling work of Dr. and Mrs S. B. Turner in the inter-war years. Not only were they instrumental in establishing the Bargoed branch but they also worked tirelessly; instructing, organising and inspiring, to ensure it went from strength to strength. Under their leadership Bargoed branch offered instruction at all levels as well as organising fund-raising and social events.

On visiting Bargoed early in 1927 to present certificates to members who had been successful in the recent examinations, Sir Herbert Lewis, Principal Secretary for the Order in Wales took the opportunity to highlight the role of St. John Ambulance Brigade in the community as well as state the case for a local depot for distribution of medical appliances. After the Great War ended the Priory distributed medical and surgical equipment from its many private wartime hospitals to local branches (local branches paid for the equipment when they had the funds to do so) across the country from where items were hired out at weekly charges (just a few pence) before being returned to the depot when no longer required. Bargoed had been just a village at the time of Sir Herbert's previous visit but by 1927 it was a congested colliery town with a population in excess of 15,000 making demands on local doctors kept busy dealing with accidents at work and there was no district nurse to serve the area. He recognised the work already done by Mrs Turner and her helpers and expressed his confidence that they could ensure Bargoed branch continued to assist the doctors and train others, especially working miners, in first aid as well as preparing to open a local comfort depot. Sir Herbert's understanding of the situation was accurate: within a few months of his visit the ladies had organised and opened a local depot and were keeping pace with the high demand for items such as bed rests, hot water bottles and bronchitis kettles in addition to rendering help to doctors and facilitating first aid training.

It was usual practice to hold a social in honour of students who had earned certificates and that held in St. Gwladys' Church Hall early in 1928 was attended by over 200 people including some from neighbouring detachments. Prior to the entertainment (singing and dancing), not only did the students receive their certificates but also a surprise presentation of an inscribed cigarette case was made to Dr. S. B. Turner in recognition of his outstanding service and energy.

Fund raising was an important part of the work of the local branch. The fact that, as *Merthyr Express* reported in Spring 1927, the local Superintendent had to issue a warning about bogus and unauthorised collectors in the locality should not be allowed to detract from the efforts of the organisation. Proceeds of Flag Days, such as the successful one held in June 1927, augmented the Priory of Wales Central Fund while local funds were swelled through regular whist drives and dances, and usually held in the Workmen's Institute. In August 1927 Bargoed branch organised their first annual Eisteddfod in the Workmen's Institute. The highlight of their annual fund-raising and social calendar was the well-publicised annual autumn whist drive and dance including a raffle of an attractive prize donated by Mr J. Petch of Cardiff. In November 1927 that prize, an expenses-paid day trip to London (or a £2 10s voucher in lieu) was won by Irene Oulde of John Street.

In the 1930s St. John Ambulance Association worked with Bargoed Mining and Technical Institute in providing Safety and First Aid classes. The Institute's 1938-39 prospectus included a 20 hour evening course on Safety First Principles in Mines culminating in the award of Safety First Badges to successful students. In the early months of 1939 students had 20 hours instruction in First Aid as applied to Mines and those successful in the examination conducted by St. John Ambulance Association gained Certificates. During the war years and the decades that followed the local St. John's Ambulance Brigade continued to adapt to changing social and economic circumstances. Dr. Iori Rees-Mathews took the St. John Ambulance classes locally in the 1960s and 1970s and the local brigade remains active today.

British Red Cross Society

Bargoed Men's Detachment of British Red Cross Society was formed 11 September 1911 with Commandant Dr. Dan Thomas J.P., Medical Officer Dr. Charles Reidy, W. Parry Williams (Pharmacist) and correspondent W. Haydon of 1 John Street. Local people still benefit from the wide range of services offered by the Society today including those helping patients discharged from hospital, as well as short-term loan of equipment such as wheelchairs. Today countless local people support the Red Cross Society as, in common with many other shopping centres across the country, the Society's shop is one of a number of Charity Shops in Bargoed's High Street and Hanbury Road.

Care

In the past, it was common for the sick and elderly to be cared for by their families, and, in the absence of families, friends and neighbours often took responsibility for such care. The age profile of the local population recorded in the 1901 and 1911 census shows a young population, as hundreds of men, some accompanied by wives and children, flocked to swell the growing communities of Bargoed and Gilfach in their search for employment. Closer examination suggests that some of the households included elderly and/or frail family members who depended on daughters or daughters-in-law for care.

This general picture has tended to change in the country in general in recent decades for a variety of reasons. It frequently became impractical for families to offer suitable ground floor accommodation to a needy relative as homes were *opened up* (walls dividing front and middle rooms in terraced houses were often demolished while some newer properties had open plan lounge/diners), and wives and mothers, increasingly likely to have paid employment outside the home, had less time and energy to offer such care. In addition, as more people are living into their eighties and beyond, not only are they likely to need support and care for longer but also their sons and daughters may well be approaching old age and its concomitant problems themselves. As a result, the caring industry has developed to cater for those who, because of sickness and/or old age, are unable to look after themselves. Sometimes, those in need of care remain in their own home with the support of family and/or non-family carers, while in other cases they move into residential care (locally in places such as Ty Clyd, Bargoed Care Home and Springfield or further afield) to receive support and care appropriate to their needs.

Some local dentists and doctors

Local dentists, with the possible exception of Herbert Naunton Davies, do not seem to have made as much impact on local society as contemporary doctors did in the first half of the twentieth century. According to Kelly's 1926 Directory there were seven dentists in Bargoed (George Henry Beckett of 34 Cardiff Road, Thomas Henry Carew of 8 Hanbury Road, Herbert Naunton Davies of 56 Gilfach Street, William John James Glassock of 22 Gilfach Street, Archie Mason of 16a High Street and Jack and Louis Symonds of 55, 57 and 58 High Street), while there was one in Gilfach (Arthur Wilmot of Park Place). Many local people may recall that dentists Mr McCucheon and J. K. Mason (son of Archie) served the local communities during the 1950s and 1960s while Eric Ricketts, who was born in Bargoed and educated in Lewis School Pengam, joined and later took over the High Street practice.

There are still a number of local people who recall visiting doctors' surgeries in the early years of the NHS that were very different from the purpose-built surgeries, with their computer-assisted facilities, up-to-date medical equipment and clerical and nursing staff as well as doctors, where most local people are registered today. Currently, two of the four local surgeries have been built on sites that many local people still associate with other buildings while the other two are in Cardiff Road. Bryntirion Surgery incorporating *Boots* Chemist is on the West Street site formerly occupied by Bargoed Mining and Technical Institute while South Street Surgery occupies the site where the Primitive Methodist Chapel formerly stood. Bargoed Hall practice occupies the upper floor of the Cardiff Road premises while the former Park Place Surgery is on the ground floor, in what was formerly Bryntirion Surgery. A number of local doctors in the decades before the creation of the National Health Service were men who, although brought up and educated elsewhere, made their homes in Bargoed and Gilfach and became key figures in the community in which they practiced medicine, while some of those of the post-NHS era were brought up locally. What follows are brief accounts of the life and work of some of the doctors who have practiced locally as well as an attempt to outline how the former practices have given rise to the current situation.

Trade Directories shed light on some of the medical practitioners in the local area in the late nineteenth and early twentieth centuries. Drs William Owen and Thomas Henry O'Shaughnessy (although the latter was not in Bargoed for long before he returned to his native Ireland) were listed in Kelly's Directory in 1895, practicing medicine locally before Bargoed Colliery was sunk. At the turn of the century Dr. William Owen served the expanding local community. Born in Caernarvonshire about 1863, he qualified as a doctor in Scotland in 1893. In 1895 he was listed in Kelly's Directory as of High Street, probably Brynmeddyg, High Street, where he was enumerated in 1901 as head of a household of four that included his wife (Elizabeth whom he had married January 1895), their female domestic servant and Thomas Nevin, a dispenser born in Scotland about 1848. Dr. Owen may have died soon after as he was not named in the Medical Register of 1903.

According to a town Directory of 1911 the rapidly growing communities in Bargoed and Gilfach were served by Ds. Daniel J. Thomas, J.P. of Cardiff Road (whose surgery was in Church Place), E. R. Bowen of Hanbury Road, Charles Reidy of High Street, J. J. Jones of Capel Street, Llewellyn of Cardiff Road and H. C. Hocken of Gilfach. By 1914 the following were listed: Drs McCrae of Church Place, Phillips of Cardiff Road, E. R. Bowen of Hanbury Road, Charles Reidy of High Street, J. J. Jones of Capel Street and S. B. Turner of Gilfach. It is not clear when or how Bargoed and District Medical Aid Society operated but it was listed in a town Directory of 1914 with a general surgery in High Street and a surgery in Gilfach's Commercial Street (as well as surgeries in Aberbargoed, Deri and Pengam). At that time its doctors were Stephens, Connelly, Avis and Wallace and its secretary was Evan Luke.

Dr. John Josiah Jones was born in Cardiganshire about 1850. He studied medicine in Glasgow and after qualifying in 1872, he practiced medicine in west Glamorgan. Arriving in Bargoed about the turn of the century, he was described as a physician and surgeon when, with his wife (he had married Hannah Edwards in 1877) and their 24-year old daughter Rachel, he was enumerated at 13 Hanbury Road in 1901. The family remained in Bargoed and he was resident in 6 Capel Street when he died 29 April 1915. Dr. Frederick Thomas Fisher of Hillside Park was registered as a doctor in 1911 and probably only practiced medicine in the local area for a short period during World War I

Irish-born Dr. Charles Reidy practiced medicine in the Rhymney Valley for over forty years, first in Maesycwmmer before arriving in Bargoed probably between 1903 and 1907. He ran his practice in High Street for the first ten years or so before moving to Cardiff Road. Dr. Walter Chapman practiced with him for a short time but he had left the area before 1923 but Dr. S. B. Turner's association with him lasted much longer. Dr. Sydney Booth Turner, son of a Methodist minister, was born in Lancashire about 1881. He qualified as a doctor in 1905 and, after experience in Sheffield and Birkenhead, he arrived in Bargoed before the outbreak of World War I to work with Dr. Reidy. It is not clear where he was living when he arrived in Bargoed but by the 1920s he and Mrs (formerly Mabel Lucy Pottier) Turner were resident in Hillcrest, and together they contributed much to life in Bargoed in the first half of the twentieth century and especially to the local branch of St. John's Ambulance Brigade. His son, Dr. John Turner, practiced with Dr. Alun Williams in Park Place, Gilfach. Dr. John Turner was one of the first of the local doctors who can be regarded as a local boy and he made his home in Gilfach Fargoed (before the R.A.F.A. Club moved there). Today this practice occupies the ground floor surgery in Cardiff Road mentioned below.

Physician and surgeon, Dr. Daniel Jenkins Thomas was Medical Officer of Health to G.U.D.C. prior to World War I. After full-time war service in the RAMC (Royal Army Medical Corps) he returned to his duties and, following his marriage in 1921 he settled down to live in Bargoed. His wife, formerly Mabel Hughes, had a long association with London's Great Ormond Street Hospital for Sick Children including serving as its Assistant Matron. Early September 1923, he resigned the post of Medical Officer of Health, refusing the offer of a salary of £760 on condition he agreed to give up private practice.

County Councillor Dr. Benjamin Henry Edward McCrea was born in 1862 in the Kent parish where his father, a respected academic and educationalist, was vicar. He was educated at Tonbridge Grammar School before he studied medicine in London. Following registration in 1891 he practiced medicine and took an active part in public life in the London area for over twenty years until he moved to Bargoed probably about 1913 where he was to continue in the same vein. Married in 1886, he was widowed before he and two infant daughters were enumerated with his widowed mother in the 1891 census. The girls were enumerated with their grandmother again in 1901 and Dr. McCrea married his second wife shortly afterwards and perhaps the children of his second marriage were born before the family arrived in Bargoed. During World War I Dr. McCrea took an active interest in the welfare of service personnel: he was Medical Officer in charge of troops under Western Command for the local area and he served on various medical and pensions boards. His wartime ambulance classes, often some seventy strong, for instruction of members wishing to join the RAMC were the largest such classes held locally. After the war ended Dr. McCrea continued as instructor and examiner for St. John's Ambulance Brigade and instructed the Bargoed colliery ambulance team that, in 1916, won the Martin Shield, the blue riband of the ambulance world, against competition from teams from across south and west England and South Wales. At the conclusion of the war, Dr. McCrea was associated with all sections of the community and politics in forming the Welcome Home Fund. As its Chairman for the first twelve months, he worked hard raising subscriptions by taking the platform at local venues and so laid the foundation of what became the Bargoed and District Memorial Fund. Dr. McCrea was a quick-thinker and able debater who was inclined to impatience with those who took time to reach conclusions. In Bargoed he continued his interest in public service and local politics serving the local community in numerous capacities. He was a leading Conservative in the Rhymney Valley: a prominent member of the Caerphilly Division Conservative Association and, in the early 1920s, he was Chairman of Lenox Constitutional Club. He was member of Glamorgan County Council for some years and he served as a Gelligaer School Governor.

Dr. McCrea's Church Place medical practice, conducted from the end property of a row of houses, now demolished, grew rapidly and he was a life-long member of the British Medical Association being a member of its Council of South Wales and Monmouthshire. Both his daughter and his son entered the medical profession. His daughter, active in the Girl Guide movement, local church and welfare work in Bargoed, left the area in 1924 to pursue a medical career at King's College Hospital, London. His son, John Alexander Vereker McCrea continued the Church Place practice but, unlike his father (who lived in The Gables, Hillside Park), he did not live in Bargoed but at Cloverdale, Pontlottyn. Over the years, Dr. J. A. V. McCrea had various partners in the practice, including Dr. Jenkins, Irish-born Dr. Dunphy who lived in Hillside Park until he emigrated to Canada, and Dr. John Merrill who, prior to his premature death in the 1960s, took the practice into the Cardiff Road practice of Dr. St. John Rees.

Dr Elias Ranson Bowen (1861-1941) gained his first medical qualifications in 1896 and he practiced in Swansea and Barry Dock before gaining further qualifications in 1906 and 1907. He probably arrived in Bargoed about 1903 where he was in practice for some three decades before retiring to his native Swansea. He was listed in a town Directory of 1911 as Hon. Secretary of the Rhymney Valley Medical Association which had been formed in 1907. His first home in Bargoed was 54 Hanbury Road, and in Kelly's Directory of 1926 his address was given as 16 Cross Street but later he moved to live in Darnley, Hillside Park. His practice had extended into Aberbargoed by 1920 when he was joined by an assistant, Dr. Hywel Tegid Prys-Jones of Pontypridd, whose father was a well-known Temperance lecturer and Methodist who visited Bargoed on numerous occasions.

The medical practice at 16 Cross Street was continued by well-respected Drs Kennedy and Redvers Davies before Dr. Iori Rees Mathews joined the practice in the early 1950s. Born in Gilfach, Dr. Rees Mathews practiced in Bargoed from the early 1950s until his retirement in the 1980s. Dr. David Williams, a Bargoed boy and former pupil of Lewis School Pengam, joined him in 1962, just a few years before the practice moved from Cross Street to Bryntirion, and remained in the practice until his retirement in 1995. The local connection in the practice continued when, in the 1980s, Dr. Michael Sheen joined the practice. Although born in Ystrad Mynach, Dr. Sheen's grandfather had lived in Bargoed.

Dr. Thomas E. Richards and his wife were well-known members of Bargoed society in the early decades of the twentieth century. It is said that, one day in 1915, Dr. Richards knocked on the door of Bargoed Hall and told builder and owner Horace Davies that he wanted to purchase the property. He extended the property and was the first of a series of doctors to live at Bargoed Hall. He was a Justice of the Peace in the counties of Brecon and Glamorgan and was High Sheriff of Breconshire in 1922. Over the years, *Merthyr Express* carried numerous references to the life and work of Dr. and Mrs Richards including 17 February 1923 it noted that Dr. Richards was recovering from illness, and 2 August 1924 that Dr. and Mrs Richards attended a Garden Party at Buckingham Palace. Using her love and knowledge of fine art and talent Mrs Richards, systematically, shrewdly and judiciously, built up what was described in *Merthyr Express* 28 July 1923 as probably, apart from those in some old mansions and castles, Wales' finest private collection of rich and rare china, old silver and glass, antique furniture and clocks, as well as paintings. Their elder son, Lieut. William Islwyn Richards, studied law but their second son, Dr. Arthur Hywel Richards (1896-1970) qualified as a doctor in 1919. He had several years' hospital experience before joining his father in general practice in Bargoed in 1926. He soon became popular with his father's patients, his skill and sympathetic approach winning their respect and appreciation and he remained in general practice in Bargoed until his retirement. Before 1948 he was an active member of the local hospital committee and of Rhymney Valley Medical Society. Following the creation of the NHS he was an active member of British Medical Association, being a representative at annual meetings in 1948 and 1949 and Chairman of Cardiff Division 1955-1956. His obituary in *Medical Journal* October 1970 records that, outside medicine and his family, Dr. A. H. Richards had two main interests, namely sport and the theatre. In his youth he played rugby for Epsom College and St. Mary's Hospital and while in Bargoed he became a low-handicap golfer and was an active member of the South Wales Golfing Alliance. He and his wife, who predeceased him in 1966, were regular visitors to Cardiff's New Theatre.

Both Drs Thomas and Arthur Richards lived in Bargoed Hall and practiced across the road at 13 Cardiff Road. For some years Dr. St. John Rees, a rugby player of note who played in the very successful Cardiff teams of the 1940s and had a utility cap for Wales, was a partner in this practice. Dr. Trevor Lewis joined the practice when Dr. Richards retired and later, brought his family from Cyncoed, Cardiff and made Bargoed Hall his home. Dr. Kurian Mampilly joined the practice, to be followed by Dr. Ramnani and Dr. Daz. Later Dr. Daz left the practice and set up his own practice in South Street (in premises constructed on the site formerly occupied by the Primitive Methodist chapel).

The link between Bryntirion and medical practice started with Somerset-born Dr. Edward Lawrence Phillips who studied medicine in Edinburgh in the 1890s and spent most, if not all, of his working life in Glamorganshire. He was enumerated in the Rhondda Valley as a Medical Practitioner in 1901. He married later that year and his only son, Ronald Arthur Phillips (who also became a doctor), was born the following year. Dr. E. L. Phillips moved from the Rhondda Valley before 1914 and he made his home in Bryntirion, Cardiff Road. His son, educated in Lewis School Pengam 1912-1916 and Epsom, graduated from Corpus Christi College Cambridge at the age of 21 in 1924 and after that he went to St. Thomas' Hospital London for medical studies. The link between medical practice and Bryntirion was broken when Dr. Phillips and his family moved to Hengoed in the 1920s and the house passed to Powell Duffryn Steam Coal Company ownership. It was the home of Mr Murray who was the Company's Transport Officer as well as being secretary of Trinity Congregational Chapel. After his time it became N.C.B. offices and remained so until 1964 at which point two medical practices (that of Drs Iori Rees-Mathews and David Williams of 16 Cross Street and that of Drs Arthur Richards and St. John Rees in Cardiff Road) bought Bryntirion and set up a modern surgery housing the two practices – one at each end. For two years in the 1980s Bryntirion Surgery operated from a temporary surgery housed in Bargoed Workmen's Institute while its modern purpose-built surgery was constructed on the site of the former surgery. On the redevelopment the practices were on two floors: the Bryntirion practice of Drs David Williams, Michael Sheen and John Wisbey occupied the lower floor while the Bargoed Hall Practice of Drs Kurian Mampilly and Ramnani was on the upper floor. The Bargoed Hall Surgery still occupies its premises but, in the early twenty-first century Bryntirion Surgery has moved to another new purpose-built surgery incorporating *Boots* Chemist on the West Street site formerly occupied by Bargoed Mining and Technical Institute leaving its ground floor Cardiff Road surgery which now houses the former Park Place Surgery.

CHAPTER 15
WELSH LANGUAGE AND CULTURE

For centuries before the Industrial Revolution it was unlikely that many local people had much contact with people who did not speak Welsh, and, in the nineteenth and early twentieth century, the Welsh language was so widely used in the local community that, it was reported, some English incomers had found it necessary to learn Welsh. One such person who learned Welsh was Michael McCarty (his surname occurs in various spellings) who was born in Ireland about 1850. It is not clear when he arrived in the local area but about 1872 he married Bedwellty-born Miriam a monoglot Welsh speaker, and they went on to have at least six sons and four daughters over the following twenty years. The family was enumerated at 10 Factory Road in 1891 when Michael spoke both English and Welsh while Miriam was described as Welsh-speaking, although she probably understood some English as their children spoke English only. By 1901 the family had moved to Bristol Terrace when Michael and Miriam were described as speaking both languages. In his History of Lewis School, Arthur Wright quoted a 1912 letter by a son of former headmaster Mr Pullin in which he wrote *I was at school from the age of 10 to 14, All conversation was in Welsh in the playground and I seemed to understand what was going on, although I was never able to carry out a conversation in the* language. Local people were proud of their Welshness as witnessed in an 1886 newspaper report on the leading residents' desire to help the young Welsh lad, local collier's son David J. Williams, pursue his studies in Llandovery College. However, over the decades some Welsh families ceased using Welsh in the home and, by the inter-war era the main language of the streets and homes of Bargoed and Gilfach was English.

Welsh language

The turn of the century was a crucial time as far as the Welsh language was concerned as not only was the English language used in contemporary commerce and industry but also compulsory education through the medium of English ensured that many of those born after 1870 became proficient in English no matter what their parents' native language. The 1891, 1901 and 1911 censuses asked for information as to whether or not the people enumerated in Bargoed and Gilfach could speak Welsh only, English only or both languages. According to a town directory published on the eve of World War I *Thirty years ago the neighbourhood was purely Welsh, but to-day, though a fair percentage of the Celtic stock remains, the town has become quite Cosomopolitan, business people from all parts of this and other Countries having settled here.*

The Bowen, Roberts and Richards families, enumerated in Bristol Terrace in 1901, illustrate three different contemporary Welsh language family scenarios. Some families retained their Welsh language even though they had spent some time away from Wales. Evan Bowen, a mason born in Pembrokeshire in the early 1860s, his wife, a native of Merthyr Tydfil, and four sons were enumerated at 17 Bristol Terrace in 1901. The two older sons were born in Brisbane, Australia, about 1889 and 1891, while the younger boys were born in Ferndale (about 1896) and Cadoxton (about 1898). In spite of the family's links with Australia, the 1901 census shows that all six family members were able to speak Welsh as well as English. Other families illustrate the way in which compulsory elementary education through the medium of English was affecting the Welsh language. The Roberts family (Thomas and his wife Sarah, together with two sons and three daughters aged from 26 down to 11) was enumerated in 20 Bristol Terrace in 1901. Both coal-hewer Thomas, born in Merthyr Tydfil about 1845, and Sarah, born in rural Cardiganshire about 1850, were monoglot Welsh. However all five of the younger generation, born in Bargoed, were able to speak both Welsh and English. The language of the hearth was Welsh, but the children, having learned English in school, held the key to the continued use of the Welsh language in whatever community they lived in the following decades. The 1901 census shows that John Richards, a railway signalman born in Gelligaer parish about 1868, and his wife, Bedwas-born Sarah, spoke both Welsh and English while the children, born in Gelligaer parish between 1893 and 1900, spoke English only. Such parents probably thought that their children did not need the Welsh language and inadvertently played a crucial role in the decline of the Welsh language.

By the inter-war era, a significant time in the history of the Welsh language in many parts of Wales, it was clear that English was gaining ground as the language of the homes and streets of Bargoed and Gilfach especially as more and more Welsh-speaking parents were indifferent to their children's command of the language.

Having recently drawn up a report on the teaching of Welsh in each local education authority, School Inspector, Mr T. Powell of Neath told his audience at the opening of South Bargoed Boys' School in Park Crescent in January 1923 that while the local authority was trying to uphold the Welsh language in the curriculum of its elementary schools and those teachers who were able to teach Welsh were enthusiastic and zealous for the language, the number of teachers able to teach Welsh in the local area was very low. However, he emphasised that the survival of the Welsh language, with its splendid history and noble literature, was not wholly dependent upon teaching in the elementary schools: it needed the sympathy of the home and it was clear that an high percentage of parents who could speak Welsh did not. He knew that some people complained that the time spent teaching Welsh would be more profitably spent on subjects such as Latin, French or mathematics, but he considered it to be a mistake to disregard the Welsh language in schools and the home. A few years later, in 1928, a Linguistic Survey of the 244 pupils on roll in Bargoed Secondary School showed that, although 76 children came from homes where both parents spoke Welsh and 50 from homes with one Welsh-speaking parent, only 21 pupils could speak Welsh, while a further 64 were able to understand, but not speak, Welsh, and only 18 came from homes where Welsh was the home language and 52 where Welsh was partially the home language.

The decline in the Welsh language was also evident in local chapels where Welsh had been the language of worship. In 1924 Bargoed Cymrodorion Society was urged to pass a resolution and send missionaries to all the Welsh places of worship to remind them to do their duty to the Welsh language. Many Welsh-speaking parents took their children to Ainon, Bethania, Calfaria and Noddfa where the services were conducted in the Welsh language. The older people understood the Welsh services but it was becoming increasingly common for the Welsh sermons to include some English for the benefit of the younger people who did not understand the Welsh language, while in the Sunday Schools, they read the Bible in Welsh before the teachers explained it in English. In late April 1926, Jeremiah Williams B.A. presided over East Glamorgan District of the Union of Welsh Societies' Conference in Bargoed's Bethania chapel. In his address to the Conference, he referred to the contemporary indifference to the Welsh language and national conscience and the growing acceptance of English standards and views in the Bargoed and Gilfach area. He believed that children should keep the Welsh language and Rev. D. L. Jenkins said they should fight to save the Welsh language in the area. At the time the language was holding its own in the Rhymney Valley but he knew that some incomers from North and West Wales were not keeping the Welsh language and that even some members of the local Cymrodorion Society spoke English at home.

Local Eisteddfodau

It had long been the custom to celebrate with music and poetry as shown by Pontaberbargoed's annual Pastai-y-bont and by the later nineteenth century local eisteddfodau were attracting local people as well as those from more distant places. The local press carried a detailed report on an Eisteddfod held in Calfaria on New Year's Day 1885 when Rev. W. Griffiths and Jonathan Williams presided and Rev. J. Volander Jones was the conductor. Both the afternoon and evening sessions opened with addresses by the bards before the competitions started. There were a number of local winners including Rhys Davies who sang *Y dryw bach* to take the prize for the alto solo while Mr J. Evans (Ioan ab Dewi) won both the competition for the best epigram to *Toothache* as well as the best descriptive song on the views of Elyrch Vale. Today's local historians would be very interested to know if any copies of the written entries have survived as the competitions included a composition entitled *The present state of the parish of Gelligaer, social and religious* as well as letters from a son or daughter in England to parents in Wales. The 15 shilling prize for the rendition of *Rwy'n cau dweyd yr hanes* by juvenile choirs was shared between the two entrants, Caersalem and Calfaria chapels, while Bargoed United Choir (conducted by Mr M. Morgan) won the £1 prize for the best rendering of *Crugybar*.

During the first half of the twentieth century numerous local organisations, both religious and secular, held eisteddfodau to raise funds. Many of these events were held annually and attracted large audiences and engendered keen competition while others, such as those held to raise money for the local canteen fund during the 1926 strike, were one-off events. Not only were they important entertainment events to look forward to but they also did much to develop the skills and confidence of the competitors, many of whom started their eisteddfod careers at a young age. One such boy was Douglas, son of local conductor and baritone W. Deri Bowen, and in 1924 the local press reported on his successes at eisteddfodau in Cardiff, Markham, Newport (semi-national Eisteddfod), Oakdale and Ystrad Mynach.

Bargoed and District Cymrodorion Society

Despite English immigration and the effects of the education system, the Welsh language and culture was important in Bargoed and Gilfach at least until the mid twentieth century. It is not clear when Bargoed and District Cymrodorion Society was formed but it was active in 1902 as the local press reported on well-attended meetings in Hanbury Cafe when members delivered papers on various topics including John Penry and Martin Luther. According to an entry about the Society in a 1911-1912 town Directory *Its members are ardent and enthusiastic Welshmen who cherish the name and traditions of Wales, and who render every countenance to anything that is essentially Welsh, and which goes to enhance the position and importance of their native land as a nation, and improve the welfare of the sons and daughters of Gwalia.* The Society was still active in the inter-war era holding monthly meetings in Bargoed Workmen's Institute in Cardiff Road. The members, many of whom were in the teaching profession, were interested in Welsh culture and issues affecting Wales as illustrated by reports in the local press. In February 1923 members heard a lecture on Welsh craft, music and literature before voting unanimously in favour of a resolution opposing Warrington Corporation's proposed acquisition of over 13,000 acres for a reservoir in the Ceiriog Valley. Other talks show that, even though many of the members, like headmaster J. Sylvan Evans and Miners' Agent Walter Lewis, J.P., were first generation residents, they were interested in the history and heritage of the local area that they had quickly come to call home. The 1923-1924 winter season started with a talk by Canon Thomas Jesse Jones of Gelligaer on the *Antiquities of the Parish*. In December 1923 members heard a lecture on Taliesin's prophesy when Prof. Gwili Jenkins M.A., B.Litt. traced the attempts to subjugate the Welsh as a nation and show that despite all counter forces the Welsh language had survived and the Welsh nation had preserved its identity. At the meeting the following month David Davies B.A. spoke on the derivation of local place names, with particular reference to a map of 1762 (it is not clear which map this was) and the farms Heolddu, Penygarreg and Pencaedrain. In the discussion that followed David Davies' talk, the members criticised their council's spelling of *Gellygaer* as well as its adoption of what members considered unsuitable names for some new streets in the locality. In March 1926 they put on a fine performance of *Llo Aur a Lloi Eraill* to a disappointingly small audience in the Workmen's Institute and rounded off that winter's programme with a social and concert (ymgomwest) that including Welsh Folk Dances by girls from South Bargoed Girls' School.

Local places of worship

It was not only in the Cymrodorion Society that aspects of Welsh cultural life were discussed. *Merthyr Express* 15 March 1924 reported that H. D. Jones, B.A. of Pengam County School addressed a meeting of Calfaria YPG on methods of collecting and classifying old melodies of Welsh folk songs and this was illustrated with some renditions accompanied by Walter Jones.

Nonconformist chapels, as well as the other local places of Christian worship, played an important role in influencing and guiding the moral and spiritual life of the population in the rapidly expanding Bargoed and Gilfach communities in the later nineteenth century and early decades of the twentieth century. Reports in the local press show that the clergy, diaconate and leading members of local nonconformist places of worship aimed to uphold the values (such as abstinence from alcohol and Sabbath observance) that had become part of Welsh chapel-going life in the nineteenth century.

They were at the forefront of local Temperance activities and from time to time the large Nonconformist chapels hosted such events. When, in September 1900 Temperance advocate Tennyson Smith arrived at Bargoed railway station to start a week-long campaign in Hanbury Road Baptist Chapel, he was greeted by cheering temperance workers before New Tredegar Town Brass Band led a procession of about five hundred people under The Temperance Society's banner *Hope, Faith and Charity*. The opening lecture later that evening was well-attended. The highlight of the week was a dramatic *Trial of Alcohol*, described by *Western Mail*'s reporter as *an amusing incident* as the *prisoner*, supposedly a bottle of beer purchased at a local public house had been tampered with and the beer replaced with water.

Walter Lewis, J.P., well-known and respected in the community as Miners' Agent and a staunch member of Noddfa Welsh Baptist congregation, was one of a number of local Nonconformists who upheld Sabbath observance. In February 1921 he was in debate with County Councillor Morgan Jones (later M.P.) on Sunday Labour and in January 1923 his opinion carried sway when an application for an extension of Bargoed Workmen's Institute's dancing licence was granted to 11 p.m. rather than midnight.

It was not unusual for Nonconformist congregations (both Welsh and English) to express disapproval of certain aspects of local life in the pre World War II era as witnessed by a report in *Merthyr Express* in July 1927. Boxing tournaments were popular in Bargoed in the early twentieth century and some had been organised to raise funds to help alleviate local distress during the 1926 strike. It is not clear whether or not any particular incident had given rise to the resolution protesting against the debasing exhibition of boxing that was unanimously passed by most of the local Nonconformist congregations. The Hanbury Road Baptist congregation went further by adding a rider protesting against what they described as *obscene cinema pictures* being posted on local public buildings in the hope that other congregations would follow their lead.

Welsh medium education

The following extract from the Log Book of Bargoed Infants' School 7 October 1963, refers to the first Welsh day school in Bargoed and Gilfach:

The Welsh Class was inaugurated today. Mrs Eirlys Thomas is the new Welsh Teacher. Nine children were admitted today. A few of these children have attended a class held on Saturday morning in the Hanbury Road Baptist Chapel Vestry. Several people visited the school today -- the parents of the new entrants to Welsh class, Mr Saunders and Mr Jones and Mr Davies – all visited the Welsh Class and other classes.

Before and after the opening of this class, Welsh Inspector, Eric Evans, visited the school frequently, equipment arrived for the class and staff were trained. In the next few years, as numbers on roll increased and more staff were employed, it became obvious that the Welsh Department would need more room and, by the summer of 1968, they started to discuss transfer of the Welsh Department to Gilfach School. The move from Bargoed Infants' School was hastened as the classrooms were needed by the neighbouring Girls' Secondary Modern, augmented by the pupils rendered school-less following a fire in their school in Pontlottyn, and the Department opened in Gilfach in late January 1970. At first, pupils progressed from primary Welsh-medium education in Gilfach to secondary in Rhydfelin but by the 1980s the local area was served by Ysgol Gyfun Cwm Rhymni (see chapter on education).

Welsh culture in the local English-medium schools

Despite English immigration and the impact of English-medium elementary education, reports in local newspapers and entries in School Log Books show that generations of local school children have celebrated Welsh language and culture. The greatest celebrations came as they marked St. David's Day with patriotic activities instead of the normal timetable in the morning and, for many years, a celebratory half holiday in the afternoon. Sometimes such events were school-based, with each class having activities in their classroom or all classes combining to celebrate together in the school hall, while on other occasions the pupils' activities extended into the community. On 1 March 1912, the headmaster of Gilfach School wrote in the school log book that *this morning was spent singing Welsh Hymns, rehearsing the life of Dewi Sant, and an address on Patriotism. Half-holiday given in the afternoon.* In 1917, the pupils of Bargoed Higher Elementary School having had the usual special programme in the morning of 1 March, repeated it in the evening when those described as *outsiders* in the headmaster's entry in the school log book could, on payment of 1 shilling, enjoy the same programme in the evening. He also entered the accounts of the event in the log book together with a note thus *Of this Balance of £11.17.8, the sum £2.2.0 was used to pay off the debt due in respect of wool for soldiers' comforts referred to on page 189 supra. The remainder has been invested in the school War Savings Association, viz £9.15.8.* On page 189 headmaster, J. Sylvan Evans, noted that, in December 1916, he had covered the cost of the khaki wool sent from the War Office and given to girl pupils for them to knit socks, mittens or scarves for soldiers. During February 1917, the decision had been taken to form The Bargoed Higher Elementary War Savings Association (registered number 253A/25).

In 1922, David Davies, headmaster of Bargoed Boys' School, recorded in the school log book that the very wet weather prevented Bargoed pupils processing through the town to Trafalgar Square in the morning as they had done in previous years. Successive headteachers of Bargoed Infants' School frequently wrote the programme for the school's morning St. David's Day celebrations in the log book and the following extract is one of the few that mentions the Welsh language:

The morning session was spent commemorating St. David. The whole school assembled in the Hall for the school concert. Items were given by all the classes were excellent and greatly enjoyed by all. The programme was wholly in Welsh and was a follows

Rhaglen Dydd Gwyl Dewi 1952

Pawb – Emyn – 'Er Teeid iw y lili'

Dosbarth 8 Dawns

Dosbarth 7 Chwarae 'Pump Dyn Bach'

Dosbarth 6 Band Jâs

Over the years, it became increasingly common for children's appearance to reflect their Welshness while listening to their teachers speaking about Welsh history and customs, or taking part in musical and/or dramatic items, on St. David's Day. Sometimes they wore daffodils or carried a Welsh flag while on other occasions they wore a Welsh costume: girls dressed in Welsh flannel skirts, white blouses and aprons, shawls and stove pipe hats while boys adopted miners' garb. More recently, both boys and girls have frequently worn rugby shirts, perhaps a reflection of the modern face of national feeling.

Children in the local English–medium schools have been exposed to Welsh language and culture in other ways. An inspection report of June 1951 noted that Bargoed Girls' County Secondary School held a Welsh assembly one morning each week, a practice that was repeated in most, if not all, local English-medium schools. Such an assembly typically included a bible reading in Welsh and a Welsh hymn followed by the school uniting to say the prayer beginning *Ein Tad* (The Lord's Prayer). In addition the Urdd movement was active in some of the local schools. Arthur Wright noted in his history that the Lewis' School branch was established in 1927. In his report to parents at Speech Day 20 December 1937, headmaster J. J. Davies noted that meetings of the

Urdd were well attended and highly successful in Bargoed Secondary School, and other local schools were, and still are, involved with such activities.

Other expressions of Welsh identity

Reports in the local press show that it was not only in local schools that St. David's Day was celebrated. In 1924 *Merthyr Express* reported on the Lenox Constitutional Club's first annual dinner in celebration of St. David. About 150 members sat down to a meal at Hanbury Hotel (where Mr and Mrs Jones were landlord and landlady) before they heard speeches and enjoyed musical entertainment.

Exiles then as now often celebrate their Welsh identity. On a Saturday in May 1927, young Douglas Bowen of Bargoed sang at a Welsh Day in Minety, Malmesbury, and on the following day he was invited to sing in a historic church near Cirencester where the rector was Rev. R. H. Wells, whose mother was still resident in his native Bargoed.

Today, the number of adults learning Welsh is increasing across the country. Adults from Bargoed and Gilfach enrol on part-time classes in Welsh in local Adult Learning Centres and number among those who attend the occasional full-day and weekend courses at more distant venues.

Conclusion

Today, although the language of the majority of the homes and streets of Bargoed and Gilfach is English, many local people, including those whose ancestors moved to the area from outside Wales, retain a love of Wales and Welsh culture. They may not uphold Nonconformist values in the way that previous generations did or organise eisteddfodau as in the past, but the daffodils or leeks on display on St. David's Day or the sea of red rugby shirts as people make their way to Cardiff and the Millennium Stadium on the morning of a home international rugby match is a reflection of their feeling.

This stone with the school motto is set in a wall of the present St. Gwladys' Primary School in north Bargoed.

This photograph (courtesy of Menna Hughes) was taken in 1969 and shows her mother Lillian While and Gwen, wife of Reg While, dressed to celebrate the Investiture of Prince Charles as the Prince of Wales. Not only are they wearing Welsh costume but the front window of the terraced house was decorated with a Welsh dragon and a portrait of Prince Charles.

This photograph also provides a good example of a typical style of local house architecture with its stone walls and pale yellow brickwork surrounding the windows and doors. This house did not have a front garden but where there was a front garden it was common for the garden wall to replicate this style.

331

CHAPTER 16
TODAY AND TOMORROW

Regeneration

In the first decade of the twenty first century, Bargoed and Gilfach together with Aberbargoed and Britannia on the east side of the river are united in what has become known as Greater Bargoed. Angel Way and Parc Coedtir Bargod have taken the place of Bargoed colliery and its world-famous coal tip. Angel Way takes through traffic away from Gilfach and Bargoed, while branches off its roundabouts give residents and visitors easier access to each of the local communities. The cycle and bridle paths in Parc Coedtir Bargod, Caerphilly County Borough's newest country park, allow local people and visitors to enjoy its wildlife and artwork. At the time of writing, local people await Bargoed's new town centre as, since through traffic has been removed from Bargoed and Gilfach, vital work is proceeding on updating the area between Trafalgar Square and Bargoed Railway Station. North Bargoed's new integrated public transport system, railway station with associated park and ride car park and nearby bus station, is operational but work on the main shopping area has not yet been completed.

Today, after years of commitment and cooperation by a variety of agencies, organisations and individuals too numerous too mention, local people have a tantalising glimpse of a better future for Bargoed and Gilfach. Since the 1970s the lives of those who lived along Commercial Street, Park Place and Gilfach Street have been blighted by a constantly-increasing stream of through traffic. At the same time shoppers and shopkeepers witnessed the chaos in Hanbury Road and High Street as cars, buses and delivery vehicles competed for space in a town centre that came together when rail and horse-drawn transport was the order of the day. Now residents, shoppers and business people can look forward to an enhanced quality of life and work, and enjoy with pride the improved Gilfach and Bargoed.

The demolition of the library built in 1972 created a gaping hole soon to be occupied by a Morrisons supermarket while Hanbury Road Baptist Chapel, a familiar part of central Bargoed's townscape for several generations, is about to enter a new phase in its history as, following extensive and imaginative refurbishment, it opens not only as a place of worship but also with a library as well as a range of other community facilities.

Memories

During the research for this work, it has become increasingly obvious that the communities of Bargoed and Gilfach have touched the lives of countless individuals. This written history has attempted to show how the area has changed over time and especially in the decades between 1858, when Bargoed Railway Station opened, and the outbreak of World War II. It provides some insight into a variety of aspects of life and work in Bargoed and Gilfach but readers, local residents and exiles, have many more stories to tell. The memories of former residents, Rev. Gwilym Thomas and George Thompson, as well as those of many present day residents and exiles have contributed much to increase the knowledge and enhance the understanding of how and why Bargoed and Gilfach developed into the communities of today.

It is hoped that this work might encourage its readers not only to think about their experiences but also to tell their story. Gelligaer Historical Society will be pleased to hear from anyone with memories, photographs or artefacts relating to the local area. Readers can do this by contacting the Society website www.gelligaerhistoricalsociety.co.uk or calling in at Bargoed Library.

BIBLIOGRAPHY

This local history is based on wide variety of sources (including trade directories, parish tithe award, census returns, local newspapers and OS maps) in the custody of various bodies including Bargoed Library, Winding House (Caerphilly County Borough's Museum), Glamorgan Archives, National Library of Wales and National Archives. While there are many works on the history of the coal industry, transport and life and work in the past that are relevant to the history of Bargoed and Gilfach the following list of published and unpublished works are of specific interest in the context of the history of Bargoed and Gilfach and other relevant works are mentioned within the text.

Published works

Andersson, Kjell-Åke, and Wiström, Mikael, *Gruvarbetare i Wales* (*Miners of Wales*, 1977)

Bargod Grammar Technical School, *The Story of Bargod Grammar Technical School 1910-1960*, (1964)

Broomfield, Stuart and Felstead, Richard, *Take Me Home to Mam, Child Colliers in the Rhymney Valley* (Rhymney Valley District Council)

Heolddu Comprehensive School *Bargoed Bygones*,

James, Paul, *The History of Bargoed and Gilfach in photographs*, Volumes 1, 2 and 3 (Old Bakehouse Publications, Abertillery)

Jones, Judith, *Gelligaer and Merthyr Common, a South Wales landscape past and present*, (Merton Priory Press, 2003)

Kidner, R. W., *The Rhymney Railway,* (Oxford, 1995)

Lawrence, Ray, *The South Wales Coalfield Directory*, (1988)

Saunders, E. John, and others, *The Gelligaer Story* (Gelligaer Urban District Council, 1959)

Turner, Kenneth Graham, *Looking Back, Times Remembered*, (Caerphilly County Borough Council, 1997)

Williams, Nesta, *Bargoed Settlement 1933-1998*

Wright, Arthur, *The History of Lewis School, Pengam.* (Newtown, published by the author, 1929)

Articles

There are numerous relevant articles in issues of *Gelligaer*, The Journal of Gelligaer Historical Society and these are indexed on Gelligaer Historical Society website www.gelligaerhistoricalsociety.co.uk

In addition the following have appeared in journals of other bodies:

Brown, Roger L., The parish of Gelligaer in the nineteenth century and the foundation of the parish of Bargoed, Morgannwg, Vol. XLVI (2002) pp 21-56.

Owen, Annie, Powys-born people enumerated in Bargoed and Gilfach 1901, <u>Cronicl Powys</u>, Vol. 79 (April 2010) pp 19-22.

Unpublished works

Ellis, Margaret R. Law and order in the Bargoed area of the Rhymney valley, parish of Gelligaer, 1908-1918, (1997) M.A. thesis Cardiff.

John, William G., G.U.D.C. Public Transport, Memories of an apprentice, (2010)

Morgan, Andrew Paul, Secondary School Entrance in the Nineteen Twenties. A Socio-Economic Analysis of the Situation of the Pupils of Lewis' School, Pengam, and Howard Gardens Municipal Secondary School for Boys in 1926-1927. (1977) M.Ed. dissertation

Owen, Annie, Heolddu's Silver Jubilee in 1998, (2002)

Thomas, Gwilym, Memories of a childhood in Bargoed, (early 1960s)

Thompson, George, Tua'r Goleuni, (South Australia, 1991)

APPENDIX
CONVERSION TABLES

Height and distance	
12 inches in one foot	
3 feet in one yard	
1760 yards in one mile	

Inches	Millimetres
1	25.4
4	100
20	500
40	1000
60	1500

Feet	Metres
5	1.5
10	3
100	30.5
500	152
1000	305
2000	610
3000	914

Miles	Kilometres
1	1.6
5	8
10	16
50	80.5
100	161

Temperature	
°F	°C
25	-3.9
32	0
50	10
70	21

Weights	
16 oz (ounces) in 1 lb (pound)	
14 lb in 1 stone	
112 lb in 1 cwt (hundredweight)	

Avoirdupois	Metric
1 oz	0.03kg
8 oz	0.23kg
1 lb	0.45 kg
1 stone	6.35 kg
1 cwt	50.8 kg

Volume	
2 pints in one quart	
8 pints in one gallon	

Imperial	Metric
1 pint	0.47 litres
2 pints (1 quart)	0.95 litres
8 pints (1 gallon)	3.79 litres

Sterling and decimal coinage	
12d in one shilling	
20 shillings in £1	

£ s d (sterling)	Decimal
6d (penny)	2½p
1 shilling	5p
2s 6d (half a crown)	12½p
10 shillings	50p
£1	100p
21 shillings (1 guinea)	£1.05

These tables are intended as a rough guide to help readers, whether accustomed to working in imperial or metric values, to better understanding of this work.